Computational Mechanics and Applied Mathematics

Computational Mechanics and Applied Mathematics

Guest Editor

Matjaž Skrinar

 Basel • Beijing • Wuhan • Barcelona • Belgrade • Novi Sad • Cluj • Manchester

Guest Editor
Matjaž Skrinar
Faculty of Civil Engineering,
Transportation Engineering
and Architecture
University of Maribor
Maribor
Slovenia

Editorial Office
MDPI AG
Grosspeteranlage 5
4052 Basel, Switzerland

This is a reprint of the Special Issue, published open access by the journal *Mathematics* (ISSN 2227-7390), freely accessible at: https://www.mdpi.com/journal/mathematics/special_issues/Q84910I41K.

For citation purposes, cite each article independently as indicated on the article page online and as indicated below:

Lastname, A.A.; Lastname, B.B. Article Title. *Journal Name* **Year**, *Volume Number*, Page Range.

ISBN 978-3-7258-3547-8 (Hbk)
ISBN 978-3-7258-3548-5 (PDF)
https://doi.org/10.3390/books978-3-7258-3548-5

Contents

About the Editor

Matjaž Skrinar

Matjaž Skrinar is an associate professor and Head of the Chair of structural mechanics at the University of Maribor, Faculty of Civil Engineering, Transportation Engineering and Architecture, and former Visiting Professor in postgraduate courses at the University North in Varaždin (2020-2023), and visiting researcher at the University of Zagreb, University of Rijeka, University of Trieste and University of Cosenza.

He is the author of 17 student textbooks for various levels of study and of more than 100 scientific contributions published in the form of papers in reputed journals, chapters in books from respected publishers, and papers at international conferences.

His main research interests include mechanics, numerical methods, finite element methods, structural dynamics, and inverse identification.

He was awarded the title of Fellow of the Wessex Institute of Great Britain by the Wessex Institute of Technology, Southampton, Great Britain (2003).

Preface

Structural engineering and mathematics have always existed mutually. Structural engineering deals with mechanics, providing complex, adequate computational models, while mathematics provides computational solution algorithms. Structural analysis is, therefore, one of the most important and demanding engineering processes as it combines several elements which, although carried out separately, lead to reliable and safe solutions as a whole: proper structural computational model selection, the implementation of suitable mathematical methods, the critical evaluation of the results with the possible modification or upgrade of the computational model and recalculation, and the execution of details following the obtained results. The almost natural synergy between mathematics and mechanics thus presents a potent tool in computational structural mechanics, allowing engineers to design structures reliably without the help of experiments.

The evident and rapid progress in computational mechanics in recent decades (both in mathematical models and computational algorithms) has already improved the level of knowledge through various numerical methods (such as finite volume, finite element, boundary element, and meshless methods) and simulations for various problems in the fields of computational mechanics and engineering. This progress, supported by the simultaneous development of computer technology, has allowed new models and approaches to become more comprehensive and complex (including more information and detail), fast (i.e., computationally more efficient), robust, and accurate.

Nevertheless, there is still room for improvement and, moreover, recent natural disasters have reinforced the need for advanced and thorough constitutive modelling and structural analyses.

The present reprint contains the 10 articles that were, after strict reviews, accepted for publication in the Special Issue "Computational Mechanics and Applied Mathematics" of the MDPI *Mathematics* journal. These articles cover a wide range of themes connected to the two topics and are related to applying new mathematical models, methods, or techniques in computational engineering mechanics, including the analytical, semi-numerical, and numerical-based computational modelling and analysis of structural engineering problems.

Because of its topicality, it can be expected that this reprint will be of interest and value for specialists working in the complex areas of Computational Mechanics and Applied Mathematics, either simply at the level of applying new knowledge or as inspiration for the foundation for new knowledge development.

The Guest Editor is himself part of the team that made the Special Issue possible. As the Guest Editor of the Special Issue, I am firstly grateful to all authors of the papers for their quality contributions, to the thorough reviewers for their valuable comments and suggestions for the improvement of the submitted works, and finally, to the helpful administrative staff of the MDPI publications team for their assistance in completing this project. Last but not least, very special thanks are in order for the Section Managing Editor, Ms. Rebecca Xue, for her outstanding and fruitful collaboration as well as valuable and prompt support.

Matjaž Skrinar
Guest Editor

 *mathematics*

Article

Computational Modeling of Natural Convection in Nanofluid-Saturated Porous Media: An Investigation into Heat Transfer Phenomena

Janja Kramer Stajnko [1,*], Jure Ravnik [2], Renata Jecl [1] and Matjaž Nekrep Perc [1]

[1] Faculty of Civil Engineering, Transportation Engineering and Architecture, University of Maribor, Smetanova 17, 2000 Maribor, Slovenia; renata.jecl@um.si (R.J.); matjaz.nekrep@um.si (M.N.P.)
[2] Faculty of Mechanical Engineering, University of Maribor, Smetanova 17, 2000 Maribor, Slovenia; jure.ravnik@um.si
* Correspondence: janja.kramer@um.si

Citation: Kramer Stajnko, J.; Ravnik, J.; Jecl, R.; Nekrep Perc, M. Computational Modeling of Natural Convection in Nanofluid-Saturated Porous Media: An Investigation into Heat Transfer Phenomena. *Mathematics* **2024**, *12*, 3653. https://doi.org/10.3390/math12233653

Academic Editor: Ilya Simanovskii

Received: 10 October 2024
Revised: 11 November 2024
Accepted: 19 November 2024
Published: 21 November 2024

Abstract: A numerical study was carried out to analyze the phenomenon of natural convection in a porous medium saturated with nanofluid. In the study, the boundary element method was used for computational modeling. The fluid flow through a porous matrix is described using the Darcy–Brinkman–Forchheimer momentum equation. In addition, a mathematical model for nanofluids was used, which follows a single-phase approach and assumes that the nanoparticles within a fluid can be treated as an independent fluid with effective properties. A combination of single- and sub-domain boundary element methods was used to solve the relevant set of partial differential equations. The method was originally developed for pure flow scenarios, but also proves to be effective in the context of fluid flow through porous media. The results are calculated for the case of two- and three-dimensional square cavities. In addition to various values of dimensionless control parameters, including the porous Rayleigh number (Ra_p), Darcy number (Da), porosity (ϕ) and nanoparticle volume fractions (φ), the effects of the inclination angle of the cavity on the overall heat transfer (expressed by the Nusselt number (Nu)) and fluid flow characteristics were investigated. The results indicate a pronounced dependence of the overall heat transfer on the introduction of nanoparticles and inclination angle. The heat transfer in a two-dimensional cavity is increased for higher values of Darcy number in the conduction flow regime, while it is suppressed for lower values of Darcy number in the Darcy flow regime. In the case of a three-dimensional cavity, increasing the volume fraction of nanoparticles leads to a decrease in heat transfer, and furthermore, increasing the inclination angle of the cavity considerably weakens the buoyancy flow.

Keywords: porous media; nanofluids; natural convection; boundary element method

MSC: 65N38; 76S99; 76R10

1. Introduction

A nanofluid is a colloidal suspension containing nanoparticles between 1 and 100 nm in size, including materials such as metals, oxides and carbides, dispersed in a base liquid such as water, oil or ethylene glycol. This breakthrough concept has been proven to improve the efficiency of cooling and heating processes in various industries and was originally introduced by Choi [1]. Recent efforts include both experimental and theoretical studies aimed at investigating the effects of improved heat transfer properties in various configurations and applications. A comprehensive overview of these studies can be found in the references [2–4]. Convective heat transfer plays a central role in various natural and engineering systems, including heating and cooling systems, geothermal systems and drying processes. The efficiency of heat transfer in these systems is considered crucial and can be significantly improved by the incorporation of nanoparticles, as described in the literature [5–8].

The thermal efficiency of several industrial applications, such as heat exchangers, can be improved by utilizing porous media (due to their large surface areas) and, furthermore, with the addition of nanoparticles. Most recent applications have been of microchannel heat sinks as innovative cooling devices, as introduced by Deng et al. [9] and Ghazvini and Shokouhmand [10]. Moreover, recent advances are comprehensively reviewed in the references [11–15], highlighting some recurring observations. In particular, the fusion of porous media and nanofluid leads to higher heat transfer rates, due to the presence of larger surface areas and more intense mixing. Nevertheless, there are still some unresolved issues, including the need for efficient numerical methods, exploring nanofluid flow in porous media under turbulent flow conditions, and conducting experimental studies involving different geometries and flow conditions.

Various mathematical models have been used in published studies to describe buoyancy-driven flow in porous media. Darcy's law is the most commonly used mathematical model for the governing momentum equation, which is particularly valid in the laminar flow regime (when Reynolds number is $Re < 10$), where viscous forces dominate over inertial forces at low velocities. In analogy to the Navier–Stokes equations, an extension of the governing momentum equations was established that includes the Brinkman term to account for viscous diffusion and the Forchheimer term to study the inertial effects in free convection [16].

There are two main approaches to the mathematical modelling of nanofluids: the single-phase and two-phase models. The single-phase approach assumes that nanoparticles behave similarly to water molecules and have similar local velocities. This assumption is particularly valid for low concentrations of nanoparticles (2.5–5%) and for solid particles with a size between 1 and 100 nm [17]. However, the two-phase model is better suited to describing mixtures of nanoparticles and base liquids in a physically correct way. This model includes mechanisms that consider the relative motion between the liquid and the nanoparticles, including Brownian diffusion and thermophoresis [18].

Various numerical methods have been used to investigate the complexity of heat transfer in porous media and to model the flow of fluids. These include the finite element method, the finite difference method, and the finite volume method, which are frequently used. Recently, the boundary element method (BEM) has emerged as an alternative, and is particularly popular for its efficiency in solving potential problems in fluid mechanics, such as inviscid flow and heat conduction. The main advantage of the BEM lies in its ability to solve partial differential equations by determining the boundary unknowns alone, bypassing the need to discretize the entire domain. However, this advantage is compromised if a suitable fundamental solution cannot be found, resulting in contributions of the domain remaining in the integral equation. In scenarios with inhomogeneous and non-linear problems such as diffusion–convection problems, the classical BEM is extended to treat domain integrals in addition to boundary integral equations. In particular, the evaluation of domain matrices becomes a central problem, since they are completely filled and asymmetric and require a lot of memory. Various strategies have been proposed to overcome this complication, including methods based on the expansion of the integral kernel [19], the dual reciprocity method [20] or the compression of the resulting complete matrices [21]. The numerical algorithm used in this study is divided into a single-domain and a sub-domain BEM, where the single-domain BEM deals with the kinematic aspect, while the sub-domain BEM is used to solve diffusion–advection type equations [22].

Previous studies have predominantly examined two-dimensional geometries in the context of convective flow within nanofluid-saturated porous media, with limited attention given to three-dimensional configurations. This research addresses this gap by presenting enhanced numerical simulations of convective flow within both two- and three-dimensional rectangular enclosures filled with a porous medium saturated with nanofluid. The study of three-dimensional geometry enables a more comprehensive understanding of fluid dynamics and heat transfer behavior in complex, real-world applications such as thermal management in electronic devices, enhanced geothermal systems and industrial heat exchangers. These simulations provide insights that can be used to design and optimize systems where precise control of heat transfer and fluid flow is critical. Furthermore, the study investigates the effect of the cavity's inclination angle on flow behavior and heat transfer characteristics, offering a more comprehensive understanding of the dynamics involved in such systems. As a test case, a suspension of solid Cu nanoparticles in water is used as the base fluid. The calculations were performed using a BEM-based algorithm. The fluid flow in porous media is characterized by the Darcy–Brinkman–Forchheimer momentum equation. A single-phase nanofluid mathematical model is used since low concentrations of nanoparticles (2.5–5%) are considered. The effectiveness of the numerical code has been demonstrated in various applications, including pure fluid flow scenarios [22,23] and flow simulations in porous media [24,25]. In this study, the effects of inclination angle and nanoparticle volume fraction on convective heat transfer are systematically examined within both conduction-dominated and convection-dominated regimes. The combined influence of these parameters leads to complex interactions within the convective flow field. In a conduction-dominated regime, a low inclination angle can enhance the effects of the increased volume fraction of nanoparticles and maximize heat transfer. In contrast, in a convection-dominated regime at larger inclination angles, the effects of nanoparticles limit the enhancement of heat transfer. This nuanced understanding enables targeted optimization for specific applications where precise control of heat transfer is essential.

2. Mathematical Model

2.1. Equations Governing Flow in Porous Media

The mathematical model for the heat transfer of nanofluids in porous media is based on the conservation equations for mass, momentum and energy. These equations are derived from the Navier–Stokes equations, which are normally formulated at the microscopic level for pure fluid flows. However, due to the irregular and generally complex geometry of porous media, a microscopic description is impractical for modeling fluid flows. Therefore, all equations are averaged over the representative elementary volume (REV), taking into account only a part of the computational domain for the flow. The specific details of the averaging procedure described by Bear [26] are not discussed in this article.

The continuity equation expresses the conservation of mass for an incompressible fluid:

$$\vec{\nabla} \cdot \vec{v} = 0. \tag{1}$$

Here, the symbol $\vec{v}$ represents the volume-averaged velocity vector.

The Brinkman–Forchheimer momentum equation is used in the present study, which reads as

$$\frac{1}{\phi}\frac{\partial \vec{v}}{\partial t} + \frac{1}{\phi^2}\left(\vec{v}\cdot\vec{\nabla}\right)\vec{v} = \frac{1}{\rho_{nf}}\vec{\nabla}p - \beta_{nf}(T - T_0)\vec{g} + \frac{1}{\phi}\frac{\mu_{nf}}{\rho_{nf}}\nabla^2\vec{v} - \frac{1}{K}\frac{\mu_{nf}}{\rho_{nf}}\vec{v} - \frac{F\vec{v}\left|\vec{v}\right|}{K^{\frac{1}{2}}}. \tag{2}$$

In the provided context, ϕ represents porosity, t signifies time, p denotes pressure, T stands for temperature, $\vec{g}$ represents gravitational acceleration, K denotes permeability, F represents the Forchheimer coefficient, ρ_{nf} represents the density of nanofluid, β_{nf} represents the nanofluid thermal expansion coefficient, and μ_{nf} denotes the dynamic viscosity of nanofluid.

The Brinkman–Forchheimer momentum equation comprises two viscous and two inertia terms:

–   The Brinkman viscous term positioned third on the r.h.s., accounts for viscous forces and ensures compliance with non-slip boundary conditions along a boundary. It has similarities with the Laplacian term found in the Navier–Stokes equations formulated for pure fluid flow [16].

- The Darcy term, positioned fourth on the r.h.s., is a linear term that establishes a connection between the velocity field and pressure difference. This relationship involves fluid viscosity and permeability (K), which is contingent upon the geometry of the porous medium and typically represents a second-order tensor. In the case of assuming an isotropic porous medium, the permeability becomes a scalar.

- The Forchheimer term, positioned as the last term on the r.h.s., also referred to as the dimensionless form-drag constant, varies based on the characteristics of the porous medium and can be expressed using the Ergun model, as proposed in Nield and Bejan [16]:

$$K = \frac{\phi^3 d_p^2}{a(1-\phi)^2}, \quad F = \frac{b}{\sqrt{a\phi^3}}. \tag{3}$$

Here, Ergun's constants are denoted by a and b, with specific values assigned as $a = 150$ and $b = 1.75$, as per [27]. Additionally, d_p represents the average particle size of the bed.

Finally, the energy equation can be formulated as follows:

$$\sigma \frac{\partial T}{\partial t} + \left(\vec{v} \cdot \vec{\nabla}\right) T = \frac{k_e}{(\rho c_p)_{nf}} \nabla^2 T, \tag{4}$$

here, σ stands for the specific heat ratio, defined as $\sigma = \phi + (1-\phi)(\rho c_p)_p / (\rho c_p)_{nf}$, where $(\rho c_p)_p$ and $(\rho c_p)_{nf}$ denote the heat capacities of the solid phase and the nanofluid phase, respectively. In addition, k_e stands for the effective conductivity of the porous medium. Following the work of [28], it is assumed that the thermal properties of the solid matrix and the nanofluid are identical, which leads to $\sigma = 1$ and $k_e = k_{nf}$.

2.2. Non-Dimensional Equations

To render Equations (1), (2) and (4) into non-dimensional form, the following dimensionless variables are utilized:

$$\vec{v} \to \frac{\vec{v}}{v_0}, \quad \vec{r} \to \frac{\vec{r}}{L}, \quad t \to \frac{v_0 t}{L}, \quad \vec{g} \to \frac{\vec{g}}{g_0}, \quad p \to \frac{p}{p_0}, \quad T \to \frac{(T - T_0)}{\Delta T} \tag{5}$$

In the given expressions, the parameters are defined as follows: the characteristic velocity (v_0) is expressed as $v_0 = k_f / (\rho c_p)_f L$, where k_f represents the fluid thermal conductivity, $(\rho c_p)_f$ denotes the heat capacity for the fluid phase, and L is the characteristic length. Additionally, the characteristic temperature (T_0) is determined as $T_0 = (T_2 - T_1)/2$, and the characteristic temperature difference (ΔT) is given by $\Delta T = (T_2 - T_1)/2$. The characteristic pressure (p_0) is established as $p_0 = 1$ bar, and the gravitational acceleration is denoted as $g_0 = 9.81$ m/s^2.

2.3. Velocity–Vorticity Formulation

The governing equations are reformulated through the introduction of the velocity–vorticity formulation, effectively dividing the computational scheme into kinematic and kinetic components. The vorticity vector is defined as the curl of the velocity, $\vec{\omega} = \vec{\nabla} \times \vec{v}$, ensuring that both the velocity and vorticity fields adhere to the solenoidal condition, $\vec{\nabla} \cdot \vec{v} = 0$, $\vec{\nabla} \cdot \vec{\omega} = 0$. The kinematics equation, derived from the mass conservation law (Equation (1)), is a vector elliptic partial differential equation of a Poisson type and can be expressed as follows:

$$\nabla^2 \vec{v} + \vec{\nabla} \times \vec{\omega} = 0. \tag{6}$$

Applying the curl operator to the momentum equation (Equation (2)) allows for the derivation of the vorticity transport equation which represents the kinetic computational aspect along with the energy transport equation:

$$\left(\vec{v}\cdot\vec{\nabla}\right)\vec{\omega} = \left(\vec{\omega}\cdot\vec{\nabla}\right)\vec{v} - C_A \mathrm{Pr} Ra_T \, \phi^2 \, \vec{\nabla} \times T \, \vec{g} + C_B \mathrm{Pr}\phi \, \nabla^2\vec{\omega} - $$
$$C_B\frac{Pr}{Da}\phi^2\vec{\omega} - \frac{F}{Da}\phi^2\left|\vec{v}\right|\vec{\omega}, \tag{7}$$

$$\left(\vec{v}\cdot\vec{\nabla}\right)T = C_C \, \nabla^2 T. \tag{8}$$

The independent non-dimensional parameters featured in the momentum equation are as follows:

- The fluid Rayleigh number:

$$Ra_T = \frac{g\,\beta_T\,\Delta T\,L^3\,\rho_f\,\left(\rho c_p\right)_f}{\left(\mu_f\,k_f\right)}, \tag{9}$$

- The Prandtl number:

$$Pr = \frac{\mu_f\,c_p}{k_f}, \tag{10}$$

- The Darcy number:

$$Da = \frac{K}{L^2}. \tag{11}$$

Furthermore, the porous Rayleigh number can be defined in dependance of the fluid Rayleigh number Ra_T and Darcy number Da as:

$$Ra_P = Ra_T \cdot Da. \tag{12}$$

In the equations provided above, the parameters C_A, C_B, and C_C represent the properties of the nanofluid and are defined by the following expressions:

$$C_A = \frac{\mu_{nf}}{\mu_f}\frac{\rho_f}{\rho_{nf}}, \quad C_B = \frac{\beta_{nf}}{\beta_f}, \quad C_C = \frac{\alpha_{nf}}{\alpha_f}, \tag{13}$$

here α_{nf} represents the thermal diffusivity of the nanofluid, defined as $\alpha_{nf} = k_{nf}/\left(\rho c_p\right)_{nf}$ where α_f is the thermal diffusivity of the pure fluid, given by $\alpha_f = k_f/\left(\rho c_p\right)_f$. The nanofluid properties are determined using the expressions outlined in the next section. For simulating pure fluid flow, the parameters are set as $C_A = C_B = C_C = 1$. As this paper focuses solely on steady flow simulations, the vorticity and energy transport equations are considered without time derivatives $\partial\vec{\omega}/\partial t = \partial T/\partial t = 0$.

The general momentum equation (Equation (2)) contains the pressure term in gradient form, which can lead to numerical instabilities. In the velocity–vorticity formulation, the pressure term is removed from the momentum equation as a primary variable, resulting from the application of the curl operator.

The determined partial differential Equations (6)–(8) form a non-linear system of equations that controls the unknown fields of velocity, vorticity and temperature. The characterization of the heat and mass transfer in the area of the porous media domain is clearly determined by the specification of the buoyancy coefficient, the Rayleigh, Prandtl, Lewis and Darcy numbers as well as the relevant initial and boundary conditions.

2.4. Nanofluid Properties

Nanofluid properties are expressed in terms of the relationships between the properties of the pure fluid and the pure solid. In all subsequent expressions, the indices f and s denote the fluid and solid phases, respectively.

Initially, the nanofluid's solid volume fraction (φ) is established as the proportion of the solid particles' volume (V_s) to the combined volume of solid particles and fluid ($V_s + V_f$):

$$\varphi = \frac{V_s}{V_s + V_f}. \tag{14}$$

Different models are used to describe the relationships between nanofluid and pure fluid properties, and a thorough investigation of different models can be found in [29]. For this study, the nanoparticles are assumed to have a spherical shape and all the assumed models apply to scenarios characterized by small temperature gradients.

The expressions for the density (ρ_{nf}), the effective dynamic viscosity μ_{nf}, the heat capacity of nanofluid $\left(\rho c_p\right)_{nf}$ and the thermal expansion coefficient $(\rho\beta)_{nf}$ are as follows:

$$\rho_{nf} = (1 - \varphi)\rho_f + \varphi\rho_s, \tag{15}$$

$$\mu_{nf} = \frac{\mu_f}{(1 - \varphi)^{2.5}}, \tag{16}$$

$$\left(\rho c_p\right)_{nf} = (1 - \varphi)\left(\rho c_p\right)_f + \varphi\left(\rho c_p\right)_s, \tag{17}$$

$$(\rho\beta)_{nf} = (1 - \varphi)(\rho\beta)_f + \varphi(\rho\beta)_s. \tag{18}$$

The Wasp model [30] provides the expression for effective thermal conductivity (k_{nf}) as follows:

$$k_{nf} = k_f \frac{k_s + 2k_f - 2\varphi\left(k_f - k_s\right)}{k_s + 2k_f + \varphi\left(k_f - k_s\right)}. \tag{19}$$

Additional assumptions for the model used include that the nanoparticles are in thermal equilibrium with the base fluid and that the boundary condition of slip resistance is met. The fluid flow is assumed to be laminar, stationary, Newtonian and incompressible. The relationship between density and temperature can be described using the Boussinesq approximation as follows:

$$\rho_{nf} = \rho_0\left(1 - \beta_{nf}(T - T_0)\right). \tag{20}$$

here, the subscript 0 denotes a reference state.

3. The Boundary Element Method

The BEM-based algorithm is used to solve the relevant non-linear partial differential equations (Equations (6)–(8)). Although the classical boundary element method (BEM) has been extended to incorporate domain integrals, several key advantages persist, justifying its use in the present study. The extended BEM can significantly reduce computational demands compared to fully volume-based methods, as it requires discretization primarily on boundaries rather than throughout the domain. This boundary-centric approach delivers high accuracy in scenarios where boundary interactions are essential. Furthermore, even though domain integrals in non-linear problems produce fully populated matrices, the BEM's boundary-focused framework generally results in lower memory usage, especially in sparse or boundary-dominant cases. Overall, the extended BEM provides a versatile and efficient computational framework, particularly advantageous in boundary-dominated or unbounded domain problems, as it reduces computational overheads while enhancing precision at critical boundary regions.

In order to determine exact values for the boundary vortices, the algorithm is divided into components for a single domain and for sub-domains. The kinematics equation

(Equation (6)) is solved with the single-domain BEM, which provides the values for the boundary vorticity. The sub-domain BEM then solves the vorticity and energy transport equations (Equations (7) and (8)) to determine the unknown values for vorticity and temperature. The algorithm was originally developed for pure fluid flow simulations [22] and subsequently adapted for nanofluids [23] and flow simulations in porous media [24,25].

The computational approach leads to a completely filled system of equations, which limits the maximum grid size due to memory constraints. To mitigate this drawback, the fast BEM is used, which utilizes sparse approximations of the full matrices [31]. The main advantage of using a single-domain BEM for boundary vortex values is the ability of the algorithm to preserve the mass in complicated geometries—a property that is not present when using velocity derivatives to compute boundary vortex values.

The numerical algorithm is structured as follows: At the beginning, the boundary conditions, which can be of Dirichlet or/and Neumann type, for velocity and temperature are specified. These conditions are used to solve the kinematic equation (Equation (6)) for the velocity values of the domain and the energy equation (Equation (8)) for the temperature values of the domain. In addition, temperature and temperature flux conditions are defined on the solid walls, together with the imposition of no-slip boundary conditions. The initial boundary conditions for vorticity values are unknown and are determined as part of the algorithm using the single-domain BEM from the kinematics equation (Equation (6)) [32]. The vorticity values within the domain are calculated by employing a sub-domain boundary element method (BEM) applied to the vorticity transport equation (Equation (7)). The overall structure of the numerical algorithm is as follows:

- Determination of fluid and porous media properties.
- Calculation of vorticity values on the boundary using single-domain BEM from the kinematics equation (Equation (6)).
- Computation of velocity values within the domain using the sub-domain BEM from the kinematics equation (Equation (6)).
- Determination of temperature values within the domain using the sub-domain BEM from the energy equation (Equation (8)).
- Determination of vorticity values within the domain using the sub-domain BEM from the vorticity equation (Equation (7)).

Checking of convergence—repeat steps 2 to 5 until all flow fields achieve the required accuracy.

3.1. Integral Formulation of Governing Equations

All governing equations are expressed in integral form through the application of Green's second identity. This involves the use of the fundamental solution u^* of the diffusion operator for the two unknown field functions:

$$u^* = \frac{1}{4\pi \left| \vec{\xi} - \vec{r} \right|},$$

(21)

here $\vec{\xi}$ is a source or collocation point on the boundary Γ and $\vec{r}$ integration point in the domain Ω. The unknown boundary vorticity values are acquired by applying the single-domain BEM to the kinematics equation (Equation (6)), which needs to be expressed in its tangential form:

$$c\left(\vec{\xi}\right)\vec{n}\left(\vec{\xi}\right) \times \vec{v}\left(\vec{\xi}\right) + \vec{n}\left(\vec{\xi}\right) \times \int_\Gamma \vec{v}\,\vec{\nabla}u^* \cdot \vec{n}\,d\Gamma =$$
$$\vec{n}\left(\vec{\xi}\right) \times \int_\Gamma \vec{v} \times \left(\vec{n} \times \vec{\nabla}\right)u^*d\Gamma + \vec{n}\left(\vec{\xi}\right) \times \int_\Omega \left(\vec{\omega} \times \vec{\nabla}u^*\right)d\Omega,$$

(22)

Here, Ω represents the computational domain, and $\Gamma = \partial\Omega$ is the boundary of the domain. The geometric factor $c\left(\vec{\xi}\right)$ is defined as $c\left(\vec{\xi}\right) = \theta/4\pi$, where θ is the inner angle with the origin at $\vec{\xi}$. If $\vec{\xi}$ lies inside the domain, then $c\left(\vec{\xi}\right) = 1$; if $\vec{\xi}$ lies on a smooth boundary, then $c\left(\vec{\xi}\right) = 1/2$. Additionally, $\vec{n}$ is a vector normal to the boundary.

3.2. Kinematics Equation

The sub-domain BEM is applied to the kinematics equation (Equation (6)) to compute the velocity values within the domain. The integral equation is given by

$$c(\xi)\vec{v}(\xi) + \int_{\Gamma} \vec{v}\left(\vec{n}\cdot\vec{\nabla}\right)u^*d\Gamma = \int_{\Gamma} \vec{v} \times \left(\vec{n} \times \vec{\nabla}\right)u^*d\Gamma + \int_{\Omega}\left(\vec{\omega} \times \vec{\nabla}u^*\right)d\Omega. \tag{23}$$

The main advantage of these formulations is that the resulting integral equation does not contain any derivatives of the velocity or vorticity fields. This property makes it possible to set the source point exclusively at the function nodes. The calculation of the values for the range velocity is based on the known boundary values of the velocity from the initial boundary conditions, where the values for the range and the boundary of the vorticity are known from the previous iteration.

3.3. Vorticity and Energy Equations

To obtain the integral representation of the equations for vorticity and energy, we use the same fundamental solution of Laplace's equation as mentioned above. The final integral form of the vorticity transport equation is given by

$$
\begin{aligned}
c\left(\vec{\xi}\right)\omega_j\left(\vec{\xi}\right) + \int_{\Gamma} \omega_j \vec{\nabla}u^*\cdot\vec{n}\,d\Gamma &= \int_{\Gamma} u^*q_j\,d\Gamma \\
+ \frac{1}{Pr}\frac{1}{C_B}\frac{1}{\phi}\int_{\Gamma}\vec{n}\cdot\left\{u^*\left(\vec{v}\omega_j - \vec{\omega}v_j\right)\right\}d\Gamma &- \frac{1}{Pr}\frac{1}{C_B}\frac{1}{\phi}\int_{\Omega}\left(\vec{v}\omega_j - \vec{\omega}v_j\right)\cdot\vec{\nabla}u^*\,d\Omega \\
- Ra_T\frac{C_A}{C_B}\,\phi\int_{\Gamma}\left(u^*T\vec{g}\times\vec{n}\right)_j d\Gamma &- Ra_T\frac{C_A}{C_B}\,\phi\int_{\Gamma}\left(T\vec{\nabla}\times u^*\vec{g}\right)_j d\Omega \\
+ \frac{1}{Da}\phi\int_{\Omega}\omega_j u^*d\Omega &+ \frac{F}{Pr\sqrt{Da}}\frac{1}{C_B}\phi\left|\vec{v}\right|\int_{\Omega}\omega_j u^*d\Omega.
\end{aligned}
\tag{24}
$$

Finally, the integral representation of the energy transport equation is expressed as

$$
\begin{aligned}
c\left(\vec{\xi}\right)T\left(\vec{\xi}\right) + \int_{\Gamma} T\vec{\nabla}u^*\cdot\vec{n}\,d\Gamma \\
= \int_{\Gamma} u^*q_T\,d\Gamma + \frac{1}{C_C}\left[\int_{\Gamma}\vec{n}\cdot\left\{u^*\left(\vec{v}T\right)\right\}d\Gamma - \int_{\Omega}\left(\vec{v}T\right)\cdot\vec{\nabla}u^*\,d\Omega\right].
\end{aligned}
\tag{25}
$$

In the given equations, q_j denotes a component of vorticity flux, and q_T represents the heat flux.

Within the sub-domain BEM method, a mesh is created for the entire domain Ω, where each mesh element is referred to as a sub-domain. Equations are formulated for each of these sub-domains. Shape functions are employed to interpolate the field functions, as well as the flux across the boundary and within the domain. In this study, hexahedral sub-domains comprising 27 nodes were employed, allowing for continuous quadratic interpolation of field functions. The boundary of each hexahedron is composed of six boundary elements. Flux interpolation on each boundary element is carried out using a discontinuous linear interpolation scheme with four nodes. The use of discontinuous interpolation mitigates definition problems in corners and edges. The resultant discrete system of equations is over-determined and is addressed through a least squares solver [22].

4. Test Examples

The examined scenario involves examples of two- and three-dimensional cavities (Figure 1), filled with a porous medium and entirely saturated with nanofluid. The horizontal walls are treated as adiabatic, while the vertical walls are differentially heated with constant temperatures on opposite walls. Owing to the temperature contrast along the vertical walls, variations in fluid density occur, giving rise to buoyancy forces that induce convective motion. The fluid ascends along the hot wall, initiating heat transport toward the cold wall. The magnitude of heat flux is contingent upon the fluid type, the nature and quantity of the added nanoparticles, and the permeability of the porous medium. The assumptions made include the non-deformability, isotropy and homogeneity of the porous medium as well as the additional assumption that there is no heat transfer between the solid and liquid phases.

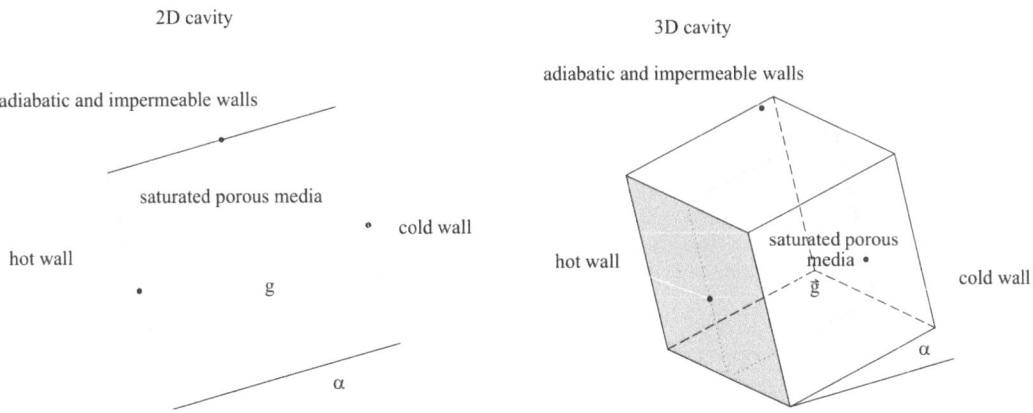

Figure 1. Two-dimensional (2D) and three-dimensional (3D) geometric representations of the examined case.

The wall heat flux is evaluated to quantify the overall heat transfer of nanofluids through porous media, which is characterized by the average Nusselt number. For nanofluids, the Nusselt number can be expressed as

$$Nu = \frac{k_{nf}}{k_f} \int_{\Gamma} \vec{\nabla} T \cdot \vec{n} \, d\Gamma \qquad (26)$$

where Γ represents the surface through which the heat flux is computed, $\vec{n}$ is the unit normal vector to this surface, k_{nf} is the thermal conductivity of the nanofluid, and k_f is the thermal conductivity of the base fluid.

The Cu nanoparticles were considered to be added to the water as a base fluid. The thermophysical properties of both are given in Table 1.

Table 1. Thermophysical properties of water and Cu nanoparticles, adapted from [25].

	c_p [J/kg K]	ρ [kg/m^3]	K [W/m K]	β [$\times 10^{-5}$ K^{-1}]	α [$\times 10^{-7}$ m^2/s]
Water	4179	997.1	0.613	21	1.47
Cu	385	8933	400	1.67	1163

Validation Tests

To achieve a grid-independent solution, a grid sensitivity analysis was first carried out. Four different non-uniform grids (21×21, 41×41, 61×61 and 81×81) were tested for the Cu–water nanofluid and $Pr = 6.2$, $Da = 10^{-2}$, 10^{-4} and 10^{-6}, respectively, $Ra_p = 1000$, $\phi = 0.4$ and $\varphi = 0.05$, which are listed in Table 2 together with the resulting average Nusselt numbers. Based on the grid independence test, the non-uniform 41×41 grid was selected for further analysis.

Table 2. Grid sensitivity analysis for 2D geometry; comparison of average Nusselt number for $Ra_p = 1000$, $Pr = 6.2$, $Da = 10^{-2}$, 10^{-4}, and 10^{-6}, $\phi = 0.4$, and $\varphi = 0.05$.

$Ra_p = 1000$	$Ra_T = 10^5$	$Ra_T = 10^7$	$Ra_T = 10^9$
Nonuniform Gird	$Da = 10^{-2}$	$Da = 10^{-4}$	$Da = 10^{-6}$
21×21	3.416	9.076	13.185
41×41	3.400	9.132	12.911
61×61	3.401	9.132	12.992
81×81	3.400	9.131	12.991

In the case of the 3D geometry example, four non-uniform grids ($12 \times 12 \times 12$, $20 \times 8 \times 20$, $22 \times 10 \times 22$, and $30 \times 10 \times 30$) for the Cu–water nanofluid and $Pr = 6.2$, $Da = 10^{-2} - 10^{-5}$, $Ra_p = 1000$, $\phi = 0.4$ and $\varphi = 0.0$ were tested. Based on the results presented in Table 3, the $20 \times 8 \times 20$ grid, with 28,577 nodes, demonstrated acceptable accuracy and was selected for further analysis.

Table 3. Grid sensitivity analysis for 3D geometry; comparison of average Nusselt number for $Ra_p = 100$, $Pr = 6.2$, $\phi = 0.4$, $\varphi = 0.0$ and various Da.

$Ra_p = 100$	$Ra_T = 10^3$	$Ra_T = 10^4$	$Ra_T = 10^5$	$Ra_T = 10^6$	$Ra_T = 10^7$
Grid	$Da = 10^{-1}$	$Da = 10^{-2}$	$Da = 10^{-3}$	$Da = 10^{-4}$	$Da = 10^{-5}$
$12 \times 12 \times 12$	1.0423	1.5428	2.3432	2.9784	3.3008
$20 \times 8 \times 20$	1.0394	1.5329	2.3313	2.9575	3.2950
$22 \times 10 \times 22$	1.0393	1.5327	2.3307	2.9552	3.2945
$30 \times 10 \times 30$	1.0393	1.5325	2.3303	2.9541	3.2934

The numerical code was validated using several test cases with different geometries and control parameters. A subset of the results is shown in Tables 4 and 5, in which the Nusselt number values (Nu) for different parameters are compared with values stated in the literature [28,33,34]. The high agreement between the calculated results and the published data confirms the accuracy of the developed numerical algorithm and it can be used for further calculations.

Table 4. Comparison of the average Nusselt number (Nu) for natural convection in porous media saturated with pure fluid ($Pr = 1.0$) across various governing parameters with the data from [28,33,34].

Da	Ra_p	Ra_T	[28]	[33]	[34]	Present
				$\phi = 0.4$		
	10	10^3	1.005	1.008	-	1.008
10^{-2}	100	10^4	1.404	1.359	-	1.371
	1000	10^5	3.159	2.986	-	3.049
	10	10^5	1.064	1.062	-	1.067
10^{-4}	100	10^6	2.580	2.702	-	2.671
	1000	10^7	7.677	8.903	-	8.377

Table 4. *Cont.*

Da	Ra_p	Ra_T	[28]	[33]	[34]	Present
10^{-6}	10	10^7	1.074	1.072	1.07	1.092
	100	10^8	2.969	2.975	3.07	3.224
	1000	10^9	11.699	11.892	12.80	12.519
				$\phi = 0.6$		
10^{-2}	10	10^3	1.012	1.010	-	1.012
	100	10^4	1.489	1.533	-	1.503
	1000	10^5	3.430	3.602	-	3.499
10^{-4}	10	10^5	1.066	1.065	-	1.070
	100	10^6	2.686	2.764	-	2.777
	1000	10^7	8.452	9.454	-	9.174
10^{-6}	10	10^7	1.074	1.072	-	1.093
	100	10^8	2.982	2.980	-	3.241
	1000	10^9	12.098	11.924	-	12.895
				$\phi = 0.9$		
10^{-2}	10	10^3	-	1.015	-	1.017
	100	10^4	-	1.667	-	1.643
	1000	10^5	-	4.075	-	3.980
10^{-4}	10	10^5	-	1.066	-	1.073
	100	10^6	-	2.817	-	2.867
	1000	10^7	-	9.947	-	9.917
10^{-6}	10	10^7	-	1.072	1.07	1.093
	100	10^8	-	2.986	3.09	3.252
	1000	10^9	-	12.069	13.29	13.164

Table 5. Comparison of the average Nusselt number (Nu) for natural convection in porous media saturated with nanofluid ($Pr = 6.2$) across various governing parameters with the data from [28].

Ra_p	Da	Ra_T	[28]	Present	[28]	Present	[28]	Present
				$\varphi = 0.05$				
				$\phi = 0.4$		$\phi = 0.6$		$\phi = 0.8$
1000	10^{-2}	10^5	3.433	3.400	3.850	3.826	4.162	4.145
1000	10^{-4}	10^7	9.117	9.132	9.590	9.743	9.901	10.154
1000	10^{-6}	10^9	11.778	12.991	11.899	13.128	11.976	13.195
				$\phi = 0.4$				
				$\varphi = 0.0$		$\varphi = 0.025$		$\varphi = 0.05$
10	10^{-2}	10^3	1.007	1.008	1.081	1.083	1.160	1.162
1000	10^{-2}	10^5	3.302	3.282	3.370	3.345	3.433	3.400
1000	10^{-6}	10^9	11.867	13.238	11.847	13.131	11.778	12.991

5. Results and Discussion

The heat transfer and flow properties were further investigated, focusing on the effects of the geometry, the inclination angle, the volume fraction of the nanoparticles and other governing parameters. Table 6 shows the results of the average Nu number for $Ra_p = 1000$, $Pr = 6.2$, $\phi = 0.4$ and different values of Darcy number, nanoparticle volume fraction φ and inclination angle α for two- and three-dimensional geometry.

Table 6. Nusselt number values for the cases of 2D and 3D geometry, $Ra_p = 1000$, $Pr = 6.2$, $\phi = 0.4$, various Da numbers, volume fraction of nanoparticles φ and inclination angle α.

$Ra_p = 1000, Pr = 6.2, \phi = 0.4$			
$\alpha = 0°$			
$Ra_T = 10^5, Da = 10^{-2}$		2D	3D
	0.0	3.282	3.072
φ	0.025	3.345	2.977
	0.05	3.400	2.884
$Ra_T = 10^7, Da = 10^{-4}$			
	0.0	9.072	8.528
φ	0.025	9.115	8.097
	0.05	9.132	7.727
$Ra_T = 10^9, Da = 10^{-6}$			
	0.0	13.238	14.270
φ	0.025	13.131	13.664
	0.05	12.991	13.078
$\alpha = 15°$			
$Ra_T = 10^5, Da = 10^{-2}$		2D	3D
	0.0	2.847	2.653
φ	0.025	2.909	2.574
	0.05	2.966	2.497
$Ra_T = 10^7, Da = 10^{-4}$			
	0.0	7.466	6.935
φ	0.025	7.494	6.176
	0.05	7.503	6.313
$Ra_T = 10^9, Da = 10^{-6}$			
	0.0	10.726	11.684
φ	0.025	10.626	11.185
	0.05	10.496	10.686
$\alpha = 30°$			
$Ra_T = 10^5, Da = 10^{-2}$		2D	3D
	0.0	2.266	2.123
φ	0.025	2.335	2.070
	0.05	2.401	2.017
$Ra_T = 10^7, Da = 10^{-4}$			
	0.0	5.137	4.749
φ	0.025	5.175	4.537
	0.05	5.206	4.337
$Ra_T = 10^9, Da = 10^{-6}$			
	0.0	7.143	7.637
φ	0.025	7.076	7.304
	0.05	6.998	6.980
$\alpha = 60°$			
$Ra_T = 10^5, Da = 10^{-2}$		2D	3D
	0.0	1.276	1.249
φ	0.025	1.269	1.240
	0.05	1.261	1.231
$Ra_T = 10^7, Da = 10^{-4}$			

Table 6. *Cont.*

	$Ra_p = 1000, Pr = 6.2, \phi = 0.4$		
φ	0.0	1.522	1.474
	0.025	1.501	1.462
	0.05	1.487	1.451
$Ra_T = 10^9, Da = 10^{-6}$			
φ	0.0	1.568	1.563
	0.025	1.554	1.557
	0.05	1.513	1.548

Furthermore, Figures 2 and 3 present the three-dimensional temperature and velocity fields for various values of Da and Ra_p at $Pr = 6.2$, $\varphi = 0.05$, and $\phi = 0.4$. Figure 4 presents isotherms and streamlines with maximum values of stream function $|\psi_{max}|$ for $Ra_p = 1000$, $Pr = 6.2$, $Da = 10^{-6}$, and $\varphi = 0.05$, at inclination angles of $0°$, $15°$, $30°$, and $60°$ at the horizontal midsection of the 3D cavity. Figures 5 and 6 also show graphically the dependence of the angle of inclination and the volume fraction of the nanoparticles on the average heat transfer.

The results in Table 6 demonstrate that, within 2D geometry, the overall heat transfer increases with higher nanoparticle volume fractions at low inclination angles ($\alpha < 30°$) and in a conduction-dominated regime ($Da \geq 10^{-4}$). Conversely, in 3D geometry, changes in nanoparticle volume fraction do not significantly influence heat transfer under comparable conditions.

From the presented temperature and velocity fields it can be observed that at low Rayleigh numbers ($Ra_p = 10$, $Ra_T = 10^7$) heat transfer is primarily governed by conduction, resulting in a nearly linear temperature distribution across the enclosure or cavity. Temperature variations exhibit a steady gradient from the hot wall to the cold wall, with minimal deviation throughout the domain. In this regime, the fluid remains predominantly stationary, leading to a stable velocity field characterized by near-zero or very low velocities, primarily consisting of slight movements near the boundaries.

Conversely, at higher Rayleigh numbers ($Ra_p > 100$, $Ra_T = 10^8$), the convective motion becomes more pronounced, leading to a temperature field characterized by non-linear gradients, well-defined boundary layers, and curvature of isotherms that follow the flow patterns. This regime also exhibits potential temperature stratification, where warmer fluid rises and cooler fluid descends, resulting in active convective currents throughout the domain. The velocity field in this case reflects the dynamic movement of the fluid, illustrating the influence of buoyancy-driven convection on heat transfer processes within the enclosure.

Figure 3 illustrates the influence of the Darcy number on the temperature and velocity fields at a fixed porous Rayleigh number. In all three cases, the high Rayleigh number indicates that convection is the dominant heat transfer mechanism, with its effects becoming more pronounced at lower Darcy numbers. As the Darcy number decreases, the strength of the convective flow intensifies, leading to the distortion or bending of isotherms. Correspondingly, the velocity field is characterized by significant fluid movement, highlighting the enhanced convective activity in this regime.

Figure 4 clearly shows that increasing the angle of inclination of the cavity suppresses the convective movement. At an inclination angle of $60°$, the isotherms approach linearity, indicating that conductive heat transfer predominates. Nevertheless, two opposing flows can be observed in the flow field, which illustrates the complex interplay between the angle of inclination and fluid movement in the cavity.

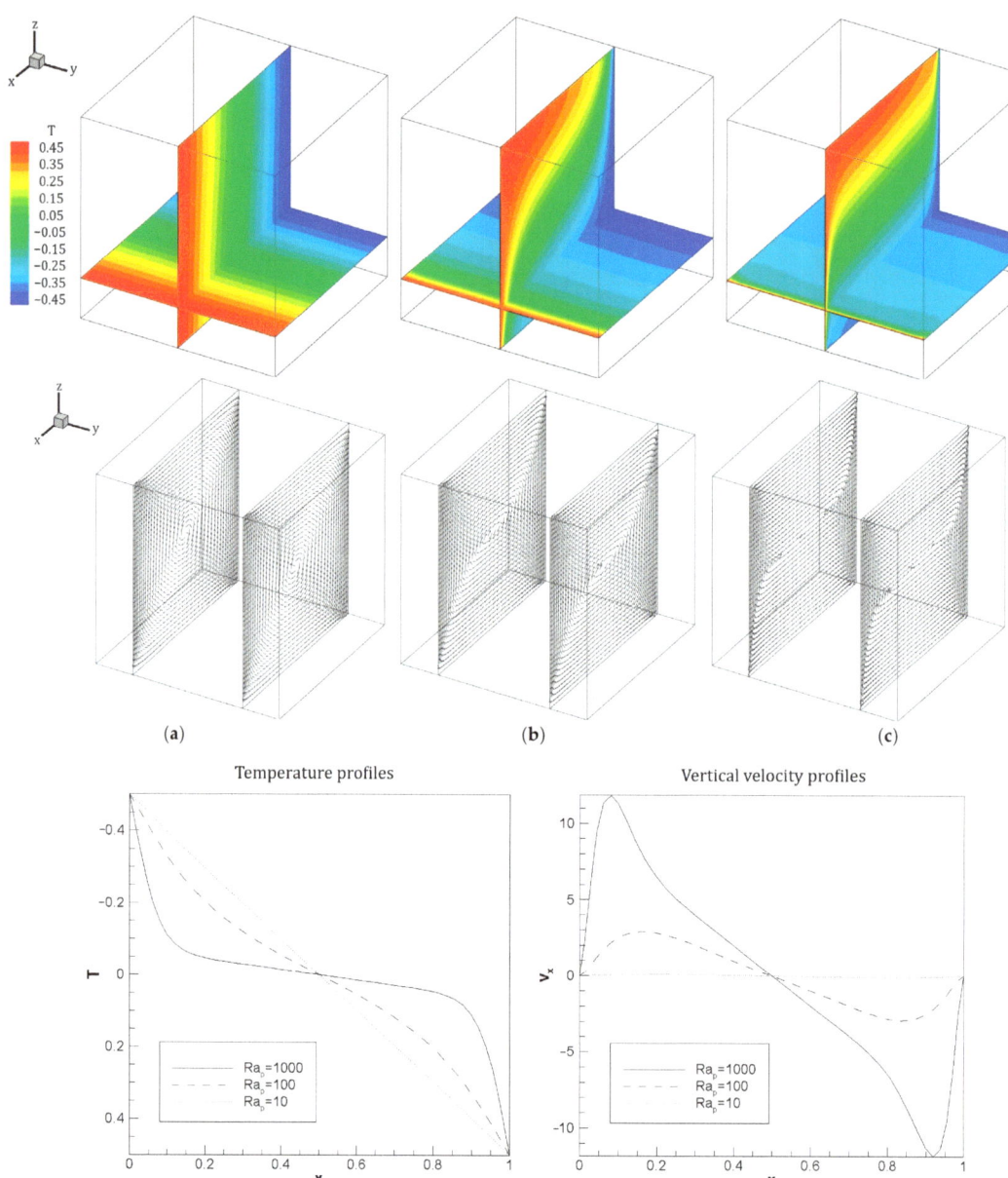

Figure 2. Temperature and velocity fields and their profiles for $Da = 10^{-6}$ at different values of Ra_p: (**a**) $Ra_p = 10$ ($Ra_T = 10^7$), (**b**) $Ra_p = 100$ ($Ra_T = 10^8$), (**c**) $Ra_p = 1000$ ($Ra_T = 10^9$), $\varphi = 0.05$ and $\phi = 0.4$.

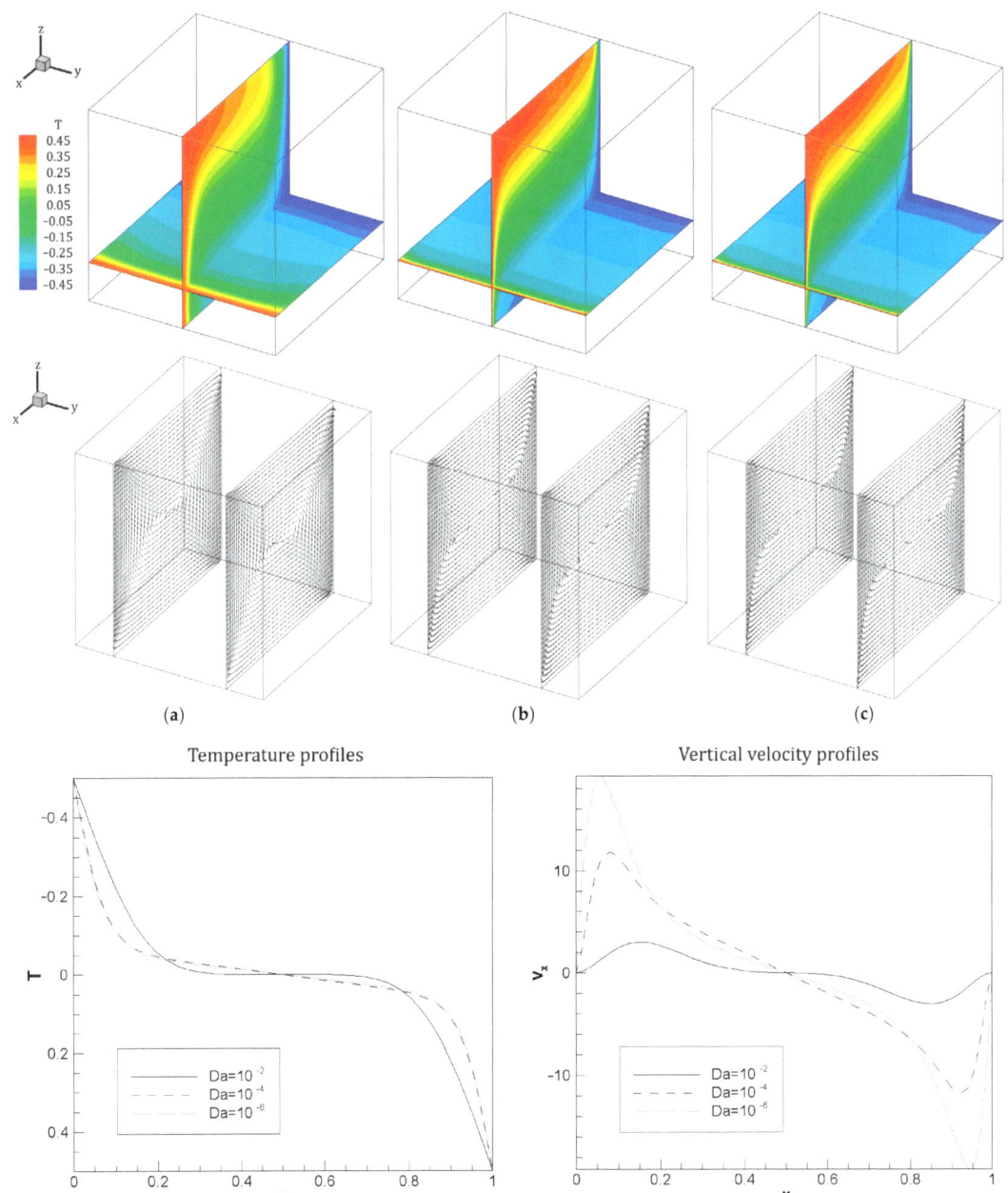

Figure 3. Temperature and velocity fields and their profiles for $Ra_p = 1000$ at different values of Da: (**a**) $Da = 10^{-2}$ ($Ra_T = 10^5$), (**b**) $Da = 10^{-4}$ ($Ra_T = 10^7$), (**c**) $Da = 10^{-6}$ ($Ra_T = 10^9$), $\varphi = 0.05$ and $\phi = 0.4$.

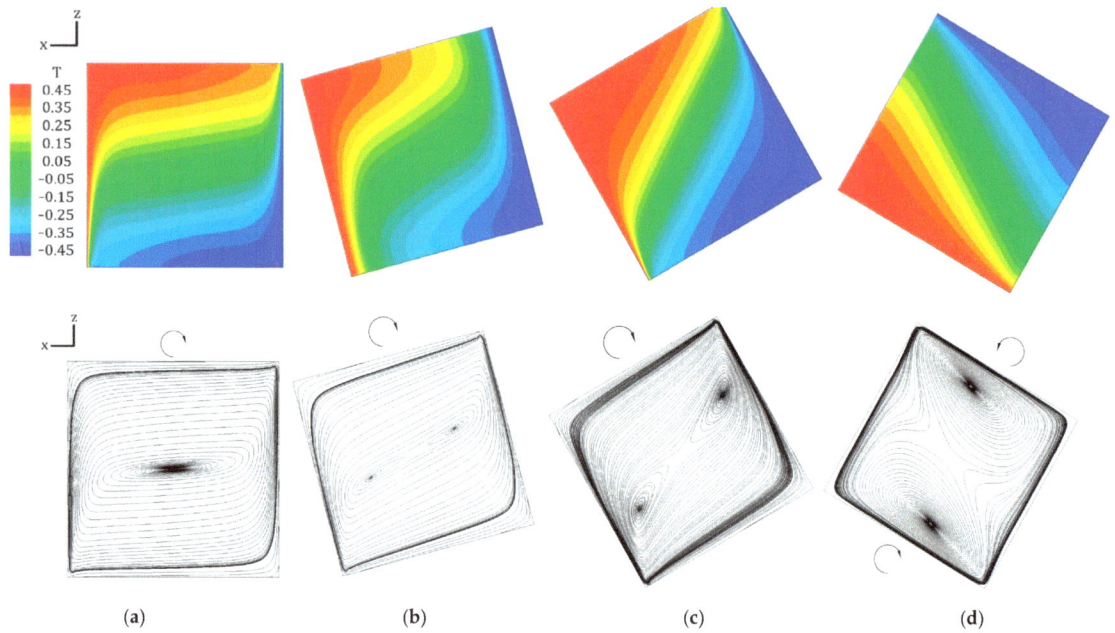

Figure 4. Temperature fields and streamlines at the midplane of 3D cavity for $Ra_p = 1000$, $Da = 10^{-6}$ ($Ra_T = 10^9$), $\varphi = 0.05$, $\phi = 0.4$ and different values of inclination angles: (**a**) $\alpha = 0°$ ($|\psi_{max}| = 20.500$), (**b**) $\alpha = 15°$ ($|\psi_{max}| = 17.463$), (**c**) $\alpha = 30°$, $|\psi_{max}| = 12.258$) (**d**) $\alpha = 60°$, $|\psi_{max}| = 2.600$).

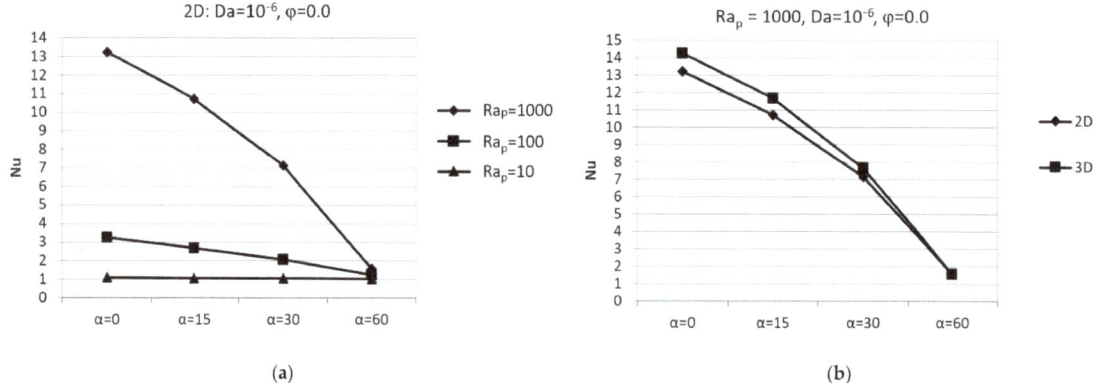

Figure 5. Average Nu for $Da = 10^{-6}$, $\varphi = 0.0$, various α and (**a**) 2D geometry, various Ra_p and (**b**) 2D and 3D geometry at $Ra_p = 1000$.

Figure 5 shows that increasing the Rayleigh number at low inclination angles improves the overall heat transfer. However, as the angle of inclination increases, the effectiveness of convective heat transfer is suppressed. In particular, the heat transfer is more pronounced in the case of the three-dimensional cavity than for low-dimensional configurations.

Figure 6 shows that in the case of 2D geometry at high Darcy numbers ($Da = 10^{-2}$), the total heat transfer increases with an increase in the volume fraction of the nanoparticles at inclination angles below $30°$. In the 3D geometry, on the other hand, the increase in the nanoparticle volume fraction does not lead to a higher heat transfer rate for any of the Darcy numbers investigated.

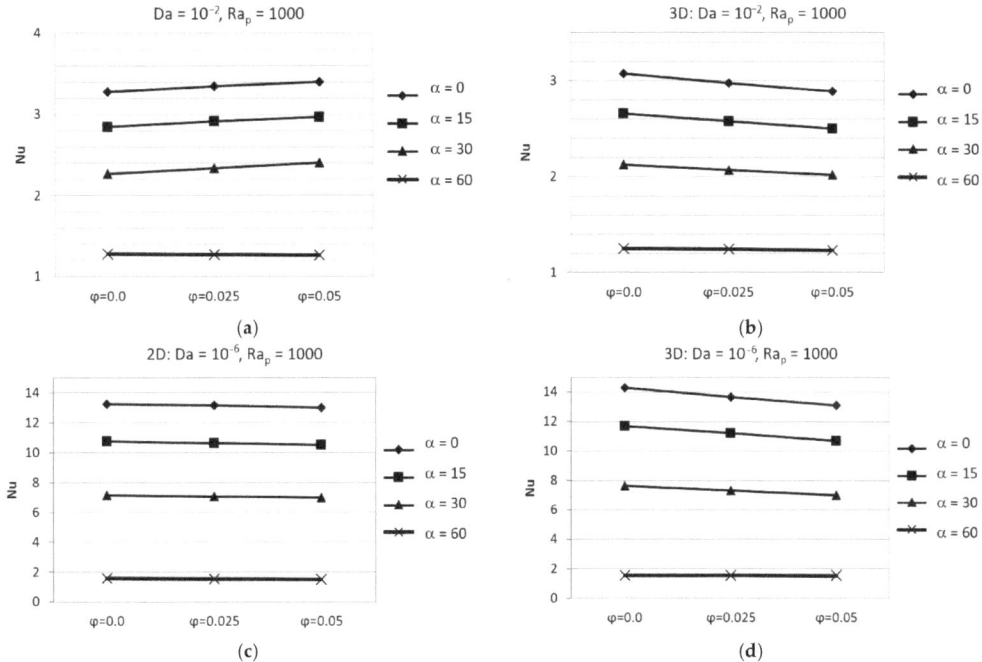

Figure 6. Average Nu for 2D and 3D geometry, $Ra_p = 1000$, various α and φ and (**a**,**b**) $Da = 10^{-2}$ and (**c**,**d**) $Da = 10^{-6}$.

5.1. Effect of the Darcy Number

Based on the average values of the Nusselt number (Nu) observed in both two- and three-dimensional geometries, a decrease in the Darcy number (Da) improves heat transfer within the cavity, which can be seen from the numerical results in Table 5 and from the temperature fields in Figures 2 and 3. The Darcy number influences the value of the Darcy term in Equation (2). As the Darcy number increases, the flow regime gradually shifts towards a Darcy flow regime and thus more closely matches the properties described by Darcy's law. At low Darcy numbers, the flow is primarily controlled by the resistance of the porous medium, resulting in a regime with minimal convective effects and significantly restricted fluid movement. This flow behavior is primarily determined by conduction rather than convection. As a result, the overall permeability of the medium is low, which promotes conductive heat transfer and suppresses advective heat transport. In this state, the system approximates the behavior of classical Darcy flow, where the effects of inertia and convection are negligible, and the flow is primarily determined by the pressure gradient and the permeability of the medium.

5.2. Effect of the Nanoparticle Volume Fraction

The solid volume fraction of nanoparticles (φ) significantly influences the fluid velocity in nanofluid flows. With increasing φ, the effective viscosity of the nanofluid usually increases due to the higher particle concentration, which leads to increased flow resistance. This increase in viscosity generally leads to a decrease in fluid velocity, especially in convection-dominated regions where the higher resistance dampens convective flows.

In conduction-dominated regimes, the influence of φ on velocity is less pronounced, as the flow is mainly driven by conduction rather than convection. However, in convection-dominated flows, higher φ values can lead to slower fluid movement, lower momentum transfer and weaker convection flows, which affect the overall heat transfer dynamics.

The results in Table 5 and Figure 6 show that in a 2D geometry, increasing the volume fraction of nanoparticles improves the overall heat transfer in the conduction-dominated regime ($Da > 10^{-4}$) and at inclination angles $\alpha \leq 30°$. However, in the convection-dominated region ($Da \leq 10^{-4}$), the addition of nanoparticles reduces convective heat transfer, resulting in lower Nusselt numbers at higher nanoparticle volume fractions. In 3D geometry, increasing the nanoparticle volume fraction suppresses convective motion in both the conduction- and convection-dominated regimes.

5.3. Effect of the Inclination Angle

The inclination angle significantly influences fluid flow and heat transfer characteristics in both 2D and 3D geometries. As the inclination angle increases, the buoyancy-driven flow is altered, which can weaken or enhance convective currents depending on the specific conditions.

In the present case, the flow tends to be more robust at lower inclination angles (e.g., $\alpha \leq 30°$), with strong convective motions contributing to higher heat transfer rates, especially in convection-dominated regimes. This is characterized by well-defined thermal boundary layers and increased Nusselt numbers (Figure 4). As the angle of inclination increases further (e.g., $\alpha > 30°$), convective motion is increasingly suppressed, and heat transfer becomes more conduction dominated. The weakening of the convection currents at larger inclination angles leads to almost linear isotherms, as observed in Figure 4, and a lower overall heat transfer, which is reflected in lower Nusselt numbers. In extreme cases, e.g., near-vertical configurations, convection can be almost completely suppressed, resulting in a significant reduction in heat transfer efficiency.

5.4. Insights into 2D and 3D Heat Transfer Mechanisms

In the 2D configuration, an increase in the volume fraction of nanoparticles improves heat transfer in the areas dominated by thermal conduction, especially at inclination angles of $\alpha \leq 30°$. This enhancement indicates an improvement in thermal conductivity due to the incorporation of nanoparticles, which facilitates efficient heat transfer in these scenarios. Conversely, under convection-dominated conditions, the introduction of nanoparticles has a detrimental effect on convective heat transfer, resulting in a decrease in Nusselt number at higher volume fractions. This decrease can be attributed to the increased viscosity of the fluid, which hinders fluid movement and reduces the efficiency of convective heat transfer.

In contrast, the 3D geometry shows a consistent suppression of convective motion as the volume fraction of nanoparticles increases, affecting both conduction- and convection-dominated regimes. This suppression indicates a more pronounced effect of nanoparticle concentration in the 3D context, likely due to enhanced fluid interactions and increased drag caused by the presence of nanoparticles. As a result, the ability of the fluid to facilitate convective heat transfer is reduced, regardless of the predominant heat transfer mechanism.

Overall, 2D systems show improved heat transfer in conduction-dominated scenarios, with increased volume fractions of nanoparticles but a decrease in convective efficiency in convection-dominated conditions. In contrast, 3D geometries consistently suppress convective motion due to the influence of nanoparticles, highlighting the complex interplay between geometric configuration, nanoparticle volume fraction and heat transfer mechanisms, which should be further explored. This comparison emphasizes the need to consider geometric configurations when evaluating heat transfer performance in nanofluids.

6. Conclusions

A numerical analysis of natural convection in two- and three-dimensional cavities fully filled with nanofluid-saturated porous media was performed utilizing the boundary element method. A single-phase mathematical nanofluid model was used in the study, assuming a low nanoparticle concentration of up to 5% and that the nanoparticles behave analogously to water molecules. The conservation of momentum was described using the Brinkman–Forchheimer momentum equation, which takes inertial effects into account. The numerical approach integrated both the single-domain and sub-domain boundary element methods to solve the velocity–vorticity formulation of the governing equations.

The proposed numerical code was validated by comparing its results with those available in the literature over a broad spectrum of governing parameters. The study further investigated the influence of different types of nanoparticles on heat transfer enhancement, with a particular emphasis on nanoparticle volume fraction and various properties of the porous media. The results indicate that, while the addition of nanoparticles enhanced the thermal conductivity of the fluid, it generally suppressed natural convection phenomena within the porous media, particularly evident in the results obtained from the three-dimensional cavity analysis.

In the non-Darcy regime (high Da values), the effect of the Brinkman viscous term in the momentum equation was significant, leading to enhanced overall heat transfer through the nanofluid-saturated porous cavity compared to the pure fluid. As the Da number decreased, the model approached the Darcy regime, and the addition of nanoparticles resulted in a reduction in overall heat transfer.

The three-dimensional analysis reveals complex interactions between the flow structure and heat transfer characteristics within the nanofluid-saturated porous cavity. The 3D temperature and velocity fields demonstrate how variations in parameters such as the Darcy number (Da), inclination angle (α) and nanoparticle volume fraction (φ) affect convection patterns and overall thermal performance. At higher Da values in three-dimensional geometries, convective motion is more pronounced due to the increased permeability of the porous medium, which promotes stronger flow circulation and enhanced heat transfer. However, the addition of nanoparticles generally reduces the overall heat transfer in the three-dimensional cavity.

Inclination angles further modify the convection dynamics; lower angles sustain strong convective loops, whereas higher angles (e.g., $\alpha = 60°$) suppress convection, leading to more stratified temperature distributions. This is characterized by nearly linear isotherms, indicating a predominance of conductive heat transfer.

The extended boundary element method presented in this study has proven to be an efficient alternative for solving complex non-linear diffusion-convection problems.

This study offers important insights into natural convection in nanofluid-saturated porous media, a field of significant industrial relevance for understanding heat transfer mechanisms. In geothermal reservoirs, nanofluids enhance thermal conductivity, improving heat recovery and efficiency. Additionally, natural convection in these materials is critical for developing thermal insulation and phase change materials for energy storage, thereby increasing energy efficiency in buildings and transportation. Furthermore, it aids in thermal management for groundwater remediation, where accurate temperature control is vital for process effectiveness.

Future challenges and directions in the field of natural convection in nanofluid-saturated porous media include the validation of theoretical and computational models through experimental studies and the evaluation of their effectiveness in practical applications. Research will focus on optimizing the properties of nanofluids, such as particle size and concentration, to improve thermal conductivity and stability. Advances in multiscale computational models will improve the prediction of heat transfer behavior. In addition, research into hybrid nanofluids and the development of innovative porous media structures with optimized pore sizes will further improve natural convection and heat transfer efficiency. These efforts aim to deepen the understanding and practical applications in this field.

Author Contributions: Conceptualization, J.K.S. and J.R.; Methodology, J.K.S. and J.R.; Software, J.K.S. and J.R.; Formal analysis, J.K.S. and R.J.; Resources, J.R. and R.J.; Data curation, J.K.S. and M.N.P.; Writing—original draft, J.K.S.; Writing—review & editing, J.K.S., R.J. and M.N.P.; Visualization, J.K.S. and M.N.P.; Supervision, J.R. and R.J. All authors have read and agreed to the published version of the manuscript.

Funding: The authors acknowledge the financial support from the Slovenian Research Agency (research core funding No. P2-0196).

Data Availability Statement: Data are contained within the article.

Conflicts of Interest: The authors declare no conflict of interest.

Nomenclature

a	Ergun's constant, $a = 150$
b	Ergun's constant, $b = 1.75$
$c\left(\vec{\xi}\right)$	geometric coefficient
c_p	specific heat at constant pressure [J/(kg · K)]
d_p	average particle size of the bed [m]
Da	Darcy number
F	Forchheimer coefficient
$\vec{g}$	acceleration due to gravity [m/s^2]
k	thermal conductivity [W/(m·K)]
K	permeability of porous medium [m^2]
L	characteristic length [m]
$\vec{n}$	unit normal vector
Nu	Nusselt number
p	pressure [Pa]
q	vorticity flux
q_T	temperature flux
$\vec{r}$	position vector [m]
Pr	Prandtl number
Ra_p	porous thermal Rayleigh number; $Ra_p = Ra_T \cdot Da$
Ra_T	fluid Rayleigh number
t	time [s]
T	temperature [K]
u^*	fundamental solution of the Laplace equation
V	volume [m^3]
$\vec{v}$	velocity vector [m/s]
Greek Symbols	
α	thermal diffusivity [m^2/s]
β	thermal expansion coefficient [1/°C]
Γ	boundary of the computational domain
ζ	inner angle
θ	boundary shape function
ϑ	boundary shape function for flux
Θ	domain shape function
$\vec{\xi}$	source or collocation point
φ	solid volume fraction of nanoparticles
ρ	density [kg/m^3]
μ	dynamic viscosity [N·s/m^2]
ϕ	porosity
σ	specific heat ratio [J/(kg·K)]
$\vec{\omega}$	vorticity vector [1/s]
Subscripts	
0	reference (average value)
c	cold wall
f	fluid phase
h	hot wall
nf	nanofluid
p	solid phase of porous medium
s	solid phase of nanofluid

References

1. Choi, S.U.S. Enhancing Thermal Conductivity of Fluids with Nanoparticles. *Am. Soc. Mech. Eng. Fluids Eng. Div. (Publ.) FED* **1995**, *231*, 99–105.
2. Trisaksri, V.; Wongwises, S. Critical Review of Heat Transfer Characteristics of Nanofluids. *Renew. Sustain. Energy Rev.* **2007**, *11*, 512–523. [CrossRef]
3. Godson, L.; Raja, B.; Mohan Lal, D.; Wongwises, S. Enhancement of Heat Transfer Using Nanofluids-An Overview. *Renew. Sustain. Energy Rev.* **2010**, *14*, 629–641. [CrossRef]
4. Gupta, M.; Singh, V.; Kumar, R.; Said, Z. A Review on Thermophysical Properties of Nanofluids and Heat Transfer Applications. *Renew. Sustain. Energy Rev.* **2017**, *74*, 638–670. [CrossRef]
5. Solangi, K.H.; Kazi, S.N.; Luhur, M.R.; Badarudin, A.; Amiri, A.; Sadri, R.; Zubir, M.N.M.; Gharehkhani, S.; Teng, K.H. A Comprehensive Review of Thermo-Physical Properties and Convective Heat Transfer to Nanofluids. *Energy* **2015**, *89*, 1065–1086. [CrossRef]
6. Vanaki, S.M.; Ganesan, P.; Mohammed, H.A. Numerical Study of Convective Heat Transfer of Nanofluids: A Review. *Renew. Sustain. Energy Rev.* **2016**, *54*, 1212–1239. [CrossRef]
7. Kakaç, S.; Pramuanjaroenkij, A. Single-Phase and Two-Phase Treatments of Convective Heat Transfer Enhancement with Nanofluids—A State-of-the-Art Review. *Int. J. Therm. Sci.* **2016**, *100*, 75–97. [CrossRef]
8. Vallejo, J.P.; Prado, J.I.; Lugo, L. Hybrid or Mono Nanofluids for Convective Heat Transfer Applications. A Critical Review of Experimental Research. *Appl. Therm. Eng.* **2022**, *203*, 117926. [CrossRef]
9. Deng, B.; Qiu, Y.; Kim, C.N. An Improved Porous Medium Model for Microchannel Heat Sinks. *Appl. Therm. Eng.* **2010**, *30*, 2512–2517. [CrossRef]
10. Ghazvini, M.; Shokouhmand, H. Investigation of a Nanofluid-Cooled Microchannel Heat Sink Using Fin and Porous Media Approaches. *Energy Convers. Manag.* **2009**, *50*, 2373–2380. [CrossRef]
11. Kasaeian, A.; Azarian, R.D.; Mahian, O.; Kolsi, L.; Chamkha, A.J.; Wongwises, S.; Pop, I. Nanofluid Flow and Heat Transfer in Porous Media: A Review of the Latest Developments. *Int. J. Heat Mass Transf.* **2017**, *107*, 778–791. [CrossRef]
12. Mahdi, R.A.; Mohammed, H.A.; Munisamy, K.M.; Saeid, N.H. Review of Convection Heat Transfer and Fluid Flow in Porous Media with Nanofluid. *Renew. Sustain. Energy Rev.* **2015**, *41*, 715–734. [CrossRef]
13. Hemmat Esfe, M.; Bahiraei, M.; Hajbarati, H.; Valadkhani, M. A Comprehensive Review on Convective Heat Transfer of Nanofluids in Porous Media: Energy-Related and Thermohydraulic Characteristics. *Appl. Therm. Eng.* **2020**, *178*, 115487. [CrossRef]
14. Xu, H.J.; Xing, Z.B.; Wang, F.Q.; Cheng, Z.M. Review on Heat Conduction, Heat Convection, Thermal Radiation and Phase Change Heat Transfer of Nanofluids in Porous Media: Fundamentals and Applications. *Chem. Eng. Sci.* **2019**, *195*, 462–483. [CrossRef]
15. Nabwey, H.A.; Armaghani, T.; Azizimehr, B.; Rashad, A.M.; Chamkha, A.J. A Comprehensive Review of Nanofluid Heat Transfer in Porous Media. *Nanomaterials* **2023**, *13*, 937. [CrossRef]
16. Donald, A.; Nield, A.B. *Convection in Porous Media*, 4th ed.; Springer: Berlin, Germany; New York, NY, USA, 2013.
17. Tiwari, R.K.; Das, M.K. Heat Transfer Augmentation in a Two-Sided Lid-Driven Differentially Heated Square Cavity Utilizing Nanofluids. *Int. J. Heat Mass Transf.* **2007**, *50*, 2002–2018. [CrossRef]
18. Buongiorno, J. Convective Transport in Nanofluids. *J. Heat Transf.* **2006**, *128*, 240–250. [CrossRef]
19. Bebendorf, M. Numerische Mathematik Approximation of Boundary Element Matrices. *Numer. Math.* **2000**, *86*, 565–589. [CrossRef]
20. Eppler, K.; Harbrecht, H. Fast Wavelet BEM for 3d Electromagnetic Shaping. *Appl. Numer. Math.* **2005**, *54*, 537–554. [CrossRef]
21. Popov, V.; Power, H.; Škerget, L. (Eds.) *Domain Decomposition Techniques for Boundary Elements: Applications to Fluid Flow*; WIT Press: Southampton, UK, 2007.
22. Ravnik, J.; Škerget, L.; Žunič, Z. Combined Single Domain and Subdomain BEM for 3D Laminar Viscous Flow. *Eng. Anal. Bound. Elem.* **2009**, *33*, 420–424. [CrossRef]
23. Ravnik, J.; Škerget, L.; Hriberšek, M. Analysis of Three-Dimensional Natural Convection of Nanofluids by BEM. *Eng. Anal. Bound. Elem.* **2010**, *34*, 1018–1030. [CrossRef]
24. Kramer, J.; Ravnik, J.; Jecl, R.; Škerget, L. Simulation of 3D Flow in Porous Media by Boundary Element Method. *Eng. Anal. Bound. Elem.* **2011**, *35*, 1256–1264. [CrossRef]
25. Stajnko, J.K.; Ravnik, J.; Jecl, R. Natural Convection in a Square Cavity Filled with a Non-Darcy Porous Medium Saturated with Nanofluid by the Boundary Element Method. *J. Porous Media* **2017**, *20*, 921–939. [CrossRef]
26. Bear, J. *Dynamics of Fluids in Porous Media*; Dover: New York, NY, USA, 1972.
27. Ergun, S. Fluid Flow through Packed Columns. *Chem. Eng. Prog.* **1952**, *48*, 89–94.
28. Nguyen, M.T.; Aly, A.M.; Lee, S.W. Natural Convection in a Non-Darcy Porous Cavity Filled with Cu–Water Nanofluid Using the Characteristic-Based Split Procedure in Finite-Element Method. *Numer. Heat Transf. Part A Appl.* **2015**, *67*, 224–247. [CrossRef]
29. Haddad, Z.; Oztop, H.F.; Abu-Nada, E.; Mataoui, A. A Review on Natural Convective Heat Transfer of Nanofluids. *Renew. Sustain. Energy Rev.* **2012**, *16*, 5363–5378. [CrossRef]
30. Wasp, E.J.; Kenny, J.P.; Gandhi, R.L. *Solid-Liquid Flow Slurry Pipeline Transportation*; Trans Tech Publications: Clausthal, Germany, 1977.

31. Ravnik, J.; Škerget, L.; Žunič, Z. Comparison between Wavelet and Fast Multipole Data Sparse Approximations for Poisson and Kinematics Boundary—Domain Integral Equations. *Comput. Methods Appl. Mech. Eng.* **2009**, *198*, 1473–1485. [CrossRef]

32. Ravnik, J.; Škerget, L.; Žunič, Z. Velocity-Vorticity Formulation for 3D Natural Convection in an Inclined Enclosure by BEM. *Int. J. Heat Mass Transf.* **2008**, *51*, 4517–4527. [CrossRef]

33. Nithiarasu, P.; Ravindran, K. A New Semi-Implicit Time Stepping Procedure for Buoyancy Driven Flow in a Fluid Saturated Porous Medium. *Comput. Methods Appl. Mech. Eng.* **1998**, *165*, 147–154. [CrossRef]

34. Lauriat, G.; Prasad, V. Non-Darcian Effects on Natural Convection in a Vertical Porous Enclosure. *Int. J. Heat Mass Transf.* **1989**, *32*, 2135–2148. [CrossRef]

 *mathematics*

Article

Analysing Flexural Response in RC Beams: A Closed-Form Solution Designer Perspective from Detailed to Simplified Modelling

Denis Imamović and Matjaž Skrinar *

Faculty of Civil Engineering, Transportation Engineering and Architecture, Chair of Mechanics of Structures, University of Maribor, Smetanova 17, SI-2000 Maribor, Slovenia; denis.imamovic@um.si
* Correspondence: matjaz.skrinar@um.si; Tel.: +386-(2)-22-94-358

Abstract: This paper presents a detailed analytical approach for the bending analysis of reinforced concrete beams, integrating both structural mechanics principles and Eurocode 2 provisions. The general analytical expressions derived for the curvature were applied for the transverse displacement analysis of a simply supported reinforced concrete beam under four-point loading, focusing on key limit states: the initiation of cracking, the yielding of tensile reinforcement and the compressive failure of concrete. The displacement's results were validated through experimental testing, showing a high degree of accuracy in the elastic and crack propagation phases. Deviations in the yielding phase were attributed to the conservative material assumptions within the Eurocode 2 framework, though the analytical model remained reliable overall. To streamline the computational process for more complex structures, a simplified model utilising a non-linear rotational spring was further developed. This model effectively captures the influence of cracking with significantly reduced computational effort, making it suitable for serviceability limit state analyses in complex loading scenarios, such as seismic impacts. The results demonstrate that combining detailed analytical methods with this simplified model provides an efficient and practical solution for the analysis of reinforced concrete beams, balancing precision with computational efficiency.

Keywords: reinforced concrete structures; non-linear behaviour; transverse displacement; moment–curvature diagram; rotational spring model

MSC: 74K10

Citation: Imamović, D.; Skrinar, M. Analysing Flexural Response in RC Beams: A Closed-Form Solution Designer Perspective from Detailed to Simplified Modelling. *Mathematics* **2024**, *12*, 3327. https://doi.org/10.3390/math12213327

Academic Editor: Yiu Yin Raymond Lee

Received: 27 September 2024
Revised: 17 October 2024
Accepted: 20 October 2024
Published: 23 October 2024

1. Introduction

Reinforced concrete (RC) is one of the fundamental building materials. Consequently, it is utilised regularly throughout a plethora of structures worldwide within modern civil engineering [1]. Its exceptional features like economy, stiffness and load-bearing capacity have made it a primary resource for many infrastructure structures, from viaducts and bridges to high-rise structures. Nevertheless, challenges arise when using RC, with cracking being one of the key issues arising from the complex non-linear behaviour of concrete.

Cracks in concrete indicate that the tensile strength of the material has been exceeded, and they are not just a cosmetic concern. A comprehensive analysis of the behaviour of RC structures over time is necessary to understand this process fully. With the appearance of the first cracks, a structure that initially exhibits linear behaviour transitions to non-linear behaviour due to crack propagation. In this context, the concrete takes on the compressive force, while the rebar bears the tensile force. As cracks propagate, the load-carrying capacity of the structural element undergoes changes. Therefore, a meticulous analysis of the impact of cracks on the structure is essential.

Load capacity analysis is crucial for guaranteeing the safety and durability of complex structures, such as bridges, power stations and tunnels. The creation of mathematical models and computational approaches is pivotal to accurately determining load-bearing capacity and ensuring structural safety [2,3]. The structural engineer is thus frequently challenged with designing an idealised mathematical model of the structure to ensure that the ensuing analysis accurately accounts for all the essential attributes of the actual structure, as far as is feasible.

Experimental verification of RC structures is crucial in enhancing the precision of structural analysis and design within the field of civil engineering. Incorporating a broader scope of material traits and integrating them into analytical models can lead to superior simulation of the structure's behaviour under realistic circumstances. This, in turn, results in safer and more efficient construction practices. To further emphasise the importance of analysing structural behaviour, it is noteworthy that beams, as integral members of structures, have been studied extensively. This is particularly true for composite beams, where studies have included deflection [4], buckling [5] and dynamic analyses [6]. These investigations highlight important aspects of structural performance and provide valuable insights into the complexities of load-bearing members.

To conduct precise computational analyses of RC structures, it is imperative to establish quality performance (stress–strain) diagrams for concrete and steel. The fundamental material characteristics of concrete and steel are their compressive and tensile strength, which can be determined via straightforward uniaxial tensile and compressive tests. Additionally, these tests enable the assessment of the complete stress–strain behaviour of both materials. Although these two fundamental properties (strengths) hold paramount importance, the precise determination of performance diagrams requires the use of additional material properties such as the modulus of elasticity, elongation at yield of steel, or failure of concrete.

In contrast to steel, it is challenging to determine the mathematical model parameters of concrete in the compressive and tensile zones due to its wider spectrum of values obtained from experiments. Conducting additional experimental verifications, e.g., three-point or four-point bending tests of RC beams, enables a more comprehensive assessment of its mechanical properties, including crack and deformation development during loading, up to ultimate failure [7–11].

RC structures exhibit a highly non-linear behaviour, particularly under extreme tensile loads. Cracks form even at relatively low bending loads, caused by the bending moment surpassing the concrete's tensile strength, leading to stiffness changes and consequent non-linear behaviour. In civil engineering, 1D finite element (FE) models are generally utilised for global analyses of non-linear responses in RC structures comprising primarily beams and columns. The non-linear region of 1D structural elements can be most simply and efficiently modelled using plastic hinges, which are simulated by non-linear rotational spring in the bending analyses [12]. Essentially, plastic hinges represent a concentrated area of the structure where the non-linear behaviour of materials is assumed. The rest of the structure is treated as linearly elastic.

The use of a non-linear rotational spring in 1D models allows for simulating the bending behaviour of a structure at loads beyond its elastic limits with sufficient accuracy. This is especially crucial in extreme conditions like seismic loads, where deformation and cracking may be limited to certain areas [13]. The precision of these analyses within the inelastic area of the structure relies predominantly on defining the moment–rotation diagram of the rotational spring stiffness.

Research on reinforced concrete beams' response has increasingly focused on enhancing their structural efficiency and durability through innovative materials and methodologies, with particular emphasis on steel bars. Recent studies have developed analytical displacement solutions for statically determinate beams, employing bi-linear stress–strain behaviour with a horizontal top branch for steel and concrete to define a trilinear moment–curvature model for predicting deflection under various loading conditions [14]. Hybrid reinforcement strategies, combining basalt fibre-reinforced polymer (BFRP) and steel bars, have demonstrated significant improvements in flexural behaviour, particularly for under-reinforced configurations [15].

The use of high-strength and high-toughness (HSHT) steel bars has further enhanced energy absorption and crack control in reinforced concrete beams [16]. Due to the broad applicability of high-strength steel bars, not only their standard bending capacity but also their behaviour at elevated temperatures is being investigated [17]. Additionally, steel–basalt fibre composite bars (SBFCBs) have shown promise in addressing corrosion issues while maintaining ductility, indicating the potential for hybrid reinforcement [18].

Constant resistance energy (CRE) steel reinforcement has outperformed traditional high-strength bars in flexural performance, highlighting its advantages in design applications [19]. Research on two-layer fibre-reinforced concrete beams has confirmed that an optimised fibre distribution enhances load-carrying capacity and ductility [20]. Furthermore, hybrid GFRP–steel reinforced concrete beams exhibit superior impact resistance compared to conventional configurations [21]. For very harsh and extreme environmental conditions, such as marine ones, the application of Negative Poisson's Ratio (NPR) steel bars was also studied [22].

The exploration of stainless steel (SS) as a reinforcement has revealed improved moment capacity, especially at lower reinforcement ratios, presenting an alternative to conventional steel [23]. An analytical approach for ultra-high-performance concrete (UHPC) has also been proposed, offering a flexible design methodology for achieving the desired structural performance [24]. Finally, studies on hybrid FRP–steel reinforced beams have provided new insights into predictive modelling for cracking moments and deflections [25]. This paper focuses on analyses of the bending behaviour of RC structures using an analytical model in accordance with the Eurocode 2 standard, assimilating the principles of structural mechanics. The new general analytical expressions derived for the curvature as a function of the bending moment and considering the actual state of stresses and strains in the cross-section were first derived. Afterwards, the derived expressions were implemented for the bending analysis of a beam under four-point loading. The choice of analysing this kind of structure was motivated by the availability of experimental data for this specific loading condition, allowing for a comprehensive investigation and validation of the proposed analytical model. Key aspects such as the first crack initiation, the loss of load-carrying capacity of the steel reinforcement and the ultimate failure of the concrete were examined in detail. This study contributes to the theoretical understanding and mathematical modelling of the RC structure's behaviour. In the end, it also discusses a new practical computational model with a discrete crack modelled by a rotational spring for predicting its response.

2. Determination of the Closed-Form Solution for the Three-Linear Moment—Curvature Diagram of the Rectangular Cross-Section

In this paper, a new analytical model is developed to calculate the structure's transverse displacement, taking into account the principles of structural mechanics and assimilating the principles and provisions of the Eurocode 2 standard. The elementary hypothesis is thus the Euler–Bernoulli hypothesis, which is in accordance with the Eurocode 2 standard. The most thorough constitutive law for concrete under compression from the code was used for the uniaxial stress–strain state, which does not explicitly demonstrate any fracture theory. This is standard practice in the flexural design of reinforced concrete members to several standards, not just Eurocode 2 [26–29].

This study can be divided in the following two main steps:

1. Determination of the closed-form solutions for the three-linear moment–curvature (flexural strength) diagram of the beam cross-section;
2. Determination of the transverse displacement in the considered point of the structure using the elastic Euler–Bernoulli bending theory based on the moment–curvature diagram of the cross-section provided in point 1.

Further, the simplified beam finite element analysis is presented as a promising potential expansion of the computational process, implementing non-linear rotational spring stiffness. The determination of the closed-form solution for this spring, which implements the three-linear moment–rotation diagram, is based on the first two derivation steps. The complete flexural strength response of the RC rectangular section shows a highly non-linear response to bending due to the both very different constitutive materials. This response has been divided into three primary behavioural phases. The first phase is the elastic non-cracked limit phase (I), followed by the crack propagation limit phase (II) and the bottom reinforcement yielding limit phase (III). These phases are defined by the identification of three limit points. For each of these phases, the moment–curvature relationship (M-κ) is assumed to be linear. Further, these three phases together constitute a simplified three-linear diagram of the cross-section (see Figure 1). The key points in this regard are the occurrences of the initial crack in the concrete ($M = M_{cr}$, $\kappa = \kappa_{cr}$), the initiation of reinforcement yielding ($M = M_y$, $\kappa = \kappa_y$) and the failure of the concrete in the compression zone ($M = M_u$, $\kappa = \kappa_u$).

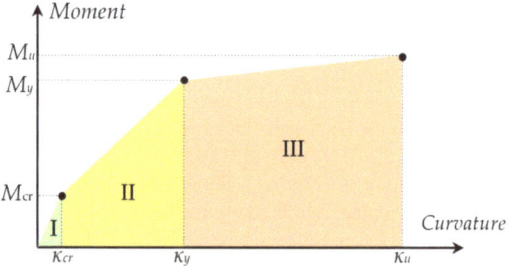

Figure 1. Tri-linear moment–curvature diagram of cross-section.

The fundamental requirement for determining the moment–curvature diagram of the RC cross-section is to know the behaviour of the two constituent materials. Numerous empirical formulae have been proposed for both concrete [30–32] and steel to determine their uniaxial stress–strain behaviour. In this study, in accordance with Eurocode 2 (EC2 [33]), the non-linear constitutive parabola–rectangle stress–strain behaviour of concrete in the compression zone is assumed to be as

$$\sigma_c(\varepsilon_c) = \begin{cases} f_c\left(1 - \left(1 - \frac{\varepsilon_c}{\varepsilon_{c2}}\right)^2\right) & for \quad 0 \le \varepsilon_c \le \varepsilon_{c2} \\ f_c & for \quad \varepsilon_{c2} \le \varepsilon_c \le \varepsilon_{c3} \end{cases}, \tag{1}$$

where f_c is the concrete compressive strength, ε_{c2} is the strain at reaching the maximum strength and ε_{c3} is the ultimate strain. It should be noted that the compressive strains and strength in Equation 1 are considered as positive.

An elasto-plastic approximation, as per the EC2 and given by Equation (2), is assumed to idealise the behaviour of the steel in tension and compression as

$$\sigma_s(\varepsilon_s) = \begin{cases} E_s\varepsilon_s & for \quad -\varepsilon_y \le \varepsilon_s \le \varepsilon_y \\ f_y & for \quad \varepsilon_s > \varepsilon_y \\ -f_y & for \quad \varepsilon_s < -\varepsilon_y \end{cases} \tag{2}$$

where E_s is the elastic modulus of steel, f_y is the yield strength and $\varepsilon_y = f_y/E_s$ is the yield strain.

The other following basic assumptions were made to determine the moment–curvature diagram of an RC cross-section [34]:

- A straight cross-section before bending remains straight after bending;
- A perfect bond exists between the reinforcement and the concrete;
- Since the tensile strength of concrete is relatively small compared to its compressive strength, a linear distribution of tensile stresses was considered for the non-cracked tensioned part of the cross-section. After a crack occurs, the tensile strength of concrete in the cracked section is neglected;

- The ultimate cross-section flexural capacity is achieved once the ultimate failure deformation ε_{c3} is reached in the top concrete compression fibre at the ultimate stage.

2.1. Determination of the Limit Characteristic Point for $M = M_{cr}$ and $\kappa = \kappa_{cr}$

The cross-section characteristics include the cross-section width (b), the cross-section height (h), the distance of the bottom rebar from the top edge of the section (d), the distance of the top rebar from the top edge of the section (d'), the area of the bottom rebar (A_s) and the area of the top rebar (A_s').

It is assumed that in this phase, there is a linear relationship between the normal stresses and strains in concrete. This is due to the short first non-cracked limit phase leading to the onset of the first crack in the cross-section and the relatively low compressive stresses. Before the formation of the first crack, the complete cross-section is considered to be in an elastic state, as shown in Figure 2. In the absence of axial force, the neutral axis $y_n = y_{cr}$ (given with respect to the top edge) and is given as

$$y_{cr} = \frac{\frac{bh^2}{2} + (n-1)(A_s'd' + A_sd)}{bh + (n-1)(A_s' + A_s)}, \tag{3}$$

where $n = E_s/E_c$ represents the ratio between the elastic modulus of steel (E_s) and concrete (E_c).

The moment of inertia of the adjusted (with $A_2 = (n-1)A_s'$ and $A_3 = (n-1)A_s$, representing adjusted cross-sections of the rebars) cross-sectional centroid $I_n = \sum_{i=1}^{3} I_i + A_i(y_i - y_{cr})^2$, accounting for the small and entirely negligible centroid moment of inertia of the rebar ($I_s = I_2 = I_3 \approx 0$), is calculated as

$$I_n = \frac{bh^3}{12} + bh\left(\frac{h}{2} - y_{cr}\right)^2 + (n-1)\left(A_s'(d' - y_{cr})^2 + A_s(d - y_{cr})^2\right). \tag{4}$$

The limit moment M_{cr} and the corresponding curvature $\kappa_{cr} = \frac{d\varepsilon_c(y)}{dy}$ at the point when the first crack appears are as follows:

$$M_{cr} = \frac{f_{ct} I_n}{h - y_{cr}}, \tag{5}$$

and

$$\kappa_{cr} = \frac{f_{ct}}{E_c(h - y_{cr})} = \frac{\varepsilon_{ct}}{h - y_{cr}}, \tag{6}$$

where ε_{ct} represents the maximum tensile strain of the concrete.

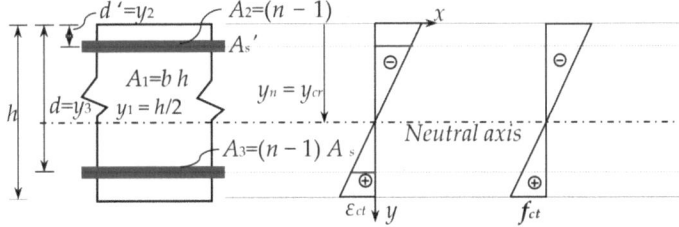

Figure 2. Stress and strain distribution over the cross-section height at the first crack initiation.

2.2. Determination of the Limit Characteristic Point for $M = M_y$ and $\kappa = \kappa_y$

In determining the limit moment M_y at which the tensile reinforcement starts to yield, the strain (ε_s) and the resultant force (F_s) in the bottom (tensile) reinforcement have been taken into account as

$$\varepsilon_s = \varepsilon_y, \tag{7}$$

and consequently,

$$F_s = f_y A_s. \tag{8}$$

The normal stresses in concrete, as given by Equation (1), occur only in the compression zone and are expected to be only parabolically distributed along the height of the non-cracked part of the cross-section, within the limits $0 \geq \varepsilon_c \geq \varepsilon_{c2}$ shown in Figure 3, where parabolic distribution is presented. The figure illustrates the additional required parameters, including the maximum compressive strain in the top fibre of the concrete (ε_{cc}), strain in the top reinforcement (ε_s'), the resultant compressive force in the concrete (F_c), the resultant force in the top reinforcement (F_s'), and the linear function of the strains over the section height $\varepsilon_c(y)$ when the bottom reinforcement reaches yielding.

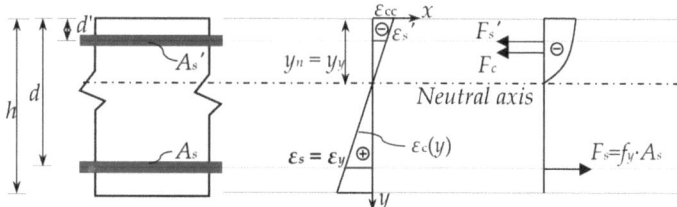

Figure 3. Stress and strain distribution over the cross-section height at the initiation of the yielding of the tension (bottom) reinforcement.

At the beginning of the yielding of the bottom reinforcement in the cross-section (assuming that the stresses in the compression zone of the concrete are exclusively distributed by the parabola), the compressive forces in concrete F_c and the top reinforcement F_s', depending on the position of the neutral axis $y_n = y_y$, must be determined as follows:

$$F_c = b \int_0^{y_y} \sigma_c(y) dy = b \int_0^{y_y} f_c \left(1 - \left(1 - \frac{\varepsilon_c(y)}{\varepsilon_{c2}}\right)^2\right) dy, \tag{9}$$

and

$$F_s' = \varepsilon_s' A_s' (E_s - E_c) = \varepsilon_c (y = d') A_s' (E_s - E_c), \tag{10}$$

assuming that the top rebar is still behaving elastically.

The strain $\varepsilon_c(y)$ can be expressed as a linear function by considering boundary conditions $\varepsilon_c(y = d) = \varepsilon_y$ and $\varepsilon_c(y = y_y) = 0$. Therefore, the strain function is

$$\varepsilon_c(y) = \frac{\varepsilon_y (y - y_y)}{d - y_y} \quad for \ \ 0 \leq y \leq h. \tag{11}$$

Considering Equation (11) in Equation (9), the resultant force in the concrete (F_c) is now

$$F_c = -\frac{b f_c y_y{}^2 \varepsilon_y \left(3 d \varepsilon_{c2} + y_y (\varepsilon_y - 3\varepsilon_{c2})\right)}{3 \varepsilon_{c2}{}^2 (d - y_y)^2}, \tag{12}$$

where the correct orientation of F_c is already presented in Figure 3.

The neutral axis position y_y is established by balancing all the forces acting on the cross-section $F_c + F_s' + F_s = 0$ (considering that F_c and F_s' are obtained with negative signs). As a result, the cubic characteristic polynomial is formed:

$$\sum_{i=1}^{4} \beta_{i,y} y_y{}^{i-1} = 0, \tag{13}$$

where the constants $\beta_{i,y}$ ($i = 1, 2, 3, 4$) are defined as

$$
\begin{aligned}
\beta_{1,y} &= 3d\varepsilon_{c2}{}^2\big(A_s d f_y + A'_s \varepsilon_y d'(E_s - E_c)\big) \\
\beta_{2,y} &= -3\varepsilon_{c2}{}^2\big(2A_s d f_y - A'_s \varepsilon_y (d+d')(E_s - E_c)\big) \\
\beta_{3,y} &= 3\varepsilon_{c2}\big(A_s f_y \varepsilon_{c2} - \varepsilon_y(A'_s \varepsilon_{c2}(E_s - E_c) + bd f_c)\big) \\
\beta_{4,y} &= b f_c \varepsilon_y (3\varepsilon_{c2} - \varepsilon_y)
\end{aligned}
\tag{14}
$$

The neutral axis position y_y at reinforcement yielding initiation in the tensile zone is determined using the relevant cubic polynomial solution, as follows:

$$
y_y = \sum_{j=1}^{2}\left(\left(-\frac{1}{2} + (-1)^{j+1}\frac{i\sqrt{3}}{2}\right)\sqrt[3]{-q + (-1)^j\sqrt{q^2 + p^3}}\right) - \frac{\beta_{3,y}}{3\beta_{4,y}},
\tag{15}
$$

where the coefficients p and q are defined as

$$
\begin{aligned}
p &= \frac{3\beta_{4,y}\beta_{2,y} - \beta_{3,y}{}^2}{9\beta_{4,y}{}^2} \\
q &= \frac{2\beta_{3,y}{}^3 - 9\beta_{2,y}\beta_{3,y}\beta_{4,y} + 27\beta_{1,y}\beta_{4,y}{}^2}{54\beta_{4,y}{}^3}
\end{aligned}.
\tag{16}
$$

The two remaining obtained solutions of the cubic polynomial for this problem are irrelevant as they lie outside the boundaries of the cross-section area.

The characteristic limit moment M_y is determined by utilising the moment equilibrium of all the resulting forces in the cross-section:

$$
M_y = M_c + F'_s d' + F_s d,
\tag{17}
$$

where $M_c = b\int_0^{y_y}\sigma_c(y)y\,dy$ represents the moment of resulting force (F_c) of the non-cracked concrete section, which is denoted as follows:

$$
M_c = -\frac{b f_c y_y{}^3 \varepsilon_y\big(4d\varepsilon_{c2} + y_y(\varepsilon_y - 4\varepsilon_{c2})\big)}{12\varepsilon_{c2}{}^2(d - y_y)^2}.
\tag{18}
$$

The corresponding curvature, obtained as $\kappa_y = \frac{d\varepsilon_c(y)}{dy}$, follows as

$$
\kappa_y = \frac{\varepsilon_y}{d - y_y}.
\tag{19}
$$

The closed-form solution for M_y and κ_y is restricted to cases where the bottom reinforcement yields prior to the strain in the concrete reaching ε_{c2} from Equation (1). A necessary condition for the validity of the application of the derived expressions is therefore $\varepsilon_{cc} = \varepsilon_c(y = 0) \geq \varepsilon_{c2}$.

2.3. Determination of the Limit Characteristic Point for $M = M_u$ and $\kappa = \kappa_u$

The value of the characteristic ultimate moment M_u is determined by considering that, at the initiation of compression failure of the top concrete fibre, the maximum compressive edge strain in the concrete is $\varepsilon_{cc} = \varepsilon_{c3}$. The linear strain function $\varepsilon_c(y)$ is therefore acquired under the following two conditions, $\varepsilon_c(y = 0) = \varepsilon_{cc} = \varepsilon_{c3}$ and $\varepsilon_c(y = y_u) = 0$. Thus, the strain function is

$$
\varepsilon_c(y) = \varepsilon_{c3}\left(1 - \frac{y}{y_u}\right).
\tag{20}
$$

At the initiation of concrete failure at the top compressive edge of the cross-section, the total resulting force (F_c) in the concrete non-cracked area is calculated by combining the resulting forces of two sub-areas. These areas include the region where the concrete strain is within the limits of $\varepsilon_{c2} \geq \varepsilon_c \geq \varepsilon_{c3}$ and the region where the concrete strain is at limit $0 \geq \varepsilon_c \geq \varepsilon_{c2}$, as illustrated in Figure 4.

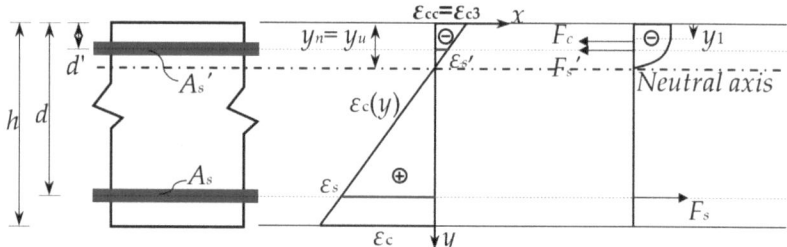

Figure 4. Stress and strain distribution over the cross-section height at the initiation of concrete failure at the top compressive fibre.

The location of the fibre separating the two stress functions across the cross-section, as derived from Equation (1), is designated as y_1, originating from the top of the cross-section, and by applying the condition $\varepsilon_c(y = y_1) = \varepsilon_{c2}, y_1$, it is defined as follows:

$$y_1 = \frac{y_u\,(\varepsilon_{c3} - \varepsilon_{c2})}{\varepsilon_{c3}}. \tag{21}$$

Considering Equation (21), the resulting force in concrete $F_c = b(\int_0^{y_1} f_c dy + \int_{y_1}^{y_u} f_c \left(\left(1 + \frac{\varepsilon_c(y)}{\varepsilon_{c2}}\right)^2 - 1\right) dy)$ can be expressed as follows:

$$F_c = \frac{1}{3} b f_c y_u \left(3 - \frac{\varepsilon_{c2}}{\varepsilon_{c3}}\right). \tag{22}$$

The forces acting on the top reinforcement (presumed in an elastic zone) and on the bottom reinforcement are

$$F_s' = \varepsilon_s' A_s' E_s = \varepsilon_c\left(y = d'\right) A_s' E_s, \tag{23}$$

and

$$F_s = f_y A_s. \tag{24}$$

It should be noted that when calculating the neutral axis $y_n = y_u$ at the initiation of the compressive failure of the concrete, it is necessary to check the following condition $|\varepsilon_s'| = |\varepsilon_c(y = d')| \le \varepsilon_y$, as it is assumed in Equation (23) that the upper reinforcement remains within the elastic region.

The position of the neutral axis y_u is determined by achieving equilibrium among the resulting forces of $F_c + F_s' + F_s = 0$ in the cross-section. As a result, the quadratic polynomial is obtained:

$$\sum_{i=1}^{3} \beta_{i,u} y_u^{\,i-1} = 0. \tag{25}$$

where the constants $\beta_{i,u}$ $(i = 1, 2, 3)$ are defined as

$$\begin{aligned} \beta_{1,u} &= -3 A_s' d' E_s \varepsilon_{c3}^{\,2} \\ \beta_{2,u} &= 3\varepsilon_{c3}\left(A_s f_y + A_s E_s \varepsilon_{c3}\right) \,. \\ \beta_{3,u} &= b f_c (3\,\varepsilon_{c3} - \varepsilon_{c2}) \end{aligned} \tag{26}$$

The position of the neutral axis y_u at the initiation of concrete collapse is defined by the solution of Equation (25), which is thus

$$y_u = \frac{\sqrt{\beta_{2,u}^{\,2} - 4\beta_{1,u}\beta_{3,u}} - \beta_{2,u}}{2\beta_{3,u}}. \tag{27}$$

The other solution of Equation (25) is irrelevant as it lies outside the boundaries of the cross-sectional area.

The characteristic moment M_u is determined by applying the moment equilibrium of all the resulting forces in the cross-section:

$$M_u = M_c + F_s'd' + F_s d, \tag{28}$$

where $M_c = b\left(\int_0^{y_1} \sigma_c y\, dy + \int_{-y_1}^{y_u} \sigma_c(y)y\, dy\right)$ denotes the moment of the stresses in the non-cracked concrete section, which is expressed as

$$M_c = \frac{b f_c y_u^2 \left(\varepsilon_{c2}^2 - 4\varepsilon_{c2}\varepsilon_{c3} + 6\varepsilon_{c3}^2\right)}{12\varepsilon_{c3}^2}, \tag{29}$$

and the corresponding curvature $\kappa_u = \frac{d\varepsilon_c(y)}{dy}$ is as follows:

$$\kappa_u = -\frac{\varepsilon_{c3}}{y_u}. \tag{30}$$

It should be noted that the presented expressions (Equations (3)–(30)), which were derived for doubly reinforced cross-sections, are applicable also to the single rebar cross-section, simply taking into account the cross-section of the top rebar as $A_s' = 0$.

3. Practical Application and Experimental Testing

The expressions derived in the previous section can be implemented for a pure bending analysis of an arbitrary rectangular cross-section with single or double reinforcement. Although they are derived in complete accordance with the laws of structural mechanics, they also include some details related to the EC2 standard requirements. To gain insight into matching the assumptions of structural mechanics and the standard's requirements, an analysis of the bending of a simply supported beam, for which the experimentally obtained values of transverse displacement at the centre were known [10], was performed using the presented expressions. Since it is a simple statically determined structure, a preliminary analysis was first performed, which led to analytical expressions for the magnitude of the transverse displacement for different phases related to the degree of cracking of different parts of the concrete beam depending on the size of the load. These derived specific expressions for the magnitude of the transverse displacement of the structure in question enabled a faster analysis of the values for comparison, but they are not necessary since all the integrals that appear in the analysis can equally be qualitatively evaluated purely numerically.

3.1. Determination of a Closed-Form Solution for the Transverse Displacement at the Centre of a Simply Supported Beam

In this section, the limit value of the Euler–Bernoulli transverse displacement at the centre of the four-point loaded RC beam from Figure 5 is calculated. The end spans and the middle span areas had different longitudinally reinforced rectangular cross-sections, with single reinforcement (subscript 1) in the end spans and double reinforcement (subscript 2) in the middle span. The beam characteristics include the total span of the beam between the two supports (l), the end span from the support to the concentrated force (l_1) and the mid-span between the concentrated forces (l_2). The beam is loaded with two vertical concentrated loads, acting at the borders of the middle span area. This load causes a constant bending moment value in the beam between both forces in the middle span area, and linear ones in both side areas.

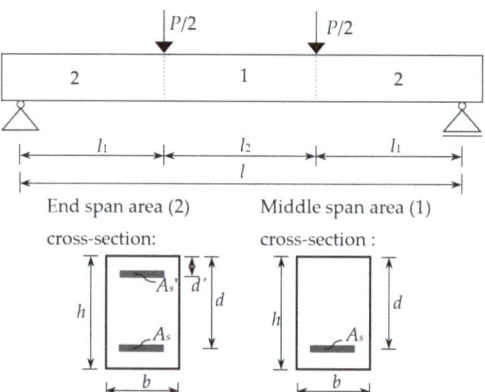

Figure 5. Four-point-loaded, simply supported RC beam with differently rebar-reinforced rectangular cross-sections in the middle span and end span areas.

Transverse displacement is calculated for all three limit moments (M_{cr}^1 at the initiation of the first crack, M_y^1 at the occurrence of the first yielding of the tensile reinforcement and M_u^1 at the compressive failure of the concrete, all appearing at the middle span area of the beam). Due to the symmetry of the beam and the loading, an alternative simplified model for the left half of the beam is considered for calculating the transverse displacements. The change in the bending stiffness, which occurs at the first crack, does not affect the linear relationship between the load and the bending moments due to the static determinacy of the structure. Therefore, the three limit moments M_i^1 ($i = cr, y, u$) that occur at the middle span area of the beam between the two forces, as shown in Figure 6, determine the two bending moment functions for the two areas:

$$M_i(x) = \frac{M_i^1}{l_1}x \qquad 0 \le x \le l_1, \tag{31}$$

and

$$M_i(x) = M_i^1 \qquad l_1 \le x \le \frac{l}{2}, \tag{32}$$

where $M_i^1 = P_i l_1 / 2$ ($i = cr, y, u$) represents the maximum bending moment at the middle span area of the beam as a function of the applied load P_i.

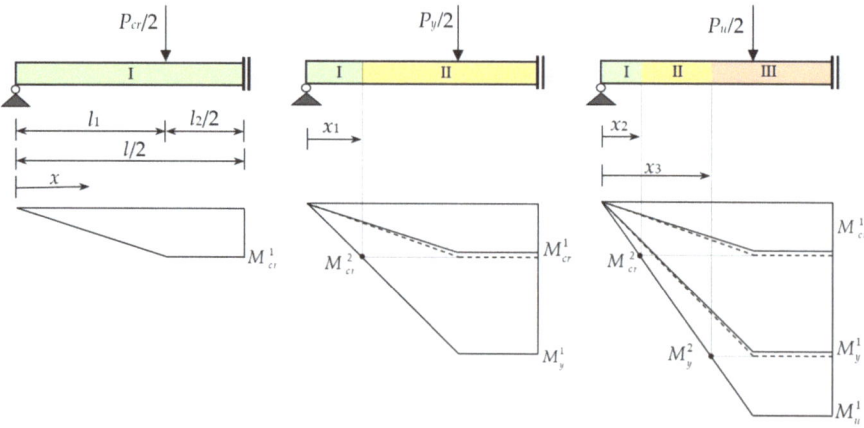

Figure 6. Moment diagrams for three characteristic moment values on the left half of the beam.

The transverse displacement of the beam at the centre (Δ) caused by bending is determined analytically for all three characteristic moments using the virtual work principle $\Delta = \int_l M(x)/EI\delta M(x) \ dx$, where $\delta M(x)$ is the moment that occurs due to a virtual vertical unit force at the centre of the beam. Considering the relation between the bending moment and the curvature, the transverse displacement Δ is expressed by the following equation:

$$\Delta = \int_0^{\frac{l}{2}} \kappa(x)x\,dx. \tag{33}$$

3.1.1. Determination of the Limit Characteristic Transverse Displacement Δ_{cr}

The transverse displacement Δ_{cr} that characterises the occurrence of the first crack in area II is determined utilising Equation (33) for the two elastic zones as

$$\Delta_{cr} = \int_0^{l_1} \kappa^2_{cr,M_{cr}^1}(x)x\,dx + \int_{l_1}^{\frac{l}{2}} \kappa^1_{cr,M_{cr}^1}x\,dx, \tag{34}$$

where the corresponding curvatures are defined as

$$\begin{aligned} \kappa^2_{cr,M_{cr}^1}(x) &= \frac{\kappa^2_{cr}}{M_{cr}^2}\frac{M_{cr}^1}{l_1}x \quad 0 \le x \le l_1, \\ \kappa^1_{cr,M_{cr}^1} &= \kappa^1_{cr} \quad l_1 \le x \le \frac{l}{2}. \end{aligned} \tag{35}$$

3.1.2. Determination of the Limit Characteristic Transverse Displacement Δ_y

The characteristic transverse displacement Δ_y at yielding initiation is determined by considering M_y^1. At the occurrence of the initial reinforcement yielding, the part of the beam from the left support to location x_1 still remains in the elastic zone (i.e., non-cracked state), while the rest of the beam from location x_1 to the centre of the beam is in the state of the crack propagation limit phase. The location x_1 is found from the moment function when considering $M(x = x_1) = M_y^1 x_1/l_1 = M_{cr}^2$. Thus, the location x_1 is

$$x_1 = \frac{M_{cr}^2}{M_y^1}l_1. \tag{36}$$

The characteristic displacement Δ_y at yielding initiation is therefore

$$\Delta_y = \int_0^{x_1} \kappa^2_{cr,M_y^1}(x)x\,dx + \int_{x_1}^{l_1} \kappa^2_{y,M_y^1}(x)x\,dx + \int_{l_1}^{\frac{l}{2}} \kappa^1_{y,M_y^1}x\,dx, \tag{37}$$

where the corresponding curvatures are defined as

$$\begin{aligned} \kappa^2_{cr,M_y^1}(x) &= \frac{\kappa^2_{cr}}{M_{cr}^2}\frac{M_y^1}{l_1}\cdot x \quad 0 \le x \le x_1, \\ \kappa^2_{y,M_y^1}(x) &= \frac{\kappa^2_{cr}-\kappa^2_y}{M_{cr}^2-M_y^2}\frac{M_y^1}{l_1}x + \frac{M_{cr}^2\kappa^2_y-M_y^2\kappa^2_{cr}}{M_{cr}^2-M_y^2} \quad x_1 \le x \le l_1, \\ \kappa^1_{y,M_y^1} &= \kappa^1_y l_1 \quad \le x \le \frac{l}{2}. \end{aligned} \tag{38}$$

3.1.3. Determination of the Limit Characteristic Transverse Displacement Δ_u

The characteristic displacement Δ_u is computed under the assumption of the bending moment reaching the value of M_u^1 in the middle span area. At the initiation of the compressive failure of the concrete, the section of the beam between the left support and location x_2 is in the elastic zone, while the section between locations x_2 and x_3 is in the cracked zone, and the area between x_3 and the centre of the beam is in the yielding zone. Locations x_2 and x_3 are determined by utilising the moment functions with respect to $M(x = x_2) = M_u^1 x_2/l_1 = M_{cr}^2$ and $M(x = x_3) = M_u^1 x_3/l_1 = M_y^2$. Thus, locations x_2 and x_3 are

$$x_2 = \frac{M_{cr}^2}{M_u^1} l_1, \tag{39}$$

and

$$x_3 = \frac{M_y^2}{M_u^1} l_1. \tag{40}$$

The characteristic displacement Δ_u at the compressive failure of the concrete is therefore

$$\Delta_u = \int_0^{x_2} \kappa_{cr,M_u^1}^2(x)x dx + \int_{x_2}^{x_3} \kappa_{y,M_u^1}^2(x)x dx + \int_{x_3}^{l_1} \kappa_{u,M_u^1}^2(x)x dx + \int_{l_1}^{\frac{l}{2}} \kappa_{u,M_u^1}^1 x dx, \tag{41}$$

where the corresponding curvatures are defined as

$$
\begin{aligned}
\kappa_{cr,M_u^1}^2(x) &= \frac{\kappa_{cr}^2}{M_{cr}^2} \frac{M_u^1}{l_1} x \quad 0 \le x \le x_2, \\
\kappa_{y,M_u^1}^2(x) &= \frac{\kappa_{cr}^2 - \kappa_y^2}{M_{cr}^2 - M_y^2} \frac{M_u^1}{l_1} \cdot x + \frac{M_{cr}^2 \kappa_y^2 - M_y^2 \kappa_{cr}^2}{M_{cr}^2 - M_y^2} \quad x_2 \le x \le x_3, \\
\kappa_{u,M_u^1}^2(x) &= \frac{\kappa_u^2 - \kappa_y^2}{M_u^2 - M_y^2} \frac{M_u^1}{l_1} x + \frac{M_u^2 \kappa_y^2 - M_y^2 \kappa_u^2}{M_u^2 - M_y^2} \quad x_3 \le x \le l_1, \\
\kappa_{u,M_u^1}^1 &= \kappa_u^1 \quad l_1 \le x \le \frac{l}{2}.
\end{aligned}
\tag{42}
$$

3.2. Experimental Verification and Discussion

Prior to the bending experiment, two preliminary tests were performed to obtain the mechanical characteristics of the steel and the concrete. The yield strength of the rebar is $f_y = 605$ MPa and represents the average value of two tensile tests performed separately of the rebar being installed. The measured strain at the yielding of the rebar is $\varepsilon_y = 3‰$. The elastic modulus of the steel (calculated from the measured stresses and strains) is $E_s = f_y / \varepsilon_y = 201.7$ GPa. The compressive mean value of the concrete strength is $f_{cm,cube} = -44.8$ MPa and represents the average of the uniaxial compressive strength of the embedded concrete on six standardised cubes.

The beam geometric characteristics from the bending experiment, which have also been implemented in the analytical model, are summarised in Table 1.

Table 1. Default beam characteristics from the bending experiment.

Parameter	Value
Beam span between supports (l)	1.45 m
Span from support to concentrated force (l_1)	0.475 m
Span between concentrated forces (l_2)	0.50 m
Cross-section width (b)	0.10 m
Cross-section height (h)	0.15 m
Distance from top edge to centroid of bottom rebar (d)	12.1 cm
Distance from top edge to centroid of top rebar (d')	2.9 cm
Area of bottom rebar (A_s)	1.571 cm^2
Area of top rebar ($A_s{}'$)	1.571 cm^2

All the remaining material properties of the concrete that were not determined experimentally during the concrete testing phase were determined using the empirical expressions defined by EC2 and are given in Table 2. As can be seen from the table, the mean values of the compressive strength ($f_c = f_{cm}$), tensile strength ($f_{ct} = f_{ctm}$) and modulus of elasticity ($E_c = E_{cm}$) of the cylinder were implemented in the analytical model for the concrete.

Table 2. Default material characteristics of concrete in analytical model in accordance with EC2.

Empirical Expressions (According to EC2)	Material Characteristics
$f_{cm} = 0.8\, f_{cm,cube}$	$f_c = f_{cm} = -35.84$ MPa
$f_{ck} = f_{cm} - 8\,\text{(MPa)}$	$f_{ck} = -27.84$ MPa
$f_{ctm} = 0.30 \cdot (f_{ck})^{\frac{2}{3}}$	$f_{ct} = f_{ctm} = 2.75$ MPa
$E_{cm} = 22 \cdot (f_c/10)^{0.3}$	$E_c = E_{cm} = 32.3$ GPa
$f_{ck} < 50$ MPa	$\varepsilon_{c2} = -2.0‰$
$f_{ck} < 50$ MPa	$\varepsilon_{c3} = \varepsilon_{cu2} = -3.5‰$

The testing device consisted of two parts, the lower support structure and the upper hydraulic piston, through which the load was introduced (Figure 7). The used hydraulic piston had a nominal force of Fv = 100 kN, and the working span of the piston was 250 mm. The piston was connected to a control unit with an analogue load display in pressure units, and the loading rate was around 32 N/s. The displacements of the concrete beam under the applied force Fv were simultaneously measured with three MarCator 1086 digital indicators located beneath the applied forces and at the mid-span of the beam. All the applied devices were calibrated by the corresponding actual testing standards.

Figure 7. Testing setup.

The analytical model has produced results which include the limit points for the moment–curvature diagrams ($M^1 - \kappa^1$ and $M^2 - \kappa^2$) of the middle span and end span areas, and the force–displacement ($P - \Delta$) diagrams. All of these results have been determined based on the data given for this case, and are conveniently summarised in Table 3.

Table 3. Results of the characteristic limit points of the analytical model.

i	cr	y	u
M_i^1 [kNm]	1.12787	9.98333	10.2068
κ_i^1 [10^{-3} rad/m]	1.17264	38.7849	106.822
M_i^2 [kNm]	1.15910	9.93093	10.1910
κ_i^2 [10^{-3} rad/m]	1.13519	37.4166	114.095
P_i [kN]	4.74891	42.0351	42.9761
Δ_i [mm]	0.25897	8.51234	19.0298

The transverse displacements from the experiment (presented in Figure 8) clearly confirm three phases for the structure in question, as was also foreseen when preparing the analytical expressions, and in the first two phases, the match between the calculated and measured values is almost perfect from the engineering point of view.

The experimental elastic phase (I) shows a slightly shorter linear range of measured transverse displacements at the centre of the beam compared to the analytical model with implemented expressions from EC2. This is due to the use of an apparent overestimation of the concrete tensile strength value (f_{ct}), obtained through the code. Therefore, the actual tensile strength is apparently much lower than assumed. On the other hand, the remaining material properties of the concrete defined according to EC2 provide a satisfactory accuracy.

In the crack propagation limit phase (II), the transverse displacements match well with the experimental results, providing an accurate representation of the real behaviour of the materials used in the analytical model.

During the reinforcement's yielding limit phase (III), when the bending moment due to the applied load approaches the ultimate limit state of bearing capacity, the analytical model exhibits a somewhat diminished agreement with the experimentally obtained values. In this phase, the stress resultant in the concrete area is an increasing function of stresses and the simultaneously decreasing function of the concrete area in compression. Such an inverse relationship between the two parameters certainly depends on the quality of both material's constitutive laws, which are, as we know, approximations. Therefore, the observed differences are attributed to the use of a simplified and conservative non-linear behaviour (in accordance to standard EC2) for both materials in the analytical model. In the preliminary experimental testing of the steel bars, the elastic limit was conservatively set at the limit of proportionality, without consideration of their non-linear elastic (i.e., with the inclined top branch of the steel design stress–strain diagram) behaviour. Nevertheless, the analytically derived definitions not only yield more than satisfactory results considering the uncertainties inherent in the experimental results in the ultimate plastic range, but the experimentally obtained results are even more favourable from the design practice point of view.

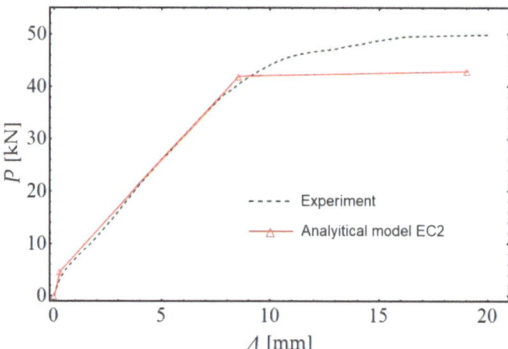

Figure 8. Comparing the experimental displacements with those predicted by the analytical model.

4. Expanding Utilisation of Detailed Solutions to Simplified Substitutive Computational Model

The analysis of the case of a simple structure in the previous study not only showed that the matching of values in the more significant engineering phase of the structural element's cracking is very good, but at the same time, it also exposed that such a thorough non-linear incremental analysis would be very time- and computational effort-consuming for more demanding structures.

When considering the serviceability limit states, where we usually focus just on the displacements, or in situations with a not accurate enough knowledge of the load (unpredictable both in magnitude as well as in direction), such as, e.g., in the analysis of the seismic load, it becomes clear that the analysis of the practically infinite possible combinations of orientations and the magnitude of the seismic load in this way is at least meaningless, if not even impossible. At the same time, it is clear that with such extreme loads, it is impossible to avoid concrete cracking, which will appear quite unpredictably (both in terms of location and size), because this is also the nature of an earthquake impact. Therefore, various standards (Eurocode 8, FEMA) enable a compromise between the thorough analysis and the complete ignoring of cracking. The impact of the cracks is thus introduced as a simple uniform reduction of bending stiffness over the entire length of each individual structural element. Such an elementary approach of including cracking is computationally straightforward, but at the same time, the quality of its results is questionable.

4.1. Determination of the Simplified Computational Model Mechanical Parameters

A much better engineering alternative, also allowed by the structural codes and also already implemented in existing software, is where the displacement response of a cracked element or beam is being modelled as a combination of two rigid parts, connected by a rotational spring (Figure 9). The position of the spring coincides with the location of the analysed displacement. The stiffness K_r of this spring must now summarise the effects from both distributions: the pure elastic deformation as well as the cracked state within the complete structural element (in contrast to the rotational spring stiffness genuine definition, which is an exclusive function of the local state of the crack, i.e., at the discrete location of the crack).

The total characteristic rotations $\varphi_{tot,i}$ ($i = cr, y, u$) in spring with rotational stiffness K_r situated at the midpoint of the beam, shown in Figure 9, which encompass both the elastic as well as non-elastic deformations in the beam, have been determined using three analytically computed characteristic transverse displacements Δ_i ($i = cr, y, u$) and the kinematic relationship that is valid for the selected substitutive model. Each total characteristic rotation $\varphi_{tot,i}$ value was thus calculated as

$$\varphi_{tot,i} = \frac{4\Delta_i}{l}. \tag{43}$$

and the obtained values are presented in the first row of Table 3.

This definition of a rotational spring is appropriate for analyses that use non-deformable line elements. However, structural computational models (like finite element models) already account for the bending elastic deformations of elastic segments. Therefore, the elastic (linear) component $\varphi_{e,i}$ is obtained through the implementation of linear constitutive moment–rotation law and similar triangles:

$$\varphi_{e,i} = \varphi_{cr} \frac{M_i^s}{M_{cr}^s} \tag{44}$$

Further, this value is subtracted from the total rotation of the rotational spring $\varphi_{tot,i}$ [35], providing the pure inelastic component for all three characteristic points ($i = cr, y, u$):

$$\varphi_{p,i} = \varphi_{tot,i} - \varphi_{e,i}. \tag{45}$$

Figure 10 shows the generalised moment–rotation diagrams for all three definitions of rotational springs.

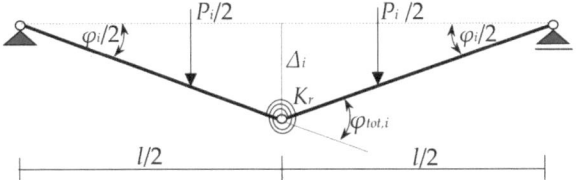

Figure 9. Transversely deformed beam with equivalent rotational spring in the mid-point.

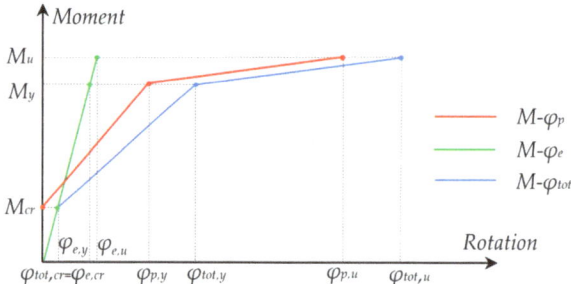

Figure 10. Generalised tri-linear moment–rotation diagram for a rotational spring.

4.2. Application Demonstration and Discussion

All of the characteristic corresponding rotation values for the previously considered beam have been determined by Equations (34), (37), (41) and (43)–(45) implementing the example data given in Section 3.2, and are conveniently summarised in Table 4. These values, combined with the corresponding moments (M_i^s) from Table 3, allow for the actual tri-linear moment–rotation diagram for a rotational spring to be constructed. Further, the corresponding rotational spring stiffness K_r value for phases II and III is obtained as the ratio of the difference of the limiting moments of each phase to the difference of the limiting rotation of the same phase (while for phase I, the stiffness value equals infinity).

Table 4. Results of the characteristic rotation limit points of the rotational spring stiffness.

i	cr	y	u
$\varphi_{tot,i}$ [10^{-3} rad]	0.71440	23.4823	52.4959
$\varphi_{p,i}$ [10^{-3} rad]	0.00000	17.1588	46.0308
$\varphi_{e,i}$ [10^{-3} rad]	0.71440	6.32356	6.46511

To demonstrate the possibilities of the alternative simplified computational model, an FE model was prepared to perform a non-linear static bending pushover analysis of the previously considered four-point-loaded, simply supported RC beam. Due to the different cross-sections of the beam, as well as the applied concentrated loads, several FEs had to be implemented (Figure 11). Since the primary goal of this model was to determine the displacement at the mid-span, i.e., at the point where the experimentally obtained values of the displacement were known, the cracked beam three-noded finite element (CB3NFE) with an embedded non-linear rotational spring (K_r), with an additional degree of freedom at the location of the rotational spring [36,37], was applied for the middle-span area (element 2). By reducing the number of degrees of freedom, the utilisation of this element allows for a slightly smaller computational model than the implementation of four standard elements, simultaneously yielding an identical quality of the results. The applied FE model allows for more convenient modelling than the analytical solving of differential equations, and at the same time significantly simplifies the modelling for the analysis performed.

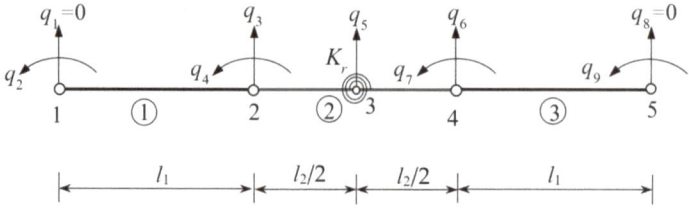

Figure 11. Idealised FE model of an RC beam using three finite elements.

In the discussed finite element analysis procedure, the bending moment at the location that governs the state and stresses in the cross-section was first obtained for each con-sidered load P. Afterwards, the bending stiffnesses in the applied finite elements was calculated by multiplying the concrete modulus of elasticity (E_c) with the moment of inertia (I_n) defined in Equation (4). Further, the implemented embedded rotational spring stiffness K_r was taken into account as a function of the applied moment, incorporating the limit points of the moment–rotation diagrams ($M^s - \varphi$) for three defined rotations, summarised in Table 4, allowing also the stiffness matrix for the second finite element to be evaluated. The additional process of analysis follows the standard steps for finite element analyses. Therefore, all three stiffness matrices of the finite elements are assembled in the structure's stiffness matrix.

For the example, for the load $P = 42.0351$ kN, the following stiffness matrix was obtained:

$$[K] = \begin{bmatrix} 8598.42 & -27152.9 & 4299.21 & 0 & 0 & 0 & 0 \\ -27152.9 & 324460. & 22265.3 & -235595. & 25462.9 & -3250.92 & 0 \\ 4299.21 & 22265.3 & 20663.5 & -52669.1 & 3250.92 & -523.309 & 0 \\ 0 & -235595. & -52669.1 & 471190. & -235595. & 52669.1 & 0 \\ 0 & 25462.9 & 3250.92 & -235595. & 324460. & -22265.3 & 27152.9 \\ 0 & -3250.92 & -523.309 & 52669.1 & -22265.3 & 20663.5 & 4299.21 \\ 0 & 0 & 0 & 0 & 27152.9 & 4299.21 & 8598.42 \end{bmatrix}$$

By also applying the load vector, discrete displacements and rotations in the model's nodes are obtained. Afterwards, this procedure is repeated for all load values of interest. However, it should be noted that the load must be applied incrementally (which is common in non-linear static analysis). Namely, when applying a load, structures redesign themselves accordingly, as the bending moment change can alter the bending stiffness, and the change of the bending stiffness in statically indeterminate structures even consequently causes a redistribution of the bending moment.

These results obtained from the presented FE model for the transverse displacement at the mid-span were identical to the results of the analytical model presented previously.

The relation established in this model between the derived tri-linear moment–curvature and moment–rotation diagrams provides a foundation for future research aimed at refining the definition of plastic hinge lengths. This link between the moment–curvature behaviour of the cross-section and the moment–rotation characteristics of a rotational spring allows for more accurate modelling of the plastic behaviour of RC beams.

5. Conclusions

This paper introduces an analytical model for predicting the transverse displacement of RC beams, using a three-linear moment–curvature diagram of the cross-section. The main contributions of the study are as follows:

- A closed-form solution for each of the three-phase moment–curvature relationships was developed, covering critical limit points: initial cracking, tensile reinforcement yielding, and ultimate concrete failure in compression;
- The model provides accurate predictions of the flexural behaviour of RC beams, validated through comparisons with experimental data, particularly in the elastic and crack propagation phases;
- The model accommodates both single and double reinforcement configurations, broadening its applicability across different beam designs;
- The analytical framework is adaptable and can be integrated into more complex structural systems to predict behaviour under varying loading conditions;
- A simplified computational model was also considered, enhancing the efficiency of the structural analysis and making it more practical for engineering applications.

Despite its strengths (efficiency and proven accuracy in the first two response phases), the model assumes perfect bonding between concrete and reinforcement and uses idealised material behaviours, which may limit its precision in more complex scenarios, such as irregular loading, high strain rates or non-standard geometries. Future research should address these limitations by refining material constitutive models, also incorporating shear effects and exploring the impact of cyclic and dynamic loading conditions.

Future studies might also build on the model with the rotational spring to develop more refined approaches that account for varying material properties, loading conditions and complex cross-sectional geometries, ultimately enhancing the reliability of plastic hinge length predictions in design and analysis.

Author Contributions: Conceptualisation, D.I.; theory development and methodology, D.I.; software, D.I. and M.S.; validation, D.I. and M.S.; formal analysis, D.I. and M.S.; writing—original draft preparation, D.I. and M.S.; writing—review and editing, D.I. and M.S.; visualisation, D.I. and M.S.; supervision, D.I. and M.S.; project administration, D.I. All authors have read and agreed to the published version of the manuscript.

Funding: This research received no external funding.

Data Availability Statement: Dataset available on request from the authors.

Acknowledgments: The second author acknowledges partial general financial support from the Slovenian Research Agency (research core funding No. P2-0129 (A) "Development, modelling and optimisation of structures and processes in civil engineering and traffic").

Conflicts of Interest: The authors declare no conflicts of interest.

References

1. Neville, A.M. *Properties of Concrete*; Longman: London, UK, 1995; Volume 4.
2. Cotsovos, D.M. A Simplified Approach for Assessing the Load-Carrying Capacity of Reinforced Concrete Beams under Concentrated Load Applied at High Rates. *Int. J. Impact Eng.* **2010**, *37*, 907–917. [CrossRef]
3. Foraboschi, P. Bending Load-Carrying Capacity of Reinforced Concrete Beams Subjected to Premature Failure. *Materials* **2019**, *12*, 3085. [CrossRef] [PubMed]
4. Akbaş, Ş.D. Large Deflection Analysis of a Fiber Reinforced Composite Beam. *Steel Compos. Struct. Int. J.* **2018**, *27*, 567–576.
5. Vodenitcharova, T.; Zhang, L.C. Bending and Local Buckling of a Nanocomposite Beam Reinforced by a Single-Walled Carbon Nanotube. *Int. J. Solids Struct.* **2006**, *43*, 3006–3024. [CrossRef]
6. Akbaş, Ş.D.; Ersoy, H.; Akgöz, B.; Civalek, Ö. Dynamic Analysis of a Fiber-Reinforced Composite Beam under a Moving Load by the Ritz Method. *Mathematics* **2021**, *9*, 1048. [CrossRef]
7. Weiss, W.J.; Güler, K.; Shah, S.P. Localization and Size-Dependent Response of Reinforced. *ACI Struct. J.* **2001**, *1*, 686–695.
8. Sumarac, D.; Sekulovic, M.; Krajcinovic, D. Fracture of Reinforced Concrete Beams Subjected to Three Point Bending. *Int. J. Damage Mech.* **2003**, *12*, 31–44. [CrossRef]
9. Fantilli, A.P.; Iori, I.; Vallini, P. Size Effect of Compressed Concrete in Four Point Bending RC Beams. *Eng. Fract. Mech.* **2007**, *74*, 97–108. [CrossRef]
10. Udovč, G. Nelinearna Računska Analiza in Eksperimentalna Verifikacija Nosilnosti Armiranobetonskega Nosilca Razpokanega Prereza. Master's Thesis, Univerza v Mariboru, Fakulteta za Gradbeništvo, Prometno Inženirstvo in Arhitekturo, Maribor, Slovenia, 2018.
11. Unuk, Ž.; Kuhta, M. Nonlinear Semi-Numeric and Finite Element Analysis of Three-Point Bending Tests of Notched Polymer Fiber-Reinforced Concrete Prisms. *Appl. Sci.* **2024**, *14*, 1604. [CrossRef]
12. Inel, M.; Ozmen, H.B. Effects of Plastic Hinge Properties in Nonlinear Analysis of Reinforced Concrete Buildings. *Eng. Struct.* **2006**, *28*, 1494–1502. [CrossRef]
13. *I.S. EN 1998-1:2005*; Eurocode 8: Design of Structures for Earthquake Resistance-Part 1: General Rules, Seismic Actions and Rules for Buildings. National Standards Authority of Ireland: Dublin, Ireland, 2005.
14. Yao, Y.; Aswani, K.; Wang, X.; Mobasher, B. Analytical Displacement Solutions for Statically Determinate Beams Based on a Trilinear Moment–Curvature Model. *Struct. Concr.* **2018**, *19*, 1619–1632. [CrossRef]
15. Liu, S.; Wang, X.; Ali, Y.M.; Su, C.; Wu, Z. Flexural Behavior and Design of Under-Reinforced Concrete Beams with BFRP and Steel Bars. *Eng. Struct.* **2022**, *263*, 114386. [CrossRef]
16. Zhang, Y.; Xiong, X.; Liang, Y.; He, M. Study on Flexural Behavior of Concrete Beams Reinforced with Hybrid High-Strength and High-Toughness (HSHT) and Ordinary Steel Bars. *Eng. Struct.* **2023**, *285*, 115978. [CrossRef]
17. Zhao, J.; Jiang, Y.; Li, X. Flexural Behavior of Concrete Beams Reinforced with High-Strength Steel Bars after Exposure to Elevated Temperatures. *Constr. Build. Mater.* **2023**, *382*, 131317. [CrossRef]
18. Sun, S.; Guo, Y.; Gui, P.; Xing, L.; Mei, K. Flexural Behaviour of Steel–Basalt Fibre Composite Bar-Reinforced Concrete Beams. *Eng. Struct.* **2023**, *289*, 116246. [CrossRef]

19. Zhang, X.; Sun, Y.; Yang, X.; Sun, L.; Wang, P. Study on the Bending Performance of High-Strength and High-Ductility CRE-Reinforced Concrete Beams. *Buildings* **2023**, *13*, 2746. [CrossRef]
20. Nematzadeh, M.; Fallah-Valukolaee, S. Experimental and Analytical Investigation on Structural Behavior of Two-Layer Fiber-Reinforced Concrete Beams Reinforced with Steel and GFRP Rebars. *Constr. Build. Mater.* **2021**, *273*, 121933. [CrossRef]
21. Yimer, M.A.; Dey, T. Dynamic Response of Concrete Beams Reinforced with GFRP and Steel Bars under Impact Loading. *Eng. Fail. Anal.* **2024**, *161*, 108329. [CrossRef]
22. Shao, S.; Shang, H.; Feng, H.; Wang, W. Study on the Mechanical Properties of NPR Steel Bars and the Bonding Properties with Marine Concrete. *Constr. Build. Mater.* **2022**, *316*, 125721. [CrossRef]
23. Ahmed, K.S.; Habib, M.A.; Asef, M.F. Flexural Response of Stainless Steel Reinforced Concrete Beam. In *Structures*; Elsevier: Amsterdam, The Netherlands, 2021; Volume 34, pp. 589–603.
24. Yao, Y.; Mobasher, B.; Wang, J.; Xu, Q. Analytical Approach for the Design of Flexural Elements Made of Reinforced Ultra-high Performance Concrete. *Struct. Concr.* **2021**, *22*, 298–317. [CrossRef]
25. Kartal, S.; Kalkan, I.; Beycioglu, A.; Dobiszewska, M. Load-Deflection Behavior of over-and under-Reinforced Concrete Beams with Hybrid FRP-Steel Reinforcements. *Materials* **2021**, *14*, 5341. [CrossRef] [PubMed]
26. Mosley, W.H.; Bungey, J.H.; Hulse, R. *Reinforced Concrete Design*; Springer: Berlin, Germany, 1999; ISBN 0-333-73956-6.
27. Avak, R. *Euro-Stahlbetonbau in Beispielen-Bemessung Nach DIN V ENV 1992-Teil 1: Baustoffe, Grundlagen, Bemessung von Stabtragwerken*; Werner Verlag: Dusseldorf, Germany, 1993; ISBN 3-8041-1044-4.
28. Bamforth, P.; Chisholm, D.; Gibbs, J.; Harrison, T. *Properties of Concrete for Use in Eurocode 2*; Institution of Structural Engineers: London, UK, 2008.
29. Ghersi, A. *Il Cemento Armato*; Dario Flaccovio: Milano, Italy, 2010.
30. Hognestad, E. *Study of Combined Bending and Axial Load in Reinforced Concrete Members*; University of Illinois at Urbana Champaign, College of Engineering: Champaign, IL, USA, 1951.
31. Mander, J.B.; Priestley, M.J.; Park, R. Theoretical Stress-Strain Model for Confined Concrete. *J. Struct. Eng.* **1988**, *114*, 1804–1826. [CrossRef]
32. Lin, C.-S.; Scordelis, A.C. Nonlinear Analysis of RC Shells of General Form. *J. Struct. Div.* **1975**, *101*, 523–538. [CrossRef]
33. *EN 1992-1-1:2004*; Eurocode 2: Design of Concrete Structures. British Standards: London, UK, 2004.
34. Paulay, T.; Priestley, M.N. *Seismic Design of Reinforced Concrete and Masonry Buildings*; Wiley: New York, NY, USA, 1992; Volume 768.
35. Ger, J.; Cheng, F.Y. *Seismic Design Aids for Nonlinear Pushover Analysis of Reinforced Concrete and Steel Bridges*; CRC Press: Boca Raton, FL, USA, 2011; Volume 2, ISBN 1-4398-3763-5.
36. Imamović, D.; Skrinar, M. Improved Finite Element of a Transversely Cracked Straight Beam with an Additional Degree of Freedom. *Lat. Am. J. Solids Struct.* **2019**, *16*, e193. [CrossRef]
37. Imamović, D. Development of New 1D Finite Elements for Numerical Modeling of Transversely Cracked Slender Beams of Rectangular Cross Section with Linear Varying Width and/or Depth. Ph.D. Thesis, University of Maribor, Faculty of Civil Engineering, Transportation Engineering and Architecture, Maribor, Slovenia, 2021.

MDPI

Article

Mathematical Modeling of the Floating Sleeper Phenomenon Supported by Field Measurements

Mojmir Uranjek [1,2], Denis Imamović [2] and Iztok Peruš [2,*]

1   Building and Civil Engineering Institute, Dimičeva 12, SI-1000 Ljubljana, Slovenia; mojmir.uranjek@um.si
2   Faculty of Civil Engineering, Architecture and Transportation Engineering, University of Maribor, Smetanova 17, SI-2000 Maribor, Slovenia; denis.imamovic@um.si
*   Correspondence: iztok.perus@um.si

Abstract: This article aims to provide an accurate mathematical model with the minimum number of degrees of freedom for describing the floating sleeper phenomenon. This was accomplished using mathematical modeling supported by extensive field measurements of the railway track. Although the observed phenomenon is very complex, the simplified single degree of freedom (SDOF) mathematical model proved accurate enough for its characterization. The progression of the deterioration of the railway track was successfully correlated to changes in the maximal dynamic factor for different types of pulse loading. The results of the presented study might enable the enhanced construction and maintenance of railroads, particularly in karst areas.

Keywords: floating sleepers; dynamic factor; pulse loading; field measurements; SDOF mathematical model

MSC: 37N15; 37N30; 74-05

Citation: Uranjek, M.; Imamović, D.; Peruš, I. Mathematical Modeling of the Floating Sleeper Phenomenon Supported by Field Measurements. *Mathematics* **2024**, *12*, 3142. https://doi.org/10.3390/math12193142

Academic Editor: Carlo Bianca

Received: 11 September 2024
Revised: 2 October 2024
Accepted: 5 October 2024
Published: 8 October 2024

1. Introduction

For a detailed analysis of the stress state in ballast railway tracks for different extreme cases such as geometrical irregularities of the rail, ballast fouling, or abrupt changes in stiffness along the railway track, realistic but also complex 2D [1] or 3D [2] numerical models are used. Simpler models, on the other hand, enable quicker characterization of the problem; however, they do not allow all factors to be considered. The simplest track model is the one introduced by Winkler in 1867, where the track was modeled as a beam on a continuous elastic foundation [3,4]. In this approach, a beam (rail) rests on a continuous elastic foundation modeled by evenly distributed linear spring stiffness. This model is suitable for assessing the static loading of a track on a soft support (i.e., wooden sleepers); however, it does not allow dynamic effects to be considered. In a more advanced approach, the track is modeled as a beam on discrete supports (e.g., Ref. [5]). Here, the rail is modeled as a Euler–Bernoulli or Rayleigh–Timoshenko beam, and rail pads by spring-damper systems. Sleepers are represented as rigid masses and ballast is modeled by spring-damper systems. To be able to consider the influence of resonance at lower frequencies, this model can be upgraded by incorporating the ballast mass [6]. The viability and applicability of this model are considered in Ref. [7] by using calibration with a 3D modeling approach. At this point, we should mention other problems that are directly related to the issues of railway infrastructure, e.g., the hunting phenomenon related to the lateral oscillation of the rail wheels [8], mathematical modeling of the deformable characteristics of railway ballast [9], and various complex mathematical analyses of the rail beam, e.g., numerical analyses of the non-uniform layered ground vibration caused by a moving railway load [10]. In the modern sustainable development of railway infrastructure, we must not forget about innovation (e.g., Cai et al. [11] identified key influencing factors in railway engineering technological innovation in complex and difficult areas) and maintenance [12–15]. Effective planning, first, and maintenance of railway infrastructure, second, could largely prevent the phenomenon of floating sleepers discussed in this article. A step toward a better understanding of this phenomenon is, therefore, presented in this article.

The main objective of this work was to develop a simplified mathematical model with the minimum number of degrees of freedom possible, which would be accurate enough and allow simple characterization of the floating sleeper phenomenon. Such an approach would enable an easy graphical presentation of the results. Therefore, this paper could improve engineering understanding of the phenomenon and the effective development of various technical solutions to deal with the problem efficiently. Within the framework of the performed analysis, a simplified mathematical model for loading and dynamic response has been used. The results in the presented study indicate that the dynamic factor for short-term pulse loading, which corresponds to a one- or two-axle passage of train composition, has relatively low values for typical track stiffness. The factor reaches very high values with decreasing track stiffness and then decreases with a small value of track stiffness. The observed phenomenon can be described as highly non-linear.

2. Methods and Field Measurements

2.1. Basic Idea and Methods Used

Solving the problem of floating sleepers can be approached in several ways—with an experimental approach, with a theoretical approach, or with a combination of both. For example, in Ref. [16], it was established with an experimental approach that the phenomenon of floating sleepers is affected by a local change in the stiffness of the rail beam, which is generally the result of several factors. These were identified based on extensive experimental work and an analysis of the obtained results, with the help of artificial neural networks. Of the factors identified in the research, welds between two adjacent rails had by far the greatest impact (40%), while 13%, 10%, 10%, 9%, 9%, and 9% were attributed to gravel, maximum rail displacement, gauge, twist, heterogeneity, and residue, respectively. However, mathematical modeling of the phenomenon of floating sleepers according to the theoretical approach is very demanding, as is also shown by the research so far, since the existing models (e.g., Refs. [2,17]) do not yet explain the phenomenon satisfactorily. The presented research proposes a combined approach that includes the results of observations obtained through field measurements and simplified mathematical models. In this proposal, first, instead of complex discretization with MDOF models (e.g., Refs. [2,17]), which also include the half-space of the rail beam, we use simple (equivalent) SDOF models, which have all the properties and loadings of the considered rail beam structure. In this way, the individual influences and states of the considered system can be identified more easily. Furthermore, the obtained results of SDOF models in the form of simpler mathematical expressions can be more effectively interpreted and understood in engineering terms. Based on the obtained results measured in the field, such a model can be calibrated relatively easily. In this way, SDOF models will not accurately summarize all the characteristics of the phenomenon, but they will enable simpler calculations and help in understanding and solving the problems of floating sleepers.

Figure 1 shows the progression of the floating sleeper phenomenon on a short stretch of track. An indicator of the beginning of the phenomenon is a slight local dusting in the vicinity of the affected sleeper (Figure 1, left). As the phenomenon progresses, dusting intensifies and can also spread to adjacent sleepers (Figure 1, top right). The final stage of the phenomenon, when the sleepers lose contact with the ground and individual sleepers practically hang from the rails, is shown in Figure 1, bottom right.

Ballast fouling reveals a change in some of the material characteristics of the track, e.g., the reduction in stiffness over time within the observed period, which, in principle, signifies the non-linear behavior of the observed phenomenon.

MORE INTENSE AND
WIDESPREAD DUSTING

SLIGHT LOCAL DUSTING

FINAL STAGE-FLOATING
SLEEPER

Figure 1. Progression of the floating sleeper phenomenon in various states on a short stretch of track.

2.2. Assumptions, Equations, and Simplified SDOF Dynamic Model

2.2.1. Basic Assumptions

Using the simplified SDOF mathematical model, in comparison with more accurate MDOF models (e.g., Ref. [17]), we considered the following assumptions, considering the facts found in the field:

- The passage of the axle of the train composition over the observed location in the idealized simplified mathematical model represents a special case of short-term pulse loading.
- In the model, a single spring is considered between the axle of the train composition, which causes the load, and the track, which carries this load.
- In the case of short-term pulse loadings, due to their relatively short-term action, the damping in the basic equation of motion can be neglected, because it has little effect on the response. Such an approach at the same time greatly simplifies the solution of the problem.
- Since we are interested in the change of influence and the effects at the location of short-term pulse loading, we neglect the influence of adjacent structural elements in the SDOF model. In this way, the absolute values of the response are somewhat imprecisely determined. However, the qualitatively calculated response still realistically describes the actual situation, especially in the case when the stiffness characteristics of the SDOF model are calibrated with actual measurements and findings from the literature.
- Since observations in the field (Figures 1 and 2) unequivocally show that the floating sleeper is a non-linear phenomenon, it should also be modeled mathematically. This would not be a problem to analyze on a simple SDOF system; a bigger problem is to predict in advance the material characteristics of the track at the considered location. For the sake of simplification and easier physical interpretation of the results, the various most probable loadings for the entire range of real values of the oscillation times of the considered structure and duration of pulse loadings were analyzed.
- The observed phenomenon is non-linear; regardless, it was treated as a linear system in discrete time windows with known (i.e., assumed) values of stiffness and mass. In most cases, stiffness and mass values change between individual discrete time points.

Figure 2. Damage of ballast in a location prone to the phenomenon of floating sleepers: (**a**) initial state after identification, (**b**) damaged state after 21 days, and (**c**) damaged state after an additional 21 days.

Figure 2 shows the different states of ballast at the location of the floating sleeper over time and the high cycle "fatigue" of the ballast track material. There is a flow of material (i.e., ballast) whereby the individual stones of the ballast behave similarly to molecules in a liquid, except that, here, the stones are of very different shapes and dimensions; unlike a normal liquid, individual stones also wear out during translational and rotational movement. This wearing down of the ballast changes its contribution to the stiffness of the system under consideration; in this specific case, the stiffness of the track decreases—the greater the wear, the lower the stiffness of the track. The last finding confirms again that the observed phenomenon is (highly) non-linear. For the needs of our simplified SDOF mathematical model, it is crucial that the considered phenomenon can be described in various short time windows with the corresponding values of the (constant) terms of the differential equation (e.g., Ref. [18]), as will be described below.

2.2.2. Equations of Motion

The behavior of the observed structure under the action of an external time-varying loading can be described by the equation of motion for discrete models with multiple degrees of freedom (MDOF) (e.g., Refs. [17,18]):

$$[M]\{\ddot{u}\} + [C]\{\dot{u}\} + [K]\{U\} = \{f(t)\}, \tag{1}$$

where $[M]$, $[C]$, and $[K]$ represent mass, damping, and the stiffness matrix, respectively; $\{\ddot{u}\}$, $\{\dot{u}\}$ and $\{U\}$ represent acceleration, velocity, and displacement vectors, respectively, and $\{f(t)\}$ represents the loading vector.

For simple systems, i.e., single degree of freedom (SDOF) models, an algebraic form of Equation (1) can be written as:

$$m\,\ddot{u} + c\,\dot{u} + k\,u = f(t), \tag{2}$$

where m, c, and k represent mass, damping, and stiffness, respectively; $\ddot{u}$, $\dot{u}$ and u represent acceleration, velocity, and displacement, respectively, and $f(t)$ represents dynamic loading.

Solving the homogeneous part of the differential Equation (2) defines the basic dynamic parameter of the structure under consideration, which is called the period of the structure and can be expressed as:

$$T = 2\pi\,\sqrt{\frac{m}{k}}. \tag{3}$$

2.2.3. Dynamic Factor of the SDOF System

Generally, we are interested in the maximum values of individual observed quantities. Since the displacements of the structure are directly proportional to the forces of the structure, we usually define the maximal dynamic factor, $D_{f,\max}$ (known also as the maximal deformation response factor, i.e., Ref. [18]), with the equation:

$$D_{f,\max} = \frac{u_{\max}}{u_0},\qquad(4)$$

where $D_{f,\max}$ represents the ratio between the maximum absolute value of the displacements ($u_{\max}$) during the time-history response, described by Equation (2), and the absolute value of the displacement at static loading (u_0), which is usually determined as the amplitude of the dynamic loading. With the known value of $D_{f,\max}$, the maximum dynamic influences on the structure can be treated as static, which significantly simplifies solving and understanding the problem.

2.2.4. Different Pulse Loadings of the SDOF System

Short-duration pulse loadings are generally described by various functions, with the key characteristic of such a loading being that its relative duration is short. Here, the parameter $\lambda = \bar{t}/T$ refers to the ratio between the duration of the short-term pulse loading ($\bar{t}$) and the period of the structure (T). Equation (2) is simplified in this case—since the influence of damping is negligible for pulse loading, the term $c\dot{u}$ can be neglected. Moreover, since the influence of damping is neglected, the transmissibility (which represents the factor that tells how much loading is transmitted to the ballast; see, e.g., Ref. [10]) can be described by the dynamic factor (Equation (4)).

Completed solutions for $D_{f,\max}$ in the case of rectangular pulse loading (Figure 3a) are given in Ref. [18]. The solution is relatively simple and can be written in its closed form as:

$$D_{f,\max} = \frac{u_{\max}}{u_0} = \begin{cases} 1 - \cos(2\pi\lambda) & \lambda \le \frac{1}{2} \\ 2 & \lambda \ge \frac{1}{2} \end{cases}.\qquad(5)$$

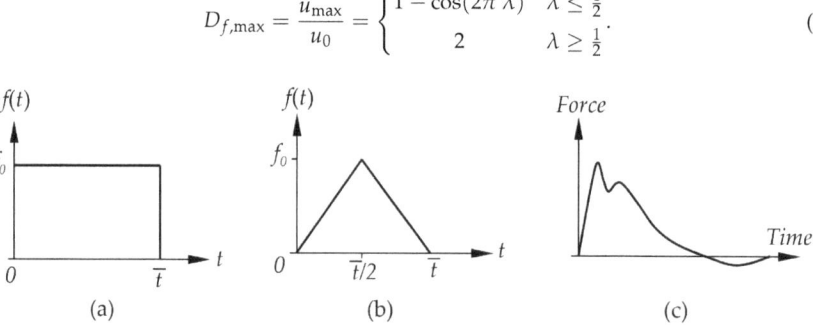

Figure 3. Different pulse loadings: (**a**) rectangular, (**b**) symmetric triangular, and (**c**) general loading.

Symmetric triangular pulse loading (Figure 3b) is more complicated as it includes the calculation of the response in three areas (the rising part of the pulse on the left, the falling part of the pulse on the right, and no pulse on the right). To make it easier to understand the results of later derivations which type of pulse loading is more suitable for the simulation of the actual load when the axle of the train composition passes over the observed track, a full derivation is given here. In the derivation, we proceed from Equation (2), noting that the displacement $u(t) = u_0 \cdot D_f(t)$ is the product of static displacement and the dynamic factor, and the loading function $f(t) = f_0 \cdot D_L(t)$ is the product of static loading and the dynamic loading factor of the symmetric triangular pulse loading. Equation (2) is further written as:

$$m \cdot u_0 \cdot \ddot{D}_f(t) + k \cdot u_0 \cdot D_f(t) = f_0 \cdot D_L(t).\qquad(6)$$

Dividing Equation (6) by $m \cdot u_0$ and considering $\frac{f_0}{u_0} = k$ and $\frac{k}{m} = \omega^2$, the following is obtained:

$$\ddot{D}_f(t) + \omega^2 \cdot D_f(t) = \omega^2 \cdot D_L(t), \tag{7}$$

where the dynamic factor of the symmetric triangular load $D_L(t)$ is defined as:

$$D_L(t) = \begin{cases} \frac{2 \cdot t}{\bar{t}} & for \quad 0 \leq t \leq \frac{\bar{t}}{2} \\ 2 - \frac{2 \cdot t}{\bar{t}} & for \quad \frac{\bar{t}}{2} \leq t \leq \bar{t} \\ 0 & for \quad t > \bar{t} \end{cases}. \tag{8}$$

Next, the time-history response of the dynamic factor in three phases is determined. The dynamic factor for the first phase (I), considering the initial conditions $D_f^I(t = 0) = 0$ and $\dot{D}_f^I(t = 0) = 0$, is given by:

$$D_f^I(t) = \frac{2 \cdot (t \cdot \omega - \sin(t \cdot \omega))}{\bar{t} \cdot \omega} \quad 0 \leq t \leq \frac{\bar{t}}{2}, \tag{9}$$

and

$$\dot{D}_f^I(t) = \frac{2 - 2 \cdot \cos(t \cdot \omega)}{\bar{t}} \quad 0 \leq t \leq \frac{\bar{t}}{2}. \tag{10}$$

The solution for the dynamic factor in the second phase (II), considering the initial conditions $D_f^{II}(t = \frac{\bar{t}}{2}) = D_f^I(t = \frac{\bar{t}}{2})$ and $\dot{D}_f^{II}(t = \frac{\bar{t}}{2}) = \dot{D}_f^I(t = \frac{\bar{t}}{2})$, is:

$$D_f^{II}(t) = \frac{2 \cdot \left(2 \cdot \sin\left(t \cdot \omega - \frac{\bar{t} \cdot \omega}{2}\right) - \omega \cdot (t - \bar{t}) - \sin(t \cdot \omega)\right)}{\bar{t} \cdot \omega} \quad \frac{\bar{t}}{2} \leq t \leq \bar{t}, \tag{11}$$

and

$$\dot{D}_f^{II}(t) = \frac{2 \cdot \left(2 \cdot \cos\left(t \cdot \omega - \frac{\bar{t} \cdot \omega}{2}\right) - \cos(t \cdot \omega) - 1\right)}{\bar{t}} \quad \frac{\bar{t}}{2} \leq t \leq \bar{t}. \tag{12}$$

The solution for the dynamic factor in the third phase (III), considering the initial conditions $D_f^{III}(t = \bar{t}) = D_f^{II}(t = \bar{t})$ and $\dot{D}_f^{III}(t = \bar{t}) = \dot{D}_f^{II}(t = \bar{t})$, is:

$$D_f^{III}(t) = \frac{8 \cdot \sin^2\left(\frac{\bar{t} \cdot \omega}{4}\right) \sin\left(t \cdot \omega - \frac{\bar{t} \cdot \omega}{2}\right)}{\bar{t} \cdot \omega} \quad t > \bar{t}, \tag{13}$$

and

$$\dot{D}_f^{III}(t) = \frac{\cos\left(t \cdot \omega - \frac{\bar{t} \cdot \omega}{2}\right) \cdot 8 \sin^2\left(\frac{\bar{t} \cdot \omega}{4}\right)}{\bar{t}} \quad t > \bar{t}. \tag{14}$$

The time at which the maximal dynamic factor occurred for the first phase is then determined. From Equation (6), it follows:

$$\dot{D}_f^I(t) = \frac{2 - 2 \cdot \cos(\omega \cdot t)}{\bar{t}} = 0 \rightarrow \cos(\omega \cdot t) = 1 \rightarrow \omega \cdot t = 2 \cdot \pi \cdot n. \tag{15}$$

Considering $T = \frac{2 \cdot \pi}{\omega}$, the time is thus:

$$t_n^I = T \cdot n; \; n = 1, 2, 3 \ldots. \tag{16}$$

Only solutions within the interval $0 \leq t \leq \frac{\bar{t}}{2}$ are considered; given that $\bar{t} = \lambda \cdot T$, the condition is:

$$\lambda \geq 2 \cdot n. \tag{17}$$

47

Substituting Equation (16) into Equation (9), the extreme value of the dynamic factor is obtained:

$$D_{f,\max}^I = D_f^I(t_n^I = T) = \frac{2\cdot n}{\lambda} \quad \lambda \geq 2\cdot n; \quad n = 1, 2, 3 \dots. \tag{18}$$

Next, the time at which the maximal dynamic factor occurred for the second phase is determined, derived from Equation (12) under the condition $\dot{D}_f^{II}(t) = 0$. The expression follows:

$$2\cdot \cos\left(t\cdot\omega - \frac{\bar{t}\cdot\omega}{2}\right) - \cos(t\cdot\omega) - 1 = 0. \tag{19}$$

Considering $T = \frac{2\cdot\pi}{\omega}$, the general four solutions of time obtained from Equation (19) are:

$$\begin{aligned}
t_{1,n}^{II} &= T\cdot(n - \alpha_1) \\
t_{2,n}^{II} &= T\cdot(n + \alpha_2) \\
t_{3,n}^{II} &= T\cdot(n - \alpha_2) \\
t_{4,n}^{II} &= T\cdot(n + \alpha_1)
\end{aligned} \quad n = 1, 2, 3\dots, \tag{20}$$

where α_i ($i = 1, 2$), in Equation (20), is defined as:

$$\alpha_i = \frac{1}{2\pi}\cdot\cos^{-1}\left(\frac{1}{2}\cdot\left(\frac{3 + (-1)^i\left(4\sqrt{2}\cos\left(\frac{\pi\cdot i}{2T}\right) - 4\sqrt{2}\cos\left(\frac{3\pi\cdot i}{2T}\right)\right)}{5 - 4\cos\left(\frac{\pi\cdot i}{T}\right)} - 1\right)\right). \tag{21}$$

Only solutions within the interval $\frac{\bar{t}}{2} \leq t = t_{i,n}^{II} \leq \bar{t}$ are considered; given that $\bar{t} = \lambda\cdot T$, the condition is:

$$\frac{\lambda}{2} \leq \frac{t_{i,n}^{II}}{T} \leq \lambda. \tag{22}$$

From Equation (22), the lower and upper bounds of parameter λ for time $t_{i,n}^{II}$ are determined. Substituting time $t_{i,n}^{II}$ from Equation (20) into Equation (11), $D_{f,\max}^{II} = D_f^{II}(t = t_{i,n}^{II})$ is obtained. Among all possible solutions, only the envelope of maximal dynamic factor values up to a parameter of $\lambda = 10$ is listed here.

$$D_{f,\max}^{II} = \begin{cases}
D_f^{II}(t = t_{4,0}^{II}) & 0.0 \leq \lambda \leq 0.5 \\
D_f^{II}(t = t_{1,1}^{II}) & 0.5 \leq \lambda \leq 2.0 \\
D_f^{II}(t = t_{2,1}^{II}) & 2.0 \leq \lambda \leq 2.5 \\
D_f^{II}(t = t_{3,2}^{II}) & 2.5 \leq \lambda \leq 4.0 \\
D_f^{II}(t = t_{4,2}^{II}) & 4.0 \leq \lambda \leq 4.5 \\
D_f^{II}(t = t_{1,3}^{II}) & 4.5 \leq \lambda \leq 6.0 \\
D_f^{II}(t = t_{2,3}^{II}) & 6.0 \leq \lambda \leq 6.5 \\
D_f^{II}(t = t_{3,4}^{II}) & 6.5 \leq \lambda \leq 8.0 \\
D_f^{II}(t = t_{4,4}^{II}) & 8.0 \leq \lambda \leq 8.5 \\
D_f^{II}(t = t_{1,5}^{II}) & 8.5 \leq \lambda \leq 10.
\end{cases} \tag{23}$$

Next, the time at which the maximal dynamic factor occurs for the third phase is determined, derived from Equation (14) under the condition $\dot{D}_f^{III}(t) = 0$. The expression follows:

$$\cos\left(t\cdot\omega - \frac{\bar{t}\cdot\omega}{2}\right)\cdot\sin^2\left(\frac{\bar{t}\cdot\omega}{4}\right) = 0. \tag{24}$$

Considering $T = \frac{2\cdot\pi}{\omega}$, the general time solution $t_{i,n}^{III}$ is:

$$t_{i,n}^{III} = \frac{t_1}{2} + T\cdot\left(n - \frac{(-1)^i}{4}\right) \quad i = 1, 2 \text{ and } n = 1, 2, 3\dots. \tag{25}$$

Furthermore, only solutions within the interval $t = t_{i,n}^{III} > \bar{t}$ are considered; given that $\bar{t} = \lambda \cdot T$, the condition is:

$$0 \leq \lambda < 2n - \frac{(-1)^i}{2} \quad i = 1,\ 2 \text{ and } n = 1,\ 2,\ 3\ldots. \tag{26}$$

Considering time $t_{i,n}^{III}$ from Equation (25) in Equation (13), it follows:

$$D_{f,\max}^{III} = D_f^{III}(t = t_{i,n}^{III}) = \frac{2 \cdot \cos(\pi \cdot \lambda) - 2}{(-1)^i \cdot \pi \cdot \lambda}. \tag{27}$$

From Equation (27), it can be observed that the magnitude of the dynamic factor $D_{f,\max}^{III}$ is independent of n. Additionally, it is evident that the dynamic factor for $i = 2$ is negative; thus, only the dynamic factor values for $i = 1$ are of interest. The dynamic factor for phase (III) is, therefore:

$$D_{f,\max}^{III} = D_f^{III}(t = t_{1,n}^{III} = t_1^{III}) = \frac{2 - 2 \cdot \cos(\pi \cdot \lambda)}{\pi \cdot \lambda} \text{ for } \lambda \geq 0. \tag{28}$$

It can be observed from Figure 4 that for phase III of the load application, the maximal dynamic factor occurs only within the interval $0 \leq \lambda \leq 0.5$. For the remaining interval $0.5 \leq \lambda \leq 10$, the maximal dynamic factor occurs during phase II of the load application.

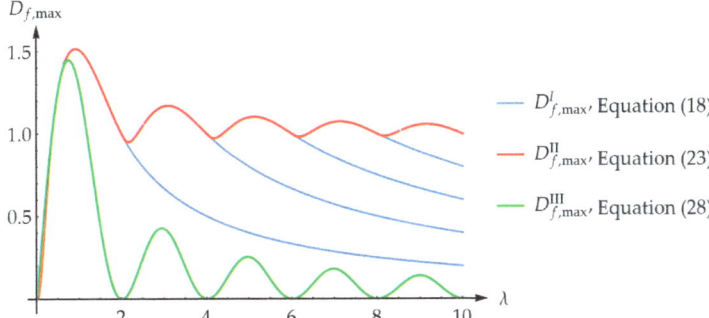

Figure 4. Maximal dynamic factor for all three phases of symmetric triangular pulse loading.

Thus, based on the dynamic factors for all three phases of load application, the final envelope $D_{f,\max}$ for the interval $0 \leq \lambda \leq 10$ is constructed in Equation (29), which is also graphically shown in Figure 5.

$$D_{f,\max} = \begin{cases} D_f^{III}(t = t_1^{III}) & 0.0 \leq \lambda \leq 0.5 \\ D_f^{II}(t = t_{1,1}^{II}) & 0.5 \leq \lambda \leq 2.0 \\ D_f^{II}(t = t_{2,1}^{II}) & 2.0 \leq \lambda \leq 2.5 \\ D_f^{II}(t = t_{3,2}^{II}) & 2.5 \leq \lambda \leq 4.0 \\ D_f^{II}(t = t_{4,2}^{II}) & 4.0 \leq \lambda \leq 4.5 \\ D_f^{II}(t = t_{1,3}^{II}) & 4.5 \leq \lambda \leq 6.0 \\ D_f^{II}(t = t_{2,3}^{II}) & 6.0 \leq \lambda \leq 6.5 \\ D_f^{II}(t = t_{3,4}^{II}) & 6.5 \leq \lambda \leq 8.0 \\ D_f^{II}(t = t_{4,4}^{II}) & 8.0 \leq \lambda \leq 8.5 \\ D_f^{II}(t = t_{1,5}^{II}) & 8.5 \leq \lambda \leq 10. \end{cases} \tag{29}$$

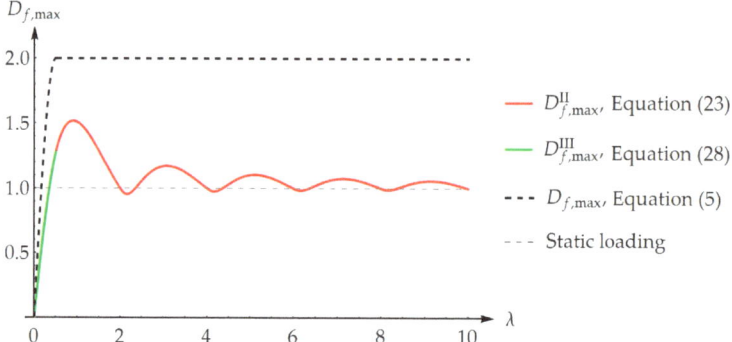

Figure 5. Envelope of the maximal dynamic factor of all three phases of symmetric triangular and rectangular pulse loading, respectively.

2.3. Performed Measurements

2.3.1. Measurement of Vertical Loads by Train Crossings

The vertical load transmitted by every single axle of the train in transit over the track was measured by the Marini SMCV measurement system. The layout of the Marini measuring system is shown in Figure 6. The system enables the measurement of:

- Dynamic or quasi-static vertical loads transmitted by each wheel/axle of the train.
- Each axle speed of the train in transit.
- The distance between two consecutive axles of the train in transit.
- Evaluation of an eventual excessive load on an axle compared to a set threshold value.
- Evaluation of an unbalanced load between the two wheels of the same axle, relative to a set threshold.

Figure 6. Layout of the Marini SMCV measuring system on the railway track.

2.3.2. Measurements of the Displacement of Sleepers

For displacement measurements (Figure 7), inductive displacement sensors were used, which made it necessary to provide a stationary reference structure. Because of this, a cantilevered scaffolding was made at each measuring point, placed about 3 m from the tracks in an area where the ground vibration amplitude due to the passing of trains was negligible in comparison to the vertical displacement amplitudes of the observed railway sleepers.

Figure 7. Measurements of the displacement of sleepers using inductive displacement sensors.

2.3.3. Measurements of Strain in the Rails

For measurements of strain on the rail (Figure 8), strain gauges were used. Before applying strain gauges to the rail surface using a special glue, the surface was smoothed and deoiled. When the surface of the structure that is the subject of measurements is deformed, the foil is also deformed, causing its electrical resistance related to strain by gauge factor to change. Consequently, strains and stresses can be calculated from the measured electrical resistance.

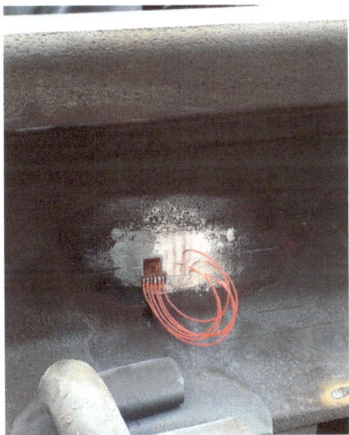

Figure 8. Strain gauge applied to the rail surface.

3. Results

3.1. Measured Loadings—Results of Load Analysis and Responses of the Rail Track

As part of the field measurements, stresses in the middle of the rail above the considered sleeper were evaluated. Based on the measured vertical normal stresses, a relatively accurate form of loading acting on the sleeper has been obtained, especially compared to previous authors who determined the final shape and length of the loading using a genetic algorithm [18].

3.1.1. Stresses in the Rail Due to the Passage of Locomotives

As the locomotive passed the measurement location, measurements were taken for all four axles. Figure 9 shows stresses σ_x, σ_y, and τ_{xy} during the locomotive's first and fourth axles passing over the measuring point. In both measurements, a time interval of 0.25 s is considered, from 16.15 to 16.40 s for axle 1 transition measurements, and from 16.86 to 17.11 s for axle 4 transition measurements. As expected, stresses are at their maximum when the locomotive axle is above the measurement point. At the passage of axle 1, i.e., at 16.30 s, stresses σ_x amount to 8.516 N/mm^2, while at the transition of axle 4 (at 17.00 s), they reach a value of 14.82 N/mm^2. In the case of vertical normal stresses σ_y, the highest value of 34.64 N/mm^2 was measured directly after the transition of axle 1 at a time of 16.3033 s. At the transition of axle 4 at a time of 17.00 s, a smaller value of 18.25 N/mm^2 was measured. In Figure 9, shear stresses τ_{xy} are equal to zero during the passage of axle 1 at the time of 16.30 s, when the axle is exactly above the measuring point, and reach their extremes immediately before and right after axle 1 passes over the measuring point; at 16.295 s, the measured value is 20.18 N/mm^2 and, in 16.3067 s, the value of -23.77 N/mm^2 is reached. Also, in the transition of axle 4, the sign of the shear stresses immediately before and after the transition is inverted, and the shear stress order of magnitude approximately coincides with the values measured in the transition of axle 1.

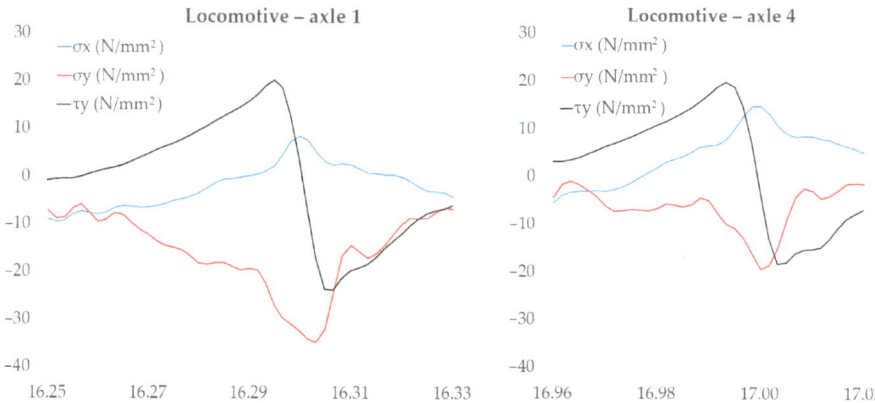

Figure 9. Stresses measured in the rail surface when axle 1 of the locomotive (**left**) and axle 4 of the locomotive (**right**) passed over the measuring point.

As can be seen, the shape of measured vertical stress σ_y coincides well with the triangular pulse loading considered in the numerical models used by other researchers. If the values measured in the passing of axle 1 and axle 4 are compared, one can acknowledge the effect of the first axle in the pair influencing the results of a neighboring axle passing through the measuring point. Vertical force at the rail–wheel contact point tends to lift the rail and sleeper at some distance from the contact point. Consequently, the passage of axle 3 influences the reduction in stresses measured by the passage of axle 4.

3.1.2. Stresses in the Rail Due to Passage of Carriages

Stresses in the rail were also measured and analyzed during the passage of train carriages. Figure 10 shows the stress curves σ_x, σ_y, and τ_{xy} during the passage of the first axle of the first carriage and the rear (140th) axle of the last carriage in the train composition over the measuring point. Like the measurements at the passage of the first axle of the locomotive, here, also, the normal stresses σ_x and σ_y and the shear stress τ_{xy} coincide well. The change in shear stresses τ_{xy} can serve as an indicator of the passage of the axle over the measuring point. During the passage of axle 1 of the first carriage in the train composition (Figure 10, left), the maximum value of the measured vertical displacement occurs slightly before (at approximately 0.03 s) the onset of extreme stress. This can be attributed to the influence of the displacements of those sleepers adjacent to the sleepers directly at the measuring point or to the time-dependent relaxation of the elements and materials of the rail track. As expected, the measured values are smaller compared to the passage of the locomotive. Horizontal stresses reach an extreme at the time of 17.257 s, i.e., 3.445 N/mm^2, and the vertical normal stresses σ_y reach an extreme at the time of 17.287 s at a value of 16.673 N/mm^2, which is approximately half the value measured during the passage of the first axle of the locomotive.

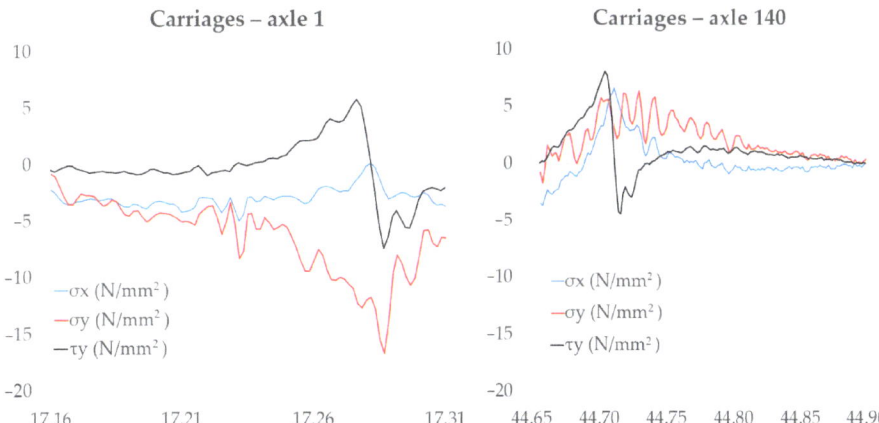

Figure 10. Stresses measured in rail surface during the passage of axis 1 of the first carriage in the train composition (**left**) and the last—140th—axle of the last wagon (**right**) over the measuring point.

3.2. Simulated Loadings and Corresponding Deformation Response Factors

The experimental measurements from Section 3.1 confirmed the theories other researchers have already considered (i.e., Ref. [19]). Namely, the actual load caused by the individual axle of the train composition when passing the observed place has an approximately symmetrical shape, which, in the first rough approximation, resembles a symmetrical, triangular shape (Figure 3b). Most of the actual loading, however, corresponds to the double triangular form, as freight wagons generally have two axles at the beginning and end of each wagon. Generally, the shape of the pulse loading must be described with a more complex function than a linear one.

Based on the displayed results of the field measurements and axle loading proposed in Ref. [19], the values of the maximal dynamic factors for different pulse loading following the procedure in Section 2.2 were calculated. Thus, all the applied loads are symmetric pulse loadings. They differ in whether it is a single or double pulse and in the shape of the function that describes the rising and falling part. Definitions and designations of pulse loadings were summarized and expanded according to Ref. [19]. Thus, all four pulse loadings can be defined and denoted as:

- **SPL-L:** single-pulse loading of linearly distributed load that decreases symmetrically concerning the geometric center of the wheel.
- **DPL-L:** double-pulse loading of linearly distributed load that decreases symmetrically for the geometric center of the wheel.
- **SPL-Q:** single-pulse loading of quadratically distributed load that decreases symmetrically concerning the geometric center of the wheel.
- **DPL-Q:** double-pulse loading of quadratically distributed load that decreases symmetrically to the geometric center of the wheel.

It should be noted that the proposed shape of pulse loading in Ref. [19] was inspired by the single wheel-induced displacement field. In Figure 11, the distribution of vertical normal stresses is shown and compared to the proposed simulated pulse loadings in this paper. Observed differences can be attributed to the influence of the multiple axle passages of a train composition. The basic data for the three supplementary impulse loads (SPL-Q, DPL-L, and SPL-Q) and the corresponding dynamic factors ($D_{f,\max}$) were obtained using the same methodology as that employed for the SPL-L case in Section 2.2. The results for the dynamic factors in all four cases are shown in Figure 12.

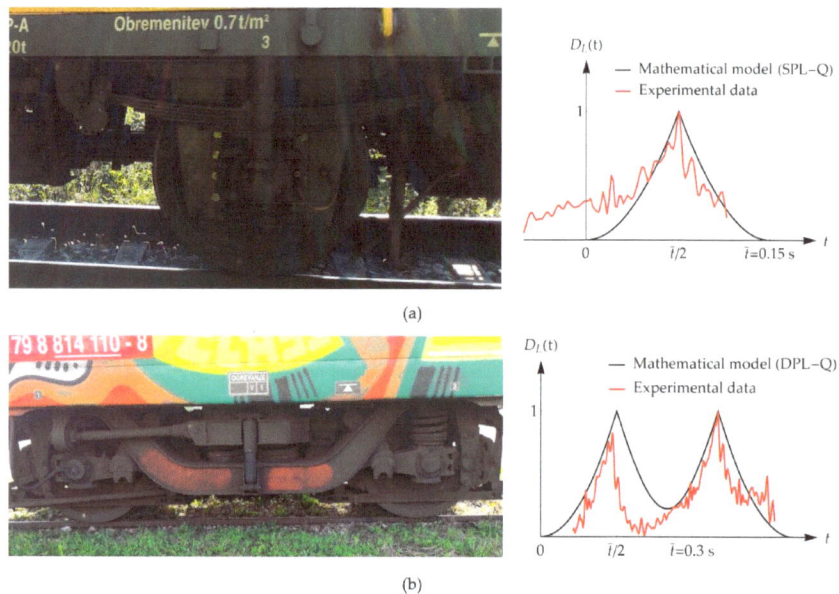

(a)

(b)

Figure 11. Normalized measured vertical normal stresses in the rail for the (**a**) one-axle and (**b**) two-axle passage of the train composition and their approximations for pulse loadings in the SDOF mathematical model.

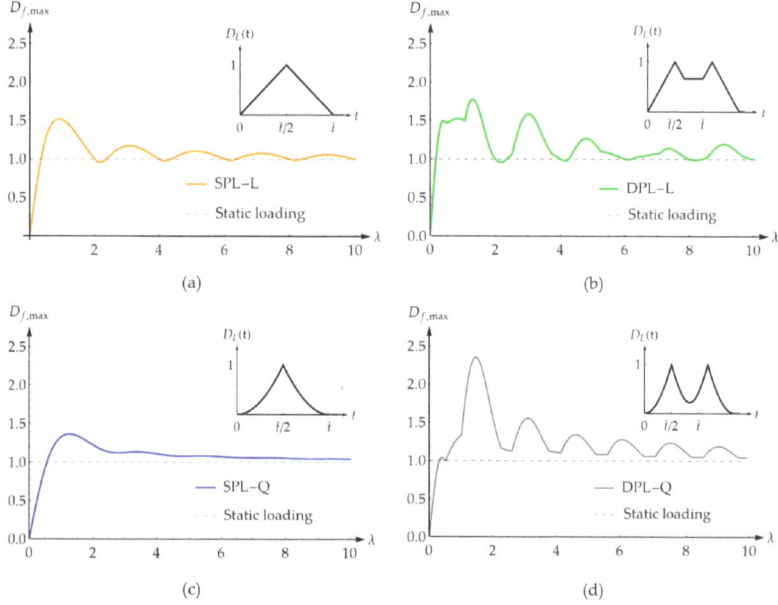

(a)

(b)

(c)

(d)

Figure 12. Different pulse loadings and the corresponding envelopes of the maximal dynamic factor of (**a**) SPL-L pulse loading, (**b**) DPL-L pulse loading, (**c**) SPL-Q pulse loading, and (**d**) DPL-Q pulse loading.

3.3. Results for the Maximal Dynamic Factor ($D_{f,max}$) Obtained by a Simplified SDOF System

The results for the dynamic factor and Figure 13 show that the maximum value (peak) of the maximum dynamic factor increases significantly with double-pulse loading. Even on average, double-pulse loadings give higher values than single ones. One of the key results of the analysis is the identification of the highest peak in the initial part of the graph, where the position of the peak is highly dependent on the type of pulse loading. We can conclude that in the initial (ideal) state, the construction of the track is relatively rigid, as is determined (and required) by the existing regulations.

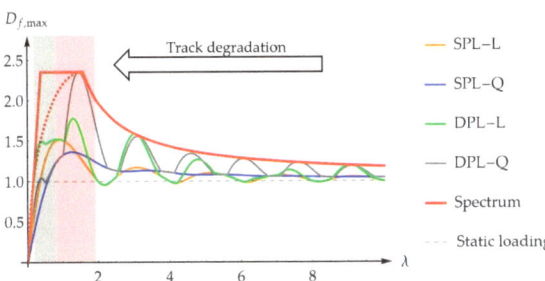

Figure 13. Comparison of the different envelopes of maximal dynamic and smoothed spectrum.

A relatively small change (reduction) in stiffness can result in a higher dynamic factor due to various influences (which have been described in the Introduction, e.g., Ref. [16]). These increase markedly with a greater reduction (large gradients of the envelope of the maximum dynamic factor) and can reach values of up to 2.5 for various pulse loadings. Such high dynamic factors in high-cycle fatigue mean high loads on the track, especially on the sleepers. The first indicator of this influence (with an increase in the dynamic factor) is mild dusting in the vicinity of the sleeper, then the dusting locally intensifies and (may) also spread to the neighboring sleepers, until the sleepers lose contact with the base and the individual sleepers practically hang from the rails (see Figure 1). With ballast fouling and the occurrence of the floating sleeper phenomenon, the stiffness is reduced significantly, which increases parameter λ. Consequently, the dynamic factor reduces to the values that are closest to the static case. Deterioration, which is a consequence of dynamic behavior, practically stops. However, the railway track is significantly damaged, due to the ballast fouling and the induced large displacements, and it urgently needs reconstruction.

The gray area indicates the λ range for the final state of the floating sleeper phenomenon, while the red area indicates the λ range of $D_{f,max}$ peaks for all four pulse loadings. It is evident that the phenomenon is highly non-linear and, as such, is hard to understand in classical engineering terms, which are related to the track's elastic characteristics. The smoothed spectrum $S(\lambda)$ is also proposed for the maximal dynamic factor of pulse loadings, which were considered in the presented study. For small λ values, the smoothed spectrum is bounded by $D_{f,max}$, calculated for DPL-Q pulse loading. It can also be observed that the proposed smoothed spectrum, which is defined by Equation (30), will, in most instances, bound the $D_{f,max}$ of DPL-Q pulse loading. Note that the dashed curve represents an alternative for a smoothed spectrum for λ values smaller than 1.58.

$$S(\lambda) = \begin{cases} 6.187 \cdot \lambda & \text{for} \quad 0 \leq \lambda \leq 0.38 \\ 2.352 & \text{for} \quad 0.38 \leq \lambda \leq 1.58 \\ 1.037 + \frac{1.356}{\lambda - 0.549} & \text{for} \quad 1.58 \leq \lambda \leq 10 \end{cases} \tag{30}$$

4. Discussion

4.1. Discussion of the Results Obtained by Field Measurement

In the case of the generally "clean" passage of a single axle of the train composition across the measurement site, a direct correlation between the maximum loading transmitted to the rail and the stresses (and displacements) may be seen. Such is, for example, the situation in the transition of the first axle of the locomotive and the axles of heavier wagons following lighter carriages. In the case of other axles, the influence of the load transfer via the adjacent sleepers becomes more important, and the correlation between maximum loading and stress flow is less obvious. This corresponds to the general laws of structural dynamics in discrete systems with several degrees of freedom, where the extremes of individual quantities do not occur at the same time.

4.2. Discussion of the Results Obtained with the Simplified SDOF Model

The proposed simplified SDOF mathematical model includes some assumptions and observations from field measurements, which allowed relatively simple modeling of the otherwise extremely complex phenomenon of floating sleepers. The results for the maximal dynamic factor show that the maximum values are possible with double loading, regardless of its shape or type. Non-linear forms of pulse loading generally result in higher values of the maximal dynamic factor. In the initial state, which corresponds to the ideal state of a newly built track (or the existing state, which is determined by modern regulations), the stiffness of the track is relatively high. The corresponding parameter λ is relatively high (the right-hand side of the graph in Figure 13) and the related maximal dynamic factor is small. Any change in the properties of the track that causes a decrease in its stiffness generally increases the value of the maximal dynamic factor. An increased maximal dynamic factor causes adverse effects on the track, manifesting themselves first as local dusting (which additionally reduces stiffness). Local dusting extends to the area of a larger number of sleepers, further reducing stiffness and increasing the value of the maximal dynamic factor. Due to the high values of the dynamic factor, the effects on the railway track are increasingly pronounced (red area in Figure 13), which finally manifests itself in the fouling of the ballast, which is the last stage of the floating sleeper phenomenon. In the last stage, the stiffness of the track continues to decrease, which results in a decrease in the value of the maximal dynamic factor (gray area in Figure 13). The phenomenon that now occurs in the equilibrium state represents the dynamic collision of the rail with the hardened surface of the fouled ballast. These dynamic effects were not covered by the proposed model, but, from observations in the field, they are minimal, and the situation is definitive. However, it is necessary to realize that this final state represents a limiting state since the large, measured displacements during the passage of the train composition do not, in any case, correspond to the safe condition of the track because, in such cases, there is a great risk of derailment.

In a continuation of this research, it would be necessary to confirm some of the presented results by using more complex mathematical models, at least in the initial and final states. The latter state corresponds to the floating sleeper phenomenon. Also, it would be beneficial to indicate other shapes/types of pulse loadings, which may produce higher values of maximal dynamic factor than those analyzed in the current paper. Based on the obtained and new results, advanced recommendations for more appropriate construction and maintenance of railroads, particularly in karst areas, could be provided.

5. Conclusions

Dynamic influences have a markedly unfavorable effect on the degradation of rail sleepers and should not be neglected. Based on the results presented in this study, it can be concluded that the complex floating sleeper phenomenon (encountered in Slovenia and many other countries) can be adequately, at least qualitatively, described by a proposed simplified SDOF mathematic model that includes one degree of freedom. Despite its simplicity, it enables the understanding of the key factors influencing the deterioration of the ballast railway track.

The results of the presented research can be summarized as follows:

- A simplified SDOF mathematical model for the quantification of the influences on the floating sleeper phenomenon has been developed.

- For mathematical modeling of the phenomenon, extensive field measurements were carried out, which yielded interesting results, enabled the identification of interesting phenomena and findings, and enabled the simplification of mathematical modeling.
- Based on the actual field measurements and some recommendations from the recent scientific literature, the loading was modeled as a pulse loading of different shapes/types.
- Calculating the maximal dynamic factor reveals that the floating sleeper phenomenon is highly non-linear. The initial response of the sleepers is elastic, but with a reduction in stiffness due to different phenomena, the maximal dynamic factor can significantly increase, which again influences a response in the form of damaged tracks. The final damaged state corresponds to the floating sleeper phenomenon, which aligns with lower values of maximal dynamic factors and relates to the dynamic collision of a rail with the hardened surface of fouled ballast, with a low value for the dynamic factor.

The presented study has detected several issues that should be addressed in future research:

- The accuracy of the applied pulse loadings should be evaluated and compared/discussed with state-of-the-art mathematical models.
- The rate of wear of the ballast and its critical threshold should be identified. Given that this sub-phenomenon is related to dynamic stability—that is, an abrupt change in the ballast's behavior, which relates to approaching the bifurcation point in the accompanying mathematical model—this could be an extremely challenging undertaking.
- As ballast wear contributes significantly to a reduction in track stiffness, the long-term implications of this wear on the safety and performance of railway tracks should be carefully addressed.
- The assumptions of the SDOF model, particularly those that ignore damping and the impact of adjacent structural elements, should be checked.
- In general, additional research (theoretical and experimental) is needed, which will confirm the obtained results and improve the explanation of the entire phenomenon of floating sleepers.

Author Contributions: Conceptualization, M.U., I.P. and D.I.; methodology, I.P. and M.U.; software, D.I.; validation, M.U., I.P. and D.I.; formal analysis, I.P. and M.U.; writing—original draft preparation, M.U. and I.P.; writing—review and editing, I.P., M.U. and D.I.; visualization, I.P. and D.I.; project administration, M.U. All authors have read and agreed to the published version of the manuscript.

Funding: This research was funded by the Ministry of Infrastructure of the Republic of Slovenia and Slovenian Research Agency (Project: Development of an innovative railway sleeper, V2-1740). The project ended on 31 March 2021.

Data Availability Statement: No additional data are publicly available. Interested readers can request/ask for the experimental field measurement data.

Conflicts of Interest: The authors declare no conflicts of interest.

References

1. Ramadan, A.N.; Jing, P.; Zhang, J.; El-Din Zohny, H.N. Numerical Analysis of Additional Stresses in Railway Track Elements due to Subgrade Settlement Using FEM Simulation. *Appl. Sci.* **2021**, *11*, 8501. [CrossRef]
2. Feng, H. 3D models of Railway Track for Dynamic Analysis. Master's Thesis, Royal Institute of Technology, Stockholm, Sweden, 2011.
3. Winkler, E. *Vorträge über Eisenbahnbau, Heft 1, 2, Verlag H*; Dominicus: Prag, Czech Republic, 1867.
4. Winkler, E. *Die Lehre von der Elasticitaet und Festigkeit—Mit Besonderer Rücksicht auf ihre Anwendung in der Technik, für Polytechnische Schulen, Bauakademien, Ingenieure, Maschinenbauer, Architekten, etc.*; Verlag H. Dominicus: Prag, Czech Republic, 1867.
5. El Moueddeb, M.; Louf, F.; Boucard, P.A.; Dadie, F.; Saussine, G.; Sorrentino, D. An Efficient Numerical Model to Predict the Mechanical Response of a Railway Track in the Low-Frequency range. *Vibration* **2022**, *5*, 326–343. [CrossRef]
6. Zhai, W.M.; Sun, X. A detailed model for investigating vertical interaction between railway vehicle and track. *Veh. Syst. Dyn.* **1994**, *23*, 603–615. [CrossRef]

7.   Rodrigues, A.F.S.; Dimitrovova, Z. Applicability of a Three-Layer Model for the Dynamic Analysis of Ballasted Railway Tracks. *Vibration* **2021**, *4*, 151–174. [CrossRef]
8.   Hurtado-Hurtado, G.; Morales-Velazquez, L.; Valtierra-Rodríguez, M.; Otremba, F.; Jáuregui-Correa, J.C. Frequency Analysis of the Railway Track under Loads Caused by the Hunting Phenomenon. *Mathematics* **2022**, *10*, 2286. [CrossRef]
9.   Kurhan, D.; Kurhan, M.; Horváth, B.; Fischer, S. Determining the Deformation Characteristics of Railway Ballast by Mathematical Modeling of Elastic Wave Propagation. *Appl. Mech.* **2023**, *4*, 803–815. [CrossRef]
10. Yao, S.; Xie, W.; Geng, J.; Xu, X.; Zheng, S. A Numerical Analysis of the Non-Uniform Layered Ground Vibration Caused by a Moving Railway Load Using an Efficient Frequency–Wave-Number Method. *Mathematics* **2024**, *12*, 1750. [CrossRef]
11. Cai, C.; Tian, S.; Shi, Y.; Chen, Y.; Li, X. Influencing Factors Analysis in Railway Engineering Technological Innovation under Complex and Difficult Areas: A System Dynamics Approach. *Mathematics* **2024**, *12*, 2040. [CrossRef]
12. Liu, H.; Rahman, M.; Rahimi, M.; Starr, A.; Durazo-Cardenas, I.; Ruiz-Carcel, C.; Ompusunggu, A.; Hall, A.; Anderson, R. An autonomous rail-road amphibious robotic system for railway maintenance using sensor fusion and mobile manipulator. *Comput. Electr. Eng.* **2023**, *110*, 108874. [CrossRef]
13. Yang, C.; Sun, Y.; Ladubec, C.; Liu, Y. Developing Machine Learning-Based Models for Railway Inspection. *Appl. Sci.* **2021**, *11*, 13. [CrossRef]
14. Offenbacher, S.; Neuhold, J.; Veit, P.; Landgraf, M. Analyzing Major Track Quality Indices and Introducing a Universally Applicable TQI. *Appl. Sci.* **2020**, *10*, 8490. [CrossRef]
15. Park, B.; Choi, Y.-T.; Hwang, S.H. Ballasted Track Status Evaluation Based on Apparent Track Stiffness Index. *Appl. Sci.* **2020**, *10*, 4729. [CrossRef]
16. Uranjek, M.; Štrukelj, A.; Lenart, S.; Peruš, I. Analysis of influential parameters for accelerated degradation of ballast railway track. *Constr. Build. Mater.* **2020**, *261*, 119938. [CrossRef]
17. Esveld, C. *Modern Railway Track*, 2nd ed.; MRT-Productions: Delft, The Netherlands, 2001.
18. Chopra, A.K. *Dynamics of Structures: Theory and Applications to Earthquake Engineering*; Pearson/Prentice Hall: Old Bridgem, NJ, USA, 2007.
19. Mezeh, R.; Mroueh, H.; Hosseingholian, M.; Sadek, M. New approach for the assessment of train/track/foundation dynamics using in-situ measurements of high-speed train induced vibrations. *Soil Dyn. Earthq. Eng.* **2019**, *116*, 50–59. [CrossRef]

 *mathematics*

Article

Strain-Rate and Stress-Rate Models of Nonlinear Viscoelastic Materials

Claudio Giorgi [1,†] and Angelo Morro [2,*,†]

1   Dipartimento di Ingegneria Civile Ambiente Territorio Architettura e Matematica, Università di Brescia, Via Valotti 9, 25133 Brescia, Italy; claudio.giorgi@unibs.it
2   Dipartimento di Informatica, Bioingegneria, Robotica e Ingegneria dei Sistemi, Università di Genova, Via All'Opera Pia 13, 16145 Genova, Italy
*   Correspondence: angelo.morro@unige.it
†   These authors contributed equally to this work.

Abstract: The paper is devoted to the modeling of nonlinear viscoelastic materials. The constitutive equations are considered in differential form via relations between strain, stress, and their derivatives in the Lagrangian description. The thermodynamic consistency is established by using the Clausius–Duhem inequality through a procedure that involves two uncommon features. Firstly, the entropy production is regarded as a positive-valued constitutive function per se. This view implies that the inequality is in fact an equation. Secondly, this statement of the second law is investigated by using an algebraic representation formula, thus arriving at quite general results for rate terms that are usually overlooked in thermodynamic analyses. Starting from strain-rate or stress-rate equations, the corresponding finite equations are derived. It then emerges that a greater generality of the constitutive equations of the classical models, such as those of Boltzmann and Maxwell, are obtained as special cases.

Keywords: viscoelastic materials; constitutive rate-type equations; nonlinear models; thermodynamic consistency

MSC: 74D05; 74C99; 74F05

Citation: Giorgi, C.; Morro, A. Strain-Rate and Stress-Rate Models of Nonlinear Viscoelastic Materials. *Mathematics* **2024**, *12*, 3011. https://doi.org/10.3390/math12193011

Academic Editor: Matjaz Skrinar

Received: 11 July 2024
Revised: 20 September 2024
Accepted: 25 September 2024
Published: 26 September 2024

1. Introduction

Viscoelasticity involves a wide domain of models of materials. In general, viscoelasticity is a property ascribed to materials whenever the mechanical response changes in time while the forces causing the deformation are removed. Furthermore, the relation between forces and deformation may be different between the loading and unloading processes, thus producing hysteresis. Accordingly, viscoelastic models are thought to involve both viscous and elastic characteristics, which in turn might be affected by the temperature. This quite general view is realized by a number of mathematical models.

As is frequent in the literature, models of viscoelasticity are set up with reference to rheological elements, mainly the Maxwell unit and the Kelvin–Voigt unit; see, e.g., [1] and [2] (Ch. 6). This results in a combination of (possibly tensorial) values of deformation, stress, and their time derivatives.

From a mathematical standpoint, viscoelasticity is modeled in different ways. A well-known description traces back to Boltzmann [3], whereby the stress at time t is affected by the strain at all times $s \leq t$. Furthermore, the stress–strain relation was assumed to be linear. Based on the Boltzmann model, much research has been undertaken for constitutive models in terms of memory functionals [4–6] in the wide domain of continuum physics and with attention to thermodynamic restrictions, initial and boundary-value problems, minimum principles, and wave propagation.

So as to obtain mathematically more tractable models, and meanwhile to allow for nonlinear effects, lately, different approaches have been developed. They are formally in differential form, and usually called *rate-type* viscoelastic models, in that they are expressed by relations between stress, strain, and their derivatives at the same time. This avoids the use of integral-type models for which the account of nonlinearities would be quite involved (see, e.g., [7]).

Physically admissible models are required to be thermodynamically consistent in the sense that the constitutive equations have to satisfy the inequality arising from the second law. While the inequality appears to place severe restrictions on the constitutive functions, a recent approach of ours enables greater generality. This occurs for two reasons. First, the entropy production is viewed as a constitutive function per se. Secondly, an appropriate exploitation of the inequality allows for possibilities that usually do not arise. There are approaches to (linear) viscoelastic models where continuum thermodynamics is not considered merely because the existence of internal energy is not assumed.

This paper develops a systematic approach to the modeling of viscoelastic materials through thermodynamically consistent schemes involving strain and stress in differential forms. Owing to the generality of the approach, we are able to recover known models from the literature and, furthermore, to find nonlinear models characterized by free energy and entropy production.

The postulate on the second law of thermodynamics leads to the CD (Clausius–Duhem) inequality, where the entropy production is provided by a constitutive function. The thermodynamic consistency is meant as the compatibility of a set of constitutive assumptions with the CD inequality. The methodology for the analysis of the consistency involves finding proper unknowns (here, stress-rate or strain-rate) through the direct application of a representation formula to the CD inequality.

Notation

The body occupies a time-dependent region Ω in the three-dimensional space. The position vector of a point in Ω is denoted by $\mathbf{x}$. For any pair of vectors $\mathbf{u}, \mathbf{w}$ or tensors $\mathbf{A}, \mathbf{B}$, the notations $\mathbf{u} \cdot \mathbf{w}$ and $\mathbf{A} \cdot \mathbf{B}$ denote the inner product. Cartesian coordinates are used, and then, in the suffix notation, $\mathbf{u} \cdot \mathbf{w} = u_i w_i$, $\mathbf{A} \cdot \mathbf{B} = A_{ij} B_{ij}$, the summation over the repeated indices can be understood. For any tensor $\mathbf{A}$, sym$\mathbf{A}$ and skw$\mathbf{A}$ denote the symmetric and skew-symmetric parts of $\mathbf{A}$. Also, Sym is the space of symmetric tensors.

2. Balance Laws and Constitutive Equations

Let R be the region occupied by the body in a reference configuration. Any point in R is associated with the position vector $\mathbf{X}$ relative to the chosen origin. The motion of the body is a C^2 function $\chi(\mathbf{X}, t) : \mathrm{R} \times \mathbb{R} \to \Omega = \chi(\mathrm{R}, t)$. We let ∇ and ∇_R denote the gradient in Ω and R. Hence, $\nabla_R \chi$ is the deformation gradient in components $F_{iK} = \partial_{X_K} \chi_i$. Let $\rho(\mathbf{x}, t)$ and $\mathbf{v}(\mathbf{x}, t)$ be the mass density and the velocity fields at $\mathbf{x}$ at time $t \in \mathbb{R}$. The symbol $\mathbf{L}$ denotes the velocity gradient, $L_{ij} = \partial_{x_j} v_i$, while $\mathbf{D} = $ sym$\mathbf{L}$ and $\mathbf{W} = $ skw$\mathbf{L}$.

Hereafter, a superposed dot denotes the total time derivative. For any function $f(\mathbf{x}, t)$ on $\Omega \times \mathbb{R}$, we evaluate $\dot{f}$ as $\dot{f} = \partial_t f + (\mathbf{v} \cdot \nabla) f$. Accordingly, the balance of mass and the equation of motion are expressed by

$$\dot{\rho} + \rho \nabla \cdot \mathbf{v} = 0, \qquad \rho \dot{\mathbf{v}} = \nabla \cdot \mathbf{T} + \rho \mathbf{b},$$

where $\mathbf{T}$ is the Cauchy stress tensor and $\mathbf{b}$ is the specific body force.

We assume the existence of a specific internal energy density ε so that $\rho(\frac{1}{2}\mathbf{v}^2 + \varepsilon)$ is the total energy density per unit volume. The balance of energy leads to

$$\rho \dot{\varepsilon} = \mathbf{T} \cdot \mathbf{D} + \rho r - \nabla \cdot \mathbf{q}, \tag{1}$$

where r is the heat supply, per unit mass, and $\mathbf{q}$ is the flux vector.

Let θ be the absolute temperature and η the specific entropy density. Letting $\mathbf{j}$ be the entropy flux, we assume the balance of entropy in the form

$$\rho\dot{\eta} + \nabla \cdot \mathbf{j} - \frac{\rho r}{\theta} = \rho\gamma,$$

where γ is the (rate of) entropy production. We let $\mathbf{b}$ and r be arbitrarily provided time-dependent fields on $\Omega \times \mathbb{R}$. Hence, we say that a process is the set $\mathrm{P} = (\rho, \mathbf{v}, \mathbf{T}, \varepsilon, \eta, \theta, \mathbf{q}, \mathbf{j}, \gamma)$, on $\Omega \times \mathbb{R}$, of the quantities entering the balance equations and the constitutive relations.

The statement of the balance of energy in the form (1) is essential for the next developments. It is worth observing that there are approaches in continuum mechanics where the existence of an energy density ε is not assumed. A distinction is made between stored and dissipated energy; the dissipated energy is determined by a rate equation involving appropriate state variables (see, e.g., [8] and Refs. therein). Still, without any assumption about the internal energy, attention is confined to a relation between stress and deformation through a transform function [9,10], the transform function being possibly expressed by fractional derivatives.

2.1. Second Law of Thermodynamics

The balance of entropy is assumed to be non-negative. Hence, the second law is stated as follows.

Postulate 1. *For every process* P *admissible in a body, the inequality*

$$\rho\dot{\eta} + \nabla \cdot \mathbf{j} - \frac{\rho r}{\theta} = \rho\gamma \geq 0 \tag{2}$$

is valid at any internal point.

Letting

$$\mathbf{j} = \frac{\mathbf{q}}{\theta} + \mathbf{k}$$

we regard $\mathbf{k}$ as the extra-entropy flux [11]. Nonzero values of $\mathbf{k}$ arise when nonlocal properties (higher-order gradients) are considered. For the present purposes, there is no loss of generality in taking $\mathbf{k} = \mathbf{0}$. Since

$$\nabla \cdot \frac{\mathbf{q}}{\theta} - \frac{\rho r}{\theta} = \frac{1}{\theta}(\nabla \cdot \mathbf{q} - \rho r) - \frac{1}{\theta^2}\mathbf{q} \cdot \nabla\theta$$

then substitution of $\nabla \cdot \mathbf{q} - \rho r$ from (1) and using the free energy $\psi = \varepsilon - \theta\eta$ results in

$$-\rho(\dot{\psi} + \eta\dot{\theta}) + \mathbf{T} \cdot \mathbf{D} - \frac{1}{\theta}\mathbf{q} \cdot \nabla\theta = \rho\theta\gamma \geq 0. \tag{3}$$

As is standard in continuum thermodynamics [11–13], the requirement (2), or (3), results in restrictions on physically admissible constitutive models. The novelty of the present approach is that, beyond the entropy flux $\mathbf{j}$, the entropy production γ is also conceptually a constitutive function to be determined. Henceforth, we apply the statement (2) to the modeling of viscoelastic materials.

While the extra-entropy flux $\mathbf{k}$ is generally associated with nonlocal effects, models of materials are characterized by the free energy ψ and the entropy production γ. Before addressing the restrictions placed by (3) and the intrinsic connections with ψ and γ, we introduce useful terminology for viscoelastic models.

2.2. Lagrangian Form of the Balance Laws

Owing to the coexistent elastic and viscous properties, viscoelasticity is described by relations involving stress, strain, and their derivatives. The occurrence of time derivatives makes the compatibility with the objectivity principle more involved, whereby the constitutive equations must be form-invariant under the group of Euclidean transformations ([14] (Section 1.13); [2] (Section 1.9)). This requirement is best satisfied by dealing within the Lagrangian description. Hence, we represent deformation and stress by using the red-Lagrange strain, $\mathbf{E}$, and the second Piola tensor, $\mathbf{T}_{RR}$,

$$\mathbf{E} = \tfrac{1}{2}(\mathbf{F}^T\mathbf{F} - \mathbf{1}), \qquad \mathbf{T}_{RR} = J\mathbf{F}^{-1}\mathbf{T}\mathbf{F}^{-T},$$

together with the referential vectors, e.g., $\mathbf{q}_R = J\mathbf{q}\mathbf{F}^{-T}$. All of them and the Jacobian $J = \det \mathbf{F}$ are in fact invariant. Under SO(3), the time derivatives $\dot{\mathbf{E}}, \dot{\mathbf{T}}_{RR}$ are also invariant. Using the identities

$$\nabla\theta = \mathbf{F}^{-T}\nabla_R\theta, \qquad \dot{\mathbf{E}} = \mathbf{F}^T\mathbf{D}\mathbf{F}$$

we have

$$\mathbf{T}\cdot\mathbf{D} = J^{-1}\mathbf{T}_{RR}\cdot\dot{\mathbf{E}}, \qquad \mathbf{q}\cdot\nabla\theta = J^{-1}\mathbf{q}_R\cdot\nabla_R\theta.$$

Consequently, multiplying (3) by J and recalling that $J\rho = \rho_R$ is the mass density in the reference configuration, we obtain the CD inequality in the form

$$-\rho_R(\dot{\psi} + \eta\dot{\theta}) + \mathbf{T}_{RR}\cdot\dot{\mathbf{E}} - \frac{1}{\theta}\mathbf{q}_R\cdot\nabla_R\theta = \rho_R\theta\gamma \geq 0. \tag{4}$$

3. Rate-Type Models for Thermo-Viscoelastic Solids

To save writing the dependence on the temperature θ and possibly the temperature gradient $\nabla\theta$, it is understood here and not written. Since we are dealing with viscoelastic models, we split $\mathbf{T}_{RR}$ into two additive parts, namely

$$\mathbf{T}_{RR} = \mathbf{G}(\mathbf{E}) + \mathbf{S}_{RR}, \tag{5}$$

with the view that $\mathbf{G}(\mathbf{E})$ is the elastic stress and $\mathbf{S}_{RR}$ the dissipative stress.

Rate-type equations involve relations, or constitutive equations, among variables $\mathbf{E}, \mathbf{S}_{RR}, \dot{\mathbf{E}}$, and $\dot{\mathbf{S}}_{RR}$. So, the variables are not independent from one another and are subject to appropriate conditions. Often, the relations are assumed in implicit form [15], namely

$$\mathcal{F}(\mathbf{E}, \mathbf{S}_{RR}, \dot{\mathbf{E}}, \dot{\mathbf{S}}_{RR}) = 0. \tag{6}$$

As a natural example, the CD inequality (4) might eventually result in the reduced form

$$\mathbf{A}(\mathbf{E}, \mathbf{S}_{RR})\cdot\dot{\mathbf{E}} + \mathbf{B}(\mathbf{E}, \mathbf{S}_{RR})\cdot\dot{\mathbf{S}}_{RR} - \gamma(\mathbf{E}, \mathbf{S}_{RR}, \dot{\mathbf{E}}, \dot{\mathbf{S}}_{RR}) = 0,$$

where $\mathbf{A}, \mathbf{B}$ are tensor functions. Depending on the function γ, this scheme allows us to obtain models of viscoelastic or viscoplastic materials with hysteresis [2] (ch. 13). To illustrate possible types of rate equations, we now show how particular cases arise from the implicit form (6).

1. Assume $\partial_{\dot{\mathbf{S}}_{RR}}\mathcal{F} \neq \mathbf{0}$. Hence, we can express $\dot{\mathbf{S}}_{RR}$ in terms of the remaining variables $\mathbf{E}, \mathbf{S}_{RR}, \dot{\mathbf{E}}$. The corresponding function

    $$\dot{\mathbf{S}}_{RR} = \mathcal{S}(\mathbf{E}, \mathbf{S}_{RR}, \dot{\mathbf{E}}), \tag{7}$$

    where $\mathcal{S}$ is a tensor-valued function, can be viewed as a constitutive function for $\dot{\mathbf{S}}_{RR}$, thus allowing models of dissipative *stress–strain-rate* materials.

2. Now let $\mathcal{F}$ be independent of $\dot{\mathbf{S}}_{RR}$ so that the condition is $\mathcal{F}(\mathbf{E}, \mathbf{S}_{RR}, \dot{\mathbf{E}}) = 0$. If further $\partial_{\mathbf{S}_{RR}}\mathcal{F} \neq \mathbf{0}$, we can solve with respect to $\mathbf{S}_{RR}$ and obtain a constitutive equation in the form

    $$\mathbf{S}_{RR} = \mathcal{S}_0(\mathbf{E}, \dot{\mathbf{E}}).$$

If, furthermore, $\mathcal{S}_0(\mathbf{E}, \dot{\mathbf{E}}) = \mathbf{S}(\mathbf{E})\dot{\mathbf{E}}$ with $\mathbf{S}$ a fourth-rank tensor-valued function, using (5), we can write

$$\mathbf{T}_{RR} = \mathbf{G}(\mathbf{E}) + \mathbf{S}(\mathbf{E})\dot{\mathbf{E}}. \tag{8}$$

Equation (8) is in a *strain-rate* form and can be viewed as a generalization of the Kelvin–Voigt model.

3.   The dual form of (7) is obtained by assuming that $\partial_{\mathbf{E}}\mathcal{F} \neq \mathbf{0}$. Hence, we obtain a constitutive function for $\dot{\mathbf{E}}$, namely

$$\dot{\mathbf{E}} = \mathcal{E}(\mathbf{E}, \mathbf{S}_{RR}, \dot{\mathbf{S}}_{RR}), \tag{9}$$

where $\mathcal{E}$ is a tensor-valued function. Equation (9) may be viewed as a *strain–stress-rate* model. If, in particular, $\mathcal{E}$ is independent of $\dot{\mathbf{S}}_{RR}$, namely $\dot{\mathbf{E}} = \mathcal{E}_0(\mathbf{E}, \mathbf{S}_{RR})$, then we can view $\mathcal{E}_0$ as describing a conservative deformation, as is the case for elastic solids.

4.   If $\mathcal{F}$ is independent of $\dot{\mathbf{E}}$ and $\partial_{\mathbf{E}}\mathcal{F} \neq \mathbf{0}$, then we can derive the constitutive equation

$$\mathbf{E} = \hat{\mathcal{E}}(\mathbf{S}_{RR}, \dot{\mathbf{S}}_{RR}).$$

This form may be referred to as a *stress-rate* model and is convenient whenever we examine the deformation determined by a time-dependent stress.

4. Stress–Strain-Rate Models

Based on the decomposition of $\mathbf{T}_{RR} = \mathbf{G}(\mathbf{E}) + \mathbf{S}_{RR}$, we look for models described by equations of the form

$$\dot{\mathbf{S}}_{RR} = \mathcal{S}(\theta, \mathbf{E}, \mathbf{S}_{RR}, \dot{\mathbf{E}}). \tag{10}$$

To allow also for heat conduction, we let

$$\theta, \mathbf{E}, \mathbf{S}_{RR}, \dot{\mathbf{E}}, \nabla_R\theta$$

be the variables for the constitutive functions

$$\psi, \eta, \dot{\mathbf{S}}_{RR}, \mathbf{q}_R, \gamma.$$

A possible dependence on $J = (\det \mathbf{C})^{1/2} = [\det(\mathbf{1} + 2\mathbf{E})]^{1/2}$ is embodied in the dependence on $\mathbf{E}$.

The CD inequality (4) can be written in the form

$$-\rho_R(\partial_\theta\psi + \eta)\dot{\theta} + (\mathbf{G}(\theta, \mathbf{E}) + \mathbf{S}_{RR} - \rho_R\partial_{\mathbf{E}}\psi) \cdot \dot{\mathbf{E}} - \rho_R\partial_{\mathbf{S}_{RR}}\psi \cdot \dot{\mathbf{S}}_{RR} - \rho_R\partial_{\dot{\mathbf{E}}}\psi \cdot \ddot{\mathbf{E}}$$
$$-\rho_R\partial_{\nabla_R\theta}\psi \cdot \nabla_R\dot{\theta} - \frac{1}{\theta}\mathbf{q}_R \cdot \nabla_R\theta = \rho_R\theta\gamma. \tag{11}$$

The quantities $\nabla_R\dot{\theta}$, $\ddot{\mathbf{E}}$, and $\dot{\theta}$ occur linearly and can take arbitrary values. Hence, (11) holds only if

$$\partial_{\nabla_R\theta}\psi = \mathbf{0}, \qquad \partial_{\dot{\mathbf{E}}}\psi = \mathbf{0}, \qquad \eta = -\partial_\theta\psi.$$

We let

$$\mathbf{G}(\theta, \mathbf{E}) = \rho_R\partial_{\mathbf{E}}\psi,$$

and hence (11) simplifies to

$$\mathbf{S}_{RR} \cdot \dot{\mathbf{E}} - \rho_R\partial_{\mathbf{S}_{RR}}\psi \cdot \dot{\mathbf{S}}_{RR} - \frac{1}{\theta}\mathbf{q}_R \cdot \nabla_R\theta = \rho_R\theta\gamma.$$

Further restrictions follow by considering (10) and $\mathbf{q}_R$ in the particular form

$$\mathbf{q}_R(\theta, \mathbf{E}, \mathbf{S}_{RR}, \nabla_R\theta).$$

It follows that $\gamma = \gamma_s + \gamma_q$, such that

$$\mathbf{S}_{RR} \cdot \dot{\mathbf{E}} - \rho_R \partial_{\mathbf{S}_{RR}} \psi \cdot \boldsymbol{\mathcal{S}} = \rho_R \theta \gamma_s \geq 0, \tag{12}$$

$$-\frac{1}{\theta} \mathbf{q}_R \cdot \nabla_R \theta = \rho_R \theta \gamma_q \geq 0, \tag{13}$$

where γ_s is independent of $\nabla_R \theta$ and γ_q is independent of $\dot{\mathbf{E}}$.

4.1. Solutions to (12)

We now look for solutions to (12) in the unknown function $\boldsymbol{\mathcal{S}}(\theta, \mathbf{E}, \mathbf{S}_{RR}, \dot{\mathbf{E}})$ subject to

$$\boldsymbol{\mathcal{S}}(\theta, \mathbf{E}, \mathbf{S}_{RR}, \dot{\mathbf{E}}) = O(|\dot{\mathbf{E}}|),$$

that is, $\boldsymbol{\mathcal{S}}(\theta, \mathbf{E}, \mathbf{S}_{RR}, \dot{\mathbf{E}}) \to 0$ as $\dot{\mathbf{E}} \to 0$.

First, we determine the general form of $\boldsymbol{\mathcal{S}}$ on the assumption that $\partial_{\mathbf{S}_{RR}} \psi \neq 0$. In this connection, we recall a representation formula [2] such that if the (second order) tensor $\mathbf{Z}$ satisfies

$$\mathbf{Z} \cdot \mathbf{N} = f, \qquad |\mathbf{N}| = 1,$$

then

$$\mathbf{Z} = f\mathbf{N} + [\mathbf{I} - \mathbf{N} \otimes \mathbf{N}]\Xi, \tag{14}$$

Ξ being an arbitrary tensor. In Equation (14), $\mathbf{I}$ denotes the fourth-order identity tensor and $\otimes$ the dyadic tensor product. Now let $\partial_{\mathbf{S}_{RR}} \psi \neq 0$ and define

$$\mathbf{N} = \frac{\partial_{\mathbf{S}_{RR}} \psi}{|\partial_{\mathbf{S}_{RR}} \psi|}$$

while Ξ is allowed to be a function of $\theta, \mathbf{E}, \mathbf{S}_{RR}$, and $\dot{\mathbf{E}}$. Hence, by (12), with $\mathbf{Z} = \boldsymbol{\mathcal{S}}$ and $f = \mathbf{S}_{RR} \cdot \dot{\mathbf{E}} - \rho_R \theta \gamma_s$, we have

$$\dot{\mathbf{S}}_{RR} = -\frac{\theta \gamma_s}{|\partial_{\mathbf{S}_{RR}} \psi|^2} \partial_{\mathbf{S}_{RR}} \psi + \frac{\partial_{\mathbf{S}_{RR}} \psi \otimes \mathbf{S}_{RR}}{\rho_R |\partial_{\mathbf{S}_{RR}} \psi|^2} \dot{\mathbf{E}} + [\mathbf{I} - \frac{\partial_{\mathbf{S}_{RR}} \psi \otimes \partial_{\mathbf{S}_{RR}} \psi}{|\partial_{\mathbf{S}_{RR}} \psi|^2}]\Xi. \tag{15}$$

This is a general formula for the stress-rate $\dot{\mathbf{S}}_{RR}$. Appropriate choices for ψ, γ_s, and Ξ lead to special models of stress-rate equations.

4.1.1. A Model for Damage and Fatigue

A rather general model arises by letting

$$\rho_R \partial_{\mathbf{S}_{RR}} \psi = \alpha(\mathbf{E}, \theta)\mathbf{S}_{RR}, \quad \gamma_s = \beta(\mathbf{E}, \theta)|\mathbf{S}_{RR}|^2, \quad \Xi = \frac{1}{\alpha(\mathbf{E}, \theta)}\dot{\mathbf{E}},$$

where $\beta > 0$ in order that $\gamma_s \geq 0$. These assumptions simplify Equation (15) to

$$\dot{\mathbf{S}}_{RR} = -\frac{\theta \beta}{\alpha}\mathbf{S}_{RR} + \frac{1}{\alpha}\dot{\mathbf{E}}. \tag{16}$$

The function α is usually assumed to be positive, which allows

$$\tau(\mathbf{E}, \theta) = \frac{\alpha(\mathbf{E}, \theta)}{\theta \beta(\mathbf{E}, \theta)} > 0 \tag{17}$$

to be viewed as a relaxation time. To integrate Equation (16), we proceed as follows. Let

$$\mathbf{Y}_{RR} = \exp[\int_{t_0}^{t} (1/\tau) d\xi]\mathbf{S}_{RR}.$$

Hence, Equation (16) provides

$$\dot{\mathbf{Y}}_{RR}(t) := \exp[\int_{t_0}^t (1/\tau)d\xi]\left(\dot{\mathbf{S}}_{RR}(t) + \frac{1}{\tau}\mathbf{S}_{RR}(t)\right) = \exp[\int_{t_0}^t (1/\tau)d\xi]\frac{1}{\alpha}\dot{\mathbf{E}}(t),$$

and then the integration on $(t_0, t]$ yields

$$\mathbf{Y}_{RR}(t) = \mathbf{Y}_{RR}(t_0) + \int_{t_0}^t \frac{1}{\alpha}\exp[\int_{t_0}^s (1/\tau)d\xi]\dot{\mathbf{E}}(s)ds.$$

Accordingly, it follows that

$$\mathbf{S}_{RR}(t) = \exp[-\int_{t_0}^t (1/\tau)d\xi]\mathbf{S}_{RR}(t_0) + \int_{t_0}^t \frac{1}{\alpha}\exp[-\int_s^t (1/\tau)d\xi]\dot{\mathbf{E}}(s)ds.$$

Then, letting $t_0 \to -\infty$ and assuming

$$\lim_{t_0 \to -\infty}\mathbf{S}_{RR}(t_0) = \mathbf{0}$$

we obtain

$$\mathbf{S}_{RR}(t) = \int_{-\infty}^t \frac{1}{\alpha}\exp\{-\int_s^t [1/\tau]d\xi\}\,\dot{\mathbf{E}}(s)ds. \tag{18}$$

Finally, if we introduce the reduced-time function

$$\mathcal{T}_r(t) = \int_{t_0}^t \frac{1}{\tau(\mathbf{E}(\xi),\theta(\xi))}d\xi,$$

where τ is named the time-temperature shift factor, Equation (18) can be rewritten as

$$\mathbf{S}_{RR}(t) = \int_{-\infty}^t \frac{1}{\alpha}\exp\{-[\mathcal{T}_r(t) - \mathcal{T}_r(s)]\}\,\dot{\mathbf{E}}(s)ds. \tag{19}$$

Note that $\mathcal{T}_r$ depends on the past values of $\mathbf{E}$, so that (19) is a *non-separable* integral representation of $\mathbf{S}_{RR}$ (see, e.g., [16]) that is able to capture damage and fatigue effects; we mention [17] where a representation of the form (19) is used to describe damage in asphalt mixture. The thermodynamic consistency of (19) is proved in the more general case of (15), which allows for nonlinearities through ψ and γ_s and any dependence, on the whole set of variables, through Ξ.

4.1.2. The Maxwell Fluid

Assume that α and β depend on θ and let the temperature θ be a known function of time. Then, α and τ are known functions of time in that

$$\alpha(t) = \hat{\alpha}(\theta(t)), \qquad \tau(t) = \hat{\tau}(\theta(t)).$$

Hence, Equation (18) takes the form

$$\mathbf{S}_{RR}(t) = \int_{-\infty}^t \frac{1}{\alpha(s)}\exp\{-\int_s^t [1/\tau(\xi)]d\xi\}\,\dot{\mathbf{E}}(s)ds. \tag{20}$$

Equation (20) is in the form of the Boltzmann model for $\mathbf{S}_{RR}$ in terms of the present value $\mathbf{E}(t)$ and the history $\mathbf{E}^t$.

If α and $\theta\beta$, introduced in (17), are constants, then Equation (16) simplifies to

$$\dot{\mathbf{S}}_{RR} = -\frac{1}{\tau}\mathbf{S}_{RR} + \frac{1}{\alpha}\dot{\mathbf{E}}, \tag{21}$$

which is just the classical Maxwell equation although in the Lagrangian formulation. The solution $\mathbf{S}_{RR}(t)$ can be obtained directly by integration. Otherwise, we observe that α and τ would be constant and then Equation (20) would read

$$\mathbf{S}_{RR} = \frac{1}{\alpha} \int_{-\infty}^{t} \exp[-\frac{1}{\tau}(t-s)]\dot{\mathbf{E}}(s)ds,$$

whence, by an integration by parts, it follows

$$\mathbf{S}_{RR}(t) = \frac{1}{\alpha}\mathbf{E}(t) - \frac{1}{\alpha\tau}\int_{-\infty}^{t} \exp[-(t-s)/\tau]\,\mathbf{E}(s)ds.$$

Since $\mathbf{T}_{RR} = \mathbf{G}(\mathbf{E}) + \mathbf{S}_{RR}$, then $\mathbf{T}_{RR}$ can be written in the form

$$\mathbf{T}_{RR}(t) = \mathbf{G}_0(\mathbf{E}(t)) + \int_{\infty}^{t} G'(t-s)\mathbf{E}(s)ds,$$

where

$$\mathbf{G}_0(\mathbf{E}) = \mathbf{G}(\mathbf{E}) + \frac{1}{\alpha}\mathbf{E}, \qquad G'(t-s) = \frac{1}{\alpha\tau}\exp[-(t-s)/\tau].$$

It reduces to the well-known linear model [4,5] if $\mathbf{G}(\mathbf{E}) = G_\infty\mathbf{E}$, $G_\infty > 0$.

In the one-dimensional case, the differences between the linear and the nonlinear model are outlined by the following numerical simulations (see Figures 1 and 2). In the first picture, we consider the linear one-dimensional model $T_{RR} = G_\infty E + S_{RR}$, where the evolution of S_{RR} is ruled by Equation (21). The resulting system

$$\begin{cases} \dot{E}(t) = \omega\cos(\omega t) \\ \dot{T}_{RR}(t) = G_0\dot{E}(t) - \frac{1}{\tau}\left[T_{RR}(t) - G_\infty E(t)\right] \end{cases} \tag{22}$$

where $G_0 = G_\infty + 1/\alpha$ describes the cycles in the $E - T_{RR}$ plane at different frequencies ω of the oscillating strain.

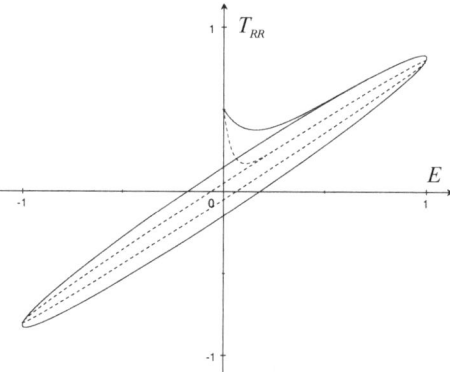

Figure 1. Stress–strain cycles at $\omega = \pi/50$ (solid) and $\omega = \pi/150$ (dashed) with $\tau = 2$, $\alpha = 5/6$, and $G_\infty = 4/5$.

Figure 2 represents the cycles at different frequencies ω of the nonlinear model obtained by letting $G(E) = G_\infty E^3$.

The resulting system

$$\begin{cases} \dot{E}(t) = \omega\cos(\omega t) \\ \dot{T}_{RR}(t) = G_0(E(t))\dot{E}(t) - \frac{1}{\tau}\left[T_{RR}(t) - G(E(t))\right] \end{cases} \tag{23}$$

where $G_0(E(t)) = G'(E(t)) + 1/\alpha$ describes the cycles in the $E - T_{RR}$ plane at different frequencies ω of the oscillating strain.

It is of interest that Figures 1 and 2 show a hysteretic evolution of the dependence $T_{RR}(E)$. Systems (22) and (23) are rate-dependent, and this is made evident by the variation in the loop shape as the frequency ω changes. Indeed, as ω goes to 0 the loop narrows until it reaches the quasi-stationary regime $T_{RR} \simeq G(E)$. On the other hand, as the frequency increases, the loop becomes narrower and narrower, thus approaching the rate-independent property at high frequencies where $\dot{T}_{RR} \simeq G'\dot{E}$. As a remark, the form of the loops associated with (23) is quite similar to the stress–strain curve occurring in foamed materials [2] (Section 13.7).

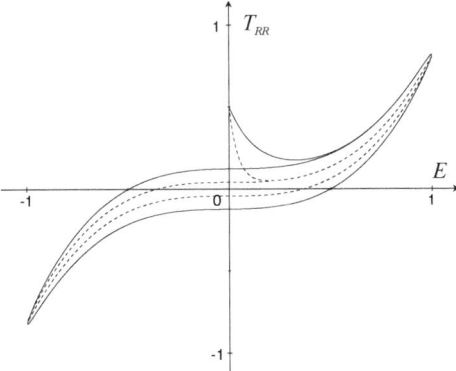

Figure 2. Stress–straincycles at $\omega = \pi/50$ (solid) and $\omega = \pi/150$ (dashed) with $\tau = 2$, $\alpha = 1$, and $G_\infty = 4/5$.

4.1.3. A Model for Bio-Soft Tissues

Consider one-dimensional settings and let $\beta = 0$, so $\gamma_s = 0$ too. Namely, materials with zero entropy production from the mechanical side are concerned. Furthermore, let α depend on the strain E as well as on the temperature. Equation (16) then simplifies to

$$\dot{S}_{RR} = f(\theta, E)\dot{E}, \qquad f(\theta, E) = \frac{1}{\alpha(\theta, E)\rho_R} \tag{24}$$

This type of rate equation is found to model the hypoelastic behavior of collagen fiber stress [18] if

$$f(\theta, E) = k\{1 - \exp[-(E/\delta)^a]\}$$

for proper values of the positive parameters k, δ, a possibly dependent on θ. Assuming that these parameters are constant, upon integration, we obtain

$$S_{RR}(t) = H(E(t)),$$

where $H'(E) = f(E)$, $H(0) = 0$.

In [18], the viscoelastic behavior of ligaments and tendons (bio-soft tissues) is determined by modeling collagen fibers and proteoglycan-rich matrix as a Maxwell-type system with two relaxation times, $\tau_1, \tau_2 > 0$. By means of the following correspondence with our notations

$$\sigma_f \to H, \qquad \sigma \to T_{RR}, \qquad E_f \to k, \qquad E_m \to h,$$

the full model (Equation (15) in [18]) can be written in the form (see Equation (16))

$$T_{RR} = G(E) + S_{RR}, \qquad \dot{S}_{RR} = -\frac{1}{\tau}S_{RR} + \frac{1}{\alpha}\dot{E}$$

where $\tau = \tau_1 + \tau_2$ and

$$G(E) = \frac{\tau}{\tau_1} H(E), \qquad \alpha(E) = \frac{1}{h - (1 - \tau_1/\tau)G'(E)}.$$

The positivity of α for each value of E is guaranteed by the condition $h \geq k\tau/\tau_1$.

4.2. Solutions to (13)

Inequality (13) holds if $\mathbf{q}_R$ is provided by a Fourier-like relation

$$\mathbf{q}_R = -\mathbf{K}(\theta, \mathbf{E})\nabla_R \theta, \tag{25}$$

with $\mathbf{K}$ a positive definite second-order tensor; the dependence on the strain $\mathbf{E}$, in addition to the temperature θ, makes the model nonlinear. However, inequality (13) allows for more general solutions $\mathbf{q}_R$.

Letting $\mathbf{N} = \nabla_R \theta / |\nabla_R \theta|$, we apply the representation formula to (13). It follows that

$$\mathbf{q}_R = \frac{\rho_R \theta^2 \gamma_q}{|\nabla_R \theta|^2} \nabla_R \theta + \left[\mathbf{1} - \frac{\nabla_R \theta \otimes \nabla_R \theta}{|\nabla_R \theta|^2}\right] \mathbf{w}, \tag{26}$$

where $\mathbf{w}$ is any vector function of $\theta, \mathbf{E}, \nabla_R \theta$. If, e.g., we select $\mathbf{w} = -\mathbf{K}\nabla_R \theta$, with $\mathbf{K}$ positive definite, then Equation (26) becomes

$$\mathbf{q}_R = -\frac{\rho_R \theta^2 \gamma_q}{|\nabla_R \theta|^2} \nabla_R \theta - \mathbf{K}\nabla_R \theta + \frac{\nabla_R \theta \cdot \mathbf{K}\nabla_R \theta}{|\nabla_R \theta|^2} \nabla_R \theta.$$

Hence, $\mathbf{q}_R$ consists of a part in the direction of $\nabla_R \theta$ and a part $-\mathbf{K}\nabla_R \theta$ subject only to $\mathbf{K} > \mathbf{0}$. This splitting is parameterized by the entropy production. Two interesting particular cases arise. Firstly, if $\gamma_q = \nabla_R \theta \cdot \mathbf{K}\nabla_R \theta / \rho_R \theta^2$, then the relation simplifies to Equation (25). Secondly, if $\gamma_q = 0$, then

$$\mathbf{q}_R = -\mathbf{K}\nabla_R \theta + \frac{\nabla_R \theta \cdot \mathbf{K}\nabla_R \theta}{|\nabla_R \theta|^2} \nabla_R \theta,$$

which is a Fourier-like relation with zero entropy production.

As a further example, let $\mathbf{w} = \alpha \mathbf{E}\nabla_R \theta$. Then, we have

$$\mathbf{q}_R = -\frac{\rho_R \theta^2 \gamma_q}{|\nabla_R \theta|^2} \nabla_R \theta + \alpha \mathbf{E}\nabla_R \theta - \alpha \frac{\nabla_R \theta \cdot \mathbf{E}\nabla_R \theta}{|\nabla_R \theta|^2} \nabla_R \theta.$$

This model shows that the deformation induces a transverse part of $\mathbf{q}_R$ relative to $\nabla_R \theta$; the CD inequality is a constraint on the longitudinal part of $\mathbf{q}_R$ while the transverse part is unconstrained.

5. Strain–Stress-Rate Models

We now consider a strain–stress-rate model in the explicit form

$$\dot{\mathbf{E}} = \mathcal{E}(\theta, \mathbf{E}, \mathbf{S}_{RR}, \dot{\mathbf{S}}_{RR});$$

for definiteness, we select $\dot{\mathbf{S}}_{RR}$, rather than $\dot{\mathbf{E}}$, as one of the variables. Accordingly, the set of variables is now

$$\theta, \mathbf{E}, \mathbf{S}_{RR}, \dot{\mathbf{S}}_{RR}, \nabla_R \theta.$$

Again, we let $\mathbf{T}_{RR} = \mathbf{G}(\mathbf{E}) + \mathbf{S}_{RR}$ and then consider the free energy

$$\rho_R \phi = \rho_R \psi - \mathbf{E} \cdot \mathbf{S}_{RR} - \mathcal{G},$$

where $\mathcal{G}$ is the elastic energy, say

$$\mathbf{G}(\mathbf{E}) = \partial_{\mathbf{E}}\mathcal{G}(\mathbf{E}).$$

Using ϕ instead of ψ, we can write the CD inequality in the form

$$-\rho_R(\dot{\phi} + \eta\dot{\theta}) - \mathbf{E}\cdot\dot{\mathbf{S}}_{RR} - \frac{1}{\theta}\mathbf{q}_R\cdot\nabla_R\theta = \rho_R\theta\gamma \geq 0.$$

Computing the time derivative of $\phi(\theta, \mathbf{E}, \mathbf{S}_{RR}, \dot{\mathbf{S}}_{RR}, \nabla_R\theta)$ and substituting, we have

$$-\rho_R(\partial_\theta\phi + \eta)\dot{\theta} - \rho_R\partial_{\mathbf{E}}\phi\cdot\dot{\mathbf{E}} - (\mathbf{E} + \rho_R\partial_{\mathbf{S}_{RR}}\phi)\cdot\dot{\mathbf{S}}_{RR} - \rho_R\partial_{\dot{\mathbf{S}}_{RR}}\phi\cdot\ddot{\mathbf{S}}_{RR}$$
$$-\rho_R\partial_{\nabla_R\theta}\phi\cdot\nabla_R\dot{\theta} - \frac{1}{\theta}\mathbf{q}_R\cdot\nabla_R\theta = \rho_R\theta\gamma \geq 0. \tag{27}$$

The arbitrariness of $\ddot{\mathbf{S}}_{RR}$, $\nabla_R\dot{\theta}$, and $\dot{\theta}$ implies that $\partial_{\dot{\mathbf{S}}_{RR}}\phi = 0$, $\partial_{\nabla_R\theta}\phi = 0$, and $\eta = -\partial_\theta\phi$. The remaining inequality is now examined by setting aside cross-coupling terms in the sense that $\mathcal{E}$ is independent of $\nabla_R\theta$ and $\mathbf{q}_R$ is independent of $\dot{\mathbf{S}}_{RR}$. Hence, the inequality (27) splits into

$$-\rho_R\partial_{\mathbf{E}}\phi\cdot\dot{\mathbf{E}} - (\mathbf{E} + \rho_R\partial_{\mathbf{S}_{RR}}\phi)\cdot\dot{\mathbf{S}}_{RR} = \rho_R\theta\gamma_S \geq 0, \tag{28}$$

and again (13), where γ_S is the value of γ at $\nabla_R\theta = 0$.

We now apply the representation Formula (14) to Equation (28). Assume $\partial_{\mathbf{E}}\phi \neq 0$ and define $\mathbf{N} = \partial_{\mathbf{E}}\phi/|\partial_{\mathbf{E}}\phi|$. Hence, by Equation (28), we obtain

$$\dot{\mathbf{E}} = \frac{\rho_R\theta\gamma_S}{|\partial_{\mathbf{E}}\phi|^2}\partial_{\mathbf{E}}\phi + \frac{\partial_{\mathbf{E}}\phi \otimes (\mathbf{E} + \rho_R\partial_{\mathbf{S}_{RR}}\phi)}{|\partial_{\mathbf{E}}\phi|^2}\dot{\mathbf{S}}_{RR} + \left[\mathbf{I} - \frac{\partial_{\mathbf{E}}\phi \otimes \partial_{\mathbf{E}}\phi}{|\partial_{\mathbf{E}}\phi|^2}\right]\Xi, \tag{29}$$

where Ξ is a tensor function of $\theta, \mathbf{E}, \mathbf{S}_{RR}, \dot{\mathbf{S}}_{RR}$. Equation (29) shows the general form of the function $\mathcal{E}$ in terms of $\theta, \mathbf{E}, \mathbf{S}_{RR}, \dot{\mathbf{S}}_{RR}$.

The simplest case follows by letting $\Xi = 0$ and $\gamma_S = 0$ (zero entropy production). Hence, we have

$$\dot{\mathbf{E}} = \mathbf{F}\dot{\mathbf{S}}_{RR}, \qquad \mathbf{F} := \frac{\partial_{\mathbf{E}}\phi \otimes (\mathbf{E} + \rho_R\partial_{\mathbf{S}_{RR}}\phi)}{|\partial_{\mathbf{E}}\phi|^2}. \tag{30}$$

The integration of (30) on $(-\infty, t)$ and the assumption $\mathbf{E}(-\infty) = \mathbf{0}$ yield

$$\mathbf{E}(t) = \int_{-\infty}^{t} \mathbf{F}(\xi)\dot{\mathbf{S}}_{RR}(\xi)d\xi.$$

An integration by parts and the assumption $\mathbf{S}_{RR}(-\infty) = \mathbf{0}$ result in

$$\mathbf{E}(t) = \mathbf{F}(t)\mathbf{S}_{RR}(t) - \int_{-\infty}^{t} \dot{\mathbf{F}}(\xi)\mathbf{S}_{RR}(\xi)d\xi.$$

These results have some analogy with a class of quasi-linear viscoelastic materials [19] where the present value of $\mathbf{B} = \mathbf{F}\mathbf{F}^T$ is provided by the history of $\dot{\mathbf{T}}$.

6. Strain-Rate Models

As a generalization of the Kelvin–Voigt constitutive equation, we now look for a function

$$\mathbf{S}_{RR} = \mathcal{S}_0(\theta, \mathbf{E}, \dot{\mathbf{E}}) = O(|\dot{\mathbf{E}}|).$$

Hence, we let

$$\theta, \mathbf{E}, \dot{\mathbf{E}}, \nabla_R\theta$$

be the variables and $\psi, \eta, \mathbf{q}_R, \gamma$ the constitutive functions. The CD inequality becomes

$$-\rho_R(\partial_\theta\psi + \eta)\dot{\theta} - \rho_R\partial_{\nabla_R\theta}\psi\cdot\nabla_R\dot{\theta} + (\mathbf{T}_{RR} - \rho_R\partial_{\mathbf{E}}\psi)\cdot\dot{\mathbf{E}} - \rho_R\partial_{\dot{\mathbf{E}}}\psi\cdot\ddot{\mathbf{E}} - \frac{1}{\theta}\mathbf{q}_R\cdot\nabla_R\theta = \rho_R\theta\gamma \geq 0.$$

The arbitrariness of $\nabla_R \dot{\theta}, \ddot{\mathbf{E}}, \dot{\theta}$ implies that

$$\partial_{\nabla_R \theta} \psi = 0, \quad \partial_{\dot{\mathbf{E}}} \psi = 0, \quad \eta = -\partial_\theta \psi.$$

The remaining inequality is

$$(\mathbf{T}_{RR} - \rho_R \partial_{\mathbf{E}} \psi) \cdot \dot{\mathbf{E}} - \frac{1}{\theta} \mathbf{q}_R \cdot \nabla_R \theta = \rho_R \theta \gamma \geq 0. \tag{31}$$

Although $\mathbf{T}_{RR}$ and $\mathbf{q}_R$ might depend jointly on $\dot{\mathbf{E}}, \nabla_R \theta$, for definiteness, we assume that

$$\mathbf{T}_{RR} = \mathbf{G}(\theta, \mathbf{E}) + \boldsymbol{\mathcal{S}}_0(\theta, \mathbf{E}, \dot{\mathbf{E}}), \quad \boldsymbol{\mathcal{S}}_0 \to 0 \quad \text{as} \quad \dot{\mathbf{E}} \to 0 \tag{32}$$

while $\mathbf{q}_R$ is independent of $\dot{\mathbf{E}}$. Hence, inequality (31) splits into two inequalities, namely

$$(\mathbf{T}_{RR} - \rho_R \partial_{\mathbf{E}} \psi) \cdot \dot{\mathbf{E}} = \rho_R \theta \gamma_E \geq 0, \tag{33}$$

and again (13), where γ_E is the value of γ at $\nabla_R \theta = 0$ and γ_q is the value of γ at $\dot{\mathbf{E}} = 0$. In light of (32), it follows from (33) that

$$\mathbf{G}(\theta, \mathbf{E}) = \rho_R \partial_{\mathbf{E}} \psi(\theta, \mathbf{E}), \quad \boldsymbol{\mathcal{S}}_0(\theta, \mathbf{E}, \dot{\mathbf{E}}) \cdot \dot{\mathbf{E}} = \rho_R \theta \gamma_E \geq 0. \tag{34}$$

6.1. Some Examples

Borrowing from [20], we now consider a model with application to human knee ligaments. Let $\mathbf{G}$ and $\boldsymbol{\mathcal{S}}_0$ be functions satisfying the requirements in (34). Let

$$I_1 = \text{tr}\, \mathbf{C} = 2\text{tr}\, \mathbf{E} + 3.$$

Hence, $\mathbf{G}$ and $\boldsymbol{\mathcal{S}}_0$ are assigned the forms

$$\mathbf{G}(\theta, \mathbf{E}) = -p\mathbf{C}^{-1} + \alpha\beta\{\exp[\beta(I_1 - 3)] - I_1\}\mathbf{1} + \alpha\beta\mathbf{C}, \quad \boldsymbol{\mathcal{S}}_0(\theta, \mathbf{E}, \dot{\mathbf{E}}) = \nu(I_1 - 3)\dot{\mathbf{E}},$$

where the parameters α, β, ν are allowed to depend on temperature. Furthermore, p is the standard pressure of the Eulerian description.

A nonlinear model is obtained by using the triples $\mathbf{J} = (J_1, J_2, J_3)$ and $\tilde{\mathbf{J}} = (\tilde{J}_1, \tilde{J}_2, \tilde{J}_3)$ of the main invariants of $\mathbf{E}$ and $\dot{\mathbf{E}}$, respectively. The requirement (34) is satisfied by letting

$$\boldsymbol{\mathcal{S}}_0(\theta, \mathbf{E}, \dot{\mathbf{E}}) = f_0(\theta, \mathbf{J})\boldsymbol{\lambda}(\dot{\mathbf{E}})$$

where $f_0 \geq 0$ and $\boldsymbol{\lambda}(\dot{\mathbf{E}}) \cdot \dot{\mathbf{E}} \geq 0$. In a more detailed form, we can assume

$$\boldsymbol{\lambda}(\dot{\mathbf{E}}) = \lambda_0(\tilde{\mathbf{J}})\dot{\mathbf{E}}, \quad \lambda_0 > 0.$$

Otherwise, we might consider the representation

$$\boldsymbol{\lambda}(\dot{\mathbf{E}}) = \lambda_0(\tilde{\mathbf{J}})\mathbf{1} + \lambda_1(\tilde{\mathbf{J}})\dot{\mathbf{E}} + \lambda_2(\tilde{\mathbf{J}})\dot{\mathbf{E}}\dot{\mathbf{E}}.$$

whence it follows that

$$\boldsymbol{\lambda}(\dot{\mathbf{E}}) \cdot \dot{\mathbf{E}} = \lambda_0(\tilde{\mathbf{J}})\tilde{J}_1 + \lambda_1(\tilde{\mathbf{J}})\tilde{J}_2 + \lambda_2(\tilde{\mathbf{J}})\tilde{J}_3.$$

In this case, the non-negative value of $\boldsymbol{\lambda}(\dot{\mathbf{E}}) \cdot \dot{\mathbf{E}}$ requires appropriate restrictions on $\lambda_0, \lambda_1, \lambda_2$.

Another class of unidimensional nonlinear strain-rate models has been proposed to describe the mechanical behavior of polymeric foams whose dynamic loading shows a dependence of the stress also on the strain-rate [2] (ch. 13.7). To include strain-rate effects, the dependence has been improved in the form [21]

$$\boldsymbol{\mathcal{S}}_0(\theta, E, \dot{E}) = f(E)h(E, \dot{E}) \tag{35}$$

where f, h may depend on the temperature θ. The literature shows various forms of the functions f, h, e.g.,

$$f(E) = a\{1 - \exp[(-c/a)E(1-E)^m]\} + b\left(\frac{E}{1-E}\right)^n, \quad h(E, \dot{E}) = 1 + (\alpha + \beta E) \ln(\dot{E}/\dot{E}_0),$$

where $a, b, c, m, n, \alpha, \beta$ are the pertinent positive parameters and $\dot{E}_0$ is a reference strain-rate (frequently $\dot{E}_0 = 10^{-3}\,\text{s}^{-1}$).

6.2. Generalizations of the Kelvin–Voigt Model

A two-parameter class of constitutive equations is considered in [15] in the form

$$\gamma \mathbf{B} + \nu \mathbf{D} = \mathcal{F}(\mathbf{T}), \quad \mathbf{B} = \mathbf{FF}^T;$$

this equation is said to model a fluid if $\gamma = 0$ and an elastic solid if $\nu = 0$. For generality, we might regard strain-rate models as those characterized by relations in the Lagrangian form,

$$\mathcal{F}_S(\theta, \mathbf{E}, \dot{\mathbf{E}}, \mathbf{S}_{RR}) = \mathbf{0} \quad \text{or} \quad \mathcal{F}_T(\theta, \mathbf{E}, \dot{\mathbf{E}}, \mathbf{T}_{RR}) = \mathbf{0},$$

where $\mathbf{T}_{RR} = \mathbf{G}(\mathbf{E}) + \mathbf{S}_{RR}$. As we show in a while, significantly different relations arise depending on the choice of the (independent) variables.

For definiteness, here, we let $\theta, \mathbf{E}, \mathbf{S}_{RR}$ be the variables. The exploitation of the CD inequality leads to

$$\partial_{\nabla_R \theta} \psi = \mathbf{0}, \quad \partial_{\mathbf{S}_{RR}} \psi = \mathbf{0}, \quad \eta = -\partial_\theta \psi$$

and the remaining inequality is (33). Assuming $(34)_1$, we have

$$\mathbf{S}_{RR} \cdot \dot{\mathbf{E}} = \rho_R \theta \gamma_E.$$

Since γ_E depends on $\theta, \mathbf{E}, \mathbf{S}_{RR}$, we look for $\dot{\mathbf{E}}$ as a function of the same variables, namely

$$\dot{\mathbf{E}} = \mathcal{E}_0(\theta, \mathbf{E}, \mathbf{S}_{RR}),$$

(see the special case of item 3). We let $\mathbf{N} = \mathbf{S}_{RR}/|\mathbf{S}_{RR}|$ and apply the representation Formula (14) to obtain

$$\dot{\mathbf{E}} := \mathcal{E}_0(\theta, \mathbf{E}, \mathbf{S}_{RR}) = \frac{\rho_R \theta \gamma_E(\theta, \mathbf{E}, \mathbf{S}_{RR})}{|\mathbf{S}_{RR}|^2} \mathbf{S}_{RR} + \left[\mathbf{I} - \frac{\mathbf{S}_{RR} \otimes \mathbf{S}_{RR}}{|\mathbf{S}_{RR}|^2}\right]\Xi, \tag{36}$$

where Ξ is a tensor function of the variables $\theta, \mathbf{E}, \mathbf{S}_{RR}$. In particular, if we take $\Xi = -\beta \mathbf{E}$, then it follows

$$\dot{\mathbf{E}} = \frac{\rho_R \theta \gamma_E + \beta \mathbf{S}_{RR} \cdot \mathbf{E}}{|\mathbf{S}_{RR}|^2} \mathbf{S}_{RR} - \beta \mathbf{E}. \tag{37}$$

A model describing a conservative strain evolution is obtained by assuming zero entropy production, $\gamma_E = 0$. If $\rho_R \theta \gamma_E = \alpha |\mathbf{S}_{RR}|^2$, we can write Equation (37) in the form

$$\dot{\mathbf{E}} + \beta \mathbf{E} = \alpha\left(1 + \frac{\beta \mathbf{S}_{RR} \cdot \mathbf{E}}{\alpha |\mathbf{S}_{RR}|^2}\right)\mathbf{S}_{RR}.$$

Inasmuch as $|\beta \mathbf{S}_{RR} \cdot \mathbf{E}/\alpha |\mathbf{S}_{RR}|^2| \ll 1$, we obtain the Kelvin–Voigt equation as an approximation of (37).

A more general constitutive equation in the form

$$\dot{\mathbf{E}} + \beta \mathbf{E} = \mathfrak{H}(\theta, \mathbf{E}, \mathbf{S}_{RR})$$

is thermodynamically consistent. This is shown by substituting

$$\Xi = \beta \mathbf{E} + \mathcal{H}(\theta, \mathbf{E}, \mathbf{S}_{RR})$$

in (36). It follows that

$$\dot{\mathbf{E}} + \beta\mathbf{E} = \mathcal{H}(\theta, \mathbf{E}, \mathbf{S}_{RR}) + \frac{\rho_R\theta\gamma_E(\theta, \mathbf{E}, \mathbf{S}_{RR}) + \beta\mathbf{S}_{RR}\cdot\mathbf{E} - \mathbf{S}_{RR}\cdot\mathcal{H}(\theta, \mathbf{E}, \mathbf{S}_{RR})}{|\mathbf{S}_{RR}|^2}\mathbf{S}_{RR}. \tag{38}$$

The right-hand side is the expected function $\mathfrak{H}(\theta, \mathbf{E}, \mathbf{S}_{RR})$, where $\beta\mathbf{E}$, $\mathcal{H}(\theta, \mathbf{E}, \mathbf{S}_{RR})$ and $\gamma_E(\theta, \mathbf{E}, \mathbf{S}_{RR})$ are involved in a proper way. This is a nonlinear generalization of the Kelvin–Voigt type. However, if $\gamma_E = 0$, then a model is obtained with zero entropy production.

If θ is a known function of time, then we can integrate (38) to obtain

$$\mathbf{E}(t) = \int_{-\infty}^t \exp\left[-\int_s^t \beta(\xi)d\xi\right]\mathfrak{H}(\theta, \mathbf{E}, \mathbf{S}_{RR})(s)ds,$$

which is again in the Boltzmann form with dependence on the histories of θ, $\mathbf{E}$, and $\mathbf{S}_{RR}$.

If instead we let $\theta, \mathbf{E}, \dot{\mathbf{E}}$ be the variables, then, applying the representation formula to $(34)_2$, it follows that

$$\mathbf{S}_{RR} := \mathcal{S}_0(\theta, \mathbf{E}, \dot{\mathbf{E}}) = \frac{\rho\theta\gamma_E(\theta, \mathbf{E}, \dot{\mathbf{E}})}{|\dot{\mathbf{E}}|^2}\dot{\mathbf{E}} + \left[\mathbf{I} - \frac{\dot{\mathbf{E}}\otimes\dot{\mathbf{E}}}{|\dot{\mathbf{E}}|^2}\right]\Xi.$$

In the simple case

$$\mathbf{G}(\mathbf{E}) = g\mathbf{E}, \qquad \rho_R\theta\gamma_E = \lambda|\dot{\mathbf{E}}|^2, \ \lambda > 0, \qquad \Xi = \mathbf{0}$$

we have

$$\mathbf{T}_{RR} = g\mathbf{E} + \lambda\dot{\mathbf{E}}.$$

6.3. Remarks about Alternative Strain-Rate Models

Let

$$\rho_R\theta\gamma_E = \alpha(J_S)|\mathbf{S}_{RR}|^2, \qquad \beta = \beta(J_S),$$

where J_S denotes the triple of main scalar invariants of $\mathbf{S}_{RR}$. Hence, in light of (37), we can write

$$\dot{\mathbf{E}} + \beta\mathbf{E} = \left(\alpha(J_S)\sqrt{J_2} + \beta\frac{\mathbf{S}_{RR}\cdot\mathbf{E}}{|\mathbf{S}_{RR}|}\right)\frac{\mathbf{S}_{RR}}{|\mathbf{S}_{RR}|}, \qquad J_2 = |\mathbf{S}_{RR}|^2. \tag{39}$$

Within the strain-limiting elastic constitutive setting [22,23], the strain $\mathbf{E}$ and the strain-rate $\dot{\mathbf{E}}$ are replaced by their linear approximations ε and $\dot{\varepsilon}$. In this setting,

$$\left|\frac{\mathbf{S}_{RR}\cdot\varepsilon}{|\mathbf{S}_{RR}|}\right| \leq |\varepsilon| \ll 1$$

so that, if $\alpha\sqrt{J_2}$ and β are comparable, then we can take the approximation

$$\varepsilon + \nu\dot{\varepsilon} = \beta_1\mathbf{S}_{RR}, \qquad \nu = 1/\beta, \quad \beta_1 = \alpha/\beta > 0. \tag{40}$$

Hence, assuming $\text{tr}\,\mathbf{S}_{RR} = 0$ and $\alpha = \hat{\alpha}(J_2) > 0$, we recover the model investigated in [22].

Remark 1. *If β and then ν are constant, then integration of (40) on $(-\infty, t]$ yields*

$$\varepsilon(t) = \int_{-\infty}^t \exp(-\beta(t-u))\,\alpha(J_S(u))\,\mathbf{S}_{RR}(u)du. \tag{41}$$

Equation (41) shows an example of separable strain-dependent modulus [16,24].

7. Stress-Rate Models

Many experimental tests may be viewed as the investigation of the strain induced by a stress process. This warrants attention regarding stress-rate models, as is the case in [25,26]. Hence, we now address equations of the form

$$\mathbf{E} = \mathbf{g}(\theta, \mathbf{T}_{RR}, \dot{\mathbf{T}}_{RR}). \tag{42}$$

To examine the compatibility of the constitutive function (42) with the second law, we let

$$\theta, \mathbf{T}_{RR}, \dot{\mathbf{T}}_{RR}, \nabla_R \theta$$

be the set of variables. Consistently, it is convenient to consider the Gibbs free energy

$$\rho_R \phi = \rho_R \psi - \mathbf{T}_{RR} \cdot \mathbf{E}$$

and observe that

$$-\rho_R \dot{\psi} + \mathbf{T}_{RR} \cdot \dot{\mathbf{E}} = -\rho_R \dot{\phi} - \dot{\mathbf{T}}_{RR} \cdot \mathbf{E}.$$

Now, $\phi, \eta, \mathbf{q}, \mathbf{E}, \gamma$ are provided by constitutive equations. Computation of $\dot{\phi}$ and substitution in the CD inequality yield

$$-\rho_R(\partial_\theta \phi + \eta)\dot{\theta} - (\mathbf{E} + \rho_R \partial_{\mathbf{T}_{RR}} \phi) \cdot \dot{\mathbf{T}}_{RR} - \rho_R \partial_{\dot{\mathbf{T}}_{RR}} \phi \cdot \ddot{\mathbf{T}}_{RR}$$

$$-\rho_R \partial_{\nabla_R \theta} \phi \cdot \nabla_R \dot{\theta} - \frac{1}{\theta} \mathbf{q}_R \cdot \nabla_R \theta = \rho_R \theta \gamma \geq 0.$$

The arbitrariness of $\ddot{\mathbf{T}}_{RR}, \nabla_R \dot{\theta}, \dot{\theta}$ implies that

$$\partial_{\dot{\mathbf{T}}_{RR}} \phi = \mathbf{0}, \quad \partial_{\nabla_R \theta} \phi = \mathbf{0}, \quad \eta = -\partial_\theta \phi$$

and

$$-(\mathbf{E} + \rho_R \partial_{\mathbf{T}_{RR}} \phi) \cdot \dot{\mathbf{T}}_{RR} - \frac{1}{\theta} \mathbf{q}_R \cdot \nabla_R \theta = \rho_R \theta \gamma \geq 0. \tag{43}$$

For reasonable simplicity, we let $\mathbf{q}$ be independent of $\dot{\mathbf{T}}_{RR}$. Hence, we let

$$\gamma = \gamma_T(\theta, \mathbf{T}_{RR}, \dot{\mathbf{T}}_{RR}) + \gamma_q(\theta, \mathbf{T}_{RR}, \nabla_R \theta),$$

both γ_T and γ_q being non-negative. Thus, it follows that

$$[\mathbf{g}(\theta, \mathbf{T}_{RR}, \dot{\mathbf{T}}_{RR}) + \rho_R \partial_{\mathbf{T}_{RR}} \phi(\theta, \mathbf{T}_{RR})] \cdot \dot{\mathbf{T}}_{RR} = \rho_R \theta \gamma_T, \tag{44}$$

$$-\frac{1}{\theta} \mathbf{q}_R \cdot \nabla_R \theta = \rho_R \theta \gamma_q \geq 0.$$

For definiteness, we consider (44) under the assumption

$$\mathbf{g}(\theta, \mathbf{T}_{RR}, \dot{\mathbf{T}}_{RR}) = \mathbf{g}_0(\theta, \mathbf{T}_{RR}) + \tilde{\mathbf{g}}(\theta, \mathbf{T}_{RR}, \dot{\mathbf{T}}_{RR}), \qquad \tilde{\mathbf{g}} \to 0 \text{ as } \dot{\mathbf{T}}_{RR} \to \mathbf{0}.$$

It follows that

$$\mathbf{g}_0(\theta, \mathbf{T}_{RR}) = -\rho_R \partial_{\mathbf{T}_{RR}} \phi(\theta, \mathbf{T}_{RR})$$

and

$$\tilde{\mathbf{g}}(\theta, \mathbf{T}_{RR}, \dot{\mathbf{T}}_{RR}) \cdot \dot{\mathbf{T}}_{RR} = \rho_R \theta \gamma_T.$$

A nonlinear dependence of $\tilde{\mathbf{g}}$ on $\mathbf{T}_{RR}$ and $\dot{\mathbf{T}}_{RR}$ can be assumed in the form

$$\tilde{\mathbf{g}}(\theta, \mathbf{T}_{RR}, \dot{\mathbf{T}}_{RR}) = g_1(\theta, \mathbf{J}_T) \boldsymbol{\lambda}(\dot{\mathbf{T}}_{RR}),$$

where $g_1 \geq 0$ and

$$\boldsymbol{\lambda}(\dot{\mathbf{T}}_{RR}) = \lambda_0(\mathbf{J}_{\dot{T}}) \dot{\mathbf{T}}_{RR}, \qquad \lambda_0 > 0.$$

8. Advantages and Disadvantages of Rate Equations

The constitutive equations of viscoelastic materials in the form of rate equations are advantageous in many respects. Relative to the Lagrangian description adopted in this paper, the dissipative properties of solids are modeled by equations involving the rates $\dot{\mathbf{E}}, \dot{\mathbf{S}}_{RR}$, most frequently through nonlinear dependencies on $\mathbf{E}$ and $\mathbf{S}_{RR}$. Nonlinear properties are then accounted for in a variety of ways, thus showing the flexibility of the approach. Furthermore, the thermodynamic consistency is established in a standard way by using the representation formula also in view of the constitutive property of the entropy production.

The nonlinearities possibly involved in the rate equations need not allow us to set the equations in the form of materials with fading memory. This shows the limited possibility of modeling through memory integrals, although increasing attention is focused on models with fractional derivatives [27–29].

It is worth mentioning that, so far, aging properties are described by memory functionals. In this connection, consider a four-rank tensor function $\mathbf{G}(t, s)$ on $\mathbb{R} \times \mathbb{R}^+$ and, in the Eulerian description, we modify the Boltzmann model of viscoelastic behavior in the form

$$\mathbf{T}(\mathbf{x}, t) = \mathbf{G}_0(t)\varepsilon(\mathbf{x}, t) - \int_{-\infty}^{t} \partial_s \mathbf{G}(t, s)\varepsilon(\mathbf{x}, s)ds,$$

where $\mathbf{G}_0(t) = \mathbf{G}(t, t)$ and ε is the infinitesimal strain tensor. The function $\mathbf{G}(t, s)$ accounts for the memory through the second variable, s, and for aging through the first variable, t. This approach is developed in [30]. The aging effect on the viscoelastic property is also described by a memory integral through a rescaling of times t, s [17,31], as illustrated above by Equation (19).

9. Conclusions

The modeling of viscoelastic or dissipative solids is often developed through memory functionals. The description through the Boltzmann functional for the stress in terms of the strain history is the best-known example in this sense. Yet, memory functionals make it more involved than any account of nonlinearity and affect compatibility with thermodynamics. That is why, alternatively, the thermodynamically consistent modeling of viscoelasticity is performed through rate-type equations whose best-known examples are those associated with rheological models.

This paper provides a general account of viscoelasticity through rate equations as relations between strain, stress, and their derivatives. To comply with the objectivity principle, we chose to follow the Lagrangian description and used as variables the Green–Lagrange strain $\mathbf{E}$ and the second Piola stress $\mathbf{T}_{RR}$, or $\mathbf{E}$ and $\mathbf{S}_{RR} = \mathbf{T}_{RR} - \mathbf{G}(\mathbf{E})$. Both $\mathbf{E}$ and $\mathbf{T}_{RR}$ are invariant under Euclidean transformations and hence so are their time derivatives $\dot{\mathbf{E}}, \dot{\mathbf{T}}_{RR}$. The inspection of thermodynamic consistency leads to the analysis of inequalities like, e.g., $\mathbf{S}_{RR} \cdot \dot{\mathbf{E}} = \rho_R \theta \gamma_s$. Equations (15), (29) and (38) describe general classes of viscoelastic models in rate-type form.

Two features, characteristic of this paper, are unusual in the literature. Firstly, the entropy production γ_S is regarded as provided by a constitutive function to be determined or chosen. Secondly, the use of a representation formula enables vector (or tensor) unknowns to comprise an arbitrary term, denoted by Ξ. Sections 4–7 show that special selections of Ξ lead to qualitatively new constitutive equations. Furthermore, the constitutive rate equations thus determined have the remarkable advantage of being consistent with thermodynamics. The main outcome of this paper is that a simple, unique scheme, consistent with the second law of thermodynamics, leads to nonlinear models of various real materials (see Sections 4.1, 6.1 and 6.3).

Although this has not been our concern here, it is worth mentioning that the same thermodynamic approach to equations involving $\dot{\mathbf{E}}$ and $\dot{\mathbf{T}}_{RR}$ enables the modeling of hysteresis in viscoplastic materials, as shown, e.g., in [6]. Regarding possibilities for future work developments, we observe that modeling through rate equations is under investigation in connection with the transition processes.

Author Contributions: Investigation, conceptualization, writing, editing: A.M. and C.G. All authors have contributed substantially and equally to the work reported. All authors have read and agreed to the published version of the manuscript.

Funding: This research received no external funding.

Data Availability Statement: Data are contained within the article.

Acknowledgments: The research leading to this work has been developed under the auspices of Istituto Nazionale di Alta Matematica-Gruppo Nazionale di Fisica Matematica.

Conflicts of Interest: The authors declare no conflicts of interest.

References

1. Gutierrez-Lemini, D. *Engineering Viscoelasticity*; Springer: Berlin/Heidelberg, Germany; New York, NY, USA, 2014.
2. Morro, A.; Giorgi, C. *Mathematical Modelling of Continuum Physics*; Birkhäuser: Cham, Switzerland, 2023.
3. Boltzmann, L. Zur Theorie der elastichen Nachwirkung. *Sizber. Kaiserl. Akad. Wiss. Wien. Math.-Naturw. Kl.* **1874**, *70*, 275–300.
4. Leitman, M.J.; Fisher, G.M.C. The linear theory of viscoelasticity. In *Encyclopedia of Physics*; Truesdell, C., Ed.; Springer: Berlin/Heidelberg, Germany, 1973; Volume VIa/3.
5. Fabrizio, M.; Morro, A. *Mathematical Problems in Linear Viscoelasticity*; SIAM: Philadelphia, PA, USA, 1992.
6. Giorgi, C.; Morro, A. Materials with memory: Viscoelasticity and hysteresis. In *50+ Years of AIMETA. A Journey through Theoretical and Applied Mechanics in Italy*; Rega, G., Ed.; Springer: Cham, Switzerland, 2022; pp. 243–260.
7. Giorgi, C.; Golden, M. Viscoelastic and electromagnetic materials with non-linear memory. *Materials* **2022**, *15*, 6904. [CrossRef] [PubMed]
8. Zanj, A.; He, F.; Breedveld, P.C. Energy-biased viscoelastic model: A physical approach for material anelastic behavior by the bond graph approach. *Simulation* **2020**, *96*, 111–127. [CrossRef]
9. Suda, M.; Nagahama, H. Physically meaningful parameters of viscoelastic models based on the general functional form of the transfer functions. *Phys. Scr.* **2023**, *98*, 105255. [CrossRef]
10. Su, X.; Yao, D.; Xu, W. A new method for formulating linear viscoelastic models. *Int. J. Engng. Sci.* **2020**, *156*, 103375. [CrossRef]
11. Müller, I. *Thermodynamics*; Pitman: New York, NY, USA, 1985.
12. Truesdell, C. *Rational Thermodynamics*; Springer: New York, NY, USA, 1983.
13. Gurtin, M.E.; Fried, E.; Anand, L. *The Mechanics and Thermodynamics of Continua*; Cambridge University Press: Cambridge, UK, 2010.
14. Eringen, A.C.; Suhubi, E.S. *Elastodynamics*; Academic Press: New York, NY, USA, 1974; Volume I.
15. Rajagopal, K.R. On implicit constitutive theories. *Appl. Math.* **2003**, *48*, 279–319. [CrossRef]
16. Fung, Y.C. Stress strain history relations of soft tissues in simple elongation. In *Biomechanics, Its Foundations and Objectives*; Fung, Y.C., Perrone, N., Anliker, M., Eds.; Prentice Hall: Englewood Cliffs, NJ, USA, 1972.
17. Schapery, R.A. On the characterization of nonlinear viscoelastic materials. *Polym. Eng. Sci.* **1969**, *9*, 295–310. [CrossRef]
18. Xi, M.; Yun, G.; Narsu, B. A mathematical model for viscoelastic properties of biological soft tissues. *Theory Biosci.* **2022**, *141*, 13–25. [CrossRef]
19. Muliana, A.; Rajagopal, K.R.; Wineman, A.S. A new class of quasi-linear models for describing the nonlinear viscoelastic response of materials. *Acta Mech.* **2013**, *224*, 2169–2183. [CrossRef]
20. Pioletti, D.P.; Rakotomanana, L.R.; Benvenuti, J.-F.; Letvraz, P.-F. Viscoelastic constitutive law in large deformations: Application to human knee ligaments and tendons. *J. Biomech.* **1998**, *31*, 753–757. [CrossRef]
21. Nagy, A.; Ko, W.L.; Lindholm, U.S. Mechanical behavior of foamed materials under dynamic compression. *J. Cell. Plast.* **1974**, *10*, 127–134. [CrossRef]
22. Rajagopal, K.R.; Saccomandi, G. Circularly polarized wave propagation in a class of bodies defined by a new class of implicit constitutive relations. *Z. Angew. Math. Phys.* **2014**, *65*, 1003–1010. [CrossRef]
23. Şengül, Y. Viscoelasticity with limiting strain. *Discr. Cont. Dyn. Syst. Ser. S* **2021**, *14*, 57–70. [CrossRef]
24. Oza, A.; Vanderby, R., Jr.; Lakes, R.S. Interrelation of creep and relaxation for nonlinearly viscoelastic materials: Application to ligament and metal. *Rheol. Acta* **2003**, *42*, 557–568. [CrossRef]
25. Erbay, H.A.; Şengül, Y. A thermodynamically-consistent stress rate type model of one-dimensional strain-limiting viscoelasticity. *Z. Angew. Math. Phys.* **2020**, *71*, 94–103. [CrossRef]
26. Duman, E.; Şengül, Y. Stress-rate-type strain-limiting models for solids resulting from implicit constitutive theory. *Adv. Cont. Discr. Mod.* **2023**, *2023*, 6. [CrossRef]
27. Fabrizio, M.; Giorgi, C.; Morro, A. Modelling of heat conduction via fractional derivatives. *Heat Mass Transfer* **2017**, *53*, 2785–2797. [CrossRef]
28. Tarasov, V.E. Generalized Memory: Fractional Calculus Approach. *Fractal Fract.* **2018**, *2*, 23. [CrossRef]
29. Brandibur, O.; Garrappa, R.; Kaslik, E. Stability of Systems of Fractional-Order Differential Equations with Caputo Derivatives. *Mathematics* **2021**, *9*, 914. [CrossRef]

30. Fabrizio, M.; Giorgi, C.; Morro, A. Two approaches to aging and fatigue models in viscoelastic solids. *Atti Accad. Peloritana Pericolanti* **2019**, *97*, A7.
31. Zink, T.; Kehrer, L.; Hirschberg, V.; Wilhelm, M.; Böhlke, T. Nonlinear Schapery viscoelastic material model for thermoplastic polymers. *J. Appl. Polym. Sci.* **2022**, *139*, 52028. [CrossRef]

Article

Topology Optimization for Quasi-Periodic Cellular Structures Using Hybrid Moving Morphable Components and the Density Approach

Pengfei Xiao [1], Chunping Zhou [1], Yongxin Qu [2], Yunfeng Luo [2,*] and Quhao Li [2,*]

[1] AVIC Research Institute for Special Structures of Aeronautical Composites, Jinan 250000, China; 13163339094@163.com (P.X.)
[2] School of Mechanical Engineering, Shandong University, Jinan 250061, China
* Correspondence: luoyunfeng@sdu.edu.cn (Y.L.); quhaoli@sdu.edu.cn (Q.L.)

Abstract: Porous hierarchical structures are extensively utilized in engineering for their high specific strength, enhanced corrosion resistance, and multifunctionality. Over the past two decades, multiscale topology optimization for these structures has garnered significant attention. This paper introduces a novel hybrid MMCs (Moving Morphable Components)–density topology optimization method for quasi-periodic cellular structures. The term 'quasi-periodic' refers to microstructures whose different macroscopic points exhibit similar topologies with varying parameters. The primary concept involves using the MMC method to describe microstructural topology, while employing variable density to depict macro layouts. This approach leverages the advantage of MMCs in explicitly describing structural topology alongside the variable density of arbitrary microstructures. Sensitivity analyses of the optimization functions concerning design variables are shown, and a gradient optimization solver is employed to solve the optimization model. The examples effectively show the efficacy of the proposed method, illustrating that quasi-periodic cellular structures outperform single-scale solid structures.

Keywords: moving morphable components (MMC) method; topology optimization; quasi-periodic structures; hybrid method

MSC: 74P05

Citation: Xiao, P.; Zhou, C.; Qu, Y.; Luo, Y.; Li, Q. Topology Optimization for Quasi-Periodic Cellular Structures Using Hybrid Moving Morphable Components and the Density Approach. *Mathematics* **2024**, *12*, 2401. https://doi.org/10.3390/math12152401

Academic Editor: Matjaz Skrinar

Received: 2 July 2024
Revised: 29 July 2024
Accepted: 31 July 2024
Published: 1 August 2024

1. Introduction

Cellular structures are abundant in natural biological entities, and are renowned for their exceptional structural performance [1]. The biomimetic emulation of these cellular structures has garnered significant interest across various industries including the aerospace, automotive, and biomedical fields. In recent years, propelled by the rapid advancements in advanced manufacturing technologies, particularly additive manufacturing, it has become feasible to fabricate cellular structures with increasingly intricate geometries [2–4]. Consequently, the systematic design of cellular structures tailored to meet specific engineering requirements has emerged as a pivotal focus.

The topology optimization (TO) method is an automated design approach that generates novel and often unexpected design solutions by determining the optimal material distribution to meet specified design objectives and constraints [5–9]. It is of great significance to search for a cellular structure with excellent performance and establish a design theory based on the TO method to promote the engineering application of hierarchical structures. Cellular structures, unlike single-scale structures, encompass two or more interconnected scales, posing challenges for topology optimization. A straightforward yet computationally costly approach involves discretizing the domain using fine meshes that span all scales. Subsequently, procedures such as those used in traditional TO can be applied [10]. However, this method typically necessitates a dense mesh, leading to significant computational overheads.

Another approach to mitigate computational demands is to separate the two scales using the multiscale finite element method [11] or homogenization method [12,13]. Combining topological optimization methods with homogenization theory, some scholars have carried out research on microstructure topology optimization methods with specific/specific properties, and obtained a large number of microstructure configurations with excellent properties, such as materials with a negative Poisson ratio, materials with zero expansion and materials with a high permeability. Notable studies include those by Rodrigues et al. [14] and Xia et al. [15,16], where both macro-scale material distribution and corresponding local microstructures were optimized concurrently. However, these methods still entail significant computational costs due to the necessity of inverse-homogenization for all macro elements, and they often lack connectivity between neighboring microstructures. To address these challenges, Yan et al. [17,18] proposed a concurrent design for periodic multiscale structures that provides simpler topological optimization formulas with fewer computational resources being required. Based on the homogenization method, the performance transfer relationship between the two scales is established, and the optimization variables of two levels are unified in a simple optimization model, and there is only one macro finite element calculation and one micro homogenization calculation for each optimization step. Therefore, this method shows advantages in terms of its simple optimization formulation, low calculation and easy implementation, and has been successfully applied to many physical problems, such as the thermodynamic coupling problem, dynamic problem, uncertainty problem and multifunctional problem. However, since such structures contain the same microscopic structure, the ability to change the material properties in the macro domain is limited, thus reducing the room for improvement in structural properties. In view of this, some scholars have proposed a TO method of periodic multiscale structure according to partitions. In this kind of algorithm, the domain can be divided into a series of regions either artificially or according to specific criteria, different regions have different microstructure configurations, and the same region is periodically filled by a single microstructure. The core problem of this method is how to find a suitable and efficient macro-structure partitioning strategy to reduce the computation while ensuring the performance.

Different to the above method, recently, some researchers focused on the design of quasi-periodic structures. The so-called quasi-periodic means that the microstructures share the same topology but different parameters. The key idea of these works is changing the parameters of a unit cell, in order to transfer the variable material property across the macro domain. Due to the invariance in topological form on the macro scale, the quasi-periodic structure avoids the discontinuity phenomenon at the boundary of the microstructure, and the spatial variation in material properties can be realized by adjusting the macro distribution of variable parameters, so it has a broader design space than the periodic cellular structure. Recently, the authors introduced a TO method for a quasi-periodic cellular structure. Previous studies achieved this by manipulating the microstructural topology using erode–dilate operators. Similar concepts have been implemented within the level set TO method [19,20], where quasi-periodic cells are described by cutting the signed distance function using different thresholds. Building upon this foundation, Zong et al. [21] introduced shape-function-based thresholds that interpolate height variables at nodes to ensure seamless geometric connections between adjacent cells. Through this formulation, the macro and micro concurrent design of a quasi-periodic double-level structure is realized. For this kind of algorithm, micro-structures at different locations have the same topological configuration but different parameters, which ensures different functional requirements at different locations, and creates a double-layer porous structure with better performance.

Compared to density or level set methods, the Moving Morphable Components (MMCs) method [22–24] offers a clear geometric representation of the design space, which simplifies the interpretation and manipulation of design variables. The above advantages make it convenient to incorporate variable parameters for quasi-periodic cellular structures. Therefore, we applied the MMCs method to describe microstructural topology. For the macro domain, the one to zero density is also used to give the optimal distribution for microstructures with different volume fractions. The study focuses on minimizing compliance under a volume constraint, and employs the Moving Asymptotes Method (MMA) [25] to solve the optimization models.

2. Problem Formulation

This section introduces a novel topological description for quasi-periodic cellular structures within the MMCs framework. First, a brief overview of the MMCs method is provided to ensure the paper is self-contained. Next, the design variables used to describe the quasi-periodic cellular structures are defined. Finally, the formulation for topology optimization is presented.

2.1. Moving Morphable Component Method

Different from the level set and density methods, the MMCs-based approach adopts a set of moving morphable components as basic building blocks for topology optimization. The implementation of the MMCs method involves optimizing the positions (center coordinates), sizes and orientations of a series of structural components to determine the final global topology description equation. This, in turn, defines the precise boundaries of the structure for its final representation. The basic forms and component descriptions are shown in Figure 1. This topological description method enables the final designed structure to have clear boundary descriptions and geometric features (such as the length and width of the components).

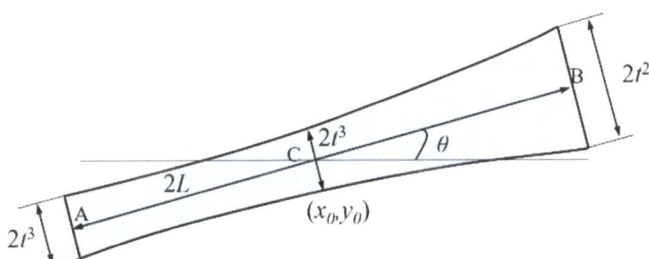

Figure 1. Parametric description of a structural component in the MMC method.

Based on the above component description, the final configuration of the structure can be obtained by designing the control parameter vectors $\mathbf{D} = \{(\mathbf{D}^1)^{\mathrm{T}}, \ldots, (\mathbf{D}^i)^{\mathrm{T}}, \ldots\}$ of multiple components. Here, $\mathbf{D}^i = (x_{0i}, y_{0i}, L_i, \theta_i, \mathbf{d}_i^{\mathrm{T}})^{\mathrm{T}}$ represents the topological control parameters of the ith component. $\mathbf{d}_i$ represents the parameters in the component control equation (such as t_i^1, t_i^2 and t_i^3 in Figure 1), and L is the length of a component. The relationship between the background element density and the global Heaviside equation determined by

$$\rho_j^{mi} = \sum_{k=1}^{4} H(\phi_k^j(\mathbf{D}^i))/4 \tag{1}$$

where ϕ_k^j represents the TD function value of the k-th node with the j-th element node. Many functions have been used to describe components, such as super-ellipses and closed B-splines (CBS). In this paper, the following TDF [26] is applied for its simplicity:

$$\phi_i(x,y) = \left(\frac{x'}{L_i}\right)^p + \left(\frac{y'}{f(x')}\right)^p - 1 \tag{2}$$

with

$$\left\{\begin{matrix} x' \\ y' \end{matrix}\right\} = \begin{bmatrix} \cos\theta_i & \sin\theta_i \\ -\sin\theta_i & -\cos\theta_i \end{bmatrix} \left\{\begin{matrix} x - x_{0i} \\ y - y_{0i} \end{matrix}\right\} \tag{3}$$

where $f(x')$ describes the thickness of the components along the x' direction. $p = 6$ is applied here. By using these parameters, the boundary and geometry features of a component can be described explicitly:

$$f(x') = \frac{t^1 + t^2 - 2t^3}{2L^2}(x')^2 + \frac{t^2 - t^1}{2L^2}x' + t^3 \tag{4}$$

where t^1, t^2 and t^3 denote the thickness of a component. The specific expression of Heaviside function is as follows:

$$H_\varepsilon(x) = \begin{cases} 1, & if\ x > \varepsilon, \\ \frac{3(1-\alpha)}{4}\left(\frac{x}{\varepsilon} - \frac{x^3}{3\varepsilon^3}\right) + \frac{1+\alpha}{2}, & if\ -\varepsilon \le x \le \varepsilon, \\ 0, & otherwise. \end{cases} \tag{5}$$

Here, ε represents the transition region as well as degree of nonlinearity in the filtering process. α is a small value for avoiding singularities for the linear equations solver.

2.2. Topological Description Formulation

Compared to the traditional density or level set-based method, the design variable in the MMC method changes from the unit density ρ_i^{mi} to the component variable $\mathbf{D}^i$ of the structure. Thus, we can easily apply the varied thickness of the components based on MMC algorithm to map the microscopic base unit cell (BUC) into a series of quasi-periodic microstructures.

Two procedures are involved in describing a quasi-periodic cellular structure. One procedure involves describing the base unit cell, while the other involves choosing a variable method to generate quasi-microstructures from BUC. Since the MMC method provides explicit parameters for describing components, it offers a more convenient approach to defining variable parameters compared to other methods. Therefore, the MMCs method is applied here to describe the topology of the BUC. The topology of the BUC can be determined by a design vector $\mathbf{D}^{mi}$. To obtain a series of quasi-periodic microstructures using a simple alterable parameter from the BUC, we define a parameter R which can scale the thickness of all components, as shown in Figure 2, this means:

$$\left[t_i^1, t_i^2, t_i^3\right]_Q = R \times \left[t_i^1, t_i^2, t_i^3\right]_B \tag{6}$$

where the subscripts Q and B represent the quasi-periodic microstructures and base unit cell (BUC), respectively. When $R < 1$, the thickness of the components decreases, resulting in microstructures with a smaller volume fraction. Conversely, when $R > 1$, the thickness of the components increases, leading to microstructures with a larger volume fraction. By gradually increasing R from zero in small increments until the cell is completely filled with solid material, different microstructures can be obtained.

After obtaining quasi-periodic microstructures, the next step is to determine the optimal macro distribution of these microstructures. The most direct approach is to set vector $\mathbf{R}_{ma}$ as the design variable. By optimizing $\mathbf{R}$ for the desired objective and constraint functions, the optimal quasi-periodic cellular structure can be achieved. However, determining the bounds of $\mathbf{R}$ in this way can be challenging. To address this problem, the element density $0 \le \rho^{ma} \le 1$ is defined as the design variable instead of $\mathbf{R}$ in the macro design. Here, $\rho_e^{ma} = 0$ and $\rho_e^{ma} = 1$ represent the void and solid, respectively. For $0 < \rho_e^{ma} < 1$, the corresponding microstructure with the same volume fraction is placed. The subscript e denotes index of the design variable.

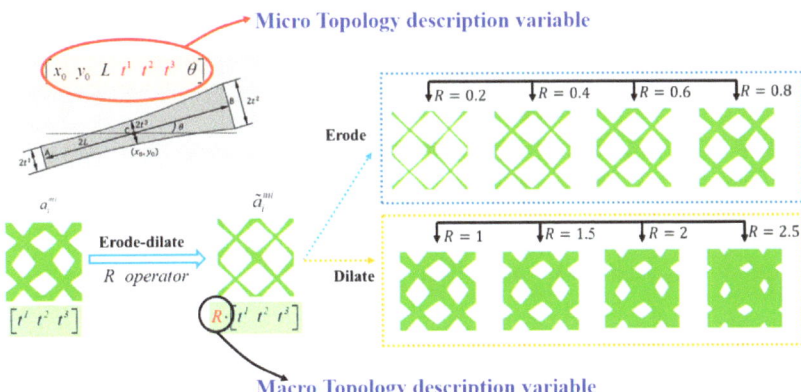

Figure 2. The two types of design variables in the proposed method.

In a conclusion, the component parameter is the Micro Topology description variable and R is the Macro Topology description variable. By optimizing the distribution of the quasi-periodic microstructures, in other words, by optimizing the distribution of the Macro Topology description variable R, a multi-scale structure with quasi-periodic microstructures can be obtained.

2.3. Optimization Formulation

In this study, the typical optimization problem of minimizing structural compliance is considered to make an easy comparison with traditional methods. By minimizing structural compliance, maximum stiffness for a prescribed force can be achieved. This function, being convex, is well-suited for finding the optimal solution and is widely applied in topology optimization to test new methods. The formulations are expressed as follows:

$$
\begin{aligned}
&\text{find} \quad \boldsymbol{\rho}^{ma}, \mathbf{D}^{mi} \\
&\text{min} \quad c = \mathbf{F}^{\mathrm{T}}\mathbf{U} = \mathbf{U}^{\mathrm{T}}\mathbf{K}\mathbf{U} \\
&\text{s.t.} \quad \mathbf{K}(\boldsymbol{\rho}^{ma}, \mathbf{D}^{mi})\mathbf{U} = \mathbf{F} \\
&\qquad \int_{D^{mi}} H(\phi^s(\mathbf{x}))dV - \overline{V}^{mi} = 0 \\
&\qquad \sum_{e=1}^{N^{ma}} \rho_e^{ma} v_e^{ma} - \overline{V}^{ma} \le 0 \\
&\qquad 0 \le \rho_e^{ma} \le 1, \ (e = 1, \ldots, N^{ma}) \\
&\qquad \mathbf{D}^{mi} \in \Xi_{\mathbf{D}}
\end{aligned}
\tag{7}
$$

where $\boldsymbol{\rho}^{ma} = \left(\rho_1^{ma}, \ldots, \rho_e^{ma}, \ldots, \rho_{N^{ma}}^{ma}\right)^{\mathrm{T}}$ and $\mathbf{D}^{mi} = \left(\left(\mathbf{D}^1\right)^{\mathrm{T}}, \ldots, \left(\mathbf{D}^i\right)^{\mathrm{T}}, \ldots \left(\mathbf{D}^{N^{mi}}\right)^{\mathrm{T}}\right)^{\mathrm{T}}$ denote the vectors of design variables. $\overline{V}^{mi}$ and $\overline{V}^{ma}$ are the upper limits for the volume constraint. N^{mi} and N^{ma} the number of design variables within the macro and micro domains, respectively. Here, the limit of the micro volume is added for a stable convergence. Here, $\overline{V}^{mi} = 0.2$ is applied in the following examples. $\Xi_{\mathbf{D}}$ is the admissible set for the design variables. c is the structural compliance which can be computed by:

$$
c = \mathbf{U}^{\mathrm{T}}\mathbf{K}\mathbf{U} = \sum_{e=1}^{N^{ma}} \mathbf{U}_e^{\mathrm{T}}\mathbf{K}_e\mathbf{U}_e
\tag{8}
$$

where $\mathbf{K}$, $\mathbf{U}$ and $\mathbf{F}$ denote the global stiffness matrix, displacement vector and load vector, respectively. The subscript e represents the element form:

$$\mathbf{K}_e = \int_{\Omega_e} \mathbf{B}^T \mathbf{D}_e^{ma} \mathbf{B} d\Omega \tag{9}$$

where Ω_e denotes the element domain. $\mathbf{D}_e^{ma}\left(\rho_e^{ma}, \mathbf{D}^{mi}\right)$ is the elastic matrix which relates to the microstructural topology and macro density. $\mathbf{B}$ is the element strain–displacement matrix.

3. Numerical Implementations

In this section, we initially outline interpolation strategies that correlate material properties with design variables. Subsequently, a sensitivity analysis of the functions is carried out using gradient-based optimization solvers.

3.1. Interpolation Scheme

Before computing the element stiffness matrix, the elastic matrices of microstructures should be given. In this study, the widely applied asymptotic homogenization (AH) method [27] is used:

$$\mathbf{D}^{\mathrm{H}} = \frac{1}{|Y|} \int_Y \left[\mathbf{D}(\mathbf{y}) - \mathbf{D}(\mathbf{y}) \varepsilon_y(\phi, \mathbf{y}) \right] d\mathbf{y} \tag{10}$$

where Y is the local coordinate in the unit cell, and $\mathbf{y}$ denotes the coordinate vector. $\mathbf{D}(\mathbf{y})$ is the elastic matrix for the elements in the microstructure. To obtain a clear 0–1 topology, the Solid Isotropic Material with Penalty method [28] is applied here as:

$$\mathbf{D}_i = \left(\underline{\rho} + (\overline{\rho} - \underline{\rho})\left(\overline{\rho}_i^{mi}\right) \right) \mathbf{D}_0 \tag{11}$$

where $\mathbf{D}_0$ is the elastic material matrix and subscript i represents the ith element in unit cell. $\underline{\rho} = 0.001$ is a small value to avoid a singular global stiffness matrix, $\overline{\rho} = 1$. $\varepsilon_y(\cdot)$ represents the strain calculator. $\phi = \left[\phi^{11}, \phi^{22}, \phi^{12}\right]$ denotes the characteristic displacements which are obtained by solving:

$$\int_Y \varepsilon_y^{\mathrm{T}}(\mathbf{v}) \left[\mathbf{D}(\mathbf{y}) - \mathbf{D}(\mathbf{y}) \varepsilon_y(\phi) \right] d\mathbf{y} = 0, \forall \phi \in V_y \tag{12}$$

where V_y denotes the function space of periodic functions. Due to computational constraints, calculating the elastic matrices $\mathbf{D}^{\mathrm{H}}$ for all microstructures generated by the BUC is challenging. As a result, only a subset of samples is selected for computation. Subsequently, cubic B-splines are employed as the basis functions, and an explicit formulation is derived using the least squares method:

$$\mathbf{D}^{\mathrm{H}}\left(\rho_e^{ma}, \rho_i^{mi}\right) = f_{spline}\left(\rho_e^{ma}, \rho_i^{mi}\right) \tag{13}$$

To prevent the occurrence of microstructures with low volume fractions, which are challenging to manufacture, a penalization scheme is implemented:

$$\mathbf{D}_e^{ma}\left(\rho_e^{ma}, \rho_i^{mi}\right) = (\rho_e^{ma})^q f_{spline}\left(\rho_e^{ma}, \rho_i^{mi}\right) \tag{14}$$

where q is the penalization power. The following values of q are suggested:

$$q = \begin{cases} 3 & \rho_e^{ma} < 0.1 \\ 0 & \rho_e^{ma} \geq 0.1 \end{cases} \tag{15}$$

3.2. Sensitivity Analysis

Since topology optimization has a large number of design variables, gradient-based optimization solver is often applied. Here, the adjoint method is used to derive the sensitivities of the functions with respect to the design variables in micro and macro domain. Frist, the general formulation of the structural compliance with respect to x_j ($=\rho_i^{mi}, \rho_e^{ma}$) can be written as:

$$\frac{\partial c}{\partial x_j} = -\sum_e^{N^{ma}} \mathbf{U}_e^T \left(\int_{\Omega_e} \mathbf{B}^T \frac{\partial \mathbf{D}_e^{ma}}{\partial x_j} \mathbf{B} dV \right) \mathbf{U}_e \tag{16}$$

where x_j ($=\rho_i^{mi}, \rho_e^{ma}$) includes the two types of the design variable. For the two design variables, the primary difference lies in the derivation of the elastic matrix $\mathbf{D}_e^{ma}$. Therefore, we will give the detail formulations of the design variables ρ_e^{ma} and ρ_i^{mi} separately.

(1) Sensitivities with respect to. ρ_e^{ma}
Differentiating Equation (14) to ρ_e^{ma} yields:

$$\frac{\partial \mathbf{D}_e^{ma}}{\partial \rho_j^{ma}} = \begin{cases} 0 & e = j \\ q\left(\rho_j^{ma}\right)^{q-1} f_{spline}\left(\rho_e^{ma}, \rho_i^{mi}\right) + \left(\rho_j^{ma}\right)^q \frac{\partial f_{spline}\left(\rho_e^{ma}, \rho_i^{mi}\right)}{\partial \rho_j^{ma}} & e \neq j \end{cases} \tag{17}$$

Then, substituting it into Equation (16), and we can obtain:

$$\frac{\partial c}{\partial \rho_e^{ma}} = \\ -p(\rho_e^{ma})^{p-1} \mathbf{U}_e^T \left(\int_{\Omega_e} \mathbf{B}^T f_{spline}\left(\rho_e^{ma}, \rho_i^{mi}\right) \mathbf{B} dV \right) \mathbf{U}_e - (\rho_e^{ma})^p \mathbf{U}_e^T \left(\int_{\Omega_e} \mathbf{B}^T \frac{\partial f_{spline}\left(\rho_e^{ma}, \rho_i^{mi}\right)}{\partial \rho_e^{ma}} \mathbf{B} dV \right) \mathbf{U}_e \tag{18}$$

where subscript $e = 1, 2, \ldots, N_{ma}$.

(2) Sensitivities with respect to. D_i^{mi}
Substituting Equation (14) to Equation (16), the sensitivity of ρ_i^{mi} can be written as:

$$\frac{\partial c}{\partial D_i^{mi}} = \frac{\partial c}{\partial \rho_j^{mi}} \cdot \frac{\partial \rho_j^{mi}}{\partial D_i^{mi}} = -\sum_{r=1}^{N^{ma}} u_r^T \cdot (\mathrm{f}(\rho_r^{ma}) \cdot \int_{\Omega_e} B^T \frac{\partial D_r(\rho_j^{mi}, \rho_e^{ma})}{\partial \rho_j^{mi}} \cdot \frac{\partial \rho_j^{mi}}{\partial D_i^{mi}} B \cdot d\Omega_e) \cdot u_r \tag{19}$$

Note that $\partial c/\partial \rho_i^{mi}$ is a summation of the elements in the macro domain:

$$\frac{\partial \rho_j^{mi}}{\partial D_i^{mi}} = \sum_{k=1}^4 (q \cdot H(\phi_k^j)^{q-1} \cdot \frac{\partial H(\phi_k^j)}{\partial D_i^{mi}})/4 \tag{20}$$

4. Results and Discussions

To validate the effectiveness of the method, two design problems including the short and long cantilever beam problems are shown here. The cantilever beam is a common design problem in structural optimization. These problems usually involve optimizing the material distribution of a structure to meet specific performance indicators under given constraints. The detailed numerical implantations and parameter settings are provided in the subsequent subsections, including an optimization model, parameter setting, optimization results, and so on. For the finite element analysis, four-node bilinear rectangular element grids are applied to discretize the domains. In two examples, the micro-design domain is discretized into 50×50 rectangular elements. The material properties of the two examples are set as Young's modulus $E = 206$ MPa and Poisson's ratio $\mu = 0.28$. To obtain a design with a smooth gradient for the density in the macro domain and prevent the phenomenon of a numerical instability such as the checkerboard scheme that occurs in the topology optimization design of a continuum structure, the density filtering technique is applied. Here, the filtering radius is set to $r^{ma} = 1.5$. The objective function of the example is the maximization of structural stiffness; that is, the minimization of structural compliance. It is the most commonly used objective function in topology optimization design because it has the characteristics of a simple form and reflects structural stiffness properties. By updating the design variables based on MMA after the sensitivity analysis, the optimal micro-structure layout of the cantilever beam can be obtained to meet the design requirements. The convergence criterion of the MMA algorithm was selected as $\max\left\|x^{i+1} - x^i\right\| \leq 10^{-3}$, and the maximum number of iteration steps was set to 300.

4.1. Short Cantilever Beam Problem

The first test case involves minimizing compliance for a short cantilever beam. Figure 3 illustrates the design domain for the short cantilever beam, including the force, boundary conditions and sizes. In this case, the size of the design domain is 20 mm by 15 mm. The degree of freedom at the left end of the short beam is completely fixed. A vertical point load of $F = 1$ KN is applied at the bottom-right corner. The short cantilever beam is discretized using a 20×15 grid of elements. The upper volume fraction of the material is 0.4.

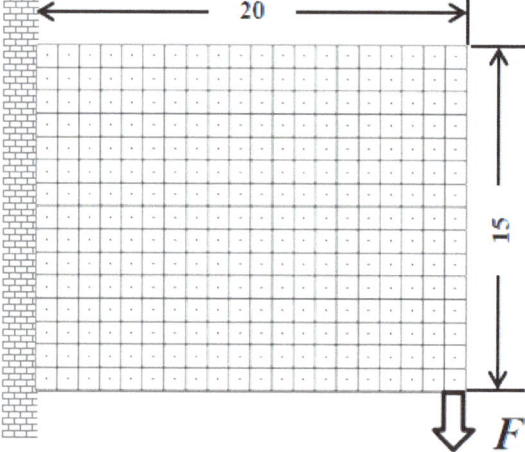

Figure 3. The design domain for the short cantilever beam, including the force, boundary conditions and sizes.

Figure 4a shows the optimized topology of the base unit cell which is described by the MMCs method, while the optimized macrostructural density layout is shown in Figure 4b. It should be noted that, here, the black color means the design variable $\rho_e^{ma} = 1$, the gray color means $0 < \rho_e^{ma} < 1$ and the white color means $\rho_e^{ma} = 0$. For different parameters of the operator R, the corresponding microstructural is shown in Figure 5. Here, we just give microstructural topology for some ρ_e^{ma}, actually we can obtain an arbitrary microstructural topology for all of the ρ_e^{ma} using the method shown in Section 2. According to the macrostructural density layout, the base unit cell with the closest volume fraction is placed at each macroscopic unit to assemble the quasi-periodic cellular structure, and the result is shown in Figure 6. The compliance of the optimized quasi-periodic cellular structure obtained by the proposed method is 21.73.

Firstly, based on the operator R described in the MMCs framework proposed in this paper, the microstructure form of the quasi-periodic cellular structure is described, and a microstructure optimization design is created.

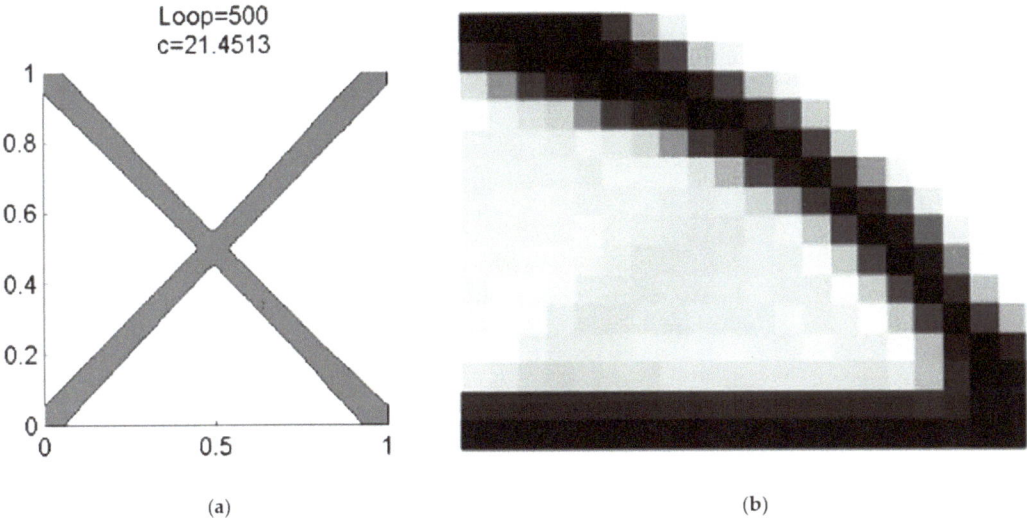

Figure 4. The optimized structure by the proposed method: $c = 21.73$. (**a**) Microstructural topology. (**b**) Macrostructural layout.

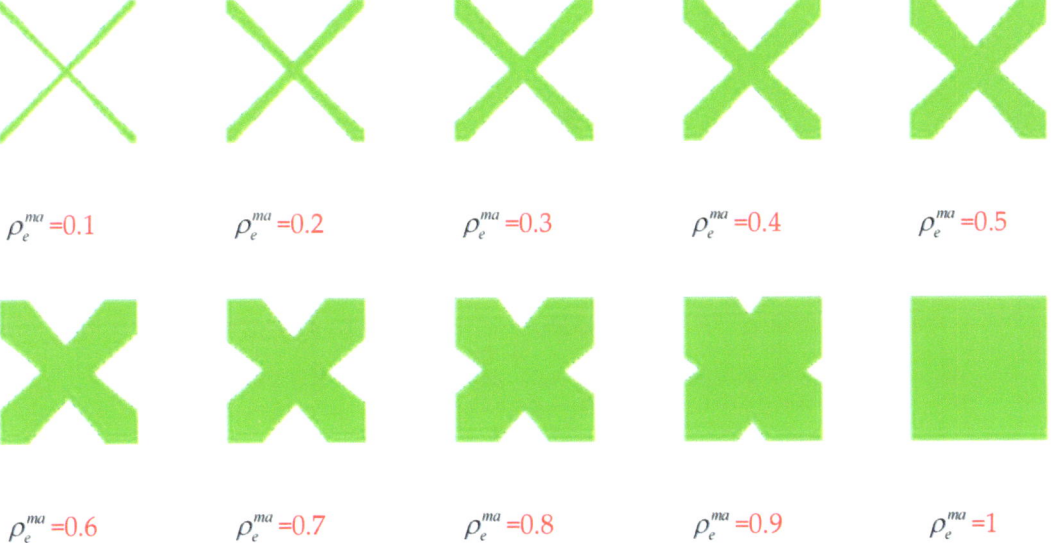

Figure 5. The microstructural topology for different parameters ρ_e^{ma}.

Furthermore, in order to further verify the effectiveness of the algorithm, the structure with less compliance can be optimized under the same condition. Therefore, the problem was solved using the classical single-scale method and periodic cellular structural design, and the results are presented in Figures 7a and 7b, respectively. The structural compliances obtained by these two methods were 27.85 and 52.81, respectively, both of which are higher than the compliance achieved by the proposed method. It also proves that the feasible domain of the structure can be greatly extended by a quasi-periodic design, and a cellular structure with a better performance can be obtained. Since the porous hierarchical structure has lager stiffness than traditional solid structures, it has been widely used in aerospace now. Often, the design results have been fabricated by additive manufacturing.

Figure 6. The optimized structure by the proposed method: $c = 21.73$.

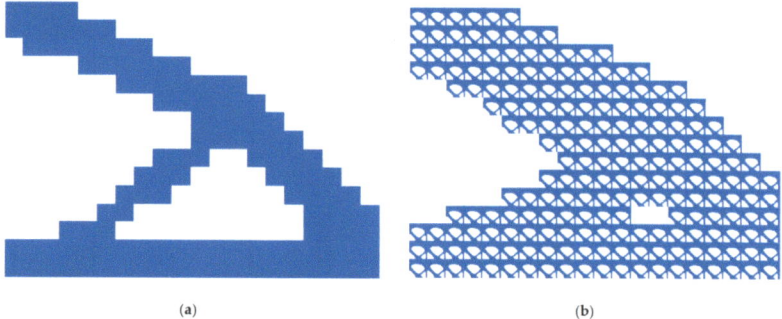

(a) (b)

Figure 7. The optimized results: (**a**) single-scale design: $c = 27.85$; (**b**) periodic design: $c = 52.81$.

4.2. Long Cantilever Beam Problem

The second case addressed here is the minimum compliance for a long cantilever beam. The design domain, depicted in Figure 8, is a rectangle measuring 120 mm by 30 mm, with the left side fixed. The domain is discretized using a 120 × 30 grid of rectangle elements, and a vertical point load of $F = 1$ KN is applied at the bottom-right corner. The volume fraction of the total material is set at 0.4. Figure 9 shows the optimization iteration curve, highlighting the change in the base cell in the micro domain and the density distribution of the macro domain with the number of optimization steps. It can be seen from the curve that the convergence of the optimization objective function is good and the volume fraction is satisfied. The slight oscillations observed in the iteration curve are due to variations in the parameters. The final optimized quasi-periodic cellular structure, with a compliance of 269.73, is presented in Figure 10. At the top of the picture is the microstructure topology optimized at the microscopic level and the base unit cell library constructed by the erode–dilate operator. The volume fraction of base unit cells varies from zero to one, corresponding to the macroscopic density layout. It can be seen from the optimization results that the microstructure topology can ensure the connectivity between cellular structures, although the volume fraction of each base unit cell is variable. At the bottom of the image is the optimal density layout obtained by macroscopic optimization. As can be seen from the figure, the external outline of the structure is solid material, and the base unit cells are mainly distributed in the middle part of the beam. These numerical examples verify the effectiveness of the proposed erode-dilate algorithm under the MMCs framework, which can improve the design space, ensure the connectivity and manufacturability of the structure and obtain cellular structures with excellent performance.

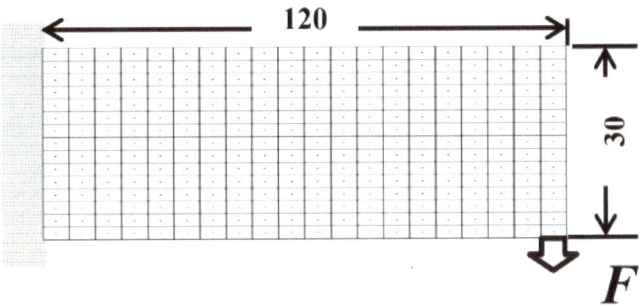

Figure 8. The design domain for the long cantilever beam, including the force, boundary conditions and sizes.

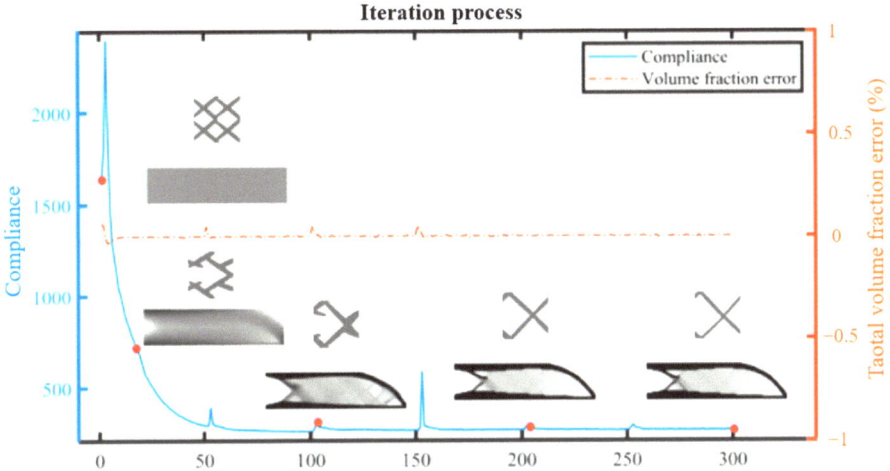

Figure 9. Iteration process.

Figure 10. The final optimized structure obtained by the proposed method: $c = 269.73$.

5. Conclusions

In this study, we developed a novel topology optimization (TO) method for designing quasi-periodic cellular structures using a hybrid material-and-morphology-based (MMCs–density) approach. This method enables integrated optimization at both macro and micro scales. The MMCs method was employed to describe the quasi-periodic microstructures by varying the thickness of the bars. The topology of the base unit microstructure is optimized to construct a library of quasi-periodic structures, followed by the macrostructure optimization to determine the distribution of these quasi-microstructures. Interpolation functions are established to derive sensitivities for use in gradient-based optimization. This approach allows us to simultaneously optimize the topology and parameters of microstructures, which vary within the macro design domain, thereby enhancing the performance of graded structures. Moreover, the resulting neighboring microstructures are seamlessly connected, facilitating rapid prototyping via additive manufacturing. The numerical examples demonstrate that quasi-periodic structures offer significant performance improvements over periodic structures, with only a modest increase in the computational cost.

Author Contributions: Conceptualization, P.X.; Methodology, Q.L.; Software, C.Z.; Validation, Y.L.; Formal analysis, Y.Q. All authors have read and agreed to the published version of the manuscript.

Funding: This work is financially supported by the National Natural Science Foundation of China (Grant Nos. 52375253 and 12202154).

Data Availability Statement: The original contributions presented in the study are included in the article, further inquiries can be directed to the corresponding author.

Conflicts of Interest: The authors declare no conflict of interest.

References

1. Duncan, O.; Shepherd, T.; Moroney, C.; Foster, L.; Venkatraman, D.P.; Winwood, K.; Allen, T.; Alderson, A. Review of Auxetic Materials for Sports Applications: Expanding Options in Comfort and Protection. *Appl. Sci.* **2018**, *8*, 941. [CrossRef]
2. Xiao, Z.; Yang, Y.; Xiao, R.; Bai, Y.; Song, C.; Wang, D. Evaluation of topology-optimized lattice structures manufactured via selective laser melting. *Mater. Des.* **2018**, *143*, 27–37. [CrossRef]
3. Tang, Y.; Dong, G.; Zhou, Q.; Zhao, Y.F. Lattice Structure Design and Optimization with Additive Manufacturing Constraints. *IEEE Trans. Autom. Sci. Eng.* **2018**, *15*, 1546–1562. [CrossRef]
4. Panesar, A.; Abdi, M.; Hickman, D.; Ashcroft, I. Strategies for functionally graded lattice structures derived using topology optimisation for Additive Manufacturing. *Addit. Manuf.* **2018**, *19*, 81–94. [CrossRef]
5. Li, Q.; Liang, G.-q.; Luo, Y.; Zhang, F.; Liu, S. An explicit formulation for minimum length scale control in density-based topology optimization. *Comput. Methods Appl. Mech. Eng.* **2023**, *404*, 115761. [CrossRef]
6. Wu, Q.; He, J.; Chen, W.; Li, Q.; Liu, S. Topology optimization of phononic crystal with prescribed band gaps. *Comput. Methods Appl. Mech. Eng.* **2023**, *412*, 116071. [CrossRef]
7. Wu, Q.; Li, Q.; Liu, S. A method for eliminating local modes caused by isolated structures in dynamic topology optimization. *Comput. Methods Appl. Mech. Eng.* **2024**, *418*, 116557. [CrossRef]
8. Zhu, J.-H.; Zhang, W.-H.; Xia, L. Topology optimization in aircraft and aerospace structures design. *Arch. Comput. Methods Eng.* **2015**, *23*, 595–622. [CrossRef]
9. Liu, S.; Hu, R.; Li, Q.; Zhou, P.; Dong, Z.; Kang, R. Topology optimization-based lightweight primary mirror design of a large-aperture space telescope. *Appl. Opt.* **2014**, *53*, 8318–8325. [CrossRef]
10. Aage, N.; Andreassen, E.; Lazarov, B.S.; Sigmund, O. Giga-voxel computational morphogenesis for structural design. *Nature* **2017**, *550*, 84–86. [CrossRef]
11. Liu, H.; Wang, Y.; Zong, H.; Wang, M.Y. Efficient structure topology optimization by using the multiscale finite element method. *Struct. Multidiscip. Optim.* **2018**, *58*, 1411–1430. [CrossRef]
12. Sigmund, O. Materials with prescribed constitutive parameters: An inverse homogenization problem. *Int. J. Solids Struct.* **1994**, *31*, 2313–2329. [CrossRef]
13. Groen, J.P.; Sigmund, O. Homogenization-based topology optimization for high-resolution manufacturable microstructures. *Int. J. Numer. Methods Eng.* **2018**, *113*, 1148–1163. [CrossRef]
14. Rodrigues, H.; Guedes, J.M.; Bendsoe, M.P. Hierarchical optimization of material and structure. *Struct. Multidiscip. Optim.* **2002**, *24*, 1–10. [CrossRef]
15. Xia, L.; Breitkopf, P. Concurrent topology optimization design of material and structure within FE2 nonlinear multiscale analysis framework. *Comput. Methods Appl. Mech. Eng.* **2014**, *278*, 524–542. [CrossRef]

16. Xia, L.; Breitkopf, P. Multiscale structural topology optimization with an approximate constitutive model for local material microstructure. *Comput. Methods Appl. Mech. Eng.* **2015**, *286*, 147–167. [CrossRef]
17. Liu, L.; Yan, J.; Cheng, G. Optimum structure with homogeneous optimum truss-like material. *Comput. Struct.* **2008**, *86*, 1417–1425. [CrossRef]
18. Yan, J.; Cheng, G.-d.; Liu, L. A uniform optimum material based model for concurrent optimization of thermoelastic structures and materials. *Int. J. Simul. Multidiscip. Des. Optim.* **2008**, *2*, 259–266. [CrossRef]
19. Wang, Y.; Chen, F.; Wang, M.Y. Concurrent design with connectable graded microstructures. *Comput. Methods Appl. Mech. Eng.* **2017**, *317*, 84–101. [CrossRef]
20. Wang, Y.; Zhang, L.; Daynes, S.; Zhang, H.; Feih, S.; Wang, M.Y. Design of graded lattice structure with optimized mesostructures for additive manufacturing. *Mater. Des.* **2018**, *142*, 114–123. [CrossRef]
21. Zong, H.; Liu, H.; Ma, Q.; Tian, Y.; Zhou, M.; Wang, M.Y. VCUT level set method for topology optimization of functionally graded cellular structures. *Comput. Methods Appl. Mech. Eng.* **2019**, *354*, 487–505. [CrossRef]
22. Guo, X.; Zhang, W.; Zhong, W. Doing Topology Optimization Explicitly and Geometrically—A New Moving Morphable Components Based Framework. *J. Appl. Mech.* **2014**, *81*, 081009–081012. [CrossRef]
23. Guo, X.; Zhang, W.; Zhang, J.; Yuan, J. Explicit structural topology optimization based on moving morphable components (MMC) with curved skeletons. *Comput. Methods Appl. Mech. Eng.* **2016**, *310*, 711–748. [CrossRef]
24. Zhang, W.; Chen, J.; Zhu, X.; Zhou, J.; Xue, D.; Lei, X.; Guo, X. Explicit three dimensional topology optimization via Moving Morphable Void (MMV) approach. *Comput. Methods Appl. Mech. Eng.* **2017**, *322*, 590–614. [CrossRef]
25. Svanberg, K. The method of moving asymptotes—A new method for structural optimization. *Int. J. Numer. Methods Eng.* **1987**, *24*, 359–373. [CrossRef]
26. Zhang, W.; Yuan, J.; Zhang, J.; Guo, X. A new topology optimization approach based on Moving Morphable Components (MMC) and the ersatz material model. *Struct. Multidiscip. Optim.* **2016**, *53*, 1243–1260. [CrossRef]
27. Papanicolau, G.; Bensoussan, A.; Lions, J.-L. *Asymptotic Analysis for Periodic Structures*; Elsevier: Amsterdam, The Netherlands, 1978.
28. Bendsøe, M.P.; Sigmund, O. Material interpolation schemes in topology optimization. *Arch. Appl. Mech.* **1999**, *69*, 635–654. [CrossRef]

Article

Concurrent Topology Optimization of Curved-Plate Structures with Double-Sided Stiffeners

Kai Xu, Fengtong Zhang, Yunfeng Luo * and Quhao Li *

Key Laboratory of High Efficiency and Clean Mechanical Manufacture of MOE, School of Mechanical Engineering, Shandong University, Jinan 250061, China; 202100161024@mail.sdu.edu.cn (K.X.); zhangfengtong@sdu.edu.cn (F.Z.)
* Correspondence: luoyunfeng@sdu.edu.cn (Y.L.); quhaoli@sdu.edu.cn (Q.L.)

Abstract: Due to their high specific stiffness, particularly in bending, along with their strong design capabilities, stiffened plates have become a prevalent structural solution in aerospace and various other fields. In pursuit of optimizing such structures, a topology optimization method named Heaviside-function-based directional growth topology parameterization (H-DGTP) was proposed in our previous work. However, this approach is limited to designing planar, single-sided stiffened structures. Thus, this paper extends the scope of this method to encompass double-sided, curved, stiffened panels, presenting a topology optimization technique tailored for such configurations. Specifically, considering the position, shape of the curved panels, and the arrangement and height of the stiffeners as design variables, while prioritizing structural stiffness as the objective, a topology optimization model for double-sided curved stiffened plate structures is established, and the corresponding sensitivities of the objective with respect to the design variables are analytically derived. Numerical examples illustrate that simultaneously optimizing the position and shape of the plate, as well as the layout and height of the stiffeners on both sides of the curved plate, results in greater stiffness compared to optimizing only part of these variables, validating the necessity and effectiveness of the proposed method.

Keywords: topology optimization; Heaviside function; curved stiffened structure

MSC: 74P05

Citation: Xu, K.; Zhang, F.; Luo, Y.; Li, Q. Concurrent Topology Optimization of Curved-Plate Structures with Double-Sided Stiffeners. *Mathematics* 2024, 12, 2213. https://doi.org/10.3390/math12142213

Academic Editor: Matjaz Skrinar

Received: 9 June 2024
Revised: 6 July 2024
Accepted: 9 July 2024
Published: 15 July 2024

1. Introduction

The stiffened plate structure, composed of a base plate and several stiffeners, is of great significance in the fields of machinery, aerospace, etc., for its high rigidity-to-weight ratio and strong design freedom. Previous studies have shown that by reasonably optimizing the plate shape and stiffener layout, the mechanical properties of the stiffened plate structure can be improved effectively [1–3]. Therefore, establishing a systematic optimization design method for a stiffened plate structure has become a research hotspot [4–7]. In recent years, applying genetic algorithms and other intelligent algorithms to optimize stiffened plate structures has made great progress [8]. However, the shortcomings of these methods, such as low computational efficiency, few achievable design variables, and limited optimization space, limit their application. Casting is a very commonly used manufacturing process for the stiffened structure due to its advantages, including cost-effectiveness, complex shape formation, and high material utilization [9]. Hence, casting provides a mature manufacturing technology for complex stiffened plate structures. However, the casting process also has requirements regarding the shape of the casting; for example, the shape of the casting should be protruding, and internal holes should be avoided [10]. If this is not the case, the casting may have defects, or casting failure may be experienced.

Topology optimization is currently one of the most powerful structural design methods. It can obtain innovative configurations with an excellent performance by seeking the optimal layout of materials under given objectives and constraints [11]. As an intelligent and systematic optimization design method, it can design products according to performance requirements and manufacturing capacity. Therefore, topology optimization is widely used to improve the structural properties of materials in aerospace and other fields [12,13]. Various topology optimization methods have been proposed in the past few decades, including homogenization-based methods [14], density-based methods [15], level set methods [16], evolution methods [17], and feature-mapping methods [18,19]. In the context of topology optimization, how to generate designs that can be manufactured by casting is of great importance. In this direction, several studies have been conducted. For example, a level-set-based method for the conceptual design shape and topology optimization of castings is proposed in the work of Wang et al. [20], and this method can conveniently consider casting constraints and traditional material volume constraints. Xu et al. [21] proposed a topology optimization method for natural frequency optimization considering casting constraints.

So far, several topology optimization methods for the stiffened layout of plate and shell structures have been developed [22–24]. Cheng and Olhoff developed a topology optimization method to design the thickness of plates to realize the optimal design of stiffened plate structures [25]. Rais-Rohani and Lokits also utilized the topology optimization method to explore the design aspects of composite stiffeners [26]. Furthermore, Krog and Olhoff [27] derived a stiffened structure by employing the homogenization method and strategically designing laminated microstructure parameters. In addition, Gersborg and Andreasen proposed a parametric interpolation format based on a three-dimensional structure to delineate stiffener height [19]. The underlying concept was to identify the interface between the solid and hollow materials along the stiffener to attain an optimal structure. Moreover, Liu et al. [28] developed a novel parametric method for the design of single-sided stiffened plate structures by using the Heaviside function, which is referred to as Heaviside-function-based directional growth topology parameterization (H-DGTP). Also, Sun et al. [29] proposed a multiple unidirectional material field-based topology optimization method for thin-walled structures with directional straight stiffeners. Huang et al. [30] developed a mesh-deformation-based integrated topology and shape optimization framework for stiffened curved shells. Sun et al. [31] proposed an isogeometric-analysis-based stiffness spreading method for stiffener layout optimization. Up to now, the above works have mainly focused on single-sided stiffened structures. However, the design space of a single-sided stiffened structure is not large enough to accommodate complex design requirements. Hence, developing a design theory and method for single-sided stiffened plates to increase the design space is an important direction.

Under above context, an improved H-DGTP-based topology optimization method for double-sided stiffened plates is proposed in this paper, where the main contribution is that the scope of the improved method is extended from single-sided stiffened plates to double-sided ones. In the proposed method, two types of design variables are introduced: one is used to describe the shape of the reference plate in relation to the height of the interpolation point of the reference plate; the other is used to describe the double-sided stiffener layout above and below the reference plate in relation to the density field of the bidirectional stiffener distribution and the height field describing the height of the stiffeners. Several numerical results indicate that the aforementioned optimization variables have a significant impact on the optimization outcomes, thereby validating the necessity of the collaborative optimization approach presented in this paper. Here, it is worth mentioning that the results obtained by the method proposed in this paper naturally satisfy the casting constraints of vertical stiffeners, thereby removing the barriers from design to manufacturing and greatly improving the possibility of engineering applications using the optimization method presented, and the corresponding results.

2. Topology Optimization Model

2.1. Parameterization Model for the Curved-Plate Structure with Double-Sided Stiffeners

The parameterization of double-sided curved stiffened plates is a prerequisite for achieving their topological optimization. Therefore, this section proposes a new parameterization model for such structures based on the Heaviside function. This model can simultaneously describe the shape of the curved plates and the layout of the stiffeners, as illustrated in Figure 1.

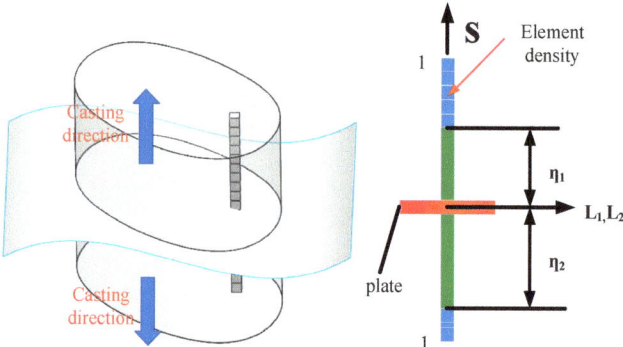

Figure 1. Illustrative sketch of the curved-plate structure with double-sided stiffeners.

To determine the location of the reference plate, a set of design variables is defined. The height values of the reference plate center are equally distributed: $\mathbf{s_{dc}} = [s_{dc0}, s_{dc2}, \ldots, s_{dcn}]^{\mathrm{T}}$. The coordinates are $\mathbf{x} = [x_0, x_2, \ldots, x_n]^{\mathrm{T}}$, and the spacing is h. In this paper, cubic spline interpolation with natural boundary conditions is applied to determine the height of any element of the reference plate center whose expression is

$$\mathbf{s_d} = \mathbf{A_1} * \mathbf{m} + \mathbf{A_2} * \mathbf{s_{dc}} \tag{1}$$

where $\mathbf{m} = [M_0, M_2, \ldots, M_n]$ can be obtained by

$$\begin{pmatrix} 2 & \lambda_0 & & & \\ \mu_1 & 2 & \lambda_1 & & \\ & \ddots & \ddots & \ddots & \\ & & \mu_{n-1} & 2 & \lambda_{n-1} \\ & & & \mu_n & 2 \end{pmatrix} * \begin{pmatrix} M_1 \\ M_2 \\ \vdots \\ M_{n-1} \\ M_n \end{pmatrix} = \begin{pmatrix} d_0 \\ d_1 \\ \vdots \\ d_{n-1} \\ d_n \end{pmatrix} \tag{2}$$

where $\mathbf{d} = [d_0, d_1, \ldots, d_n]$ is computed by

$$\mathbf{d} = \frac{3}{h^2} \begin{pmatrix} 0 & \cdots & \cdots & \cdots & \cdots & 0 \\ 1 & -2 & 1 & & & \\ & 1 & -2 & 1 & & \\ & & \ddots & \ddots & \ddots & \\ & & & 1 & -2 & 1 \\ 0 & \cdots & \cdots & \cdots & \cdots & 0 \end{pmatrix} * \mathbf{s_{dc}} \tag{3}$$

In addition, $\mathbf{A_1}$ and $\mathbf{A_2}$ are given as follows:

$$\mathbf{A_1} = \begin{pmatrix} \mathbf{u}(1) & \mathbf{v}(1) & & \\ & \mathbf{u}(2) & \mathbf{v}(2) & \\ & & \ddots & \ddots \\ & & & \mathbf{u}(m) & \mathbf{v}(m) \end{pmatrix} \quad \mathbf{A_2} = \begin{pmatrix} \boldsymbol{\alpha}(1) & \boldsymbol{\beta}(1) & & \\ & \boldsymbol{\alpha}(2) & \boldsymbol{\beta}(2) & \\ & & \ddots & \ddots \\ & & & \boldsymbol{\alpha}(m) & \boldsymbol{\beta}(m) \end{pmatrix} \tag{4}$$

where **u**, **v**, α and β are computed by

$$
\begin{aligned}
\mathbf{u}(i) &= \frac{(x(j)-i)^3-(x(j)-i)^2*h^2}{6*h}, & x(j-1) < i \le x(j), \quad j = 2,3,\ldots,n \\
\mathbf{v}(i) &= \frac{(i-x(j-1))^3-(i-x(j-1))^2*h^2}{6*h}, & x(j-1) < i \le x(j), \quad j = 2,3,\ldots,n \\
\boldsymbol{\alpha}(i) &= \frac{x(j)-i}{h}, & x(j-1) < i \le x(j), \quad j = 2,3,\ldots,n \\
\boldsymbol{\beta}(i) &= \frac{i-x(j-1)}{h}, & x(j-1) < i \le x(j), \quad j = 2,3,\ldots,n
\end{aligned}
\tag{5}
$$

Through the above formulations, the specific position of the center of a series of reference plate centers in the X and Y directions can be determined.

The thickness of the reference plate is δ_d. Thus, when only considering the influence of the reference plate, the density of any element in the design domain can be obtained:

$$
X_{1e} = H_1\left(s_e, s_{dj}\right), \text{ where } H_1\left(s_e, s_{dj}\right) = \begin{cases} 1 & \left|s_e - s_{dj}\right| \le \frac{\delta_d}{2} \\ 0 & \left|s_e - s_{dj}\right| > \frac{\delta_d}{2} \end{cases}
\tag{6}
$$

where $s_e = x/l \in [0,1]$ is a normalized coordinate of the center point of any element in the Z direction, s_{dj} is the height of any element on the reference plate to the lower boundary of the design domain, and H_1 is the first Heaviside function, whose specific expression is as follows:

$$
H_1(s_e, s_d) = e^{-\frac{1}{2}\left(\frac{2(s_e-s_d)}{\delta_d}\right)^{2\beta_1}}
\tag{7}
$$

where the parameter $\beta_1 > 0$ determines the smoothness of the approximate function. The larger the β_1 value, the steeper the approximation, as shown in Figure 2.

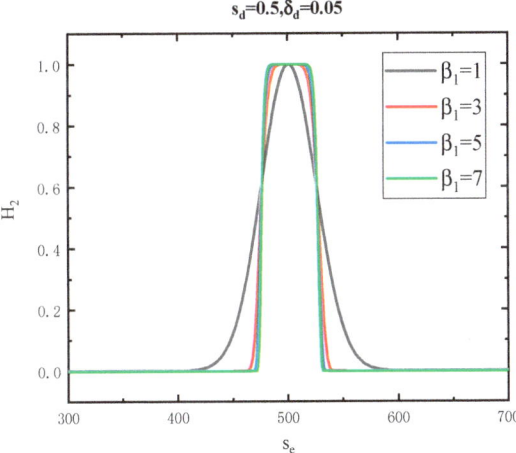

Figure 2. The second smooth Heaviside function with different β_1 values.

Now, after the reference plate has been determined, the next step is to model the stiffeners. The direction of the stiffener is first determined, and sets of elements above and below the reference plate (usually judged by the position of the center point of the element) are regarded as two stiffeners. Here, four design values are defined: the design variable that describes the layout of the stiffeners above the reference plate L_1, the design variable that describes the height of the stiffeners above the reference plate η_1, the design variable that describes the layout of the stiffeners below the reference plate L_2, and the design variable that describes the height of the stiffeners below the reference plate η_2. Thus, when considering the influence of stiffeners, the density of any element is formulated as follows:

$$X_{2e} = \begin{cases} L_{1j} \cdot H_1(\eta_{1j}, s_{1e}) \ above \\ L_{2j} \cdot H_1(\eta_{2j}, s_{2e}) \ below \end{cases} \tag{8}$$

where

$$H_2(\eta_{ij}, s_{ie}) = \begin{cases} 1 \ s_{ie} < \eta_{ij} \\ 0 \ s_{ie} \geq \eta_{ij} \end{cases} \quad i = 1,2 \tag{9}$$

where $s_{ie} = x_i / l_i \in [0,1]$ is the normalized coordinate of the center point of any element above/below the reference plate; η_{ij} is the height of the j-th stiffener above/below the reference plate; H_2 is the second Heaviside function; and $L_{ij} \in [0,1]$ is the density of the j-th stiffener above/below the base surface which can be penalized to 0 or 1. Because the Heaviside function is a sudden-change function and its first derivative is discontinuous, in order to adopt a gradient optimization algorithm, it usually needs to be approximately smoothed. In this paper, the Sigmoid function commonly used in artificial neural network theory is used to approximate the Heaviside function, and the modified form is as follows:

$$H_2(\eta_i, s_i) = \frac{e^{\beta_2 *(\eta_i - s_i)}}{1 + e^{\beta_2 *(\eta_i - s_i)}} \quad i = 1,2 \tag{10}$$

where the parameter β_2 is similar to β_1, which determines the smoothness of the approximate function, and the larger the β_2 value, the steeper the approximation, as is shown in Figure 3.

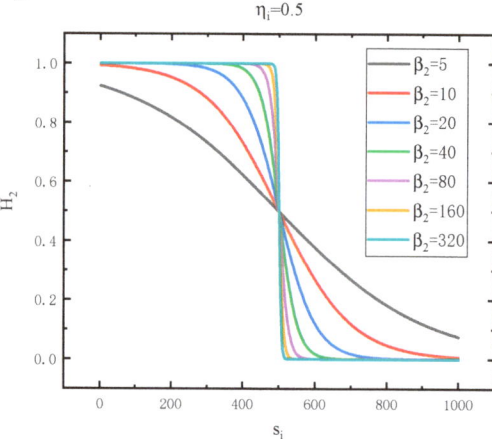

Figure 3. The first smooth Heaviside function with different β_2 values.

When the two conditions of the stiffeners and the base plate are considered simultaneously, the relations of their values with the density of all elements are determined, as shown in Table 1.

Table 1. The relationship between ρ_e and X_1, X_2.

Different Combinations of X_1, X_2	Interpolated Elemental Density
$X_1 = 1$	$\rho_e = 1$
$X_1 = 0, X_2 = 1$	$\rho_e = 1$
$X_1 = 0, X_2 = 0$	$\rho_e = 0$

Therefore, as is shown in Figure 4, the density of all elements in the 3D design domain can be interpolated as follows:

$$\rho_e = X_1 + X_2(1 - X_1) \tag{11}$$

$$\rho_e = X_1 + X_2\left(1 - X_1\right)$$

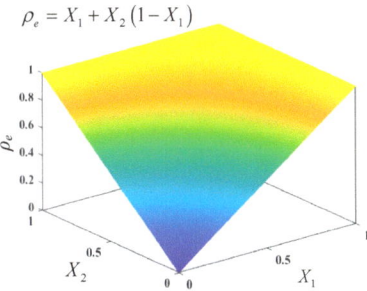

Figure 4. The interpolation function for element density ρ_e.

Now, Equation (11) is the final developed parameterization model for the curved-plate structure with double-sided stiffeners, and it is used to realize the topology optimization of such structures in the next section.

2.2. Topology Optimization Model

In this paper, the compliance optimization problem is considered. The optimization formulation is given as follows:

$$
\begin{aligned}
&\text{min} && c = \mathbf{U}^{\mathrm{T}}\mathbf{F} \\
&\text{subject to} && \mathbf{K}(\rho_e)\mathbf{U} = \mathbf{F} \\
& && g \leq 0 \\
& && 0 \leq \boldsymbol{\eta_1}(i), \boldsymbol{\eta_2}(i), \mathbf{L_1}(i), \mathbf{L_2}(i), \mathbf{s_{dc}}(i) \leq 1 \quad\text{for}\quad i = 1, \dots, m \\
&\text{find} && \boldsymbol{\eta_1}(i), \boldsymbol{\eta_2}(i), \mathbf{L_1}(i), \mathbf{L_2}(i), \mathbf{s_{dc}}(i) \in \mathbf{R}^m
\end{aligned}
\tag{12}
$$

where c is the compliance, $\mathbf{U}$ is the displacement vector, $\mathbf{F}$ is the external load vector, and $\mathbf{K}$ is the global stiffness matrix, which can be assembled by

$$
\mathbf{K}(\rho) = \sum_{e=1}^{N}\left(\underline{\rho} + (\bar{\rho} - \underline{\rho})\rho_i^p\right)\mathbf{K_e}
\tag{13}
$$

where $\mathbf{K_e}$ is the element stiffness matrix and N is the number of elements. $\underline{\rho} = 0.001$ is the lower limit of density to avoid the singularity of the global stiffness matrix; $\bar{\rho} = 1$ is the upper limit of density. p is a penalization parameter, and is set as 3 in this paper. Because of only considering volume constraint in this paper, the constraint function can be expressed by

$$
g = \frac{\sum\limits_{e=1}^{N} \rho_e v_e}{\gamma V} - 1
\tag{14}
$$

where v_e is the element volume, γ is the allowed volume fraction, and V is the total volume of the design domain.

3. Sensitivity Analysis

The sensitivity of the objective function c with respect to the design values $\mathbf{s_{dc}} = [s_{dc1}, s_{dc2}, \dots, s_{dcn}]^{\mathrm{T}}$ can be obtained by the chain rule as follows:

$$
\frac{\partial c}{\partial s_{dc}} = \sum_{i=1}^{Ne} \frac{\partial c}{\partial \rho_e}\left(\frac{\partial \rho_e}{\partial X_1}\frac{\partial X_1}{\partial s_d}\frac{\partial s_d}{\partial s_{dc}} + \frac{\partial \rho_e}{\partial X_2}\frac{\partial X_2}{\partial s}\frac{\partial s}{\partial s_d}\frac{\partial s_d}{\partial s_{dc}}\right)
\tag{15}
$$

where Ne is the number of elements in the design domain, and $\partial \rho_e / \partial X_1$ can be written as

$$
\frac{\partial \rho_e}{\partial X_1} = 1 - X_2
\tag{16}
$$

In addition, the term $\partial X_1/\partial s_d$ can be formulated as

$$\frac{\partial X_1}{\partial s_d} = \frac{\partial H_1}{\partial s_d} = \frac{2\beta_1}{\delta_d}\left(\frac{2(s_e - s_d)}{\delta_d}\right)^{2\beta_1-1} e^{-\frac{1}{2}\left(\frac{2(s_e-s_d)}{\delta_d}\right)^{2\beta_1}} \tag{17}$$

Also, $\partial s_d/\partial s_{dc}$ is the sensitivity of the height of the reference plate to the equally distributed height of the reference plate s_{dc}, which can be expressed by

$$\frac{\partial s_d}{\partial s_{dc}} = A_1 \cdot \frac{\partial m}{\partial s_{dc}} + A_2 = A_1 \cdot \begin{pmatrix} 2 & \lambda_0 & & & \\ \mu_1 & 2 & \lambda_1 & & \\ & \ddots & \ddots & \ddots & \\ & & \mu_{n-1} & 2 & \lambda_{n-1} \\ & & & \mu_n & 2 \end{pmatrix}^{-1} \cdot \frac{\partial d}{\partial s_{dc}} + A_2 \tag{18}$$

Now, $\partial \rho_e/\partial X_2$, $\partial X_2/\partial s$ can be similarly written as follows:

$$\frac{\partial \rho_e}{\partial X_2} = 1 - X_1 \tag{19}$$

$$\frac{\partial X_2}{\partial s_i} = -L_i \frac{\beta_2 e^{\beta_2 * (\eta_i - s_i)}}{\left(1 + e^{\beta_2 * (\eta_i - s_i)}\right)^2} \quad i = 1,2 \tag{20}$$

Based on the relationship between s and s_d, say that

$$s = \begin{cases} s_1 = \frac{s_e - s_d}{1 - s_d} & s_e \geq s_d \\ s_2 = \frac{s_d - s_e}{s_d} & s_e < s_d \end{cases} \tag{21}$$

The term $\partial s/\partial s_d$ can be expressed by

$$\frac{\partial s}{\partial s_d} = \begin{cases} \frac{\partial s_1}{\partial s_d} = \frac{s_e - 1}{(1 - s_d)^2} & s_e \geq s_d \\ \frac{\partial s_2}{\partial s_d} = \frac{s_e}{(s_d)^2} & s_e \geq s_d \end{cases} \tag{22}$$

According to Equations (1), (10), and (11), the sensitivity of the objective function c to the design values η_1, η_2, L_1, L_2 by the chain rule can be obtained as follows:

$$
\begin{aligned}
\frac{\partial c}{\partial \eta_1} &= \sum_{e=1}^{Ne_1} \frac{\partial c}{\partial \rho_e}\left(\frac{\partial \rho_e}{\partial X_1}\frac{\partial X_1}{\partial \eta_1} + \frac{\partial \rho_e}{\partial X_2}\frac{\partial X_2}{\partial \eta_1}\right) = \sum_{e=1}^{Ne_1} \frac{\partial c}{\partial \rho_e}\frac{\partial \rho_e}{\partial X_2}L_1\frac{\partial H_2(\eta_1, s_1)}{\partial \eta_1} \\
\frac{\partial c}{\partial L_1} &= \sum_{e=1}^{Ne_1} \frac{\partial c}{\partial \rho_e}\left(\frac{\partial \rho_e}{\partial X_1}\frac{\partial X_1}{\partial L_1} + \frac{\partial \rho_e}{\partial X_2}\frac{\partial X_2}{\partial L_1}\right) = \sum_{e=1}^{Ne_1} \frac{\partial c}{\partial \rho_e}\frac{\partial \rho_e}{\partial X_2}H_2(\eta_1, s_1) \\
\frac{\partial c}{\partial \eta_2} &= \sum_{e=1}^{Ne_2} \frac{\partial c}{\partial \rho_e}\left(\frac{\partial \rho_e}{\partial X_1}\frac{\partial X_1}{\partial \eta_2} + \frac{\partial \rho_e}{\partial X_2}\frac{\partial X_2}{\partial \eta_2}\right) = \sum_{e=1}^{Ne_2} \frac{\partial c}{\partial \rho_e}\frac{\partial \rho_e}{\partial X_2}L_2\frac{\partial H_2(\eta_2, s_2)}{\partial \eta_2} \\
\frac{\partial c}{\partial L_2} &= \sum_{e=1}^{Ne_2} \frac{\partial c}{\partial \rho_e}\left(\frac{\partial \rho_e}{\partial X_1}\frac{\partial X_1}{\partial L_2} + \frac{\partial \rho_e}{\partial X_2}\frac{\partial X_2}{\partial L_2}\right) = \sum_{e=1}^{Ne_2} \frac{\partial c}{\partial \rho_e}\frac{\partial \rho_e}{\partial X_2}H_2(\eta_2, s_2)
\end{aligned} \tag{23}
$$

where Ne_1 is the number of elements in a stiffener above the reference plate, Ne_2 is the number of elements in a stiffener below the reference plate, and $\partial c/\partial \rho_e$ is the sensitivity of compliance to element density, whose expression is

$$\frac{\partial c}{\partial \rho_e} = -p(\bar{\rho} - \rho)\rho_e^{p-1}U_e^{\mathsf{T}}K_eU_e \tag{24}$$

where $\mathbf{U_e}$ is the displacement vector of the element and $\mathbf{K_e}$ is the stiffness matrix of the element. $\partial H_2 / \partial \eta_i$ is the sensitivity of the Heaviside function with respect to the design variable η_i, which can be expressed by

$$\frac{\partial H_2}{\partial \eta_i} = \frac{\beta_2 e^{\beta_1 * (\eta_i - s_i)}}{\left(1 + e^{\beta_2 * (\eta_i - s_i)}\right)^2} \qquad i = 1, 2 \qquad (25)$$

The values of parameters β_1 and β_2 determine the size of the transition domain of the Heaviside function, so choosing reasonable values of parameters β_1 and β_2 is very influential to the optimization process. To determine their value, numerical experiments were carried out to show that the height of the stiffeners η_i varied by 0.0001 steps from 0 to 1, and the other design variables were all 1. For different β_1 values, the curves of the objective function on the variable are shown in Figure 2.

4. Numerical Implementations

Next, the process of topology optimization with the parameterized methods is summarized. First of all, we need to determine the position of the reference plate by setting the initial design variable, and then substituting the initial design variable into cubic spline interpolation to obtain the height of the reference plate with a set of elements in the X direction. The height of each set of elements in the Y direction is the same, so the height of all elements on the reference plate can be obtained. The element density within the thickness of the reference plate is 1. The direction of the stiffeners is positive and negative in the Z direction. Secondly, the element density should be calculated by the parameterized optimization method, which is the key to the realization of the algorithm. Third, a new iterative process is started by updating the design variables through MMA. The specific optimization process is as follows:

Step 1: Initialize design variables. Determine the position of the base surface and set up the direction of the stiffeners and the maximum design variable change $\Delta \rho_{\max}$, maximum iterations $i_{\max} = 400$, and the iteration counters $i = 0$, $\beta_1 = 5$, and $\beta_2 = 1$. Set up the system of equations and choose the filter method, etc.

Step 2: While $\max \lVert \rho^{i+1} - \rho^i \rVert > \Delta \rho_{\max}$ and $i \leq i_{\max}$, then $i = i + 1$ and go to Step 3, else go to Step 9.

Step 3: Calculate element density from design variables.

Step 4: Solve elastic problems.

Step 5: Calculate objective function and constraint function.

Step 6: Solve sensitivity.

Step 7: Update design variables based on MMA optimization algorithm.

Step 8: If $\mathrm{mod}(i, 30) = 1 \parallel \max \lVert \rho^{i+1} - \rho^i \rVert < 0.01$, then $\beta = \min(\beta + \Delta\beta, 128)$ and go to Step 2.

Step 9: Post-processing after optimization convergence.

5. Numerical Examples

Based on the topology optimization method presented above, the topology optimization design is carried out for two typical examples. In the examples, the material is isotropic, the elastic modulus is $E = 1$ MPa, and Poisson's ratio is $\nu = 0.3$. The design domain is divided by a hexahedral eight-node grid. The interpolation parameters p for the SIMP interpolation start at 1 and increase by 1 for every quarter of the operation. The maximum is 3. Sensitivity filtering is used to avoid the checkerboard phenomenon and grid dependence, and the filtering radius is 2.5. The design variables are updated based on the MMA algorithm. A parameter is introduced in order to describe the dispersion of the optimization results, which is

$$Mnd = \frac{\sum\limits_e 4\rho_e (1 - \rho_e) v_e}{\sum\limits_e v_e} \qquad (26)$$

where ρ_e is the element density and v_e is the element volume. The smaller the value of *Mnd*, the closer the optimized element density is to the 0–1 distribution, and the better the optimization effect.

5.1. Example 1: Simply Supported Plate

In this section, the structure of a simply supported plate is designed, as shown in Figure 5, to obtain the optimal reference surface position, stiffener height, and layout simultaneously. The design range is a 192 × 192 × 128 cube, and the four edges of the lower end face are fixed in three directions. Vertical point loads F are applied to the upper bottom, as shown in Figure 5. In order to better optimize the structure, select the element near the load and constraint as the undesignable domains.

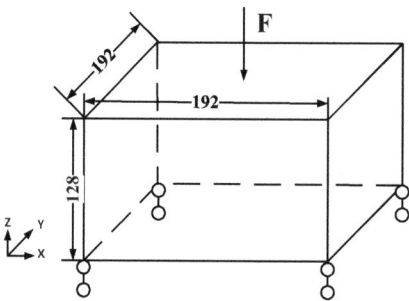

Figure 5. The design domain of the simply supported plate structures.

First, the topological optimization results obtained by the four methods are shown in Figure 6 with a volume fraction of 40%. The red represents the reference plate, the green represents the stiffener structure, and the remaining colors are gray elements. Figure 6a is the result of the topology optimization under the condition where the reference plate is a flat plate and the height is fixed to 0.5. It can be seen that there are more gray elements around the reference plate, and the final objective function value is 328.8133. Figure 6b is the topological optimization result under the condition where the reference plate is a flat plate and the height is a design variable. It can be seen that there are fewer gray elements around the reference plate, and the final objective function value is 317.1167. Figure 6c is the topological optimization result under the condition where the reference plate is a curved plate interpolated by spline and both ends of the curved plate are fixed at 0.5. It can be seen that compared with the result of a flat plate, the structure is more reasonable and there are fewer gray elements. The final objective function value is 303.8884. Figure 6d is the topological optimization result under the condition where the reference plate is a curved plate interpolated by spline and both ends of the curved plate are highly free. Compared with the optimization results of the previous three methods, the final objective function value is smaller (294.7610), as shown in Table 2.

Table 2. Initial and final values of the objective function for the considered four cases.

Method Category	Method 1	Method 2	Method 3	Method 4
Initial value of the objective function	1201	1201	1201	1201
The final value of the objective function	328.81	317.12	303.89	294.76

The iterative curves of the optimization process of the four methods are given in Figure 7. The small oscillation of the curve during the optimization iterative process is mainly caused by the changes in the values of β_1 and β_2. The sudden increase in the objective function near steps 100 and 200 is due to the increase in the penalty factor p. Through optimization, the four methods, respectively, reduce the objective function from the same initial value of 1201 to 328.81, 317.12, 303.89, and 294.76, corresponding to increases in structural stiffness of 3.65, 3.79, 3.95, and 4.07 times, respectively. Thus, it can be seen from these results that the optimized result for Method 4 is the best, where the reference plate is curved with its shape freely optimized, including the location at the boundaries. Furthermore, optimized structures with different volume fractions are also provided, as shown in Figure 8. It can be observed that there are differences in the optimized results with different volume fractions, indicating that volume fraction can influence the optimal structure.

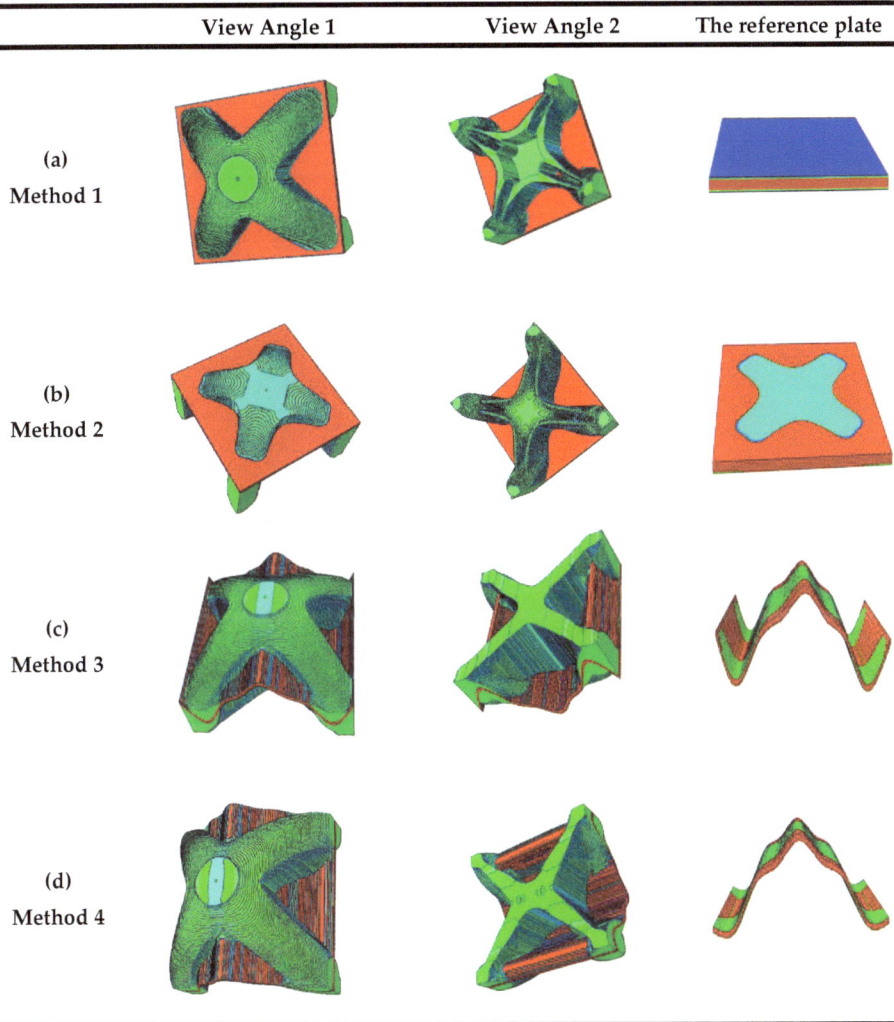

Figure 6. Topologically optimized structures of the four methods. (**a**) Method 1: The reference plate is flat and its location in the height direction is fixed at 0.5. (**b**) Method 2: The reference plate is flat and its location in height direction is considered as a design variable. (**c**) Method 3: The reference plate is curved with its shape optimized but with fixed locations at the boundaries (fixed as 0.5). (**d**) Method 4: The reference plate is curved with its shape freely optimized, including the locations at the boundaries.

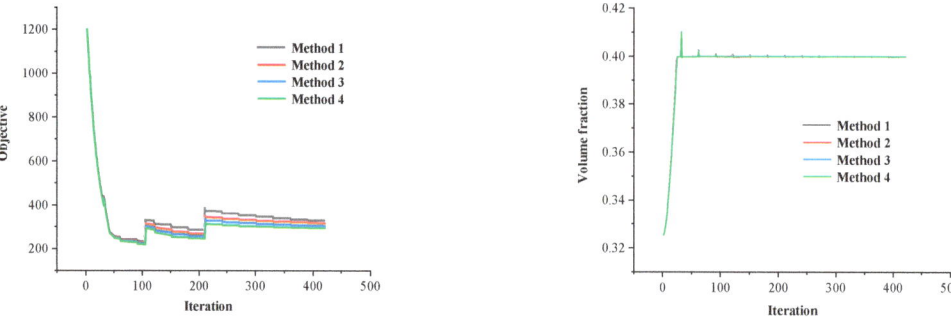

Figure 7. Iteration curves of objective function and constraint function.

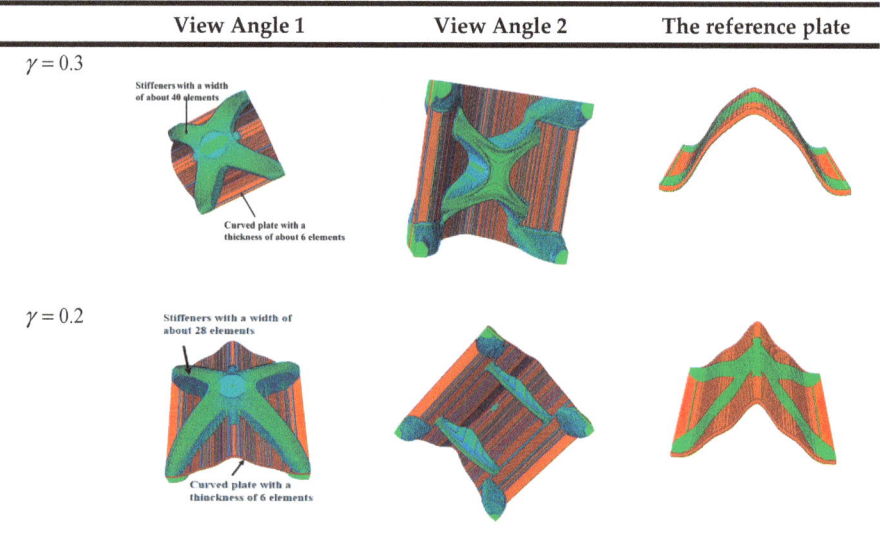

Figure 8. Optimized structures with different volume fractions.

Also, it should be noted that the computational efficiency of the proposed method is poorer than the existing H-DGTP-based method (for the above considered examples, the computational efficiency of the proposed method is approximately 20% to 30% lower than for existing methods), and this is because the new method has far more design variables, which will increase the computational time of the sensitivity analysis and optimization solver.

5.2. Cantilever Beam

In this section, the structure of the cantilever beam is designed, as shown in Figure 9, to obtain the optimal base reference position, stiffener height, and layout simultaneously. The design domain is a 384 × 64 × 128 cube, whose left side is fixed in three directions. Vertical point loads F are applied to the right end of the reference surface, as shown in Figure 9. The discrete domain of an eight-node brick element is used for finite element analysis. The volume fraction is set to 40%.

As shown in Figure 10, the optimized results indicate that the shape of the optimal structure plate is curved rather than flat, validating the necessity for the optimization of the stiffened plate's shape. Additionally, it can be observed that there are stiffening structures on both sides of the plate. Therefore, it can be concluded that, through the method proposed in this paper, stiffened plates with stiffeners on both sides can be obtained. This once again confirms the effectiveness of the method proposed in this paper.

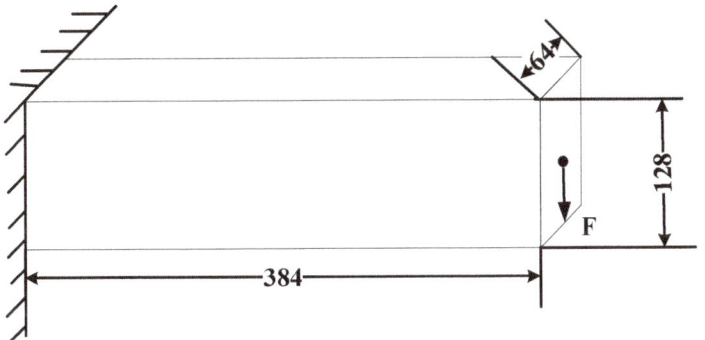

Figure 9. The design domain of the cantilever beam example.

View angle 1

View angle 2

The plate

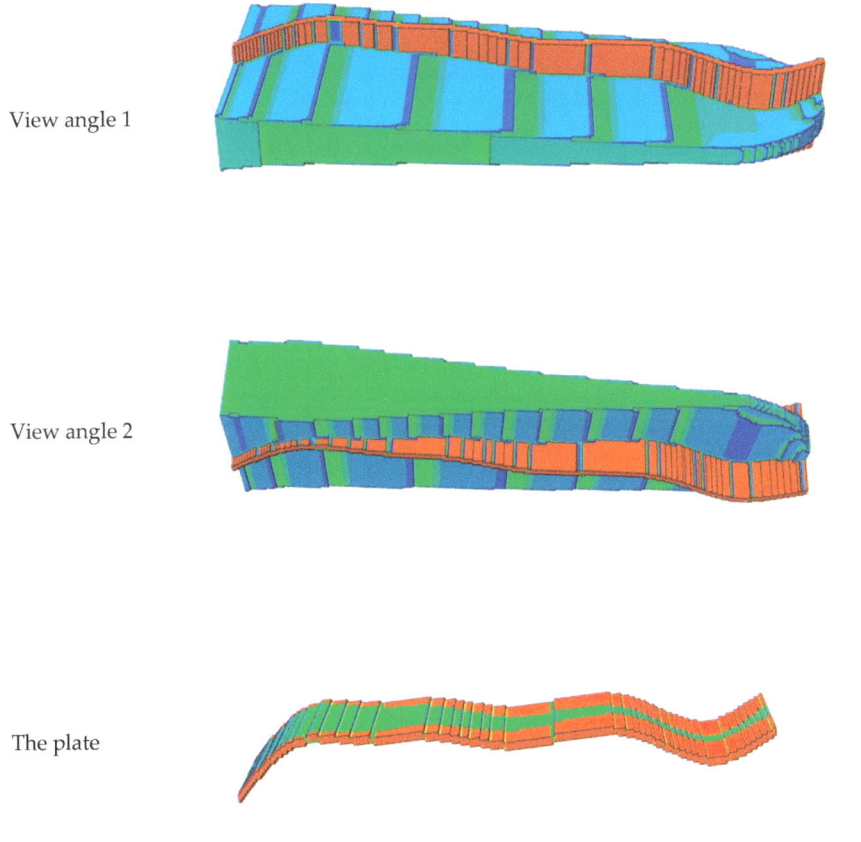

Figure 10. Different view angles of the optimized structures.

6. Conclusions

This paper proposed an improved H-DGTP method (Heaviside-function-based directional growth topology parameterization method) for stiffened plate structures. This enhanced approach extends the method's scope from planar and single-sided stiffened plates to curved and double-sided ones. It specifically considers the positioning and shape of curved panels, along with the arrangement and height of stiffeners, as design variables. Emphasizing structural stiffness as the optimization objective, a topology optimization model is established for double-sided curved stiffened plate structures, followed by a comprehensive sensitivity analysis. Numerical examples demonstrate that optimizing both the position and shape of the plate, along with the layout and height of the stiffeners on both sides of the curved plate simultaneously, yields greater stiffness than optimizing only a subset of these variables. This underscores the necessity and effectiveness of the proposed method.

In this article, only the mechanical stiffness optimization problem is considered. In the future, this method will be extended to more complex design problems, such as thermomechanical coupling and thermo-vibration coupling problems.

Details on the numerical implementation for replicating the results are provided in Section 4, with the pseudo-code and the optimization parameters. The design problems, mesh size, and boundary conditions are given in Section 5. If the information provided in the paper is not enough, we sincerely welcome scientists or interested parties to contact us for further explanation.

Author Contributions: Methodology, K.X., F.Z., Y.L. and Q.L.; Validation, K.X., F.Z., Y.L. and Q.L.; Writing—original draft, K.X. and F.Z.; Writing—review & editing, Y.L. and Q.L. All authors have read and agreed to the published version of the manuscript.

Funding: This work was financially supported by the National Natural Science Foundation of China (Grant Nos. 52375253 and 12202154) and the Dreams Foundation of Jianghuai Advance Technology Center (No. 20240102).

Data Availability Statement: The original contributions presented in the study are included in the article, further inquiries can be directed to the corresponding authors.

Conflicts of Interest: The authors declare that they have no conflicts of interest.

References

1. Zhang, S.; Norato, J.A. Optimal design of panel reinforcements with ribs made of plates. *J. Mech. Des.* **2017**, *139*, 081403. [CrossRef]
2. Hao, P.; Wang, B.; Tian, K.; Li, G.; Du, K.; Niu, F.J. Efficient optimization of cylindrical stiffened shells with reinforced cutouts by curvilinear stiffeners. *AIAA J.* **2016**, *54*, 1350–1363. [CrossRef]
3. Zhu, J.-H.; Gu, X.-J.; Zhang, W.-H.; Beckers, P. Structural design of aircraft skin stretch-forming die using topology optimization. *J. Comput. Appl. Math.* **2013**, *246*, 278–288. [CrossRef]
4. Chen, B.; Liu, G.; Kang, J.; Li, Y. Design optimization of stiffened storage tank for spacecraft. *Struct. Multidiscip. Optim.* **2007**, *36*, 83–92. [CrossRef]
5. Ding, Y.; Zhou, Z.; Wang, Z.; Liu, H.; Wang, K. Bionic Stiffener Layout Optimization with a Flexible Plate in Solar-Powered UAV Surface Structure Design. *Appl. Sci.* **2019**, *9*, 5196. [CrossRef]
6. Shroff, S.; Acar, E.; Kassapoglou, C. Design, analysis, fabrication, and testing of composite grid-stiffened panels for aircraft structures. *Thin-Walled Struct.* **2017**, *119*, 235–246. [CrossRef]
7. Ji, J.; Ding, X.; Xiong, M.J. Optimal stiffener layout of plate/shell structures by bionic growth method. *Comput. Struct.* **2014**, *135*, 88–99. [CrossRef]
8. Kaufmann, M.; Zenkert, D.; Mattei, C. Cost optimization of composite aircraft structures including variable laminate qualities. *Compos. Sci. Technol.* **2008**, *68*, 2748–2754. [CrossRef]
9. Ahn, H.-K.; De Berg, M.; Bose, P.; Cheng, S.-W.; Halperin, D.; Matoušek, J.; Schwarzkopf, O. Separating an object from its cast. *Comput.-Aided Des.* **2002**, *34*, 547–559. [CrossRef]
10. Xia, Q.; Shi, T.; Wang, M.Y.; Liu, S. A level set based method for the optimization of cast part. *Struct. Multidiscip. Optim.* **2010**, *41*, 735–747. [CrossRef]
11. Li, B.; Huang, C.; Xuan, C.; Liu, X. Dynamic stiffness design of plate/shell structures using explicit topology optimization. *Thin-Walled Struct.* **2019**, *140*, 542–564. [CrossRef]

12. Zhu, J.-H.; Zhang, W.-H.; Xia, L. Topology optimization in aircraft and aerospace structures design. *Arch. Comput. Methods Eng.* **2016**, *23*, 595–622. [CrossRef]
13. Li, B.; Hong, J.; Liu, Z. Stiffness design of machine tool structures by a biologically inspired topology optimization method. *Int. J. Mach. Tools Manuf.* **2014**, *84*, 33–44. [CrossRef]
14. Bendsøe, M.P.; Kikuchi, N. Generating optimal topologies in structural design using a homogenization method. *Comput. Methods Appl. Mech. Eng.* **1988**, *71*, 197–224. [CrossRef]
15. Bendsøe, M.P.; Sigmund, O. *Topology Optimization—Theory, Methods, and Applications*; Springer: Berlin/Heidelberg, Germany, 2003.
16. Wang, M.Y.; Wang, X.M.; Guo, D.M. A level set method for structural topology optimization. *Comput. Methods Appl. Mech. Eng.* **2003**, *192*, 227–246. [CrossRef]
17. Xie, Y.M.; Steven, G.P. A simple evolutionary procedure for structural optimization. *Comput. Struct.* **1993**, *49*, 885–896. [CrossRef]
18. Wein, F.; Dunning, P.D.; Norato, J.A. A review on feature-mapping methods for structural optimization. *Struct. Multidiscip. Optim.* **2020**, *62*, 1597–1638. [CrossRef]
19. Gersborg, A.R.; Andreasen, C.S. An explicit parameterization for casting constraints in gradient driven topology optimization. *Struct. Multidiscip. Optim.* **2011**, *44*, 875–881. [CrossRef]
20. Wang, Y.; Kang, Z. Structural shape and topology optimization of cast parts using level set method. *Int. J. Numer. Methods Eng.* **2017**, *111*, 1252–1273. [CrossRef]
21. Xu, B.; Han, Y.S.; Zhao, L.; Xie, Y.M. Topology optimization of continuum structures for natural frequencies considering casting constraints. *Eng. Optim.* **2019**, *51*, 941–960. [CrossRef]
22. Bojczuk, D.; Szteleblak, W. Optimization of layout and shape of stiffeners in 2D structures. *Comput. Struct.* **2008**, *86*, 1436–1446. [CrossRef]
23. Luo, J.; Gea, H.C. Optimal stiffener design for interior sound reduction using a topology optimization based approach. *J. Vib. Acoust.* **2003**, *125*, 267–273. [CrossRef]
24. Zhang, H.; Ding, X.; Dong, X.; Xiong, M. Optimal topology design of internal stiffeners for machine pedestal structures using biological branching phenomena. *Struct. Multidiscip. Optim.* **2018**, *57*, 2323–2338. [CrossRef]
25. Cheng, K.-T.; Olhoff, N. An investigation concerning optimal design of solid elastic plates. *Int. J. Solids Struct.* **1981**, *17*, 305–323. [CrossRef]
26. Rais-Rohani, M.; Lokits, J. Reinforcement layout and sizing optimization of composite submarine sail structures. *Struct. Multidiscip. Optim.* **2007**, *34*, 75–90. [CrossRef]
27. Krog, L.A.; Olhoff, N. Optimum topology and reinforcement design of disk and plate structures with multiple stiffness and eigenfrequency objectives. *Comput. Struct.* **1999**, *72*, 535–563. [CrossRef]
28. Liu, S.; Li, Q.; Chen, W.; Hu, R.; Tong, L. H-DGTP—A Heaviside-function based directional growth topology parameterization for design optimization of stiffener layout and height of thin-walled structures. *Struct. Multidiscip. Optim.* **2015**, *52*, 903–913. [CrossRef]
29. Sun, Z.; Wang, Y.; Gao, Z.; Luo, Y. Topology optimization of thin-walled structures with directional straight stiffeners. *Appl. Math. Model.* **2023**, *113*, 640–663. [CrossRef]
30. Huang, L.; Gao, T.; Sun, Z.; Wang, B.; Tian, K. An integrated topology and shape optimization framework for stiffened curved shells by mesh deformation. *Eng. Comput.* **2023**, *40*, 1771–1793. [CrossRef]
31. Sun, Y.; Zhou, Y.; Ke, Z.; Tian, K.; Wang, B. Stiffener layout optimization framework by isogeometric analysis-based stiffness spreading method. *Comput. Methods Appl. Mech. Eng.* **2022**, *390*, 114348. [CrossRef]

Article

A Robust Flexible Optimization Model for 3D-Layout of Interior Equipment in a Multi-Floor Satellite

Masoud Hekmatfar [1,2], M. R. M. Aliha [1,*], Mir Saman Pishvaee [2] and Tomasz Sadowski [3,*]

1   Welding and Joining Research Center, School of Industrial Engineering, Iran University of Science and Technology (IUST), Narmak 16846-13114, Iran; m_hekmatfar97@ind.iust.ac.ir
2   School of Industrial Engineering, Iran University of Science and Technology (IUST), Narmak 16846-13114, Iran; pishvaee@iust.ac.ir
3   Department of Solid Mechanics, Lublin University of Technology, Nadbystrzycka 40 Str., 20-618 Lublin, Poland
*   Correspondence: mrm_aliha@iust.ac.ir (M.R.M.A.); t.sadowski@pollub.pl (T.S.)

Abstract: Defanging equipment layout in multi-floor satellites consists of two primary tasks: (i) allocating the equipment to the satellite's layers and (ii) placing the equipment in each layer individually. In reviewing the previous literature in this field, firstly, the issue of assigning equipment to layers is observed in a few articles, and regarding the layout, the non-overlapping constraint has always been a challenge, particularly for components that do not have a circular cross-section. In addition to presenting a heuristic method for allocating equipment to different layers of the satellite, this article presents a robust flexible programming model (RFPM) for the placement of equipment at different layers, taking into account the inherent flexibility of the equipment in terms of placement and the subject of uncertainty. This model is based on the existing uncertainty between the distances between pieces of cuboid equipment, which has not been addressed in any of the previous research, and by comparing its outputs with cases from past studies, we demonstrate a significantly higher efficiency related to placing the equipment and meeting the limit of non-overlapping constraints between the equipment. Finally, it would be possible to reduce the design time in the conceptual and preparatory stages, as well as the satellite's overall size, while still satisfying other constraints such as stability and thermal limitations, moments of inertia and center of gravity.

Keywords: satellite components/equipment 3D layout; uncertainty; proposed robust flexible programming model (RFPM); optimization algorithm

MSC: 90C17

Citation: Hekmatfar, M.; Aliha, M.R.M.; Pishvaee, M.S.; Sadowski, T. A Robust Flexible Optimization Model for 3D-Layout of Interior Equipment in a Multi-Floor Satellite. *Mathematics* **2023**, *11*, 4932. https://doi.org/10.3390/math11244932

Academic Editor: Matjaz Skrinar

Received: 28 October 2023
Revised: 5 December 2023
Accepted: 7 December 2023
Published: 12 December 2023

1. Introduction

In the system design phase of a satellite, layout design is the key step that determines whether the aggregation of functional components from different subsystems can operate normally and smoothly in the space environment throughout its design lifespan or not.

The main aim of satellite layout design is to place the objects or equipment (called components) in the proper positions and orientations to meet various engineering requirements or constraints [1].

As the problem of component layout in a satellite occurs in a limited 3D space, the study of three-dimensional layout would help us to investigate and find the best choices for satellite components' layout. Another important criterion in satellite component layout is the multi-floor concept, due to the space of the satellite containing different layers. Ahmadi, A., et al. [2] undertook a comprehensive survey of multi-floor layouts, and provided a complete overview of the models and solution methods applied for multi-floor facility layout problems.

One of the practical problems with satellite layout is related to the measurement of the distance between pieces of equipment under uncertainty. This type of planning is related to epistemic uncertainty, in which either the data are incomplete or the essence of the problem has an imprecise definition. Here, the opinion of the decision-maker (DM) is not considered, and the uncertainty is related to the data of the problem. On the other hand, flexible programming is used when the constraints are soft and flexibility is considered for the final value of the objective function. Here, the DM has the flexibility required to satisfy the constraints or the value of the objective function, and even though the data are certain, the DM can comment on the uncertainty of the information.

The uncertainty concept plays a significant role in determining the distances between cuboid equipment to solve the overlapping issue in satellite layout by applying flexible programming in determining the distances between pieces of equipment, which is the major contribution of this article.

The rest of this article is structured as follows: A thorough analysis of earlier investigations is provided in Section 1.1. The multi-layer satellite equipment layout problem and related mathematical model are presented in Section 1.2. The problem statement and solution of the integration optimization problem are presented in Section 2, which includes two steps of equipment allocation to bearing layers and then a thorough description of the layout of each layer.

The findings of the sensitivity analysis applied to case studies are presented in Section 3, along with a discussion. Finally, Section 4 presents the conclusions.

1.1. Literature Review

The works of [3,4] probably contain the first uses of numerical optimization methods in the layout of spacecraft equipment during the conceptual phase. Rocco, E.M., et al. [5] also presented a multi-objective optimization method for a set of satellites to minimize time-limited fuel consumption. A detailed study of approaches and solution algorithms for the arrangement of three-dimensional equipment was presented by [6]. They showed that the use of CAD software for designing the arrangement of equipment, especially in the arrangement of electrical board parts, is very common, while the three-dimensional arrangement of this software is not very efficient and innovative, and meta-innovative methods such as genetic algorithm and simulated annealing (SA) (such as in the research of [7], who used the SA algorithm to investigate the location of three-dimensional equipment with unknown geometric shapes) have been used more widely in this field.

Articles published in the field of satellite layout are summarized in Table 1. In this table, the methods for allocating equipment to the carrier plates or locating the equipment on each plate are specified, and the details of the problems mentioned by the articles as case studies or numerical examples can be observed in this table. As demonstrated in the table, there are only four articles discussing the allocation of equipment between carrier plates, and the rest only considered the DM's opinion or used arrangements from previous articles.

In addition, regarding the dimensions of problem-solving, as illustrated in Table 1, only 11 articles examined issues related to the design of four carrier plates. Three papers by [8–10] adapted the data from [1] to a multi-cabin satellite with 120 components and eight layers, as opposed to the single-cabin satellite of the original article. These three articles, which established the concept of docking two satellites, are excluded from Table 1. In the remaining cases, the layout of the equipment is either described for a smaller number of plates or is limited to the satellite's cabin, with the latter being more suitable for cube-shaped satellites. In the following, most of the research that has been published in the field of satellite equipment arrangement will be introduced.

Table 1. Solution methods and dimensions of case studies on satellite component layout in previous articles.

No	References	Allocation Phase	Solving Method for Non-Overlap Constraints	Solving Method for Other Mechanical Constraints (Moment of Inertia, Center of Gravity, …)	Problem Dimensions			
					Ex. 1		Ex. 2	
					Layers–Components	Component Shapes	Layers–Components	Component Shapes
1	[11]	equally allocated	analytic geometrical and heuristics methods	dynamical equilibrium constraints	2–26	Cuboid and Cylinder		
2	[12]	centripetal balancing method	GA to reach feasible solution near optimality, plus ACO to adjust the situation of each component	centripetal balancing method	4–53	Cuboid and Cylinder		
3	[13]	predetermined	Heuristic artificial individuals adding rules to the initial population of GA	human-guided GA	4–51	Cuboid and Cylinder		
4	[14]	equally allocated	differential evolution (DE) and local search for cylindrical components	combined GA and PSO	2–14	Cylinder		
5	[15]	predetermined	Human–Algorithm knowledge based on the support of GA		4–51	Cuboid and Cylinder		
6	[1]	Hopfield neural network (HNN)	Geometrical Analysis of Compaction and separation algorithms for nonconvex polygons	hybrid GA and PSO	4–32	Cuboid and Cylinder	4–60	Cuboid and Cylinder
7	[16]	predetermined	hybrid knowledge-based method on the basis of human–computer cooperative GA		4–53	Cuboid and Cylinder		
8	[17]	predetermined	heuristic algorithm of oriented bounding box trees	cooperative co-evolutionary scatter search	1–9	Cylinder	4–60	Cuboid and Cylinder
9	[18]	predetermined	Human-Computer Cooperative Coevolutionary Genetic Algorithm (HCCGA)		3–45	Cuboid and Cylinder		

Table 1. *Cont.*

No	References	Allocation Phase	Solving Method for Non-Overlap Constraints	Solving Method for Other Mechanical Constraints (Moment of Inertia, Center of Gravity, …)	Problem Dimensions			
					Ex. 1 Layers–Components	Ex. 1 Component Shapes	Ex. 2 Layers–Components	Ex. 2 Component Shapes
10	[19]	-	Analytic Geometrical Method for two circular or two rectangular components	ACO	1–40	Rectangle		
11	[20]	predetermined	Dual-System Variable-Grain Cooperative Coevolutionary Genetic Algorithm (DVGCCGA) to avoid "premature convergence" problem		4–60	Cuboid and Cylinder	2–18	Cylinder
12	[21]	-		two quasi-physical optimization methods for solving the circle packing problem	1–50	Circle		
13	[22]	-	VBA in Excel and SOLIDWORKS		Satellite Cabin-8	Cuboid		
14	[23]	-	MATLAB, NSGA and SOLIDWORKS	a multi-objective methodology by CAD	Satellite Cabin-27	Cuboid and Cylinder		
15	[24]	predetermined	Finite Circle Method (FCM)	simulated annealing (SA) optimization and quasi-Newton method	2–18	Cylinder	3–17	Cuboid and Cylinder
16	[25]	predetermined	projection and no-fit polygon methods	local search and heuristics	4–51	Cuboid and Cylinder	4–53	Cuboid and Cylinder
17	[26]	-	NSGA and SOLIDWORKS		Satellite Cabin-15	Cuboid and Cylinder		
18	[27]	Genetic Algorithm (GA)	heuristic positioning rule	a combined method of ACO and PSO	4–60	Cuboid and Cylinder		
19	[28]	predetermined		Hybrid GA and gradient-based Sequential Quadratic Programming (SQP) considering natural frequency and attitude control constraints	4–53	Cuboid and Cylinder		

Table 1. *Cont.*

No	References	Allocation Phase	Solving Method for Non-Overlap Constraints	Solving Method for Other Mechanical Constraints (Moment of Inertia, Center of Gravity, …)	Problem Dimensions			
					Ex. 1		Ex. 2	
					Layers–Components	Component Shapes	Layers–Components	Component Shapes
20	[29]	-	Hybrid GA and gradient-based Sequential Quadratic Programming (SQP) for cylindrical and spherical shapes		1–9	Cylinder		
21	[30]	predetermined	Analytic Geometrical Method	Dual-System Cooperative co-evolutionary detecting Particle Swarm Optimization	4–60	Cuboid and Cylinder	2–29	Cuboid and Cylinder
22	[31]	-	developed PSO		1–40	Circle		
23	[32]	Genetic Algorithm (GA) and Tabu Search (TS)	differential evolution (DE)		2–19	Cuboid and Cylinder		
24	[33]	-	the Optimal Latin Hypercube (OLH) method	Nondominated Sorting Genetic Algorithm (NSGA)	Satellite Cabin-15	Cuboid and Cylinder		
25	[34]	equally allocated	Finite Circle Method (FCM)	developed PSO	2–18	Cylinder	2–16	Cuboid and Cylinder
26	[35]	equally allocated	Hybrid Differential evolution (DE) and gradient-based Sequential Quadratic Programming (SQP) for cylindrical shapes		2–14	Cylinder	2–40	Cylinder
27	[36]	a heuristic algorithm based on stepwise regression	a pseudo-algorithm employing differential evolution (DE)		4–60	Cuboid and Cylinder		
28	[37]	predetermined	Developed PSO and Phi-Function Method/FCM		4–60	Cuboid and Cylinder	2–16	Cuboid and Cylinder
29	[38]	equally allocated	Improved Niching Method (developed GA for cylindrical components)		2–14	Cylinder		

One of the essential constraints in satellite layout is the non-overlapping of components in all bearing plates, named layers. One common method is based on integrating Computer-Aided Design (CAD) tools, engineering analysis packages and optimization algorithms. Coupling optimization algorithms with Computer-Aided Design (CAD) and engineering analysis packages to find the optimal layout of spacecraft equipment was first proposed by [39]. After that, this method was applied in the studies of [22,23,26,33,40,41].

The following are the most important articles in the field of satellite equipment arrangement, and they present various methods in approaching the subject of non-overlapping.

For the first time, ref. [11] studied the arrangements of equipment on several satellite layers, and then analyzed the three-dimensional layout problem on a rotating vessel. Because of the spiral rotation movement of the vessel, they took into account dynamic equilibrium constraints and used the heuristic algorithms constructed by [42] for non-convex polygons to determine the amount of overlap among objects.

Sun, Z.G. et al. [12] introduced a centripetal balancing heuristic algorithm to allocate objects between bearing plates. To distribute objects in a bearing plate, they applied a Genetic Algorithm (GA) to produce random populations and finally to reach a feasible (near-optimal) solution. Eventually, they developed an Ant Colony Optimization (ACO) method to refine the positions of each object in a detailed design on bearing surfaces.

Huo, J. et al. [13] developed a human-guided GA, and compared its results with the GA library to demonstrate the efficacy of their algorithm for the two-dimensional layout of objects in a satellite. They added artificial individuals to the population of GA to cope with overlapping components.

Liu, Z. et al. [15] presented a Human–Algorithm–Knowledge approach with the support of GA to design the layout of equipment in a satellite, and used the CAD software to derive previous knowledge for use in their GA.

Zhang, B. et al. [1] developed a two-stage model for the layout optimization of satellites. The first stage concerned allocating objects to different bearing plates, and the second one dealt with the detailed design of each bearing plate such that no overlapping occurred. To develop an optimal layout in each bearing plate, they applied a combinatorial method including GA and Particle Swarm Optimization (PSO) metaheuristics. They explained that GA is inherently suited to finding global convergence, while PSO is the proper method for local convergence, and the disadvantage of GA in local convergence was compensated for using PSO to replace the random population in the initial phase of GA and the weakness of PSO in terms of global converge was satisfied using the best solution of GA to replace the first population of PSO. To tackle the overlapping issue, they applied the concept of the compaction and separation algorithm introduced by [43], who applied locality heuristics for star-shaped non-convex polygons.

Huo, J.Z. et al. [16] presented a co-evolutionary method in which a genetic algorithm (GA) was used to determine the rotation angle of the final layout scheme of the equipment, and a heuristic combination–rotation method was introduced to determine the entire layout scheme with reference to the rotation strategy of a heuristic constraint rubik cube method (CRCM).

Teng, H.F. et al. [20] proposed an evolutionary method called the dual-system variable-grain algorithm to decompose the satellite layout system into several sections, and also to avoid premature convergence problems. In their model, they took into account the constraints of interference between objects, the centroid offset of the satellite system and constraints of inertia angles. They applied analytic geometry to handle the discontinuous constraints related to overlapping volumes. Li, Z. et al. [27] presented a three-step strategy for distributing equipment throughout the layers of a satellite and then determining the location of each component inside its assigned layer. In the initial phase, each piece of equipment was assigned to one of the four bearing layers using a genetic algorithm (GA). In the second step, they applied a heuristic positioning rule to address the challenge of satisfying overlapping constraints between circles and rectangles in the precise 2D design of equipment for each layer. In this step, an ACO algorithm and a heuristic adjustment approach are used to manage the detailed design of each layer. Lastly, they presented a PSO algorithm to combine subproblems and attempt to minimize errors in the mass center and moment of inertia, while preserving the other components of the objective function. Liu, J. et al. [25] proposed a hybrid method based on local and heuristic search algorithms to find the optimal arrangement of satellite equipment. They calculated the amount of equipment overlap based on geometric shapes. In this way, if two devices were rectangular, or one was rectangular and the other was circular, projection and no-fit polygon methods were used, respectively. The second method is utilized for the non-overlapping of polyhedra, in which all possible placements of a polyhedron in relation to others are illustrated, and the topic of overlapping between two polyhedra is relegated to overlapping between a polyhedron and a vector that is more computationally efficient. Cui, F.Z. et al. [30] represented a new dual algorithm combining the detecting of PSO and a cooperative co-evolution method for use in a multi-layer satellite. Similar to [20], here, analytic geometry was the method they proposed to deal with the problem of overlapping among components. Ref. [32] presented an integrated method for satellite equipment assignment and layout design. They used GA and Tabu Search (TS) to reassign equipment before attempting to lay out 19 components in two layers using the Differential Evolution (DE) method. Ref. [36] stated that the assignment of satellite equipment can be achieved based on the Multiple Bin Packing Problem (MBPP) approach. They offered a method based on stepwise regression to assign equipment, and after comparing the assignment schemes, the optimal one was chosen as the input for the layout phase, which was solved using a pseudo-algorithm employing DE and a random mutation operation. Refs. [37,44] evaluated the overlap between equipment in the satellite's central plane utilizing the method given in the paper by Chernov et al. (2012) [45] and the phi-function method. For two components, if the value of the phi-function is positive, the two components will not overlap; if the value of the function is zero, they are tangential to each other, and if it is negative, they intersect. Also, unlike most of the research done in this field, they here considered the interaction between the pieces of equipment. They studied five examples of different satellites. The first example involved six equilateral triangles in a circular enclosure, the second example involved resolving an overlapping problem between two diagonally placed rectangles, the third example concerned cylindrical satellites, the fourth example was for nano-satellites, and the final example concerned overlapping between parts in cube-shaped satellites. They solved the third and fifth instances using an adaptive PSO approach, and the fourth example using the Finite Circle Method (FCM), all of which were developed by [34]. Finally, the existing limitations associated with this method were also addressed, and it was shown that, due to the use of geometric non-linear and non-convex restrictions, the proposed model does not provide a sufficient solution for some conditions, and it is necessary that in the future, efficient and effective algorithms be produced to solve this problem.

In the field of uncertainty, defined uncertainty as the difference between the amount of information needed and the amount of information available to perform a task [46]. The uncertainty related to decision-making arises under conditions of incomplete information. Ref. [47] divided the discussion of uncertainty between issues of flexibility in limitations and the different levels of acceptability of goals, and those related to uncertainty in input data. In this way, the flexibility in the constraints takes into account the decision-maker's preferences. Ref. [48] divided decision-making conditions into two groups according to the quality of available information: decision-making under conditions of certainty (when information is fully available) and decision-making under conditions of uncertainty (when information is incomplete). Ref. [49] indicated that developments in robust optimization have taken place in three historical waves. The first wave, begun by [50], concerned robust optimization related to a scenario-based stochastic planning approach. Refs. [51,52] then developed this approach further. The second wave, known as robust convex programming, was first introduced by [53–55]. Here, the cone programming method is used to solve convex problems due to the existence of complexities, which is achieved according to duality theorems and optimality conditions. The third wave, pioneered by [56], presented different approaches to robust planning. They demonstrated that robust fuzzy mathematical programming (RFMP) can be divided into two parts: possibilistic programming and flexible programming.

As the analyses in the literature demonstrate, there are two fundamental aspects to the satellite layout issue. First, there is the issue of component distribution across different bearing layers, and second, there is the problem of cuboid component overlapping. Accordingly, this paper addresses both problems.

In the next section, the mathematical modeling of satellite components' layout is described.

1.2. Mathematical Modeling

Conceptual design, preliminary design, and detailed design are the three basic stages of satellite design. One of the fundamental subjects of the detailed design phase is layout design, which encounters the issue of whether operational components from various subsystems can function properly and effectively when integrated in a unique environment, such as a space that is constantly exposed to cosmic rays.

The major goal of designing satellite equipment is to optimize a satellite's stability, control, and dimensions, which will result in a reduction in the size and weight of the satellite, and so this kind of optimization can have a direct impact on the satellite's launch success, as well as its continuity and durability in space.

Numerous factors, such as size, stability, and optimum system performance, contribute to the best satellite layout, and result in more variables and limitations. This intricacy emphasizes the need for industrial engineering optimization solutions rather than the typical trial-and-error methods used in mechanical engineering in this field. The challenge of placing many pieces of equipment in a cylinder, cube, or polygonal volume on different floors, and deploying multiple distinct plates within the satellite, is known as a problem related to optimizing telecommunication and measurement satellite equipment.

The layout optimization problem of a communication satellite module can be described as follows.

A total number of n components will be located in a cylindrical satellite module with two floors. Four plates, including the upper and lower and two middle plates of the inner space of the satellite, attached to a standing column in the module, are used to hold all the components, and in this proposed methodology, all the components are given simple cylindrical and cubic shapes and regarded as rigid bodies with uniform mass allocation.

There is an even distribution of mass across every piece of equipment, which are shaped as cubes or cylinders.

An extensive analysis of the influencing factors, such as distance constraints, heat constraints, radiation constraints, functional constraints, and stability, is crucial because the goal of this paper is to optimize the interior space of the satellite and ultimately reduce its dimensions and weight. The problem becomes more complex after a full analysis of these constraints, necessitating the employment of specialized optimization software. Therefore, the ultimate objective is to build an optimization model and ensure its output with the aid of software, so that manufacturing units can optimally place equipment when building satellites with smaller dimensions and weights.

The objective is to reduce the satellite's size and weight while still maintaining stability, taking into account the major inertia moments, cross-inertia moments, and center of gravity, as well as distance, heat, and radiation limits. The problem of equipment placement is an NP-hard problem because of the engineering and mechanical complexity of satellites. This calls for a combination of numerous intricate and specialized approaches, in addition to the design of a sophisticated system. For example, shown in Figure 1 is a typical cylindrical configuration of a satellite, with two center plates (or four layers/floors) for holding boxes and components across the satellite's multiple floors. The shape of the equipment is cylindrical or cubic, and all of it is located on one of the two sides of these center plates. As each side of a plate is called a layer, this satellite includes four layers. Depending on the numbers, sizes and weights of the cylindrical and cubic boxes (representative of interior equipment of satellite), several solutions may be developed for the placement of the elements in the layers or floors of the satellite. Finding the optimum solution (i.e., the best layout or placement of elements, with the ability to satisfy the constraints of the problem) using optimization methods rather than trial-and-error methods is an interesting and important issue. Successful optimization methods can help the designers of satellites in reducing the time taken in designing the layout of the components and subsystems.

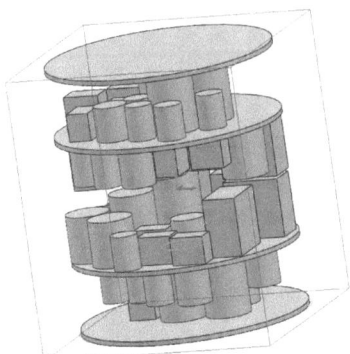

Figure 1. Example of the 3D layout of cubic or cylindrical components (boxes) of a sample satellite with two middle plates and four layers.

The assumptions of the model are as follows:

Three-dimensional layout—Difficulties in placing satellite equipment arise across three dimensions, so the Z axis is considered the main part;

Multi-layer layout—The multiple layers of a satellite represent another crucial consideration in the installation of satellite equipment. In relation to this, the model must allocate equipment to all plates or layers;

Non-interference and overlap constraints—No interference occurs between any pieces of the components;

Equilibrium constraint—The equilibrium error of the system should be as small as possible;

Thermal constraints—The performance of electronic components may be directly impacted by the thermal environment. As a result, the system's equipment is generally more efficient and reliable when heat flow is distributed uniformly.

From a thermal point of view, each piece of equipment has an effective area that can affect the performance of other equipment. Therefore, reducing the interaction space is essential to improving the uniformity of the thermal field in the satellite. In determining the thermal effects of equipment, it is assumed that some components produce a thermal radius that forms a uniform circle around the equipment. For this reason, no intersection between virtual thermal radii between equipment is allowed;

Obnoxious equipment limitations—Another constraint must be taken into account for some equipment types with a high amount of heat radiation, or "hot parts", such as batteries, radio transmitters, and photo transmitters, which must be positioned at as great a distance from one another as possible in the satellite space. In other words, there needs to be limitations placed on the presence of this hot equipment on each floor of the satellite;

Static stability constraint—The center of gravity offset of the system should be as small as possible.

The stability limit of the satellite should be such that the device can move and rotate easily in space. Therefore, the sum of the inertia moments of the system should be minimal. Physically, minimizing the sum of moments of inertia means that the satellite inherently tends towards stability, and this minimization can reduce the effort required from subsystems in stabilizing the satellite, as a result of which moments of inertia, including the axes of the main axis and impact or cross moments, must be at a minimum.

System uncertainty—There is no fixed value for the distance at which equipment should be spaced apart, so it is important to use uncertainty to determine this distance. As mentioned in the previous section, uncertainties are included in the model for a variety of reasons—one of them is uncertainty on the part of the decision-maker (DM). In the design of satellite equipment layout, it is not easy to apply non-overlap constraints to cube-shaped equipment with a rectangular cross-section as has been done for cylindrical equipment with a circular cross-section, because, when there are two items of circular equipment, the overlap between them can be easily prevented by calculating the radius and entering the distance between the two radii. On the other hand, for two pieces of equipment with a rectangular cross-section, or when there is one piece of circular equipment and another rectangular one, the non-overlap restriction cannot be easily observed. For this reason, the uncertainty argument is easily applicable, and is very effective in developing a solution.

Due to the nature of the problem, the fuzzy concept is also used here, meaning that the constraints related to equipment distances are written in fuzzy form. By adding fuzzy constraints, a decision variable (α) is defined in the model and added to the objective function with a penalty coefficient (γ).

1.2.1. Model Development

In this section, we outline the parameters, decision variables, objective functions and constraints of the basic model, derived from previous studies such as [1,12,15] and to be utilized for introducing and defining the 3D layout problem, and the optimization method is also illustrated.

Model Parameters

The model parameters are introduced as follows:

i—indicator of the equipment;
j—index of the number of layers (j = 1, 2, 3, 4)
l_j—layer j of the satellite;
a_i—the cross-sectional length of the cuboid equipment i;
b_i—the cross-sectional width of the cuboid equipment i;
r_i—radius of the cross-sectional area of the cylindrical equipment i;
h_i—the height of the equipment i;
m_i—the mass of equipment i;
θ_i—the angle between the positive direction of the x-axis and the horizontal edge of the cuboid equipment i;
c—number of pieces of cuboid equipment;
n—total number of equipment;
n_j—the number of equipment pieces located at layer j;
sM_i—a segment of the radius of the hypothetical circumferential circle of a cross-section of cuboid equipment i;
sO_i—optimistic value of a triangular fuzzy number for sM_i;
sP_i—pessimistic value of a triangular fuzzy number for sM_i;
$\widetilde{sT}_i$—a triangular fuzzy number for sM_i;
γ—the cost of the fine for each unit of violation of the soft limit;
x_e—expected coordinates in the direction of the x-axis of the satellite's center of gravity;
y_e—expected coordinates in the y-axis direction of the satellite's center of gravity;
z_e—expected coordinates in the direction of the z-axis of the satellite's center of gravity;
J_{xi}—moment of inertia of equipment in the direction of the x-axis;
J_{yi}—moment of inertia of equipment in the direction of the y-axis;
J_{zi}—moment of inertia of equipment in the direction of the z-axis;

δx_e—permissible error of deviation in the coordinates of the real center of gravity of the satellite from the expected value in the direction of the x-axis;

δy_e—permissible error of deviation in the coordinates of the real center of gravity of the satellite from the expected value in the direction of the y-axis;

δz_e—permissible error of deviation in the coordinates of the real center of gravity of the satellite from the expected value in the direction of the z-axis;

$\delta\theta_x$—permissible error of deviation in the angle between the mass moment of inertia of the satellite in the direction of the x-axis from the axis of the coordinate of the satellite in the direction of the ox axis;

$\delta\theta_y$—permissible error of deviation in the angle between the mass moment of inertia of the satellite in the direction of the y-axis and the axis of the satellite coordinates in the direction of the oy axis;

$\delta\theta_z$—permissible error of deviation in the angle between the mass moment of inertia of the satellite in the direction of the z-axis from the coordinate axis of the satellite in the direction of the z-axis.

Decision Variables of the Model

The model's decision variables are as follows:

x_i—the coordinates of equipment i in the direction of the x-axis;

y_i—the coordinates of equipment i in the direction of the y-axis;

z_i—the coordinates of equipment i in the direction of the z-axis;

x_m—coordinates of the center of gravity of the satellite in the direction of the x-axis;

y_m—the coordinates of the center of gravity of the satellite in the direction of the y-axis;

z_m—coordinates of the center of gravity of the satellite in the direction of the z-axis;

θ_x—the angle between the mass moment of inertia of the satellite in the direction of the x-axis and the axis of the satellite coordinates in the direction of the x-axis;

θ_y—the angle between the mass moment of inertia of the satellite in the direction of the y-axis and the coordinate axis of the satellite in the direction of the y-axis;

θ_z—angle between the mass moment of inertia of the satellite in the direction of the z-axis and the axis of coordinates of the satellite in the direction of the oz axis;

I_{xx}—the mass moment of inertia of the satellite in the direction of the x-axis;

I_{yy}—the mass moment of inertia of the satellite in the direction of the y-axis;

I_{zz}—the mass moment of inertia of the satellite in the direction of the z-axis;

I_{xy}—product moment of inertia used to calculate satellite imbalance in the direction of the x and y plane;

I_{xz}—product moment of inertia used to calculate satellite imbalance in the x and z plane directions;

I_{yz}—product moment of inertia used to calculate satellite imbalance in the y and z plane directions;

fr_i—the final radius of equipment i after performing the uncertainty calculations;

α_i—the minimum level of satisfaction in flexible constraints;

S_j—the space available on each layer;

S'_j—the space occupied on each layer.

There are three types of coordinate systems:

1. *Oxyz* reference coordinate system

   O—the center of this coordinate system is located on the geometric center of the lower plate of the satellite;

   z—the longitudinal symmetric axis of the satellite, which is positive in the upward direction;

   x—the axis perpendicular to the z-axis on the bottom plate of the satellite;

   y—the axis perpendicular to the z-axis on the bottom plate of the satellite and at a 90-degree angle to the x-axis.

This coordinate system is used to find the center of the satellite and determine the layout of the equipment.

2. Satellite coordinate system $O'x'y'z'$

    O'—the center of this coordinate system is located on the real center of gravity of the satellite.

    z'—the longitudinal symmetric axis of the satellite that coincides with or is parallel to the z-axis.

    x', y'—these two axes are parallel to the x- and y-axes, respectively.

This coordinate system is used to calculate the mass and product moment of inertia of the satellite.

3. The local coordinate system of the equipment $O''x''y''z''$

    O''—the center of this coordinate system is located on the center of gravity of the equipment;

    z''—the longitudinal symmetric axis of the equipment, which is parallel to the z-axis.

    x'', y''—these two axes form an angle α_i parallel to the x- and y-axes, respectively.

This coordinate system is used to calculate the moment of inertia of the equipment according to its axis.

Optimization Model

A minimal sum of the moments of inertia physically suggests that the satellite is inherently stable. This means that minimizing the sum of the moments of inertia can reduce the efforts required from the attitude control subsystem in the stabilization of the satellite.

The moments of inertia of both cubic and cylindrical components are calculated in the *xyz* direction. The total moments of inertia of all the components that need to be minimized can be expressed as follows:

$$\text{Min } f(X) = I_{xx} + I_{yy} + I_{zz} \tag{1}$$

The constraints are as below.

Non-overlap constraint:

$$g_1(X) = -(x_i - x_j)^2 - (y_i - y_j)^2 + (r_i + r_j)^2 \leq 0 \text{ for } i,j \in L_k \quad k = 1,2,3,4 \tag{2}$$

Static stability constraint:

$$g_2(X) = |x_m - x_e| - \delta x_e \leq 0 \tag{3}$$

$$g_3(X) = |y_m - y_e| - \delta y_e \leq 0 \tag{4}$$

$$g_4(X) = |z_m - z_e| - \delta z_e \leq 0 \tag{5}$$

where x_e, y_e and z_e are the expected centroid position of the satellite and δx_e, δy_e and δz_e are the allowance errors of x_m, y_m and z_m (real centroid position of the satellite), respectively.

Equilibrium constraints:

$$g_5(X) = |\theta_x - \theta_e| - \delta\theta_x \leq 0 \tag{6}$$

$$g_6(X) = |\theta_y - \theta_e| - \delta\theta_y \leq 0 \tag{7}$$

$$g_7(X) = |\theta_z - \theta_e| - \delta\theta_z \leq 0 \tag{8}$$

where θ_x, θ_y and θ_z are angles between the principal axes of inertia of the satellite and the principle axes oz, oy and oz, and $\delta\theta_x$, $\delta\theta_y$ and $\delta\theta_z$ are their allowance errors.

The objective function (1) shows the minimization of mass moments of inertia in the main direction of the coordinate axis. Constraint (2) represents the constraint of non-overlapping between pieces of equipment by requiring that the distance between the centers of two pieces of equipment be equal to or larger than the sum of their two radii. For cuboid equipment, the radius of the circumferential circle of the rectangular cross-section is considered as the radius.

Constraints (3) to (5) show static stability, where x_e, y_e and z_e coordinates are the expected center of gravity of the satellite and δx_e, δy_e and δz_e are permissible error in the coordinates of the actual center of gravity of the satellite (x_m, y_m, z_m). The deviation of the center of gravity of the satellite after the placement of all equipment should not be greater than that in the expected center of gravity of the satellite. Constraints (6) to (8) are equilibrium constraints, in which θ_x, θ_y and θ_z are the angles between the directions of the mass moments of inertia of the satellite with the major axes O_x, O_y and O_z, and $\delta\theta_x$, $\delta\theta_y$ and $\delta\theta_z$ are their allowable errors. The following shows how to calculate θ_x, θ_y and θ_z.

The center of mass of the ith component in the local xyz coordinate system can be stated as shown below:

$$x_m = \sum_{i=1}^{n} m_i x_i \div \sum_{i=0}^{n} m_i \tag{9}$$

$$y_m = \sum_{i=1}^{n} m_i y_i \div \sum_{i=0}^{n} m_i \tag{10}$$

$$z_m = \sum_{i=1}^{n} m_i z_i \div \sum_{i=0}^{n} m_i \tag{11}$$

where ($x_i.y_i.z_i$) and m_i are the coordinates of the center and the mass of the piece of equipment i, respectively. In the denominator of these equations, the sum starts from zero because, in addition to the number of pieces of equipment (n), the mass of the shell, the middle cylinder and the floors must also be taken into account in calculating the true center of gravity of the satellite.

The computational formulas of moments of inertia in the main directions of the satellite coordinate axis are as follows:

$$
\begin{aligned}
I_{xx} &= \sum_{i=1}^{n} (J_{xi}\cos^2\theta_i \ + J_{yi}\sin^2\theta_i) + \sum_{i=1}^{n} m_i(y_i^2 + z_i^2) - \sum_{i=0}^{n} m_i(y_m^2 + z_m^2) \\
&= \sum_{i=1}^{c} (\tfrac{1}{12}(m_i(b_i^2 + h_i^2)\cos2\theta_i + \tfrac{1}{12}m_i(a_i^2 + h_i^2)\sin2\theta_i) \\
&\quad + \sum_{i=c+1}^{n} \tfrac{1}{12}m_i(3r_i^2 + h_i^2) + \sum_{i=1}^{n} (m_i(y_i^2 + z_i^2) - \sum_{i=0}^{n} (m_i(y_m^2 + z_m^2)
\end{aligned} \tag{12}
$$

where J_{xi} and J_{yi} are moments of inertia of the ith component concerning the local coordinate system (to the x- and y-axes, respectively). a_i and b_i are the length and width of a cubic component, respectively, and h_i and r_i are the height and radius of the ith component (for both cubic and cylindrical components). Similarly, the derivations of moments of inertia in the y direction of both cylindrical and cubic components are shown below:

$$
\begin{aligned}
I_{yy} &= \sum_{i=1}^{c} (\tfrac{1}{12}m_i(a_i^2 + h_i^2)\cos^2\theta_i + \tfrac{1}{12}m_i(b_i^2 + h_i^2)\sin^2\theta_i) + \sum_{i=c+1}^{n} \tfrac{1}{12}m_i(3r_i^2 + h_i^2) \\
&\quad + \sum_{i=1}^{n} (m_i(x_i^2 + z_i^2) - \sum_{i=0}^{n} (m_i(x_m^2 + z_m^2)
\end{aligned} \tag{13}
$$

Similarly, the derivations of moments of inertia in the z direction of both cylindrical and cubic components are illustrated below:

$$I_{zz} = J_{zi} + \sum_{i=1}^{n} m_i(x_i^2 + y_i^2) - \sum_{i=0}^{n} m_i(x_m^2 + y_m^2) \tag{14}$$

α_i—this parameter is the placement angle of the cubic object; it equals the included angle between axis x in the positive direction and the long edge of the cubic component. Here, it is assumed that the cubic equipment only rotates 90 degrees, so the only possible values for this parameter are zero or 90.

The formulae of θ_x, θ_y and θ_z are as below:

$$\theta_x(x) = \arctan\frac{\frac{2I_{xy}}{I_{xx}-I_{xy}}}{2} \tag{15}$$

$$\theta_y(x) = \arctan\frac{\frac{2I_{xz}}{I_{xz}-I_{xx}}}{2} \tag{16}$$

$$\theta_z(x) = \arctan\frac{\frac{2I_{yz}}{I_{xz}-I_{xy}}}{2} \tag{17}$$

where I_{xy}, I_{xz} and I_{yz} are the products of moments of inertia in the $x - y$, $x - z$ and $y - z$ planes, respectively, for both cylindrical and cubic components, and are calculated as below:

$$\begin{aligned}
I_{xy} = \sum_{i=1}^{n} & (m_i(x_i - x_m)(y_i - y_m) + (J_{xi} + (y_i^2 + z_i^2) - J_{yi} - (x_i^2 + z_i^2)) \div 2) \times \sin 2\theta_i \\
&= \sum_{i=1}^{n}\left[m_i x_i y_i + \frac{J_{xi} + m_i(y_i^2 + z_i^2)}{2}\sin 2\theta_i \right] \\
&- \sum_{i=1}^{n}\left[\frac{J_{yi} + m_i(x_i^2 + z_i^2)}{2}\sin 2\theta_i \right] - \sum_{i=1}^{n} m_i x_m y_m
\end{aligned} \tag{18}$$

$$I_{xz} = \sum_{i=1}^{n} (m_i(x_i - x_m)(Z_i - Z_m)) = \sum_{i=1}^{n} m_i x_i z_i - \sum_{i=1}^{n} m_i x_m z_m \tag{19}$$

$$I_{yz} = \sum_{i=1}^{n} (m_i(y_i - y_m)(Z_i - Z_m)) = \sum_{i=1}^{n} m_i y_i z_i - \sum_{i=1}^{n} m_i y_m z_m \tag{20}$$

The moments of inertia of the ith cylindrical component are defined by J_{xi}, J_{yi} and J_{zi} in relation to the local coordinate system, as follows:

$$J_{xi} = J_{yi} = \frac{1}{12} m_i \left(3r_i^2 + h_i^2 \right) \tag{21}$$

$$J_{zi} = \frac{1}{2} m_i r_i^2 \tag{22}$$

Also, moments of inertia for the ith cubic component indicated by J_{xi}, J_{yi} and J_{zi} are shown below:

$$J_{xi} = \frac{1}{12} m_i \left(b_i^2 + h_i^2 \right) \tag{23}$$

$$J_{yi} = \frac{1}{12} m_i \left(a_i^2 + h_i^2 \right) \tag{24}$$

$$J_{zi} = \frac{1}{12} m_i \left(a_i^2 + b_i^2 \right) \tag{25}$$

2. Problem Statement and Implementation

The main issue to be investigated in this study is how to deal with the component assignment problem, along with the growing number of bearing layers and components and the complexity of technical requirements related to the satellite layout problem. In this section, we offer a heuristic solution for the assignment problem, and then the RFMP is used to evolve the distance between cuboid components.

In approaching the mentioned problem, consider Figure 2, which shows the front view of a satellite in which components and boxes (cylindrical or cubic parts) are located on two floors or four layers (levels), such that the equipment is located on the upper and lower levels of each floor. The center of gravity of the satellite shown in Figure 2 (x_m, y_m, z_m) is somewhere between levels L_2 and L_3 (i.e., between the two middle plates of the satellite). The distance between the layers and the bottom plate of the satellite is defined by H1, H2 and Ht as shown in Figure 2. The parameters introduced in Figure 2 will be explicated in the next part.

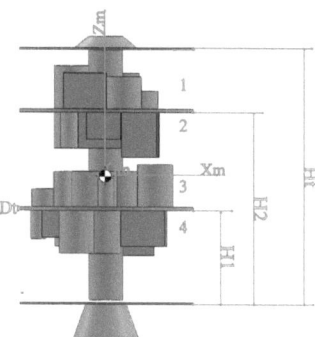

Figure 2. Front view of satellite with two middle plates and the locations of components in four layers.

2.1. Allocation and Layout

The placement of equipment in the satellite space involves two main steps: first, the allocation of equipment to floors and layers, and then their placement in each layer. As such, the problem is one of allocation and layout. Since the objective function involves minimizing mass moments of inertia, the equipment should be arranged such that the moments of inertia possess the lowest possible values in all directions of the coordinate axes (x, y, z). Since the problem involves two floors and four layers, the placement of equipment can affect the moments of inertia in two ways.

The location of equipment at different levels affects the moment of inertia in the directions of the x- and y-axes, and the layout of the equipment at each layer can affect the moment of inertia in the direction of the z-axis (I_{zz}). In other words, to change the moment of inertia in the directions of the x- and y-axes, the distances of the pieces of equipment from the $o_m x_m$ and $o_m y_m$ axes, respectively, play a decisive role. Therefore, if a component is moved between layers, its distance from the mentioned axes changes, and this affects the moment of inertia in the x and y directions. Conversely, if the distance of the equipment from the $o_m z_m$ axis remains constant, there will be no change in the moment of inertia in the direction of the z-axis. According to this, the proper allocation of equipment to different layers can play an important role in reducing the moment of inertia in the directions of the x- and y-axes (I_{xx} and I_{yy}).

2.1.1. Allocation of Components between Layers

At this stage, all components are assigned to one of four layers in the satellite such that the most optimal state is created for the intended function. As previously explained, the assignment of equipment to surfaces can affect the moments of inertia along the x- and y-axes (I_{xx} and I_{yy}). Since Equations (12) and (13) are similar, calculations are here only undertaken for one of them, and the result is generalized to the other. As is evident from Equation (26), to obtain the lowest possible value for this expression, the first three expressions must show the lowest value, and the last expression must have the maximum possible value.

$$\sum_{i=1}^{c} \left(\tfrac{1}{12} m_i \left(b_i^2 + h_i^2 \right) cos^2 \theta_i + \tfrac{1}{12} m_i \left(a_i^2 + h_i^2 \right) sin^2 \theta_i \right) + \sum_{i=c+1}^{n} \tfrac{1}{12} m_i \left(3r_i^2 + h_i^2 \right)$$
$$+ \sum_{i=1}^{n} \left(m_i \left(y_i^2 + z_i^2 \right) \right) - \sum_{i=0}^{n} \left(m_i \left(y_m^2 + z_m^2 \right) \right) \tag{26}$$

Before considering the minimization of the above expression, we must first discuss the value of z_i. This value indicates the final localization of the equipment in terms of height (z dimension) after placement. This is calculated as follows:

$$z_i = \begin{cases} H_2 + D_t + \tfrac{h_i}{2} & if \ l_j = 1 \\ H_2 - \tfrac{h_i}{2} & if \ l_j = 2 \\ H_1 + D_t + \tfrac{h_i}{2} & if \ l_j = 3 \\ H_1 - \tfrac{h_i}{2} & if \ l_j = 4 \end{cases} \tag{27}$$

Since the length, width and height (a, b, h) of cuboid equipment, and the radius and height (r, h) of cylindrical equipment, are fixed, the first three expressions of Equation (26) cannot be altered. Therefore, to change the equation, we must perform the following:

$$\sum_{i=1}^{n} \left(m_i \left(y_i^2 + z_i^2 \right) \right) - \sum_{i=1}^{n} \left(m_i \left(y_m^2 + z_m^2 \right) \right) \tag{28}$$

First, we consider the first part of the above equation. Given that the allocation of equipment to distinct layers impacts their z-axis coordinates, it suffices to minimize the first half of Formula (28) to minimize the following value:

$$\sum_{i=1}^{n} \left(m_i z_i^2 \right) \tag{29}$$

We now turn to the second part of Equation (28). According to Equations (10) and (11), which concern the coordinates of the center of mass in the directions of the axes y and z, the second expression of Equation (28) is written as follows:

$$\sum_{i=1}^{n} \left(m_i \left(\sum_{i=1}^{n} m_i y_i \div \sum_{i=1}^{n} m_i \right)^2 + m_i \left(\sum_{i=1}^{n} m_i z_i \div \sum_{i=1}^{n} m_i \right)^2 \right) \tag{30}$$

As can be observed, the denominator of both fractions in Formula (30) is the sum of the mass of all the equipment, which is a constant and can be omitted from the maximization computation. On the other hand, since in this part, the layout of equipment in each layer is not considered, and only their locations are important to the surfaces, we can omit the first part of (30), which refers to the coordinates in the direction of the y-axis. It is thus sufficient to maximize the following value to maximize the whole expression:

$$\sum_{i=1}^{n} \left(m_i \right) \left(\sum_{i=1}^{n} m_i z_i \right)^2 \tag{31}$$

Since the total mass of all equipment is a fixed value, the only part that will need to be maximized is as follows:

$$\left(\sum_{i=1}^{n} m_i z_i \right)^2 \tag{32}$$

Here, there are two expressions (29) and (31). One should take the maximum possible value, and the other should be minimized:

$$Min \sum_{i=1}^{n} (m_i z_i^2) \ and \ Max (\sum_{i=1}^{n} m_i z_i)^2 \tag{33}$$

As is known, maximizing the expression $(\sum_{i=1}^{n} m_i z_i)^2$ is equivalent to maximizing $\sum_{i=1}^{n} m_i z_i$, but in the first expression, the minimization of $\sum_{i=1}^{n} m_i z_i^2$ is considered. Therefore, as the second power in the expression of minimization indicates, this part is of higher priority than the part regarding maximization, and in principle, the heavier the mass of the equipment at lower layers, the lower the product of mass in their height will be, and so the total moment of inertia in the direction of the x-axis (I_{xx}) will assume the lowest possible value.

On the other hand, according to Equation (11) and considering that the moment of inertia is calculated according to the coordinates of the center of gravity, it can be concluded that the closer the equipment is to the center of gravity of the satellite, the lower the moment of inertia in the direction of the x-axis ((I_{xx}) and y (I_{yy})) will be. Therefore, it makes sense to place more equipment in the middle layers (layers L_2 and L_3) so as to minimize the moment of inertia. According to the above explanations, we conclude that, in order to optimize the allocation of equipment at different levels of the satellite, it is best to place heavier equipment at lower layers (L_3 and L_4 layers) and to group more items in the middle layers (layers L_2 and L_3). Now, to satisfy the abovementioned cases, the following heuristic method is presented.

Heuristic Method to Allocate Equipment to Different Layers

Step 1: Arrange all the equipment at the same time based on height (h) and mass (m). Since all equipment is symmetrical and the mass distribution is assumed to be the same, the center of mass of each item of equipment is located in the middle, and its height is equal to half the height of the equipment ($\frac{h}{2}$). Therefore, pieces of equipment that have a lower height are prioritized for placement in the initial and final layer (layers L_1 and L_4). Conversely, if the height of the equipment is great, placing it in one of the middle layers (layers L_2 and L_3) will reduce the distance between it and the center of gravity of the satellite, thus decreasing the moment of inertia along the x-axis (I_{xx}) and y-axis (I_{yy}). Step 2: The space available on each layer is displayed by S_j, and variable S_j' is refers to the amount of layer j occupied by the equipment. If more than 70% of the area on each layer ($0.7 \times S_j$) is occupied by equipment, localization here will be practically impossible, as it will not be possible to place the equipment without overlapping. Moreover, since the area occupied by the equipment at levels L_2 and L_3 must be at least two times the area occupied by the equipment on layers L_1 and L_4, the following ratio forms between the surface areas:

$$2 \times (S_1' + S_4') \leq S_2' + S_3' \leq 1.4 \times (\frac{1}{S' - 1.4}) \times (S_1' + S_4') \tag{34}$$

where

$$S' = \sum_{j=1}^{4} S_j' \tag{35}$$

Step 3: After the equipment is arranged according to height and mass, to minimize the moments of inertia, pieces of equipment with lower heights should be placed on layers L_1 and L_4, and to satisfy Equation (22), the equipment with the lowest height and mass values will be selected and placed on a list called A. This separation is necessary so that this equipment can be assigned to the two layers L_1 and L_4, and the rest of the equipment will be automatically assigned to layers L_2 and L_3. An approximate value means that one can start from Equation (36) to satisfy Equation (34) and return to this step to add the next piece of equipment to List A if the final assignment of Equation (34) is not met.

$$(S_1' + S_4') \geq S' - 1.4 \tag{36}$$

where S' is the total area available for the equipment in the four layers. There are only a few cases in which Equations (34) and (36) are met. For example, if there are a total of 60 pieces of equipment, and it is determined by the initial division that only in cases where $n_1 + n_4 = 19$, 20, 21 or 22 does the ratio of Equation (22) remain eligible, then the following steps will be performed for the feasible cases.

Step 4: The selected equipment (List A) that makes up $n_1 + n_4$ is sorted by mass from low to high.

Step 5: To allocate equipment to layer L_1, start from the lowest height and the lowest amount of mass and work up until the following ratio of the total area of the selected equipment becomes feasible,

$$0.4 \, (S'_1 + S'_4) \leq S'_1 \leq 0.6 \, (S'_1 + S'_4) \tag{37}$$

This division is intended to maintain the balance of equipment between the first and fourth layers. Therefore, with the first choice that satisfies this ratio, the allocation of equipment to the first level is completed, and the values of n_1 and S'_1 are determined.

Step 6: The rest of the equipment is assigned to layer L_4, and the values of n_4 and S'_4 are determined.

Step 7: The rest of the equipment (remaining about $\frac{2}{3}$), which makes up $n_2 + n_3$, should be assigned to the two layers L_2 and L_3. Accordingly, the equipment is ordered by height and then mass, from the greatest to the lowest value;

Step 8: Since, according to the previous description, the equipment must occupy less than 70% of the area of each layer, the remaining equipment will be assigned to the two layers L_2 and L_3 in such a way that the components are again arranged from the lowest to the highest value, and assigned to layer L_2 until the following ratios are met, after which the remaining equipment is assigned to layer L_3.

$$S'_2 \leq 0.7 S_2 \tag{38}$$

$$S'_3 \leq 0.7 S_3 \tag{39}$$

$$0.9 S'_3 \leq S'_2 \leq 1.1 S'_3 \tag{40}$$

According to the previously mentioned constraints, such as Equation (33), and the need for a balanced distribution of equipment between layers, following the completion of Equations (38) and (39), Equation (40) must also be performed with relation to these two layers. Thus, all equipment is assigned to all layers, with heavier equipment placed on layers L_3 and L_4, and equipment with the lowest height on layers L_1 and L_4.

Step 9: Upon completion of equipment allocation, the information obtained should be placed in the GAMS software (v.24.1.3), following which the problem can be considered initially solved, and the optimal local solution will be generated and stored. The assigning of an initial solution means that uncertainty is not considered at this point, and the designing of a detailed layout with equipment on each floor is done in the next section. By employing the presented heuristic method, all the cases that may produce a near-optimal solution are considered, and the best arrangements are used as inputs in the next stage.

2.1.2. Layout of Equipment in Each Layer

Since the satellite's components are cuboid or cylindrical, they can be viewed in two dimensions as a rectangle or a circle. To satisfy the non-overlap constraint between equipment, the location of each piece of equipment must be compared with the locations of others, and no overlap between any components will be allowed. Here, two types of survey are required: one for circular cross-sectioned equipment and one for rectangular cross-sectioned equipment.

Satisfying the non-overlap constraint for equipment with a circular cross-section is easily achievable. To do this, it is sufficient to rewrite constraint number 2, as follows.

$$(r_i + r_j)^2 \leq (x_i - x_j)^2 + (y_i - y_j)^2 \tag{41}$$

As indicated by the inequality in (41), the Euclidean distance between the centers of both circles must be greater than or equal to the sum of the radii of the two circles.

For equipment with a rectangular cross-section, satisfying the non-overlap constraint is not as simple as it is with circular equipment. In this article, we use flexible and robust programming to solve this problem. It is assumed that each rectangle can be represented by a circle whose center is positioned in the same location as the center of the rectangle, and after this, no overlap between these circles is allowed.

Now, if the abovementioned circle is considered as a circumscribed rectangular circle, satisfying the non-overlap constraint will increase the distance between the pieces of equipment more than is necessary, and as a result, the objective function will degrade. If the circle is designed to be so small that it becomes inscribed on the rectangle, then even though the objective function is greatly reduced and the components are positioned at shorter distances from each other, we will see the overlap of parts of the rectangular components, and the non-overlap constraint will be violated.

Therefore, it is essential to find virtual circles that, while satisfying the non-overlap constraint, can present optimal and minimal values of the objective function. To achieve the best hypothetical circle, a novel approach is applied. As shown in Figure 3, the value of sM is considered as a parameter to determine the optimal radius of the hypothetical circle. Other parameters (i.e., r, x and y) have also been defined previously.

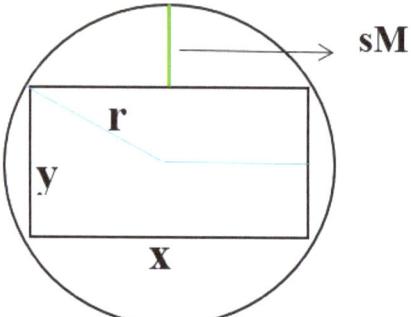

Figure 3. Defining the circle circumscribed for equipment with a rectangular cross-section in terms of sM, dimensions of the rectangle (x, y) and the radius of the circle (r).

If the hypothetical circle displayed the largest radius and we converted the circumscribed circle to a rectangle, the value of sM could be calculated as follows

$$sM_i = r(i) - \frac{\min(x(i).y(i))}{2} \tag{42}$$

where x and y are the length and width of the rectangle, respectively, and r is the radius of its hypothetical circumscribed circle.

Conversely, if the radius of the hypothetical circle is the smallest, and is set out as a circle inscribed in the rectangle, the value of sM will tend to be zero. To ensure a flexible constraint and a robust concept, fuzzy numbers are an appropriate option, because the nature of fuzzy numbers closely affects flexible robust programming [49].

2.2. Robust Flexible Programming Model (RFPM)

To cope with the difficulties associated with overlapping issues for rectangle shapes, a robust flexible programming model is proposed.

Based on the RFPM introduced by [49], fuzzy numbers are represented as triangular numbers in this paper.

To solve the problem using flexible programming, the model is first written as follows:

$$Min\ f(x) = I_{xx} + I_{yy} + I_{zz} \tag{43}$$

s.t.

$$fr_i \mathrel{\widetilde{\geq}} r_i \quad i \in cubic\ equipments \tag{44}$$

$$fr_i \geq r_i \quad i \in cylinder\ equipments \tag{45}$$

$$(fr_i + fr_{i+1})^2 \leq (x_i - x_{i+1})^2 + (y_i - y_{i+1})^2 \quad i \in cubic\ equipments \tag{46}$$

The sign of $\widetilde{\geq}$ represents the fuzzy version of $\geq$, and illustrates that the value of the right hand side of the constraint is smaller than or similar to that of the left hand side. The fuzzy number $\widetilde{sT}$ can be used to depict the flexible condition of the fuzzy constraint.

Therefore, the model can be rewritten as follows:

$$Min\ f(x) = I_{xx} + I_{yy} + I_{zz} \tag{47}$$

s.t.

$$fr_i \geq r_i - \widetilde{sT} \times (1 - \alpha_i) \quad i \in cubic\ equipments \tag{48}$$

$$fr_i \geq r_i \quad i \in cylinder\ equipments \tag{49}$$

$$(fr_i + fr_{i+1})^2 \leq (x_i - x_{i+1})^2 + (y_i - y_{i+1})^2 \quad i \in cubic\ equipments \tag{50}$$

The α parameter indicates a minimum level of satisfaction with the flexible constraint. Suppose that the fuzzy number $\widetilde{sT}$ is a triangular fuzzy number represented by three numbers ($\widetilde{sT} = (sP.sM.sO)$), which can be elucidated by the method demonstrated in Yager (1981) as follows:

$$\widetilde{sT} = \left(sM + \frac{(sO - sM) - (sM - sP)}{3} \right) \tag{51}$$

Based on constraint 2, the flexible programming model can be rewritten in the non-fuzzy mode as follows:

$$Min\ f(x) = I_{xx} + I_{yy} + I_{zz} \tag{52}$$

s.t.

$$fr_i \geq r_i - sM_i + \left(\frac{(sO - sM) - (sM - sP)}{3} \right) \times (1 - \alpha_i) \quad i \in cubic\ equipments \tag{53}$$

$$fr_i \geq r_i \quad i \in cylinder\ equipments \tag{54}$$

$$(fr_i + fr_{i+1})^2 \leq (x_i - x_{i+1})^2 + (y_i - y_{i+1})^2 \quad i \in cubic\ equipments \tag{55}$$

The expression $\left(\frac{(sO-sM)-(sM-sP)}{3} \right) \times (1 - \alpha_i)$ indicates the permissible amount of violation of the flexible constraint. It should be noted that the use of this flexible fuzzy programming method allows other fuzzy numbers to be used in the fuzzy constraint, and other fuzzy ranking methods can also be used to de-fuzzy the uncertain parameters present in the soft constraints.

Also, using α-cuts to determine the degree of violation in soft constraints can lead us to different fuzzy solutions that help decision-makers in comparing different outputs and achieving better solutions in sensitivity analysis.

In the fuzzy flexible planning model, the decision of whether to allocate the lowest level of satisfaction to the flexible constraints ($0 \leq \alpha \leq 1$) must be made by the decision-maker. In other words, this method should be reactive, and the decision-maker will achieve different results by manually changing the minimum level of satisfaction and extracting the best solutions for the fuzzy parameters.

The desirability of choices made at each stage is determined by the output of the model. The drawback of this method is that there is no guarantee of achieving the optimal level of satisfaction. For this purpose, the RFPM is represented as follows.

$$Min\ f(x) = I_{xx} + I_{yy} + I_{zz} + \gamma \times \left[sM_i + \left(\frac{(sO - sM) - (sM - sP)}{3} \right) \right] \times (1 - \alpha) \quad (56)$$

s.t.

$$fr_i \geq r_i - \left(sM_i + \left(\frac{(sO - sM) - (sM - sP)}{3} \right) \right) \times (1 - \alpha_i)\ \ i \in cubic\ equipments \quad (57)$$

$$fr_i \geq r_i \qquad i \in cylinder\ equipments \quad (58)$$

$$(fr_i + fr_{i+1})^2 \leq (x_i - x_{i+1})^2 + (y_i - y_{i+1})^2 \quad i \in cubic\ equipments \quad (59)$$

$$0 \leq \alpha \leq 1.\ I_{xx}, I_{yy}, I_{zz}, fr \geq 0 \quad (60)$$

In this model, in addition to minimizing moments of inertia, a new section has been added to the objective function, which depicts the total cost of the penalty for possible non-compliance with the flexible constraints. In essence, this phase controls the feasibility and robustness of flexible constraints.

In other words, this expression shows the difference between the minimum and maximum possible values for the flexible constraint, as follows:

$$\left(sM_i + \left(\frac{(sO-sM)-(sM-sP)}{3} \right) \right) \times (1 - \alpha_i)$$
$$= r_i - \left[r_i - \left(sM_i + \left(\frac{(sO-sM)-(sM-sP)}{3} \right) \right) \times (1 - \alpha_i) \right] \quad (61)$$
$$i \in cubic\ equipments$$

In this model, the penalty cost for each unit of violation of the soft constraint is also considered, as is represented by the parameter γ. In the RFPM, unlike the initial flexible programming model, the minimum level of satisfaction (α) is no longer a parameter and is determined by the model as a variable.

Therefore, when solving the model at once, the optimal value of this variable can be achieved, and there is no need to repeat the experiments. Because the objective function of the model seeks a balance between the robustness cost (the last expression of the objective function) and the overall performance of the system, including other expressions of the objective function (such as moments of inertia), the proposed model is called a realistic RFPM.

It should be noted that the parameter γ is an important value, and its value is determined based on the application and the subject under discussion. Here, for example, for cuboid components that need to be placed at a greater distance from other equipment, the value of the penalty parameter can be set as much greater; in this case, the variable α will tend to increase to near 1, and therefore the soft constraint for this piece of equipment will become similar to those of cylindrical components.

It should be noted that the use of the penalty parameter in the objective function helps to optimize the variable of minimum satisfaction level (α), and prevents the direct involvement of decision-makers in quantifying this variable.

3. Results and Discussion

In this section, the efficiency of the proposed model is investigated by comparing its performance with those of previous models in a review of the literature.

Since some of the constraints of the model are flexible, new parameters are introduced that are valued for their possible ability to exceed the aforementioned constraints. For this purpose, the maximum permissible flexibility for soft constraints (sT) is considered.

To analyze the sensitivity of a model based on flexible robust planning, we must first compare it with a simple flexible model with certain levels of satisfaction (for example, $\alpha = 0.0$, 0.1, 0.2, 0.3). The numerical examples used in [1,12,15] were used for this purpose. These three numerical examples have served as the foundation for numerous papers; therefore, the results shown in the eleven articles that used these numerical examples are compared to the results of the suggested model. The multi-layer satellites investigated in the following case studies have a similar structure and layout to those of the geostationary communications satellites of the INTELSAT III series that were designed, assembled, and finally launched successfully several times between 1968 and 1970. The use of new optimization methods and algorithms can reduce the time required for satellite layout design and the related steps, and can help in improving the mass properties as well as the stability and controllability parameters of real satellite projects.

- Case Study 1: Investigating the work of [12]

In this example, there are 53 pieces of equipment, of which 24 are cuboids and 29 are cylindrical. In this example, the satellite equipment is arranged across two levels and four layers. As shown in Figure 2, the parameters of the satellite body are as follows: the radius of the circular cross-section of the satellite surface is 500 mm; the radius of the middle cylinder in the satellite connecting the surfaces is 100 mm; the H_1, H_2 and H_t parameters are 300 mm, 830 mm and 1150 mm, respectively, and the diameters of the first and second levels are 20 mm each. The empty satellite consists of four plates (two middle levels and two floor and top levels of the satellite), and the satellite shell and its middle cylinder weigh 776.53 kg. To perform more accurate calculations, it was assumed that the density of materials used in the body of this satellite was 3.006 g/cm^3 (a combination of aluminum and titanium alloys), and the thickness of the satellite's shell was 41.25 mm. Also, the two middle plates on which components are placed were considered to be hollow cylinders with inner and outer diameters of 100 and 500 mm, respectively, and the upper and lower plates were considered as complete cylinders with 100 mm diameters. According to these hypotheses, it was simple to calculate the weights of each component in the satellite, and to determine the satellite's moment of inertia (as $I_{x0} = I_{y0} = 185.24$ and $I_{z0} = 155.2$ kg.m^2). Since the moment of inertia is higher with an empty satellite than when the components are added, it is expected that the values for the moment of inertia in each of the principal directions of the coordinate axes will be greater than the values calculated for an empty satellite compartment. Also, the coordinates of the center of gravity of the empty satellite were calculated as $C_0 = (0, 0, 595)$.

This case was first introduced by [12,16], after which [25,28] also used the data of this numerical example, and compared their results with each other. Ref. [16] similarly utilized comparable data, but the coordinates of their resulting layout were not given for comparison with other studies. With the assumptions mentioned above and according to the coordinates of the equipment after placement in the mentioned articles, the moments of inertia were recalculated and the results were compared, which can be seen in Table 2.

Table 2. Comparison of moments of inertia of articles with similar data.

References	Moment of Inertia			
	I_{xx} (kg.m²)	I_{yy} (kg.m²)	I_{zz} (kg.m²)	f (kg.m²)
[12]	261	268.5	225.8	755.3
[16]	268.4	271.1	232.7	772.2
[25]—Ex. 2	264.4	261.5	222.2	748.1
[28]	270	265.7	231.9	767.7

As illustrated in Table 2, the best solution in all these articles was given by [25], wherein the achieved objective function was less than the others. Therefore, in this paper, we have used the output in this paper to determine the θ_i of cuboid equipment.

Then, using the heuristic method provided in Section 2.1.1, all conceivable modes of allocation of equipment to different layers with these data were investigated, and 25 viable models of equipment allocation were determined. Here, each of these models were implemented using the RFPM described in Section 2.1.2 and GAMS software, and the results have been compared to those of previous works that utilized these data (Table 3).

Table 3. Moments of inertia for feasible states in case study 1.

No.	I_{xx} (kg.m²)	I_{yy} (kg.m²)	I_{zz} (kg.m²)	f (kg.m²)	No.	I_{xx} (kg.m²)	I_{yy} (kg.m²)	I_{zz} (kg.m²)	f (kg.m²)
1	256.3	254.5	220.1	730.8	14	255	256.4	220.3	731.8
2	257.6	257.2	232.9	747.6	15	254.2	257.6	220.4	732.2
3	252.9	254.1	224.5	731.5	16	256.2	255.1	219.3	730.6
4	255.5	257.9	224.1	737.5	17	256.3	255.7	219.7	731.7
5	254.7	257.9	226.9	739.6	18	257.3	256.3	220.9	734.5
6	253.9	256.5	224.2	734.6	19	256.5	258.7	222.1	737.4
7	254.5	254.9	220.9	730.3	20	256.4	257.4	224.7	738.5
8	255.7	253.7	220.3	729.6	21	256.9	257.6	220.3	734.8
9	255.1	253.8	219.2	728.1	22	256.1	257.8	219.1	733
10	255.2	255.9	221.2	732.3	23	259.6	261.1	225.4	746.2
11	256.5	259.7	226.2	742.4	24	259.5	256.2	219.6	735.3
12	260.8	255.1	227.6	743.5	25	261	262.5	226.9	750.4
13	255.3	255.9	220.4	731.6					

As can be seen from the table, the minimum moment of inertia is associated with possible state number 9, in which the total moment of inertia in the main directions of the coordinate axes is equal to 728.1 kg.m², and on the other hand, in 24 of the 25 possible states, the total moment of inertia is slightly better than that given by [25]. Figures 4 and 5 and Table 4 depict the outputs of the model for a case wherein the sum of the moment of inertia is at its lowest possible value (layout of equipment on different layers of the satellite) and the coordinates of the equipment in this optimal state, respectively. In Figure 4, a total number of 29 cylindrical and 24 cubic components are finally placed in optimal locations on the four layers (i.e., L_1, L_2, L_3, L_4) or two middle plates of a satellite with a general cylindrical configuration. Figure 5 also shows the numbers and locations of cylindrical and cubic parts allocated to the four layers of the satellite based on the optimal layout.

To compare the best solutions obtained (Table 3) with a flexible model in the flexible state, we have run the model in all possible modes and compared the objective functions with each other. The results can be seen in Figure 6.

As demonstrated in Figure 6, in cases where the minimum level of satisfaction required to exceed the flexible constraints (α) is greater than 0.4, the models will not be responsive in the flexible state, because, if this parameter tends to 1, the constraint loses its flexibility and the rectangular radius of the cuboid equipment becomes equivalent to the radius of its circumference, and the limit of no overlap between the pieces of equipment will not be met.

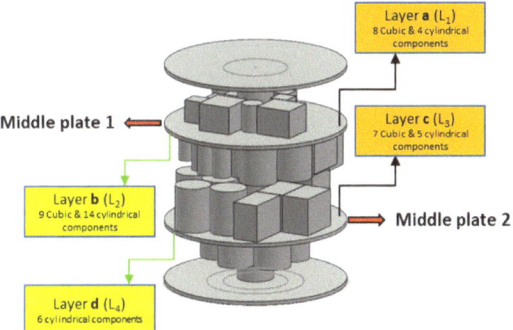

Figure 4. Layout of equipment (i.e., placement of a total of 29 cylindrical and 24 cubic components with different sizes and masses) on different layers (i.e., L_1, L_2, L_3, L_4) of the satellite in the optimal state.

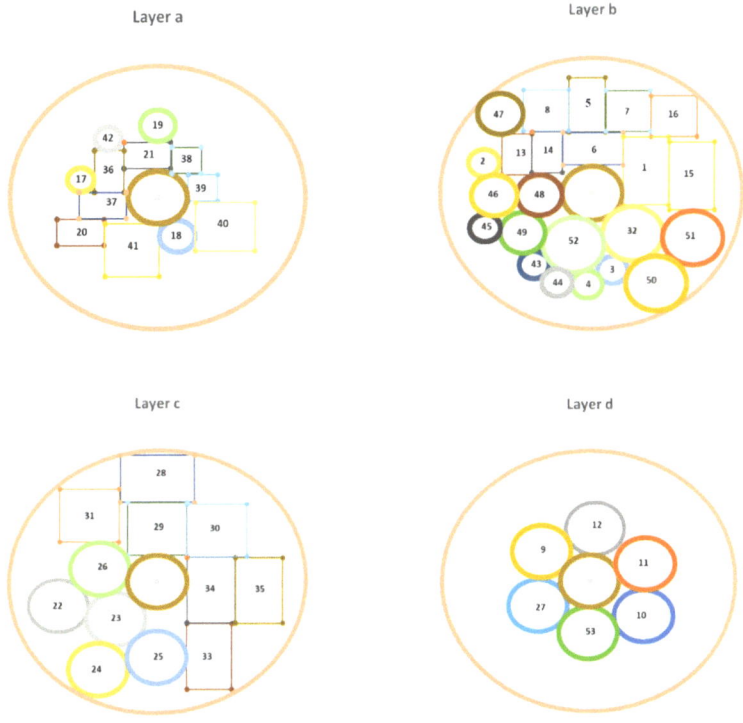

Figure 5. Top view of the optimal allocation and layout of equipment on different layers (layer (**a**) (L_1), layer (**b**) (L_2), layer (**c**) (L_3) and layer (**d**) (L_4)) of the cylindrical satellite.

Table 4. Optimal dimensions and coordinates of equipment in case study no. 1.

No	Dimensions (mm)			Mass (kg)	Optimal Coordinates		Θi (rad)	Layer
	ai/ri	bi	hi	mi	xi (mm)	yi (mm)		
1	150	250	200	22.50	329.47	64.86	$\pi/2$	L_2
2	150	250	200	22.50	177.47	82.86	$\pi/2$	L_2
3	150	250	200	22.50	174.13	−285.90	$\pi/2$	L_3
4	160	250	200	24.00	180.21	−33.62	$\pi/2$	L_3
5	160	250	200	24.00	341.89	−35.46	$\pi/2$	L_3
6	250	180	200	27.00	0.07	391.00		L_3
7	200	200	250	30.00	−0.30	200.34		L_3
8	200	200	250	30.00	200.37	193.88		L_3
9	200	200	250	30.00	−229.55	251.01		L_3
10	150	150	250	16.88	118.90	302.23	$\pi/2$	L_2
11	150	150	250	16.88	−153.95	305.58	$\pi/2$	L_2
12	150	150	250	16.88	270.27	283.38	$\pi/2$	L_2
13	100	150	200	9.00	−250.46	143.29	$\pi/2$	L_2
14	100	150	200	9.00	−149.32	150.71	$\pi/2$	L_2
15	100	100	150	4.50	98.32	140.94		L_1
16	100	100	150	4.50	153.65	36.60		L_1
17	200	185	150	16.65	228.81	−111.59		L_1
18	185	200	150	16.65	−86.89	−200.66	$\pi/2$	L_1
19	200	120	200	14.40	2.14	164.48		L_2
20	120	120	200	14.40	−18.22	325.14	$\pi/2$	L_2
21	160	100	120	1.92	−261.47	−133.58		L_1
22	160	100	120	1.92	−35.20	159.98		L_1
23	100	160	120	1.92	−165.12	99.19	$\pi/2$	L_1
24	160	160	120	1.92	−186.27	−30.91		L_1
25	100		240	26.62	−333.30	−94.41		L_3
26	100		240	26.62	−139.40	−143.42		L_3
27	100		240	26.62	−200.18	−334.88		L_3

No	Dimensions (mm)		Mass (kg)	Optimal Coordinates		Layer
	ri	hi	mi	xi (mm)	yi (mm)	
28	100	240	26.62	−1.58	−288.80	L_3
29	100	240	26.62	−193.90	49.01	L_3
30	100	180	16.97	−175.93	−95.12	L_4
31	100	180	16.97	189.11	65.10	L_4
32	100	180	16.97	19.82	199.02	L_4
33	100	180	16.97	−164.75	113.40	L_4
34	100	180	16.97	183.52	−134.83	L_4
35	100	200	18.85	211.87	−332.71	L_2
36	100	200	18.85	333.30	−164.84	L_2
37	100	200	18.85	−61.62	−190.27	L_2
38	100	200	18.85	133.97	−148.50	L_2
39	75	200	10.60	−324.88	−7.36	L_2
40	75	200	10.60	−304.87	293.12	L_2
41	75	200	10.60	−174.88	−6.50	L_2
42	75	200	10.60	−230.85	−145.67	L_2
43	50	200	4.71	−359.25	112.82	L_2
44	50	200	4.71	67.92	−283.18	L_2
45	50	200	4.71	−16.60	−336.62	L_2
46	50	200	4.71	−191.98	−264.47	L_2
47	50	200	4.71	−116.38	−329.92	L_2
48	50	200	4.71	−354.70	−128.75	L_1
49	60	150	5.09	67.08	−148.29	L_1
50	60	150	5.09	0.03	273.81	L_1
51	45	160	3.05	−168.36	223.99	L_1
52	45	160	3.05	−261.07	68.28	L_1
53	100	180	16.97	−5.59	−199.92	L_4

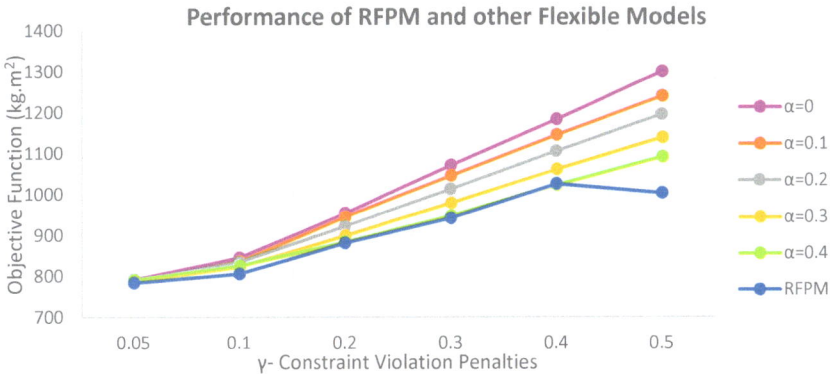

Figure 6. Comparison of the objective function of the RFPM with the flexible models.

It is also clear that when increasing the penalty coefficient for violating the flexible constraints (α) in the objective function, the values of the objective function will increase. As a result, the higher the coefficient, the faster the minimum level of satisfaction (α) will increase in a flexible model with a lower α. The reason for this is that, with a decreasing level of satisfaction, the value of $(1 - \alpha)$ will increase, and the product of the penalty for violating the soft limits by an amount of $(1 - \alpha)$ in the objective function will increase more sharply.

In the RFPM, the model provides a better solution for all cases; however, when $\gamma = 0.5$, this difference will be more pronounced than in other flexible cases, as the penalty coefficients will be increased and the model will attempt to reduce the value of the objective function, causing the minimum value of the satisfaction level (α) to increase. Comparing the values of the variables of the minimum satisfaction level (α) when $\gamma = 0.05$ and $\gamma = 0.5$, it is obvious that the satisfaction level at $\gamma = 0.5$ will have a higher value, which, as previously stated, is due to the model's goal of reducing the objective function, but this can prevent the flexibility of soft constraints increasing, and will increase the value of the moment of inertia by increasing the distances between pieces of equipment.

Therefore, moments of inertia must also be compared to infer the best penalty coefficient.

The total of moments of inertia in the principal directions of the coordinate axes has also been examined using the aforementioned models to determine with which coefficient the model yields the most accurate response. The outcomes are depicted in Figure 7.

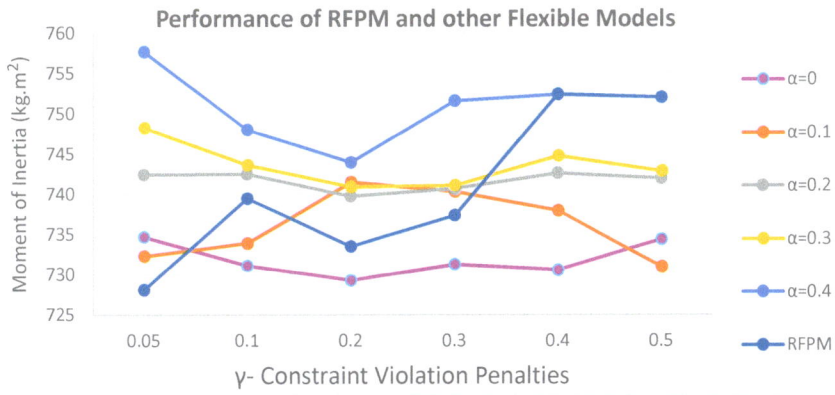

Figure 7. Comparison of the sum of moments of inertia of RFPM produced with flexible models.

As depicted in Figure 7, the greater the minimal satisfaction level (α) in flexible models, the greater the amount of the estimated radius of cuboid equipment that will become a circumscribed circle. This model tends to place pieces of equipment further apart from one another, hence increasing the total moments of inertia. An intriguing phenomenon that arises is the distinction between the modifications achieved in the trends under RFPM and flexible models in return for increasing the penalty coefficient for violating soft constraints. This indicates that when increasing the penalty coefficient, the RFPM will produce a greater sum of moments of inertia output. Consequently, the optimal instance for this model is $\gamma = 0.05$.

As this coefficient increases, to avoid increasing the objective function of the model, it tries to increase the value of the minimum satisfaction level (α), but the RFPM prevents this from occurring, such that the soft constraints are met and the value is not excessively high, causing the objective function to be greater than under flexible states. As a result, the best case for the RFPM is when the value of the penalty coefficient is $\gamma = 0.05$. In cases when the cost factor is below this value, the model loses efficiency because the penalty for violating the soft constraints on the objective function is drastically reduced. The model's minimum satisfaction level (α) tends towards zero, and the flexible constraints will be in their softest state, which increases the probability of equipment overlapping.

Now that it has been determined that the RFPM is more capable than other flexible models, we will compare this model to the models proposed in prior articles. Here, four articles that used this example in their case studies are analyzed, and the data from each article are used as input for the suggested robust model based on pre-existing equipment positions on different satellite layers. In addition, the model has been applied to these data. The outcomes are depicted in Figure 8.

Figure 8. Comparison of the sum of moments of inertia of RFPM with the results of other articles [12,16,25,28].

As shown in Figure 8, the suggested RFPM has a lower total number of moments of inertia than previous articles with all scenarios of penalty coefficients for the violation of soft constraints. Also, the proposed RFPM shows the lowest values of the sum of moments of inertia, at $\gamma = 0.05$.

There is a 1.75 percent improvement when comparing the moments of inertia achieved by [25] (741.6 kg.m^2) and the suggested RFPM (728 kg.m^2). This implies that if an identical force is required to spin these two satellites, at least 13 kg of mass could be conserved. This improvement will be vital for satellite design specialists seeking to increase the functionality of their products, where every kilogram saved could be essential to a successful mission.

As can be seen, as the penalty coefficient increases, the values of moments of inertia tend to increase due to the objective function seeking to reduce the penalty values, resulting in less flexibility in soft constraints, as a result of which the pieces of equipment are placed far apart from one another, thereby increasing the total moments of inertia.

- Case Study 2: Investigating the work of [1]

In this example, there are 60 pieces of equipment, of which 24 are cuboids and 36 are cylindrical. In this example, the satellite equipment is arranged across two levels and four layers. The parameters of the satellite body are as follows: the radius of the circular cross-section of the satellite surfaces is 500 mm; the radius of the middle cylinder of the satellite connecting the surfaces is 100 mm; the H_1, H_2 and H_t parameters are 300 mm, 830 mm and 1150 mm, respectively, and the diameters of the first and second levels are 20 mm each.

The empty satellite consists of four plates (two middle levels and two floor and top levels of the satellite), a satellite shell and the middle cylinder, the combined mass of which is 576.53 kg. To perform more accurate calculations, it was assumed that the density of materials used in the body of this satellite was 3.006 g/cm^3 (a combination of aluminum and titanium alloys) and the thickness of the satellite's shell was 24.5 mm.

Also, the two middle plates on which the components are placed were assumed to be hollow cylinders with inner and outer diameters of 100 and 500 mm, respectively, and the upper and lower plates were assumed to be complete cylinders with 100 mm diameters. Using these hypotheses, the weights of each part of the empty satellite were calculated, and the moment of inertia of the empty satellite was determined to be $I_{x0} = I_{y0} = 133.24$ and $I_{z0} = 98.4$ kg.m^2.

Since the moment of inertia is higher for an empty satellite than when the components are added, it is expected that the values obtained regarding the moment of inertia in each of the principal directions of the coordinate axes are greater than these values calculated for an empty satellite. Also, the coordinates of the center of gravity of the empty satellite were calculated as $C_0 = (0, 0, 595)$.

Since the case was first introduced by [1], five articles, including those by [17,20,30, 36,37] also used the data from this example, and compared their results with each other. Ref. [27] also utilized these numerical data, but the output localizations of the equipment were not organized diagonally, therefore the findings were not comparable. According to the assumptions mentioned above and the coordinates of the equipment placements in the mentioned articles, the moments of inertia have been recalculated and the results compared, as can be seen in Table 5.

Table 5. Comparison of moments of inertia in articles with similar data.

References	Moment of Inertia			
	I_{xx} (kg.m^2)	I_{yy} (kg.m^2)	I_{zz} (kg.m^2)	f (kg.m^2)
[1]	228.7	232.9	185.1	646.7
[17]	227.8	226	178.2	632
[20]—Ex. 2	228.3	225.8	171.4	625.5
[30]	223.5	220.7	168.4	612.6
[36]	218.2	215.6	166.2	600
[37]—Ex. 3	224.1	228.1	179.7	631.9

As depicted in Table 5, the best solution in these articles was given by [36], where the objective function was less than in other articles. Therefore, in this paper, we have used the output to determine the value of θ_i for cuboid equipment. As explained in case study no. 1, here, according to the heuristic method presented in Section 2.1.1, all possible models of equipment allocation to different layers with these data have been examined, and 25 feasible models have been obtained.

Here, each of these feasible models was implemented using the RFPM presented in Section 2.1.2 and GAMS software, and the results have been compared with those from other papers that also used this numerical example (Table 6).

Table 6. Moments of inertia for feasible states described in case study 2.

No.	I_{xx} (kg.m^2)	I_{yy} (kg.m^2)	I_{zz} (kg.m^2)	f (kg.m^2)	No.	I_{xx} (kg.m^2)	I_{yy} (kg.m^2)	I_{zz} (kg.m^2)	f (kg.m^2)
1	204.8	208.9	164. 8	578.5	14	207.9	209.3	171.2	588.5
2	206.8	208.3	164.7	579.8	15	208.3	210.9	169.6	588.8
3	207.7	206.2	166.9	580.8	16	211.3	208.3	169.7	589.3
4	210.8	199.9	170.2	580.9	17	209.1	209.9	172.8	591.8
5	206.6	208.8	167.2	582.4	18	209	212.6	170.6	592.2
6	210.9	207.1	165.8	583.7	19	211.6	210.1	171.2	592.9
7	207.9	207.9	168.2	584	20	209.7	211.3	173.2	594.2
8	209.8	209.2	165.1	584	21	210.8	210.1	174.1	594.9
9	209.8	209.45	166.3	585.5	22	210.9	211.4	173.1	595.5
10	208.2	207.9	169.8	586	23	211.3	211.1	175.3	597.7
11	207.9	208.2	170.8	586.9	24	211.9	208.4	177.7	598.1
12	208.8	208.7	169.6	587.1	25	212.4	211.5	176.5	600.4
13	208.4	207.1	171.5	587.1					

As can be seen in the table, the minimum value of the sum of moments of inertia in the main direction of the coordinate axes is equal to 578.5 kg/m^2, and in 24 of the feasible states, the sum of moments of inertia derived is slightly better than that given by [36]. Figure 9 and Table 7 show the output of the model for cases where the sum of the moments of inertia is as low as possible (layout of equipment on different layers of the satellite) and the coordinates of the equipment in this optimal model, respectively.

To compare the best solutions obtained (Table 6) with the flexible model in the flexible state, we ran the model in all possible modes and have compared the objective functions with each other. The results can be seen in Figure 10.

As illustrated in Figure 10, in cases where the minimum level of satisfaction required for exceeding the flexible constraints (α) is greater than 0.25, the models will not be responsive in the flexible state because, as in case no. 1, if this parameter tends to 1, the constraint loses its flexibility, and the rectangular radius of the cuboid equipment becomes equivalent to the radius of the circumference, and the constraint of non-overlapping between the equipment will not be met. The only difference from case study no. 1 is that, in flexible states, the minimum level of satisfaction cannot be reached if it is greater than 0.25.

This is due to the increased quantity of equipment to be positioned, which reduces the flexibility of the non-overlap constraints by increasing the (α) variable and making the model infeasible. As shown previously, the objective function values increase as the penalty coefficient for violating the flexible constraints (γ) in the objective function increases. In reality, in flexible models with a smaller (α) variable, increasing the value of (γ) will increase the objective function further. In the RFPM, the model behaves similarly to that in the first case study, and at $\gamma = 0.5$, the difference in the output of the objective function between the robust and flexible models becomes more obvious.

Comparing the values of the variables of the minimum satisfaction level (α) for $\gamma = 0.05$ and $\gamma = 0.5$, we see that greater values are obtained for the variable at $\gamma = 0.5$, but this leads to an increase in moments of inertia. This implies substantially lower values for (α) variables than those seen in case study no. 1 due to the greater quantity of equipment. It indicates that soft constraints must be set to their softest mode to prevent components from overlapping.

Table 7. Optimal dimensions and coordinates of equipment in case study no. 2.

No.	ri	hi	mi	xi (mm)	yi (mm)	Layer
1	100	150	23.56	-157.9	323	L_3
2	100	160	23.56	-162.3	119.6	L_3
3	100	160	23.56	-334	221	L_3
4	100	200	23.56	-184.4	-86.5	L_3
5	100	200	23.56	-356	19.6	L_3
6	100	250	23.56	-342.8	-206	L_3
7	100	120	23.56	-13.6	-200.3	L_4
8	100	120	23.56	175.1	-123.6	L_4
9	100	200	18.85	-323	149.9	L_2
10	100	150	18.85	182.6	81.6	L_4
11	100	150	18.85	20.6	198.9	L_4
12	100	160	15.08	-123.2	157.6	L_2
13	100	160	15.08	183.1	80.4	L_2
14	100	150	15.08	-162	117.3	L_4
15	75	160	8.48	-171.1	325.9	L_2
16	75	200	8.48	48.4	192	L_2
17	75	250	8.48	318.7	206.3	L_2
18	75	150	8.48	167.3	51.4	L_1
19	75	120	7.95	-149.1	91.6	L_1
20	75	150	7.95	65.6	162.2	L_1
21	75	200	7.95	357	54.7	L_2
22	75	250	7.95	391.5	-93.1	L_2
23	75	250	7.95	-7.2	424.2	L_2
24	75	250	7.95	242	-84.4	L_2
25	60	150	5.09	0.0	-268.1	L_1
26	60	150	5.09	-154	-43.3	L_1
27	60	150	5.09	41.1	-154.6	L_1
28	60	150	5.09	137.9	-80.9	L_1
29	60	150	5.09	-79.9	-138.6	L_1
30	60	150	5.09	-65.9	203.4	L_1

No.	ai/ri	bi	hi	mi	xi (mm)	yi (mm)	θi (rad)	Layer
31	60		150	5.09	152.1	-200.2		L_1
32	60		150	5.09	254.4	-51.7		L_1
33	60	150	250	5.09	214.8	350.9		L_2
34	60	150	250	5.09	-39.9	294.2		L_2
35	60	150	250	5.09	84.6	322.1		L_2
36	60	150	250	5.09	174.5	240.1		L_2
37	250	150	150	28.13	-70.6	-376.2		L_3
38	250	150	150	28.13	170.3	-22.3	π/2	L_3
39	250	150	200	28.13	277.3	229.5	π/2	L_3
40	160	120	250	28.13	138	-365.7		L_3
41	250	150	250	28.13	68.6	184.1		L_3
42	250	150	250	28.13	70.5	341.3		L_3
43	250	150	250	28.13	22.3	-223.5		L_3
44	250	150	250	28.13	274.5	-222.5		L_3
45	250	150	250	28.13	323.45	-22.2	π/2	L_3
46	200	160	150	19.20	-349.9	-48.2	π/2	L_2
47	200	160	250	19.20	-184	-47.6	π/2	L_2
48	200	160	120	19.20	-204.7	-64.5		L_4
49	160	120	250	15.36	-4.2	-181.1	π/2	L_2
50	160	120	250	8.64	-296.7	-213.4		L_2
51	160	120	250	8.64	-155.9	-232.2		L_2
52	160	120	120	8.64	347.9	-3.8	π/2	L_4
53	150	100	120	5.40	156.4	324.5	π/2	L_1
54	150	100	120	5.40	0.2	319		L_1
55	150	100	150	5.40	191.1	197.4	π/2	L_1
56	150	100	160	5.40	290.6	-220.1		L_2
57	150	100	160	5.40	138.3	-281.2		L_2
58	150	100	200	5.40	-16.4	-315.2		L_2
59	150	100	250	5.40	151.7	-388.2		L_2
60	150	100	250	5.40	114.1	-154.6	π/2	L_2

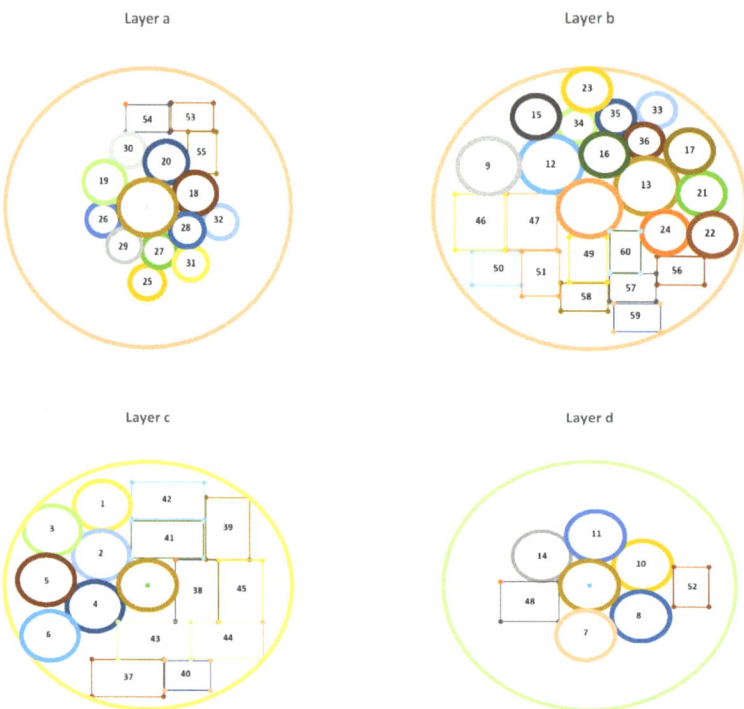

Figure 9. Top view of the optimal allocation and layout of equipment on different layers (layer (**a**) (L_1), layer (**b**) (L_2), layer (**c**) (L_3) and layer (**d**) (L_4)) of the cylindrical satellite.

Figure 10. Comparison of the objective function of the RFPM with flexible models.

Therefore, the sum of moments of inertia in the main directions of the coordinate axes has also been compared for the mentioned models, and the results can be seen in Figure 11.

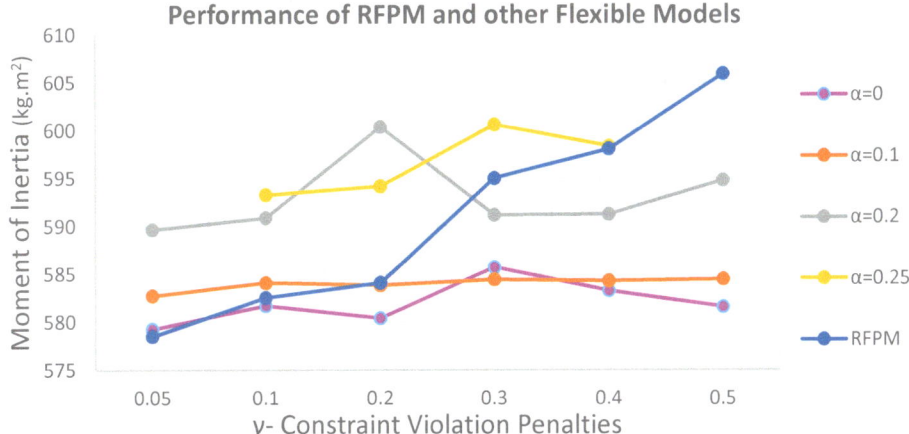

Figure 11. Comparison of the sum of moments of inertia of RFPM with those of flexible models.

As depicted in Figure 11, the behavior of the models has not changed significantly from those in case study no. 1, and it is only due to the increase in the number of equipment that the flexibility of soft constraints becomes more important; even for the flexible models where the minimum satisfaction level (α) exceeds 0.25, the model is infeasible. Similarly, when increasing the penalty factor (γ), the model in its robust form will gain more moments of inertia, due to the tendency of the model to shrink the objective function and increase the α variables, as well as the tendency of the equipment to move away from one another and raise the moments of inertia.

As a result, the best case for the RFPM is when $\gamma = 0.05$. As said before, in cases when the value of the cost factor is lower than this, the model loses its efficiency because the penalty for violating the soft constraints in the objective function is sharply reduced; the minimum level of satisfaction (α) of the model tends towards zero, and this causes the flexible constraints to enter their softest mode, increasing the likelihood of the equipment overlapping.

Now that it has been seen that the RFPM has greater capability compared to the other flexible models, we now compare this model with those proposed in similar articles. Here, five articles that used this example in their case studies have been reviewed and, according to the pre-existing equipment layouts on different satellite layers available in the articles, the data of each article have been used as input for the proposed RFPM. The results are shown in Figure 12.

As depicted in Figure 12, the sum of moments of inertia in the suggested RFPM when the penalty coefficients for the violation of soft constraints are less than 0.3 indicates a significantly better solution than in the other articles. Compared to [36], the sum of moments of inertia is increased marginally only in cases when $\gamma = 0.4$ and $\gamma = 0.5$. This confirms that the best choice for the value of the penalty coefficient is $\gamma = 0.05$, and that increasing this coefficient reduces the model's efficiency. Therefore, similar to case study no. 1, an improvement of 2.95 percent can be seen when comparing the moments of inertia between that in [36] (596.1 kg.m^2) and that achieved by the suggested RFPM (578.5 kg.m^2). This means that if an identical force is required to spin these two satellites, at least 17.6 kg of mass could be preserved.

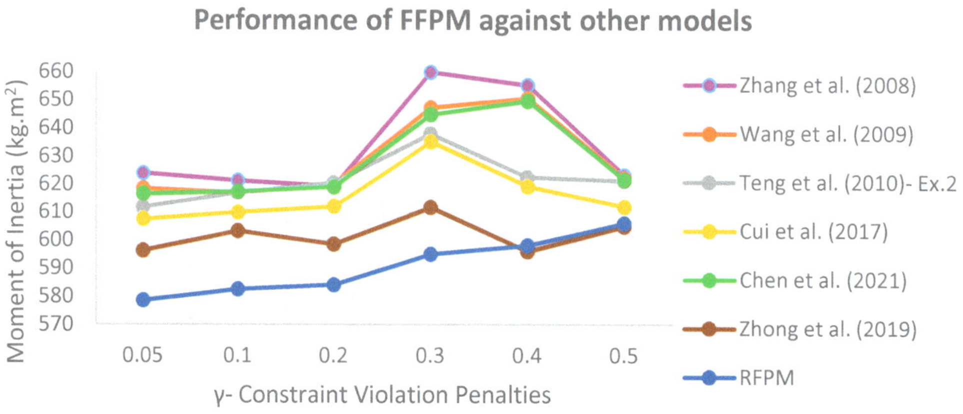

Figure 12. Comparison of the sum of moments of inertia of RFPM with the results of other articles [1,17,20,30,36,37].

- Case Study 3: investigating the work of [15]

Ref. [15] utilized the data from [57]. In this example, there are 51 pieces of equipment, of which 20 are cuboid and 31 are cylindrical. In this example, the satellite equipment is arranged across two levels and four layers. The parameters of the satellite body are as follows: the radius of the circular cross-section of the satellite surfaces is 500 mm; the radius of the middle cylinder of the satellite connecting the surfaces is 100 mm; the H_1, H_2 and H_t parameters are 500 mm, 1050 mm and 1400 mm, respectively, and the diameters of the first and second levels are 20 mm each.

The empty satellite consists of four plates (two middle levels and two floor and top levels), the satellite shell and the middle cylinder, the cumulative mass of which is 349.557 kg.

To perform more accurate calculations, it was assumed that the density of materials used in the body of this satellite was 1.766 g/cm^3 (a combination of fiberglass, Kevlar, carbon fiber, and aluminum and titanium alloys) and the thickness of the satellite shell was 20 mm. Also, the two middle plates on which equipment are placed were considered to be hollow cylinders with inner and outer diameters of 100 and 500 mm, respectively, and the upper and lower plates were considered to be complete cylinders with a 100 mm diameter. According to these hypotheses, the weight of each part of the empty chamber of the satellite was calculated, and the moment of inertia of the empty satellite was calculated, as $I_{x0} = I_{y0} = 101.556$ and $I_{z0} = 56.686$ kg.m^2.

Since the moment of inertia is higher for the empty satellite than when the equipment is added, it is expected that the values obtained for the moments of inertia in each of the principal directions of the coordinate axes will be greater than the values calculated for an empty satellite compartment. The coordinates of the center of gravity of the empty satellite were calculated as $C_0 = (0, 0, 732.96)$.

After [15], the first study to utilize these numerical data and compare their results was [25]. Ref. [13] also employed similar data, but the coordinates of their output design were not disclosed in that article to allow comparisons with other studies. According to the assumptions mentioned above and the coordinates of the placed equipment available in the mentioned articles, the moments of inertia have been recalculated and the results compared, as can be seen in Table 8.

Table 8. Comparison of moments of inertia of articles with similar data.

References	Moment of Inertia			
	I_{xx} (kg.m^2)	I_{yy} (kg.m^2)	I_{zz} (kg.m^2)	f (kg.m^2)
[15]	174.5	171.3	101	446.8
[25]—Ex. 1	163.2	162.9	93.8	420

As can be seen in Table 8, the best solution given by these two articles was produced by [25], in which the objective function was given a lower value compared to other articles. Therefore, in this paper, we have used the output to determine the θ_i value for cuboid equipment. Then, according to the heuristic method presented in Section 2.1.1, all possible models of equipment allocation to different layers using these data have been examined, and 11 feasible models have been obtained. Here, each of these models was implemented using the RFPM presented in Section 2.1.2 and GAMS software, and the results have been compared with those from other papers that used this dataset (Table 9).

Table 9. Moments of inertia for feasible states in case study 3.

No.	I_{xx} (kg.m^2)	I_{yy} (kg.m^2)	I_{zz} (kg.m^2)	f (kg.m^2)	No.	I_{xx} (kg.m^2)	I_{yy} (kg.m^2)	I_{zz} (kg.m^2)	f (kg.m^2)
1	147.7	149.5	100.7	397.9	7	149.9	150.9	96.8	397.6
2	149.2	150.7	95.7	395.6	8	148.5	149.7	98.9	397.1
3	149.4	150.7	99.8	399.9	9	149.9	150.2	97.6	397.7
4	148.5	150.4	99.6	398.5	10	149.2	150.9	98.5	398.5
5	148.6	150	101.2	399.8	11	153.6	152.1	102.7	408.4
6	149.1	149.4	100.6	399.1					

As can be seen from the table, the minimum moment of inertia correlates with the second possible state, in which the total moment of inertia in the main direction of the coordinate axes is equal to 395.6 kg.m^2, and on the other hand, in all possible states, the total moment of inertia derived is better than that achieved by [25]. Figure 13 and Table 10 show the output of the model when the value of the sum of the moments of inertia is as low as possible (layout of equipment on different layers of the satellite) and the coordinates of the equipment in this optimal state, respectively.

To compare the best solutions obtained (Table 9) with those given by the flexible model in the flexible state, we have run the model in all possible modes and compared the objective functions with each other. The results can be seen in Figure 14.

As shown in Figure 14, in cases where the minimum level of satisfaction for exceeding the flexible constraints (α) is greater than 0.3, the models will not be responsive under the flexible state because, as we saw in case studies 1 and 2, by increasing the value of (α), flexibility is lost, and the rectangular radius of the cuboid equipment becomes equivalent to the radius of the circumference. As a result, the requirement of non-overlap between the pieces of equipment will not be met.

The only difference from previous case studies is that, in flexible states, the minimum level of satisfaction becomes inapplicable if it increases from 0.3. The reason is that the equipment here occupies more space than in case study no. 1, but less compared to case study no. 2, and therefore setting $\alpha = 0.3$ also offers a feasible model. As said before, by increasing the penalty coefficient for a violation of the flexible constraints (γ) in the objective function, the objective will be increased, as the number of flexible models with a lower minimum degree of satisfaction (α) will increase dramatically as this coefficient increases.

Table 10. Optimal dimensions and coordinates of equipment in case study no. 3.

No.	Dimensions (mm)		Mass (kg)	Optimal Coordinates		Layer
	ri	hi	mi	xi (mm)	yi (mm)	
1	100	240	15.08	142.4	−140.4	L_3
2	100	240	15.08	91.8	−335.6	L_3
3	100	240	15.08	286.3	−279.3	L_3
4	100	240	15.08	329.6	−69.9	L_3
5	100	240	15.08	187.12	70.4	L_3
6	100	180	11.31	−13.4	388.6	L_2
7	100	180	11.31	184.8	329.6	L_2
8	100	180	11.31	35.2	196.9	L_2
9	100	100	11.31	−204	0.0	L_4
10	100	180	11.31	179.5	3	L_4
11	100	200	12.56	204.4	17.4	L_2
12	100	200	12.56	−97.8	−174.2	L_2
13	100	200	12.56	6.8	−342.6	L_2
14	100	200	12.56	116.6	−162.5	L_2
15	75	100	3.53	−186.8	−177.3	L_1
16	75	100	3.53	−36.9	−171.1	L_1
17	75	100	3.53	−172.7	−27.9	L_1
18	75	100	3.53	−272	84.5	L_1
19	50	200	3.14	369.1	167.6	L_2
20	50	200	3.14	375.2	−141.9	L_2
21	50	200	3.14	273.4	−134.9	L_2
22	50	200	3.14	324.7	258.3	L_2
23	50	200	3.14	354.3	−32.7	L_2
24	50	200	3.14	357.6	68.2	L_2
25	60	150	3.39	−125.2	218.4	L_1
26	60	150	3.39	103	122.4	L_1

No.	Dimensions (mm)			Mass (kg)	Optimal Coordinates		θi (rad)	Layer
	ai/ri	bi	hi	mi	xi (mm)	yi (mm)		
27	45		160	2.04	137.7	−45.4		L_1
28	45		160	2.04	167.5	39.5		L_1
29	100		180	11.31	157	−123.9		L_4
30	100		180	11.31	−28.8	−200.6		L_4
31	100		200	12.56	222.2	−328.9		L_2
32	250	150	200	15.00	−322.9	−148.1		L_2
33	250	150	200	15.00	−233.3	101.5		L_3
34	150	250	200	15.00	−228.9	−51.7		L_3
35	250	150	200	15.00	−240.9	−256.9	π/2	L_3
36	250	150	200	15.00	1.9	384		L_3
37	250	150	200	15.00	−87.8	−257.6	π/2	L_3
38	200	200	250	20.00	−8.L_3	203.9	π/2	L_3
39	200	200	250	20.00	229.9	275.9		L_3
40	200	200	250	20.00	−224.8	277.2		L_3
41	150	150	250	11.25	−334.6	5.9	π/2	L_2
42	150	150	250	11.25	−139.2	160.9	π/2	L_2
43	150	150	250	11.25	−179.1	8.7	π/2	L_2
44	150	100	200	6.00	206.5	179.3		L_2
45	150	100	200	6.00	−171.3	−324.5		L_2
46	100	100	150	3.00	−132.7	107.4		L_1
47	100	100	150	3.00	−14.9	156.1	π/2	L_1
48	200	185	150	11.10	138.1	−191.6		L_1
49	200	185	150	11.10	−9.9	203	π/2	L_4
50	200	100	200	8.00	−207.1	290.3		L_2
51	200	100	200	8.00	−317	134.4		L_2

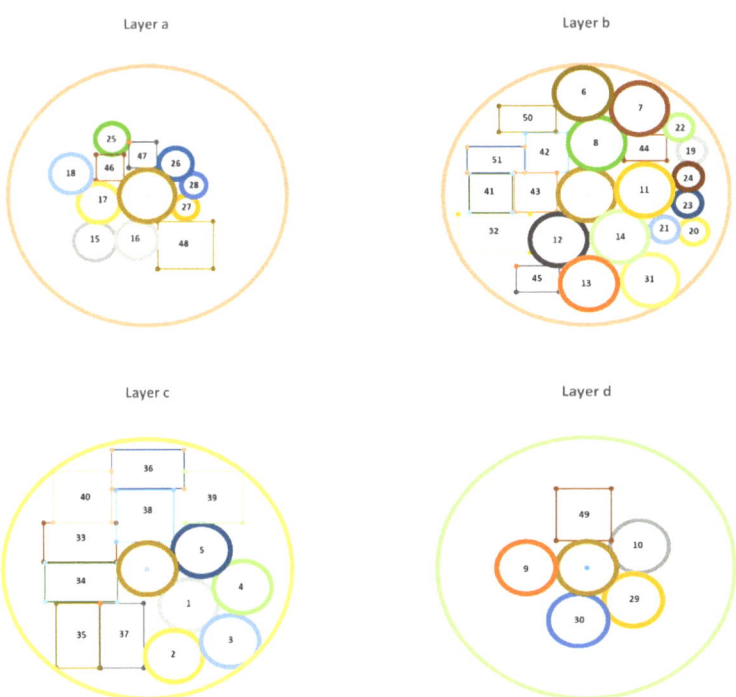

Figure 13. Top view of the optimal allocation and layout of equipment on different layers (layer (**a**) (L_1), layer (**b**) (L_2), layer (**c**) (L_3) and layer (**d**) (L_4)) of the cylindrical satellite.

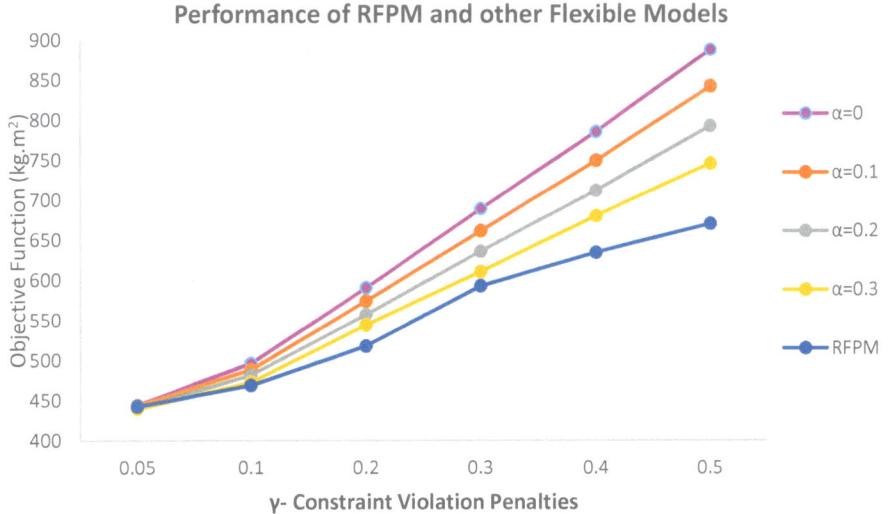

Figure 14. Comparison of the objective function of the RFPM with those of the flexible models.

In the robust state, the model acts similarly to in the previous case studies, and at $\gamma = 0.5$, the difference in the objective function for flexible models will be more obvious.

When comparing the minimum satisfaction level variables (α) for values of $\gamma = 0.05$ and $\gamma = 0.5$, it is obvious that the values obtained for the α variable at $\gamma = 0.05$ are higher than those in previous case studies, and it is only the location of the equipment that allows the robust model to limit the flexibility of soft constraints by increasing the values of the minimum satisfaction level (α) variables. As a result, these non-overlap constraints are met more easily (lower penalty in the objective function).

To offer a more detailed study, the sums of the moments of inertia in the main directions of the coordinate axes were also compared for the mentioned models, and the results can be seen in Figure 15.

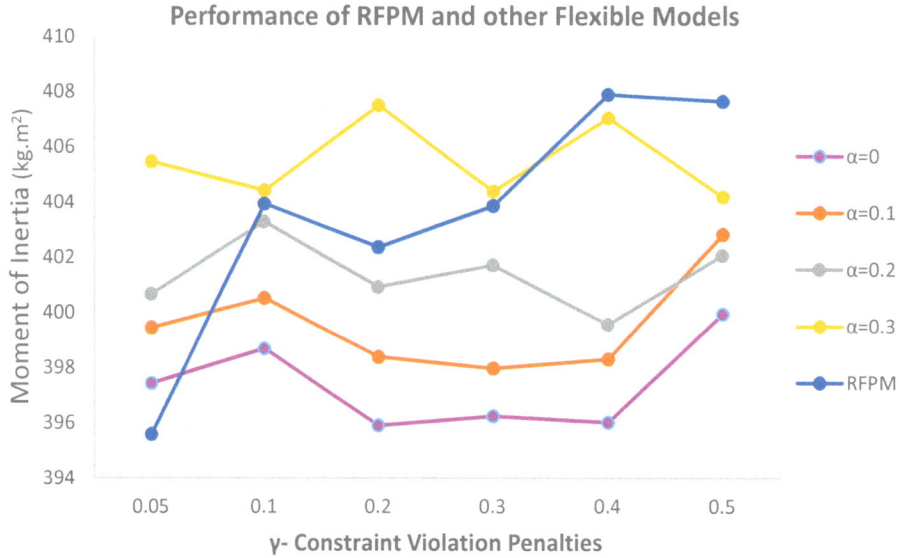

Figure 15. Comparison of the sums of moments of inertia of RFPM with those of flexible models.

As can be seen in Figure 15, in general, the behaviors of the models are not very different compared to those in previous case studies, and by increasing the penalty coefficient γ, the model can be made to gain more moments of inertia in the robust state, due to the same tendency of the model to reduce the objective function by increasing the α variables. This will result in the pieces of equipment being placed far apart from one another, thereby increasing the total moments of inertia.

Therefore, as in case studies 1 and 2, the best case for an RFPM is when $\gamma = 0.05$. As before, in cases with a cost factor below this value, the model loses its efficiency because the penalty for violating the soft constraints in the objective function is sharply reduced, and the model's minimum level of satisfaction (α) tends towards zero and leads to the flexible constraints adopting their softest state, increasing the probability of equipment overlap. As before, we now compare the robust model presented here with the models proposed in similar articles.

Here, two articles that used this example in their case studies have been examined, and, according to the pre-existing equipment layout designs for different satellite layers that are available in the articles, the data from each article have been used as the input for the proposed robust model. The results are illustrated in Figure 16.

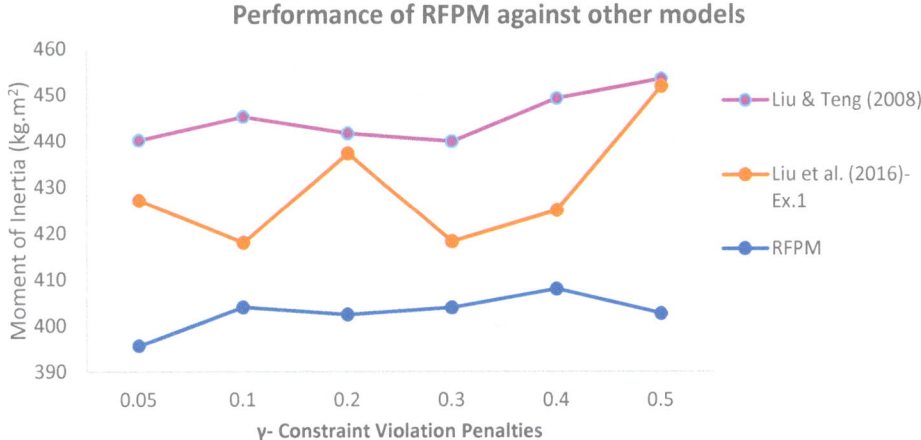

Figure 16. Comparison of the sum of moments of inertia of RFPM with the results of other articles [15,25].

As can be seen in Figure 16, the sum of moments of inertia for the proposed RFPM in all cases of penalty coefficients for the violation of soft constraints is much lower than in other articles. Also, as in previous case studies, the best and lowest values for the sum of moments of inertia can be seen in the proposed RFPM when $\gamma = 0.05$.

Similar to other case studies, an improvement of 7.35 percent may be seen when comparing the moments of inertia between [25] (427 kg.m^2) and the suggested RFPM (395.6 kg.m^2). This suggests that if an identical force is required to spin these two satellites, at least 31.4 kg of mass can be preserved.

Finally, when increasing the penalty coefficient, the values of moments of inertia tend to increase due to the objective function trying to reduce the penalty values. As a result, the soft constraints will be less flexible, as a result of which the equipment will be placed at great distances, thereby increasing the total moments of inertia.

4. Conclusions

In this study, the optimal allocation and layout of equipment in a three-dimensional satellite space are investigated. Stratified satellites were here discussed, and to measure performance, research was conducted on satellite containers with the most floors. According to the literature, the majority of satellite categories have two levels and four layers, with a total of eleven case studies discussed here using these numbers of levels and layers. In this study, the performance of the suggested model was assessed by comparison with all of the examples from these 11 publications, which were analyzed in three separate cases.

In every instance, it was demonstrated that the flexible model delivers a far superior solution compared to the models presented in prior articles.

In other words, developing an optimum solution for allocating and locating equipment using an optimization method instead of trial-and-error is the contribution of this article.

Although some authors have considered constraints related to thermal distributions, such as [23,26], no studies have taken into account the importance of the distance between components with greater thermal energy. Therefore, components that produce and emit more thermal energy must be as far away from each other as possible. For instance, to ensure better performance and a longer battery life, these components should be kept away from equipment that generates greater heat. In this case, using the concept of the obnoxious facility location problem (reviewed by Zanjirani Farahani and Hekmatfar (2009) [58]) would appropriate when locating the best positions of these components within the satellite. The concept of uncertainty can be applied here. For problematic equipment, the required distance values are unknown in advance. Possibilistic programming is useful when there is "uncertainty in the data". As a consequence, it would be feasible to model some of these problems using flexible programming under uncertainty, and some using possible programming, when it comes to problematic equipment.

Since one of the sources of uncertainty is measurement errors, and the issue of tolerance design plays a significant role in the conceptual design phase of the layout of satellite equipment, the issue of uncertainty when determining the distances between components is another appropriate use of the uncertainty concept, and this can enhance the performance of the model by satisfying the functional and equilibrium constraints, which will ultimately lead to model optimization.

Another topic that could be investigated is the satellite's temperature field, which would exert a direct influence on the operational performance of electrical components. Generally, a homogeneous distribution of heat flux within the satellite is required to maintain the optimal performance and reliability of its components. Batteries, telemetry senders, and picture senders are examples of components that emit a great deal of energy, and are therefore classified as "hot" components. These components must be positioned at specified distances from each other. Hengeveld et al. (2011a) [59] proposed that their strategy, when paired with another one that they established Hengeveld et al. (2011b) [60], was highly appropriate when distributing individual components with uneven power to different panels of a satellite so as to minimize temperature dispersion within the satellite. From a thermal perspective, each component has an effective area that influences neighboring modules; therefore, decreasing the area of intersection is comparable to increasing the uniformity of the temperature field across the satellite panels. As regards adding thermal constraints, [34] may offer the best reference.

According to all of these interpretations, regarding the calculation of the distances and thermal radii of equipment, soft constraints can be used to calculate the distances of all cuboid and cylindrical pieces of equipment such that they are no closer than a specific limit.

Author Contributions: Conceptualization, M.H. and M.R.M.A.; methodology, M.H., M.R.M.A. and T.S.; software, M.H. and M.S.P.; validation, M.H. and M.R.M.A.; formal analysis, M.H., M.S.P. and T.S.; investigation, M.H. and M.S.P.; writing—original draft, M.H. and M.S.P.; writing—review & editing, T.S.; visualization, M.H. and M.S.P.; supervision, M.R.M.A. and T.S.; Project administration, M.R.M.A. All authors have read and agreed to the published version of the manuscript.

Funding: T.S. was funded under the grant "Subvention for Science" 492 (MEiN), project No. FD-20/IL-4/046.

Data Availability Statement: The data presented in this study are available on request from the corresponding author. The data are not publicly available due to the copyright restrictions.

Conflicts of Interest: The authors declare no conflict of interest.

References

1. Zhang, B.; Teng, H.F.; Shi, Y.J. Layout optimization of satellite module using soft computing techniques. *Appl. Soft Comput.* **2008**, *8*, 507–521. [CrossRef]
2. Ahmadi, A.; Pishvaee, M.S.; Akbari Jokar, M.R. A survey on multi-floor facility layout problems. *Comput. Ind. Eng.* **2017**, *107*, 158–170. [CrossRef]
3. Ferebee, M.J., Jr.; Powers, R.B. *Optimization of Payload Mass Placement in a Dual*; Keel Space Station, NASA, Langley Research Centre: Hampton, VA, USA, 1987.
4. Ferebee, M.J.; Allen, C.L. Optimization of payload placement on arbitrary spacecraft. *J. Spacecr. Rocket.* **1991**, *28*, 612–614. [CrossRef]
5. Rocco, E.M.; Souza, M.; Prado, A. Multi-objective optimization applied to satellite constellations I: Formulation of the smallest loss criterion. In Proceedings of the 54th International Astronautical Congress (IAC'03), Bremen, Germany, 29 September–3 October 2003.
6. Cagan, J.; Shimada, K.; Yin, S. A survey of computational approaches to three-dimensional layout problems. *Comput.-Aided Des.* **2002**, *34*, 597–611. [CrossRef]
7. Jang, S. A study on three-dimensional layout design by the simulated annealing method. *J. Mech. Sci. Technol.* **2008**, *22*, 2016–2023. [CrossRef]

8.   Zhang, Z.H.; Wang, Y.S.; Teng, H.F.; Shi, Y.J. Parallel Dual-system Cooperative Co-Evolutionary Differential Evolution Algorithm with Human-computer Cooperation for Multi-Cabin Satellite Layout Optimization. *J. Converg. Inf. Technol.* **2013**, *2013*, 711–720.

9.   Zhang, Z.H.; Zhong, C.; Xu, Z.Z.; Teng, H.F. A Non-Dominated Sorting Cooperative Co-Evolutionary Differential Evolution Algorithm for Multi-Objective Layout Optimization. *IEEE Access* **2017**, *5*, 14468–14477. [CrossRef]

10.   Zhang, Z.H.; Sun, X.; Hou, L.; Chen, W.; Shi, Y.; Cao, X. A Cooperative Co-Evolutionary Multi-Agent System for Multi-Objective Layout Optimization of Satellite Module. In Proceedings of the 2017 IEEE International Conference on Systems, Man, and Cybernetics (SMC), Banff, AB, Canada, 5–8 October 2017.

11.   Teng, H.F.; Sun, S.L.; Liu, D.Q.; Li, Y.Z. Layout optimization for the objects located within a rotating vessel—A three-dimensional packing problem with behavioural constraints. *Comput. Oper. Res.* **2001**, *28*, 521–535. [CrossRef]

12.   Sun, Z.G.; Teng, H.F. Optimal layout design of a satellite module. *Eng. Opt.* **2003**, *35*, 513–529. [CrossRef]

13.   Huo, J.; Shi, Y.; Teng, H.F. Layout design of a satellite module using a human-guided genetic algorithm. In Proceedings of the 2006 International Conference on Computational Intelligence and Security, Guangzhou, China, 3–6 November 2006; pp. 230–235.

14.   Chen, W.; Shi, Y.J.; Teng, H.F. An improved differential evolution with local search for constrained layout optimization of satellite module. *Int. Conf. Intell. Comput.* **2008**, *5227*, 742–749.

15.   Liu, Z.; Teng, H. Human–computer cooperative layout design method and its application. *Comput. Ind. Eng.* **2008**, *55*, 735–757. [CrossRef]

16.   Huo, J.Z.; Teng, H.F. Optimal layout design of a satellite module using a coevolutionary method with heuristic rules. *J. Aerosp. Eng.* **2009**, *22*, 101–111. [CrossRef]

17.   Wang, Y.S.; Teng, H.F.; Shi, Y.J. Cooperative co-evolutionary scatter search for satellite module layout design. *Eng. Comput.* **2009**, *26*, 761–785. [CrossRef]

18.   Huo, J.Z.; Teng, H.F.; Sun, W.; Chen, J. Human-computer co-operative co-evolutionary method and its application to a satellite module layout design problem. *Aeronaut. J.* **2010**, *114*, 209–223. [CrossRef]

19.   Xu, Y.C.; Dong, F.M.; Liu, Y.; Xiao, R.B.; Amos, M. Ant colony algorithm for the weighted item layout optimization problem. *Comput. Sci.* **2010**, *3*, 221–232.

20.   Teng, H.F.; Chen, Y.; Zeng, W.; Shi, Y.J.; Hu, Q.H. A dual-system variable-grain cooperative Co-evolutionary algorithm: Satellite-module layout design. *IEEE Trans. Evol. Comput.* **2010**, *14*, 438–455. [CrossRef]

21.   He, K.; Mo, D.; Ye, T.; Huang, W. A coarse-to-fine quasi-physical optimization method for solving the circle packing problem with equilibrium constraints. *Comput. Ind. Eng.* **2013**, *66*, 1049–1060. [CrossRef]

22.   Lau, V.; de Sousa, F.L.; Galski, R.L.; Rocco, E.M.; Becceneri, J.C.; Santos, W.A.; Sandri, S.A. A multidisciplinary design optimization tool for spacecraft equipment layout conception. *J. Aerosp. Technol. Manag.* **2014**, *6*, 431–446. [CrossRef]

23.   Cuco, A.P.C.; Sousa, F.L.D.; Silva Neto, A.J. A multi-objective methodology for spacecraft equipment layouts. *Optim. Eng.* **2015**, *16*, 165–181. [CrossRef]

24.   Fakoor, M.; Taghinezhad, M. Layout and configuration design for a satellite with variable mass using a hybrid optimization method. *Proc. Inst. Mech. Eng. Part G J. Aerosp. Eng.* **2016**, *230*, 360–377. [CrossRef]

25.   Liu, J.; Hao, L.; Li, G.; Xue, Y.; Liu, Z.; Huang, J. Multi-objective layout optimization of a satellite module using the Wang-Landau sampling method with local search. *Front. Inf. Technol. Electron. Eng.* **2016**, *17*, 527–542. [CrossRef]

26.   Fakoor, M.; Ghoreishi, S.M.N.; Sabaghzadeh, H. Spacecraft Component Adaptive Layout Environment (SCALE): An efficient optimization tool. *Adv. Space Res.* **2016**, *58*, 1654–1670. [CrossRef]

27.   Li, Z.; Zeng, Y.; Wang, Y.; Wang, L.; Song, B. A hybrid multi-mechanism optimization approach for the payload packing design of a satellite module. *Appl. Soft Comput.* **2016**, *45*, 11–26. [CrossRef]

28.   Fakoor, M.; Mohammad Zadeh, P.; Momeni Eskandari, H. Developing an optimal layout design of a satellite system by considering natural frequency and attitude control constraints. *Aerosp. Sci. Technol.* **2017**, *71*, 172–188. [CrossRef]

29.   Shafaee, M.; Mohammadzadeh, P.; Elkaie, A.; Abbasi, S. Layout design optimization of a space propulsion system using a hybrid optimization algorithm. *Proc. Inst. Mech. Eng. Part G J. Aerosp. Eng.* **2017**, *231*, 338–349. [CrossRef]

30.   Cui, F.Z.; Xu, Z.Z.; Wang, X.K.; Zhong, C.Q.; Teng, H.F. A dual-system cooperative co-evolutionary algorithm for satellite equipment layout optimization. *Proc. Inst. Mech. Eng. Part G J. Aerosp. Eng.* **2018**, *232*, 2432–2457. [CrossRef]

31.   Qin, Z.; Liang, Y.G. Layout Optimization of Satellite Cabin Considering Space Debris Impact Risk. *J. Spacecr. Rocket.* **2017**, *54*, 1–5.

32.   Xu, Z.Z.; Zhong, C.Q.; Teng, H.F. Assignment and layout integration optimization for simplified satellite re-entry module component layout. *Proc. Inst. Mech. Eng. Part G J. Aerosp. Eng.* **2019**, *233*, 4287–7301. [CrossRef]

33.   Qin, Z.; Liang, Y.; Zhou, J. An optimization tool for satellite equipment layout. *Adv. Space Res.* **2018**, *61*, 223–234. [CrossRef]

34.   Chen, X.; Yao, W.; Zhao, Y.; Chen, X.; Zheng, X. A practical satellite layout optimization design approach based on enhanced finite-circle method. *Struct. Multidiscip. Optim.* **2018**, *58*, 2635–2653. [CrossRef]

35.   Chen, X.; Yao, W.; Zhao, Y.; Chen, X.; Zhang, J.; Luo, Y. The hybrid algorithms are based on differential evolution for satellite layout optimization design. In Proceedings of the 2018 IEEE Congress on Evolutionary Computation (CEC), Rio de Janeiro, Brazil, 8–13 July 2018; IEEE: Piscataway, NJ, USA, 2018; pp. 1–8. [CrossRef]

36.   Zhong, C.Q.; Xu, Z.Z.; Teng, H.F. Multi-module satellite component assignment and layout optimization. *Appl. Soft Comput.* **2019**, *75*, 148–161. [CrossRef]

37.   Chen, X.; Yao, W.; Zhao, Y.; Chen, X.; Liu, W. A novel satellite layout optimization design method based on phi-function. *Acta Astronaut.* **2021**, *180*, 560–574. [CrossRef]

38. Sun, J.; Chen, X.; Zhang, J.; Yao, W. A niching cross-entropy method for multimodal satellite layout optimization design. *Complex Intell. Syst.* **2021**, *7*, 1971–1989. [CrossRef]
39. Pühlhofer, T.; Baier, H. Approaches for further rationalisation in mechanical architecture and structural design of satellites. In Proceedings of the 54th International Astronautical Congress of the International Astronautical Federation, the International Academy of Astronautics, and the International Institute of Space Law, Bremen, Germany, 29 September–3 October 2003.
40. Cuco, A. Development of a Multi-Objective Methodology for Layout Optimization of Equipment in Artificial Satellites. Master's Thesis, Postgraduate Course in Space Technology and Engineering, National Institute for Space Research (INPE), Sao Paulo, Brazil, 2011.
41. Pühlhofer, T.; Langer, H.; Baier, H.; Huber, M.B.T. Multi-criteria and Discrete Configuration and Design Optimization with Applications for Satellites. In Proceedings of the 10th AIAA/ISSMO Multidisciplinary Analysis and Optimization Conference, Albany, NY, USA, 30 August–1 September 2004.
42. Albano, A.; Sapuppo, G. Optimal allocation of two-dimensional irregular shapes using heuristic search methods. *IEEE Trans. Syst. Man Cybern.* **1980**, *10*, 242–248. [CrossRef]
43. Li, Z.; Milenkovic, V. Compaction and separation algorithms for nonconvex polygons and their applications. *Eur. J. Oper. Res.* **1995**, *84*, 539–561. [CrossRef]
44. Chen, S.; Xuan, M.; Xin, J.; Liu, Y.; Gu, S.; Li, J.; Zhang, L. Design and experiment of dual micro-vibration isolation system for optical satellite flywheel. *Int. J. Mech. Sci.* **2020**, *179*, 105592. [CrossRef]
45. Chernov, N.; Stoyan, Y.; Romanova, T.; Pankratov, A. Phi-Functions for 2D Objects Formed by Line Segments and Circular Arcs. *Adv. Oper. Res.* **2012**, *2012*, 346358. [CrossRef]
46. Galbraith, J.R. *Designing Complex Organizations*; Addison-Wesley Longman Publishing Co., Inc.: Reading, MA, USA, 1973.
47. Mula, J.; Poler, R.; Garcia-Sabater, J.P. Material requirement planning with fuzzy constraints and fuzzy coefficients. *Fuzzy Sets Syst.* **2007**, *158*, 783–793. [CrossRef]
48. Klibi, W.; Martel, A.; Guitouni, A. The design of robust value-creating supply chain networks: A critical review. *Eur. J. Oper. Res.* **2010**, *203*, 283–293. [CrossRef]
49. Pishvaee, M.S.; Fazli Khalaf, M. Novel robust fuzzy mathematical programming methods. *Appl. Math. Model.* **2016**, *40*, 407–418. [CrossRef]
50. Mulvey, J.; Vanderbei, R.; Zenios, S. Robust optimization of large-scale systems. *Oper. Res.* **1995**, *43*, 264–281. [CrossRef]
51. Leung, S.C.H.; Tsang, S.O.S.; Ng, W.L.; Wu, Y. A robust optimization model for multi-site production planning problem in an uncertain environment. *Eur. J. Oper. Res.* **2007**, *181*, 224–238. [CrossRef]
52. Yu, C.S.; Li, H.L. A robust optimization model for stochastic logistic problems. *Int. J. Prod. Econ.* **2000**, *64*, 385–397. [CrossRef]
53. Ben-Tal, A.; Nemirovski, A. Robust convex optimization. *Math. Oper. Res.* **1998**, *2*, 769–805. [CrossRef]
54. Ben-Tal, A.; Nemirovski, A. Robust solutions of linear programming problems contaminated with uncertain data. *Math. Program.* **2000**, *88*, 411–424. [CrossRef]
55. El-Ghaoui, L.; Oustry, F.; Lebret, H. Robust solutions to uncertain semidefinite programs. *SIAM J. Optim.* **1998**, *9*, 33–52. [CrossRef]
56. Pishvaee, M.S.; Razmi, J.; Torabi, S.A. Robust possibilistic programming for socially responsible supply chain network design: A new approach. *Fuzzy Sets Syst.* **2012**, *206*, 1–20. [CrossRef]
57. Li, G.Q. *Research on the Theory and Methods of Layout Design and Their Applications*; Dalian University of Technology: Dalian, China, 2003. (In Chinese)
58. Zanjirani Farahani, R.; Hekmatfar, M. *Facilities Location: Concepts, Models and Applications*; Springer: Berlin/Heidelberg, Germany, 2009.
59. Hengeveld, D.W.; Braun, J.E.; Groll, E.A.; Williams, A.D. Optimal Placement of Electronic Components to Minimize heat flux nonuniformities. *J. Spacecr. Rocket.* **2011**, *48*, 556–563. [CrossRef]
60. Hengeveld, D.W.; Braun, J.E.; Groll, E.A.; Williams, A.D. Optimal Distribution of Electronic Components to Balance Environmental Fluxes. *J. Spacecr. Rocket.* **2011**, *48*, 694–697. [CrossRef]

Article

An Enhanced Hybrid-Level Interface-Reduction Method Combined with an Interface Discrimination Algorithm

Seunghee Cheon and Jaehun Lee *

Department of Mechanical Engineering, Dongguk University, Seoul 04620, Republic of Korea; s.hee.cheon@dgu.ac.kr
* Correspondence: jaehun@dgu.edu

Abstract: This study proposes an interface localizing scheme to enhance the performance of the previous hybrid-level interface-reduction method. The conventional component mode synthesis (CMS) only focuses on interior reduction, while the interface is fully retained for convenient synthesis. Thus, various interface-reduction methods have been suggested to obtain a satisfactory size for the reduced systems. Although previous hybrid-level interface-reduction approaches have addressed major issues associated with conventional interface-reduction methods—in terms of accuracy and efficiency through considering partial substructure synthesis—this method can be applied to limited modeling conditions where interfaces and substructures are independently defined. To overcome this limitation, an interface localizing algorithm is developed to ensure an enhanced performance in the conventional hybrid-level interface-reduction method. The interfaces are discriminated through considering the Boolean operation of substructures, and the interface reduction basis is computed at the localized interface level, which is constructed by a partially coupled system. As a result, a large amount of computational resources are saved, achieving the possibility of efficient design modifications at the semi-substructural level.

Keywords: parametric component mode synthesis; Craig Bampton method; interface reduction; characteristic constraint modes; hybrid-level interfaces

MSC: 70-08

Citation: Cheon, S.; Lee, J. An Enhanced Hybrid-Level Interface-Reduction Method Combined with an Interface Discrimination Algorithm. *Mathematics* **2023**, *11*, 4867. https://doi.org/10.3390/math11234867

Academic Editor: Matjaz Skrinar

Received: 8 November 2023
Revised: 29 November 2023
Accepted: 1 December 2023
Published: 4 December 2023

1. Introduction

Numerical simulations for large-scale, dynamical systems are challenging tasks even now. To mitigate these computational burdens, introducing a reduced-order model (ROM) within a surrogate modeling framework can be an attractive solution. In general, reduced-order modeling is realized by projecting a full-order system into a lower subspace using a truncated reduction basis. Traditionally, the eigenvectors of a system matrix can be a projection basis that transforms the state vector into a generalized coordinate system. By truncating the eigenvectors, one achieves a dimensionality reduction in the given system. Another type of reduction is achieved through introducing the singular value decomposition of data usually obtained from a response of the system. Such dimensionality reduction is one of the general approaches in the viewpoint of a data analysis regardless of the underlying physics of the given problems. For either the data or the system, the reduction results in efficient computations, particularly for such engineering disciplines that inevitably require heavy numerical simulations.

From the viewpoint of deriving and using appropriate reduced-order models for real industrial applications, an efficient adaptation to parametric variations is one of the most important properties that the ROM should have. Thus, the model reduction techniques have been widely investigated for real industrial systems, particularly large-scale models that undergo parametric variations. The offline–online strategy [1,2] alleviated a large amount of computation caused by repetitive evaluations with respect to parameter changes.

Once a substantial amount of data is acquired in the offline stage, prediction accuracy can be increased in the online stage. One of the major barriers that hinders applying the offline–online strategy is the number of parameters that the system contains. In particular, the offline cost dramatically increases due to the sampling of the independent parameters, which is referred to as the "curse of dimensionality". To mitigate such complexities caused by the dependencies between the parameters, various sampling strategies [3,4] have been developed within the framework of surrogate modeling and the design of experiments. To be more specific, domain-decomposition-based methods have also been developed for the spatially distributed parameters [5–7]. Such approaches have shown the possibility of offline time reduction for high dimensional parameter spaces. Some works have also developed mathematical techniques to address dimensional problems for complex finite element modeling (FEM) [8–11].

The main advantage of component mode synthesis (CMS), which stands for dynamic substructuring, is that the entire system is divided into multiple independent subsystems, and model reduction is performed at a substructural level. Therefore, design modification can be practically reflected without requiring full-system analysis with respect to design-variable changes. Based on these concepts of domain decomposition, Hurty [12] was initially conceptualized by applying normal, rigid-body, and constraint modes within the finite element modeling (FEM) framework. Subsequently, Craig Bampton [13] discovered that the treatment of interface can be simplified by considering rigid-body and redundant modes in the same manner. Bennighof and Lehoucq [14] formulated an automatic multi-level substructuring method to achieve high dimensional reduction with a similar accuracy level as modal truncation. In addition, proper consideration of residual substructural modes based on a Craig Bampton (CB) method has been suggested for enhanced accuracy by Kim [15]. The efficiency and accuracy of CMS methods are demonstrated in [12–18].

The majority of engineering systems consist of multiple materials and components. For this reason, the treatment of interface is another essential consideration for efficient and robust FEM simulation due to interaction between each domain. Peskin [19] presented the immersed boundary (IB) method to handle fluid–flexible structure interactions, such as blood flow in the heart. Based on the IB method, related works handling interfaces could be found in [20–22]. According to Craig Bampton's work, a divided substructure is separately treated for reduction as interior and interface degrees of freedom (DOFs). The fixed interface normal modes (FINMs) and static constraint modes (SCMs) are independently applied to a partitioned subsystem. This approach offers the benefit of convenience synthesis, as it ensures the interface compatibility. On the other hand, the CB method has a significant disadvantage in that it requires an additional reduction method to obtain sufficiently reduced systems. The reduced subsystems are tend to be dominated by interface DOFs under several circumstances, where fine mesh or numerous subcomponents are adopted for modeling. Therefore, to achieve a manageable size of reduced system matrices, various interface reduction techniques are presented by performing two-level reduction.

Craig and Chang [23] initially proposed the concept of interface reduction by incorporating several model reductions, such as Guyan, Ritz, and modal reduction. Castanier et al. [24] developed Craig and Chang's modal reduction method as a system-level characteristic constraint (CC) mode. The interface reduction basis is computed using secondary eigenvalue analysis to a fully synthesized system. This system-level interface-reduction method successfully represents the physical motion of the interface. Due to the constant effort for highly reduced systems, the interface reduction approach is continuously extended to various engineering fields. Traditionally, Tran [25,26] applied CMS using interface modes to the cyclic symmetry problems. Herrmann et al. [27] applied Craig and Chang's work to the acoustic fluid–structure interaction and predicted hydraulic transfer system using ROM reduced by appropriate Ritz vectors. According to recent studies, Cammarata et al. [28] presented a novel interface-reduction method for interpolation multipoint constraints by discarding dependent node selection. Hughes and Kuether [29] handled nonlinear interface for further system reduction by computing system-level CC modes and proper orthogonal interface modal derivatives. They validated this newly proposed interface reduction scheme to frictional contact system considering time transient. Additional investigations exploiting interface reduction based on dynamic substructuring to engineering fields are shown in [30–32].

The system-level CC modes approach hinders the primary advantage of CMS, which rapidly responds to parametric variations. In other words, the independence of each subsystem is no longer assured since the final reduced system is obtained after all substructures are coupled. To emphasize the flexibility of design, the local-level interface-reduction method is presented by Hong et al. [33]. The secondary eigenvalue analysis is computed at the subsystem level; exact interface compatibility should be enforced for synthesis after interface reduction. Kuether et al. [34] suggested weak compatibility at local-level interface reduction to minimize compatibility errors, constructing geometric nonlinear reduced-order models. Nevertheless, this local-level technique causes a considerable compromise in accuracy. Holzwarth et al. [35] aimed to improve the accuracy of local-level CC modes computation by adopting the Legendre polynomials. However, accuracy compromising and synthesis cumbersome remain critical concerns.

To overcome the shortcomings of the aforementioned CC modes approaches, CC modes computation to a partially synthesized system has been constantly investigated. The multilevel interface reduction presented by Wu et al. [36] performs secondary eigenvalue analysis at a localized subset level by assembling paired substructures. This method reduces computational effort and guarantees accuracy as much as the system level. Furthermore, based on the concept of Aoyama's work [37] considering a partially assembled system and separately computing CC modes, Krattiger et al. [38] recently proposed the hybrid-level (HB-level) interface reduction that allows applying boundary condition free system. These introduced methods can compromise accuracy and efficiency since constructing a single interface does not need information on disconnected substructures, but substructure connectivity is not entirely ignored. Additionally, these methods allow interface parallel computation.

Despite the CC modes computation method has substantial strengths when considering a partially synthesized system, the previous HB-level interface reduction is only applicable for modeling where each interface is independently defined and isolated. Therefore, this conventional method has difficulties in application to real industrial engineering problems. In this study, the modified HB-level interface-reduction method is proposed to provide more practical solutions for parametric studies. The proposed method aims to apply to unlimited modeling scenarios while the advantages of each localized interface set are retained. The unique numbering-based interface discrimination algorithm is integrated with the previous HB-level interface reduction [38] to address the limitation. To assess the performance of the proposed method, the graphic partitioning algorithm METIS [39] is adopted for substructuring systems. Multiple substructuring scenarios are provided to demonstrate wide applicable modeling ranges.

This paper is organized as follows. In Section 2, the CB method is described. In Section 3, the interface discrimination algorithm to build independent interface sets and a new interface reduction are proposed, with a brief review of the hybrid-level interface reduction. In Section 4, several numerical examples decomposed into multiple subdomains by METIS are presented to evaluate the performance of the proposed method.

2. Craig Bampton Method-Based Component Mode Synthesis

The conventional Craig Bampton method has been developed within the finite element discretization framework. Hence, the FEM formulation for system equation is obtained following the principle of virtual work. Further details of basic FEM formulation procedure are found in Ref. [40]. The full system equation in terms of finite element modeling is expressed as

$$\mathbf{M\ddot{u} + C\dot{u} + Ku = f}. \tag{1}$$

Equation (1) describes the global system before performing substructuring. $\mathbf{M}$, $\mathbf{C}$, and $\mathbf{K}$ represent mass, damping, and stiffness matrices, respectively. $\mathbf{u}$ and $\mathbf{f}$ are the displacement and force vectors, respectively. The size of the presented entire system is N_s. Based on the classical CB method, this proposed method is applicable to the condition that the boundary DOFs is exactly separated as nodal displacement.

In the CB-CMS, the partitioning of interiors and interfaces is essential to realize straight-forward synthesis. Following the global system matrices Equation (1), each subsystem matrix is written as

$$\begin{bmatrix} \mathbf{M}_{ii}^s & \mathbf{M}_{ib}^s \\ \mathbf{M}_{bb}^s & \mathbf{M}_{bi}^s \end{bmatrix} \begin{bmatrix} \ddot{\mathbf{u}}_i^s \\ \ddot{\mathbf{u}}_b^s \end{bmatrix} + \begin{bmatrix} \mathbf{K}_{ii}^s & \mathbf{K}_{ib}^s \\ \mathbf{K}_{bb}^s & \mathbf{K}_{bi}^s \end{bmatrix} \begin{bmatrix} \mathbf{u}_i^s \\ \mathbf{u}_b^s \end{bmatrix} = \begin{bmatrix} \mathbf{f}_i^s \\ \mathbf{f}_b^s \end{bmatrix}, \tag{2}$$

where

$$\mathbf{M}^s \ddot{\mathbf{u}} + \mathbf{K}^s \mathbf{u} = \mathbf{F}^s, \quad s = 1, 2, ..., N_d. \tag{3}$$

In this substructural system, the damping is ignored for convenience. The superscript s denotes the number of substructures, and the entire system is decomposed into total N_d subcomponents. The subscripts i and b indicate the degrees of freedom for interiors and boundaries known as interfaces.

For the sth subsystem reduction, the eigenvalue analysis is performed on interior DOFs to obtain fixed interface normal modes, one obtains the following FINMs:

$$\mathbf{\Phi}_{im}^s = [\boldsymbol{\phi}_{i,1}^s, \ \boldsymbol{\phi}_{i,2}^s, \ ..., \boldsymbol{\phi}_{i,N_m^s}^s], \tag{4}$$

where

$$\mathbf{K}_{ii}^s \boldsymbol{\phi}_{i,\xi} = \lambda_{i,\xi} \mathbf{M}_{ii}^s \boldsymbol{\phi}_{i,\xi}, \quad \xi = 1, 2, ..., N_i^s. \tag{5}$$

N_i^s is the number of interior DOFs for a sth substructure. N_m^s from Equation (4) denotes the number of selected dominant modes following the frequency cut-off method. This number should be smaller than the initial interior DOFs ($N_m^s < N_i^s$). The FINMs $\mathbf{\Phi}_{im}^s$ are derived from generalized eigenvalue analysis to satisfy the mass orthogonality, as follows:

$$[\mathbf{\Phi}_{im}^s]^T \mathbf{M}_{ii}^s \mathbf{\Phi}_{im}^s = \mathbf{I}_{mm}. \tag{6}$$

To obtain the static constraint modes for boundaries, a unit displacement is applied to the interface DOFs. In addition, an inertia force $\mathbf{f}_i^s$ is ignored for a static analysis.

$$\begin{bmatrix} \mathbf{K}_{ii}^s & \mathbf{K}_{ib}^s \\ \mathbf{K}_{bb}^s & \mathbf{K}_{bi}^s \end{bmatrix} \begin{bmatrix} \mathbf{\Psi}_{ii}^s \\ \mathbf{I}_{bb}^s \end{bmatrix} = \begin{bmatrix} \mathbf{0} \\ \mathbf{f}_b^s \end{bmatrix}, \tag{7}$$

The SCM is obtained by solving the upper part of Equation (7),

$$\mathbf{\Psi}_{ib}^s = -\mathbf{K}_{ii}^{s\,-1} \mathbf{K}_{ib}^s. \tag{8}$$

The size of SCMs for sth substructure is N_b^s, which is equal to the number of initial physical interfaces. The boundary DOFs and compatibility are fully retained by static condensation to achieve direct synthesis.

According to the above procedures, the final CB transformation for a sth substructure is expressed as

$$\mathbf{T}^s = \begin{bmatrix} \mathbf{\Phi}_{im}^s & \mathbf{\Psi}_{ib}^s \\ \mathbf{0}_{bm} & \mathbf{I}_{bb} \end{bmatrix}. \tag{9}$$

The CB-reduced mass and stiffness matrices of a sth substructure are derived by applying transformations Equation (9) to the system matrices, such that

$$\bar{\mathbf{M}}^s = [\mathbf{T}^s]^T \mathbf{M}^s \mathbf{T}^s = \begin{bmatrix} \mathbf{I}_{mm} & \bar{\mathbf{M}}^s_{mb} \\ \bar{\mathbf{M}}^s_{bm} & \check{\mathbf{M}}^s_{bb} \end{bmatrix},$$

$$\bar{\mathbf{K}}^s = [\mathbf{T}^s]^T \mathbf{K}^s \mathbf{T}^s = \begin{bmatrix} \mathbf{\Lambda}^s_{mm} & \mathbf{0}_{mb} \\ \mathbf{0}_{bm} & \check{\mathbf{K}}^s_{bb} \end{bmatrix}.$$

(10)

The bar ($\bar{\cdot}$) and check ($\check{\cdot}$) notations indicate the matrices transformed into the reduced coordinate and the generalized coordinate, respectively. The total size of sth reduced subsystem is $N^s = N^s_i + N^s_b$.

The boundary DOFs retain continuity of each subsystem without reduction. According to the interface displacement compatibility, the reduced substructural system matrices are directly synthesized as follows:

$$\tilde{\mathbf{M}}_{bb} = \sum_{i=1}^{N_d} \check{\mathbf{M}}^i_{bb}, \quad \tilde{\mathbf{K}}_{bb} = \sum_{i=1}^{N_d} \check{\mathbf{K}}^i_{bb}.$$

(11)

The tilde ($\tilde{\cdot}$) notation denotes the synthesized system, and N_d is the number of substructures. Consequently, the final displacement and transformation relationship of coupled CB system matrices is

$$\begin{bmatrix} \mathbf{u}^1_m \\ \mathbf{u}^2_m \\ \vdots \\ \mathbf{u}^s_m \\ \mathbf{u}_b \end{bmatrix} = \mathbf{P} \begin{bmatrix} \bar{\mathbf{u}}^1_i \\ \bar{\mathbf{u}}^2_i \\ \vdots \\ \bar{\mathbf{u}}^s_i \\ \mathbf{u}_b \end{bmatrix},$$

(12)

where

$$\mathbf{P} = \begin{bmatrix} \mathbf{\Phi}^1_{im} & 0 & 0 & 0 & 0 \\ & \mathbf{\Phi}^2_{im} & 0 & 0 & 0 \\ & & \ddots & 0 & \vdots \\ & & & \mathbf{\Phi}^s_{im} & 0 \\ symm & & & & \mathbf{I} \end{bmatrix}.$$

(13)

The transformation $\mathbf{P}$ is used for system recovery to approximate the full system. The subscript im indicates the reduced interior subspace of the original CB method. More details and the overview of the original CB method are presented in Ref. [13].

3. Localized Interface Reduction

This section introduces the newly proposed interface-reduction method. The presented hybrid-level interface reduction can address the issues in terms of both accuracy and efficiency. In other words, the system-level interface reduction that CC modes are computed from the fully synthesized system may be inefficient sometimes, particularly when the system needs various design modifications. On the other hand, the local-level interface reduction disregarding system connectivity compromises accuracy. Moreover, enforcing interface compatibility, which is an initial consideration for synthesis after computing CC modes at the substructural level, is a challenging task. To address these issues, this localized interface method is developed based on the key idea of the hybrid-level interface reduction initially proposed by Krattiger et al. [38].

3.1. Interface Discrimination Algorithm for Independent Interface

According to the hybrid-level interface reduction, a single interface is constructed by coupling adjacent substructures. Nevertheless, this previous method is restricted to certain modelings where each interface is clearly segregated. However, as we usually adopt a graphic partitioning algorithm for an automatic division of the whole FE model, interfaces and their reduction cannot be handled considering design parameters. This issue becomes more critical for real applications with large numbers of DOFs. To overcome this limitation, the interface discrimination algorithm is proposed by assigning a unique number based on Boolean operations. Figure 1 illustrates differences in building interface sets depending on interface reduction techniques. In addition, the process for localizing interfaces using unique numbering is described in Table 1.

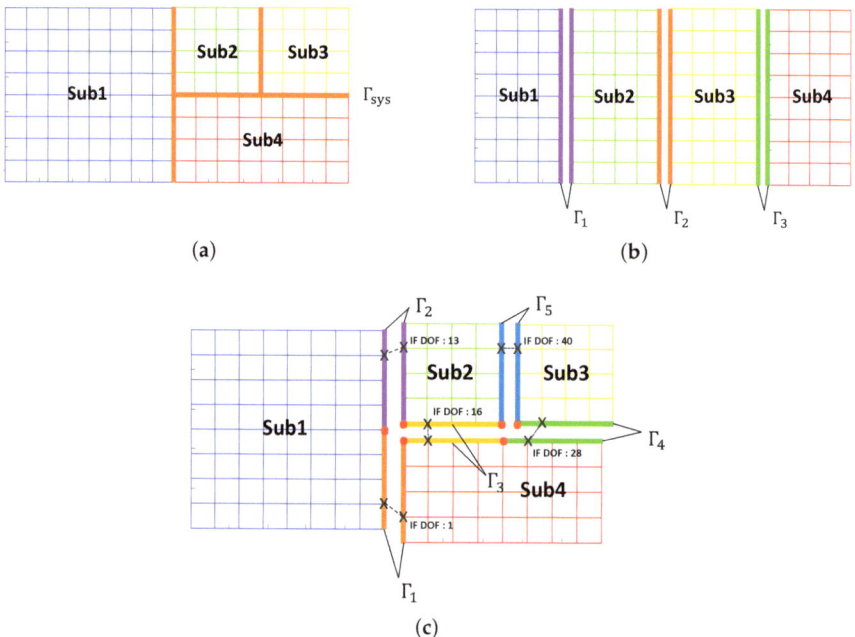

Figure 1. The comparison of interface reduction techniques between previous methods and proposed method. (**a**) System-level interface; (**b**) hybrid-level interface; (**c**) proposed semi-localized interface.

In Figure 1c, the red points are the one that contains three domains. To minimize accuracy loss, the red points sharing particularly many substructures are regarded as reduced interiors to retain without transformation. Therefore, they are excluded when we reduce the interface DOFs. Details of the algorithm for the interface discrimination are given in Algorithm 1. The example of converting binary to decimal numbers is presented in Table 1.

Table 1. Characteristic numbering for semi-localized interface reduction.

Interface DOF	Sub 1	Sub 2	Sub 3	Sub 4	Binary	Decimal	Interface Number
1	1	1	0	0	1100	12	Γ_1
13	0	1	0	1	0101	14	Γ_2
16	1	0	1	0	1010	10	Γ_3
28	0	1	1	0	0110	6	Γ_4
40	0	0	1	1	0011	3	Γ_5

Algorithm 1 Discrimination algorithm for interface localizing

---

1: **for** $s = 1, 2, ..., N_b$, **do**
2:   Describe Boolean operations between interfaces and substructures.
3:   Convert Boolean operations to a binary number.
4:   Assign a unique number by converting a binary number to a decimal number.
5: **end for**
6: Discard untransformed points as numbering.
7: Rearrange interface numbering from 1 to j.

3.2. Interface Reduction Formulations

The interface is individually defined as a single set by the interface discrimination algorithm introduced in the above subsection. This implies that the proposed method conducts the secondary eigenvalue analysis to a partially synthesized system. In this section, the interface reduction process is described, and the jth localized interface Γ_j is presented in Figure 2 for comprehensive understanding.

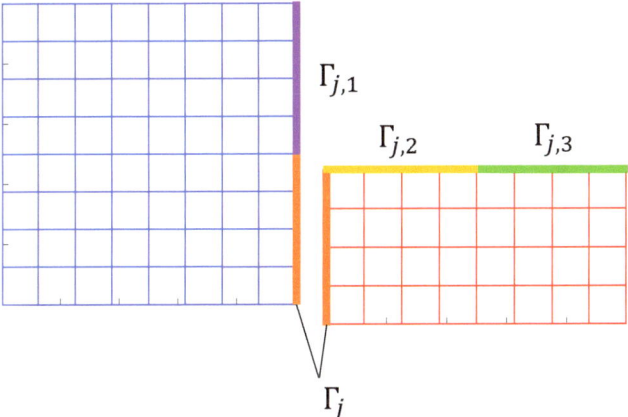

Figure 2. The jth localized interface Γ_j.

The system matrices of a jth interface are constructed by coupling relative substructures are

$$\tilde{\mathbf{M}}_{bb}^{\Gamma_j} = \sum_{i=1}^{N_k} \check{\mathbf{M}}_{bb}^i, \quad \tilde{\mathbf{K}}_{bb}^{\Gamma_j} = \sum_{i=1}^{N_k} \check{\mathbf{K}}_{bb}^i. \tag{14}$$

The N_k is the number of partially synthesized substructures to construct jth localized interface Γ_j. To obtain characteristic constraint modes, the secondary eigenvalue analysis is performed as

$$\mathbf{\Phi}_{bn}^{\Gamma_j} = [\boldsymbol{\phi}_{b,1}^{\Gamma_j}, \boldsymbol{\phi}_{b,2}^{\Gamma_j}, ..., \boldsymbol{\phi}_{b,N_n}^{\Gamma_j}], \tag{15}$$

where

$$\tilde{\mathbf{K}}_{bb}^{\Gamma_j} \boldsymbol{\phi}_{b,\xi} = \lambda_{b,\xi} \tilde{\mathbf{M}}_{bb}^{\Gamma_j} \boldsymbol{\phi}_{b,\xi}, \quad \xi = 1, 2, ..., N_b^{\Gamma_j}. \tag{16}$$

$N_b^{\Gamma_j}$ is the total number of boundary DOFs for a jth interface. The N_n is the number of selected CC modes to be used for interface reduction basis. According to modal reduction, the number of reduction basis should be $N_n < N_b^{\Gamma_j}$.

The range of CC modes computation is an important factor in obtaining guaranteed accuracy. The reduction basis for a jth interface (15) contains other interface sets dependent on synthesized substructures. In Figure 2, for example, $\mathbf{\Gamma}_{j,1}, \mathbf{\Gamma}_{j,2}, \mathbf{\Gamma}_{j,3}, \mathbf{\Gamma}_{j,4}$ are uncompleted interface sets, and connected to substructures consist of $\mathbf{\Gamma}_j$:

$$
\mathbf{\Phi}_{bn}^{\Gamma_j} = \begin{bmatrix} \mathbf{\Phi}_{bj,n}^{\Gamma_j} \\ \mathbf{\Phi}_{b1,n}^{\Gamma_{j,1}} \\ \mathbf{\Phi}_{b2,n}^{\Gamma_{j,2}} \\ \mathbf{\Phi}_{b3,n}^{\Gamma_{j,3}} \end{bmatrix}. \tag{17}
$$

Therefore, the proportion of interface set $\mathbf{\Phi}_{bj,n}^{\Gamma_j}$ is only selected as an $\mathbf{\Gamma}_j$ reduction basis. The final interface reduction basis for a jth interface is expressed as

$$
\mathbf{\Phi}_{kn}^{\Gamma_j} = \begin{bmatrix} \mathbf{\Phi}_{bj,n}^{\Gamma_j} \end{bmatrix}. \tag{18}
$$

Note that the additional sets are straightforwardly removed from Equation (17). However, it is crucial to consider these eliminated additional sets to account for the free-interface and rigid-body modes of partially synthesized systems.

In addition, the primary distinction between the previous hybrid level and this newly proposed localized interface reduction is that the points interconnected by multiple interfaces and substructures are discriminated, as presented in Figure 1a. Applying transformation to these red points may result in a significant loss of accuracy since the connection between interfaces and substructures are ignored. Thus, presented red points should be treated as CB-reduced interior DOFs and retained. Consequently, the relationship between interface-reduced CB systems is expressed as follows:

$$
\begin{bmatrix} \mathbf{U}_m \\ \mathbf{U}_{ib} \\ \mathbf{U}_n^{\Gamma} \end{bmatrix} = \begin{bmatrix} \mathbf{Q}_{im} & 0 & 0 \\ & \mathbf{I} & 0 \\ symm & & \mathbf{Q}_{kn} \end{bmatrix} \begin{bmatrix} \bar{\mathbf{U}}_i \\ \mathbf{U}_{ib} \\ \bar{\mathbf{U}}_k^{\Gamma} \end{bmatrix}, \tag{19}
$$

where

$$
\bar{\mathbf{U}}_i = \begin{bmatrix} \bar{\mathbf{u}}_i^1 \\ \bar{\mathbf{u}}_i^2 \\ \vdots \\ \bar{\mathbf{u}}_i^s \end{bmatrix}, \quad \mathbf{U}_{ib} = \begin{bmatrix} \mathbf{u}_i^1 \\ \mathbf{u}_i^2 \\ \vdots \\ \mathbf{u}_i^p \end{bmatrix}, \quad \bar{\mathbf{U}}_k^{\Gamma} = \begin{bmatrix} \bar{\mathbf{u}}_k^{\Gamma_1} \\ \bar{\mathbf{u}}_k^{\Gamma_2} \\ \vdots \\ \bar{\mathbf{u}}_k^{\Gamma_j} \end{bmatrix}. \tag{20}
$$

Following to previous procedures, interface transformation bases, $\mathbf{Q}_{im}$ and $\mathbf{Q}_{kn}$, for a final interface localized system could be written as

$$
\mathbf{Q}_{im} = \begin{bmatrix} \mathbf{\Phi}_{im}^1 & 0 & 0 & 0 \\ & \mathbf{\Phi}_{im}^2 & 0 & 0 \\ & & \ddots & 0 \\ & & & \mathbf{\Phi}_{im}^s \end{bmatrix}, \quad \mathbf{Q}_{kn} = \begin{bmatrix} \mathbf{\Phi}_{kn}^{\Gamma_1} & 0 & 0 & 0 \\ & \mathbf{\Phi}_{kn}^{\Gamma_2} & 0 & 0 \\ & & \ddots & 0 \\ & & & \mathbf{\Phi}_{kn}^{\Gamma_j} \end{bmatrix}. \tag{21}
$$

The $\mathbf{\Phi}_{im}^s$ is FINMs for interior reduction. p denotes numbering for retained points without transformation. $\mathbf{\Phi}_{kn}^{\Gamma_j}$ indicates the localized CC modes for a jth interface.

This proposed localized interface-reduction method minimizes the trade-off between accuracy and efficiency in comparison to other techniques. Design modification respecting parameter changes is more effective than system-level interface reduction, which requires assembling all substructures for CC modes computation. As a result, interface parallel computation is also possible. Regarding accuracy, the connectivity of substructures can be considered besides the local-level interface reduction, and enforcing compatibility is no longer required since straightforward synthesis can be allowed.

4. Numerical Examples

In this section, numerical examples are presented to evaluate the performance of the proposed interface-reduction method. One of the significant benefits of the proposed approach is that there is no modeling limitation to apply. To demonstrate the multiplicity of applicable models, the graphic partitioning algorithm METIS [39] is adopted for substructuring to design subdomains.

For performance verification, the original CB method [13] and the system-level interface reduced CB method with same proportion CC modes [24] are adopted as reference values. However, the previous hybrid-level interface reduction [38] cannot be applied to the systems substructured by METIS algorithm since this substructuring method provides complicated interface design, and users are not allowed to intervene for design modification. For fair comparison with the previous interface-reduction method, designed substructuring models are additionally presented with METIS substructuring. The relative error is written as

$$error_i = \frac{|\lambda_{FOM,i} - \lambda_{ROM,i}|}{\lambda_{FOM,i}}. \tag{22}$$

The subscript i denotes the ith eigenvalue of systems. Therefore, $\lambda_{FOM,i}$ indicates the ith modes of full-system, while $\lambda_{ROM,i}$ is the ith mode of the ROM. Note that the ROM could be the reference values and the proposed method. The performance evaluation of the presented systems is conducted by MATLAB R2022 in-house code under an 8-core Intel CPU running at 4.80 GHz. The finite element modeling information is summarized in Table 2. The materials for the presented structures are aluminum with the following properties: Young's modulus E = 72×10^9 Pa, Poisson ratio v = 0.33, and density ρ = 27×10^3 kg/cm^3.

Table 2. DOF information of numerical examples.

	Elem.	Node	DOFs	FINMs	CC Modes	Designed ROM	METIS ROM
Plate	128	153	459	10%	30%	13.73%	14.16%
Box–beam	360	383	2298	5%	30%	8.40%	8.77%
Wing–box	12560	12073	72438	1%	10%	-	1.75%

4.1. Cantilever Plate

The cantilever plates divided into four substructures are presented. The four-node plate element is adopted for finite element modeling, and the total number of elements and DOFs are 128 and 459, respectively. In this plate example, designed substructuring is also presented and compared with METIS substructuring. Therefore, the number of interior and interface DOFs are slightly different, while the ratios of reduced systems are similar. The details of DOF information are also presented in Table 2. The domain decomposition information and localized interfaces are described in Figures 3 and 4 for the substructuring methods. Each substructure is dependent on certain design variables, such as the thickness of a plate. The thickness is 12 mm for all substructures for both structural models.

Figure 5 shows the error verification of the proportion of CC modes. To assess the accuracy of the proposed CC modes approaches, the number of CC modes is gradually reduced from 50% to 30%. Figure 5a represents the CC modes comparison for the system performed substructuring by designers. The entire system consists of four substructures, five localized interfaces, and two untransformed points, as presented in Figure 3. For the system reduction, 38 FINMs are used for interior reduction, which is about 10% of the entire interior DOFs. In addition, 29, 24, and 19 CC modes are employed for the interface reduction, which are 50%, 40%, and 30%, proportional to the entire interfaces, respectively. In general, noticeable error gaps are observed regarding the percentage of CC modes compared to the original CMS. Nevertheless, the overall predictions are acceptable, with average relative errors of 0.3%, 1.9%, and 5.0% to the proportion of CC modes.

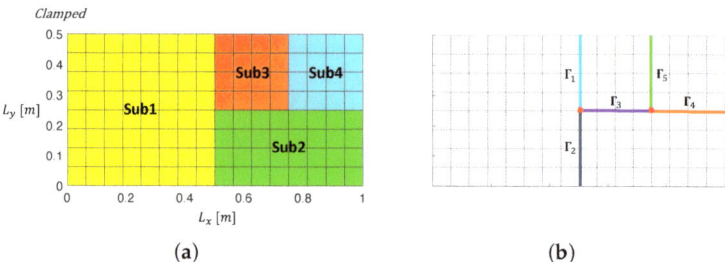

(a) (b)

Figure 3. Plate substructured by designation. (**a**) Plate with 4 design variables; (**b**) localized interfaces.

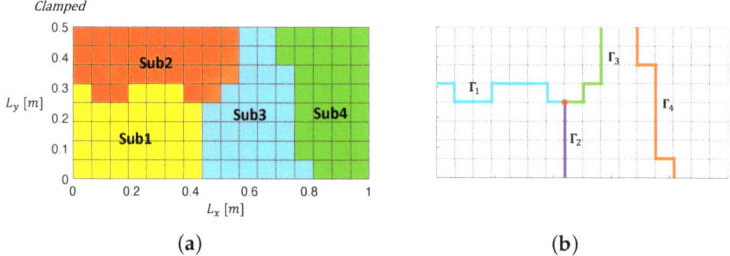

(a) (b)

Figure 4. Plate substructured by METIS. (**a**) Plate with 4 design variables; (**b**) localized interfaces.

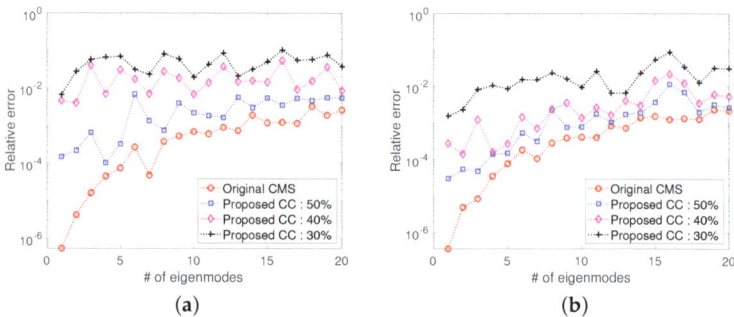

(a) (b)

Figure 5. Error verification with respect to the proportion of CC modes. (**a**) Designated substructuring plate; (**b**) METIS substructuring plate.

Regarding a plate structure performed substructuring by METIS in Figure 4, the entire system is composed of four substructures and four localized interfaces. There is an untransformed point, which is a connection of interface sets Γ_1, Γ_2, Γ_3. The same percentage of modes are adopted for the reduction in both interiors and interfaces. The interior DOFs are reduced by 35 FINMs, and 46, 36, and 27 CC modes are, respectively, used to the presented proportion of CC modes. The average errors for 50%, 40%, and 30% CC modes are 0.2%, 0.4%, and 2.1%, respectively. A higher accuracy is noticed in METIS substructuring than in the designed substructures. However, those results could not guarantee that the METIS substructuring approach performs better than the designed system. This is due to the differences in the original number of interior and interface DOFs between the two modeling, as presented in Table 3. In this presented case, a larger number of CC modes are used than designed substructuring approaches. According to the characteristic of modal system reduction, overall errors gradually increase as the number of CC modes increases, as expected, for both modeling cases.

Figure 6 compares the proposed methods and the system-level interface reduction. For a fair comparison, the total number of untransformed interface DOFs and the number of CC modes for each interface is equal to the applied number of system-level CC modes. The proposed methods show compromise in accuracy regardless of substructuring methods, while the system-level interface-reduction method presents great agreement with the original CB method. These accuracy losses are believed to be caused by system connectivity, partially considered, not a fully coupled system. Further investigation of accuracy will be presented by comparing with the previous hybrid-level interface-reduction methods in the following examples. Although the error gap is noticed, the proposed method demonstrates acceptable reliability, with presented relative errors at nearly 10^{-2}.

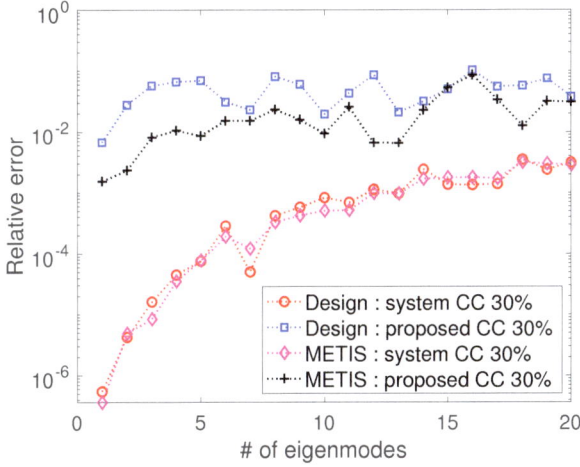

Figure 6. Error verification with respect to substructuring methods.

Table 3. The information of localized interfaces for plate.

	Interface DOFs	# of Interface Sets	Untransformed DOFs	# of CC Modes
Design domain	63	5	6	19
METIS: 4 subs	93	4	3	27

4.2. Shell Box–Beam

This section compares the performance of the proposed method with previous hybrid-level interface reduction techniques. To present the performance of the previous hybrid-level interface method, the box–beam structures are decomposed into the same number of subdomains with METIS substructuring, as illustrated in Figures 7 and 8. The system is designed to realize clearly isolated interface sets with multiple substructures, while the system designed by METIS substructuring has interconnected localized interface sets and substructures, as shown in Figure 8.

Furthermore, the applicable modeling range is also investigated with diverse box–beam substructuring designs. For FE modeling, 360 4-node flat shell elements (MITC4) [41] and 383 nodes are employed. The initial thickness is 25 mm for all presented beam models and substructures. The FE modeling details are presented by comparison of FOM and ROM in Table 2.

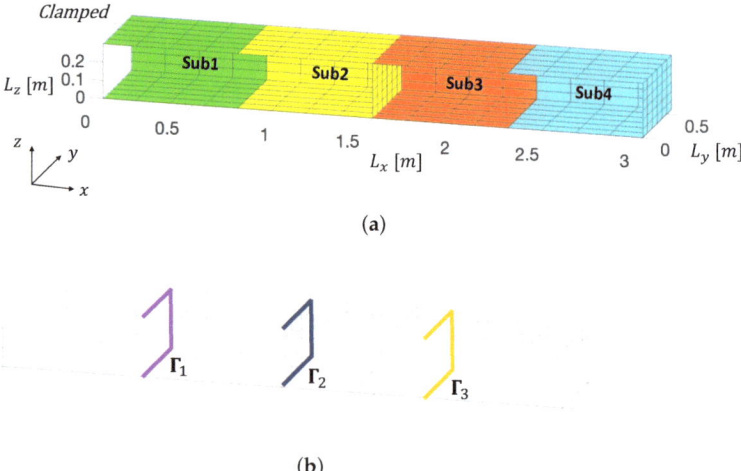

(a)

(b)

Figure 7. Box–beam substructured by designation. (**a**) Box–beam with 4 design variables; (**b**) localized interfaces.

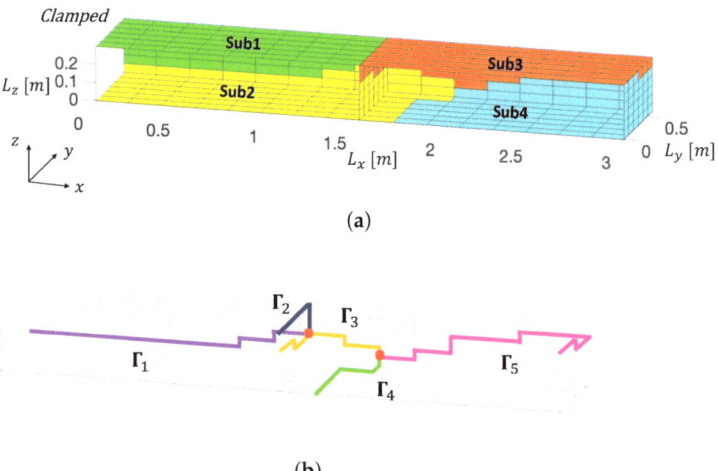

(a)

(b)

Figure 8. Box–beam substructured by METIS. (**a**) Box–beam with 4 design variables; (**b**) localized interfaces.

Figure 9 presents the error verification with respect to the proportion of CC modes for the box–beam structure. According to Figure 7, four substructures construct three independent interface sets without untransformed points to represent a modeling case applicable to the previous hybrid-level evaluation. The relative errors of the structure, which is distinctly sectioned, are presented in Figure 9a. Despite of error discrepancy in lower modes, the overall error level is comparable with the original CB method. Additionally, relative errors within 20 modes are below 10^{-3} for all presented numbers of CC modes.

In addition, Figure 9b shows the relative errors for the system performed substructuring by METIS. Compared to the original CB method, the relative errors steadily increase by considering the number of CC modes. This is a reasonable trend of modal reduction. When 30% of CC modes are used for reduction, the average relative error is 0.17%, while for 50% and 40% of CC modes, the relative errors are all below 10^{-3}.

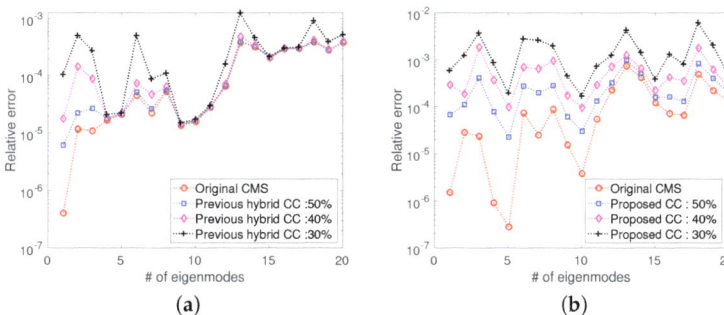

Figure 9. Error verification with respect to the proportion of CC mods for box–beam. (**a**) Previous hybrid interface reduction; (**b**) proposed localized interface reduction.

Corresponding to the previous investigation determining an appropriate number of CC modes for the box beam, it turned out that employing 30% of CC modes can achieve the desired error level, which is below 10^{-2} for the presented box model. Accordingly, the previous and proposed hybrid-level CC modes are compared using 30% CC modes in Figure 10. Furthermore, the system-level interface reduced system is also presented for more comprehensive evaluation. The proposed method shows a higher error level than the previous hybrid-level interface reduction. However, this discrepancy could not be evidence to conclude that the proposed method causes a larger compromise in accuracy than the previous method. This is because the modeling condition, such as the numbers of interior and interface DOFs, differs even when the same proportion of CC modes are employed. For instance, 102 and 95 CC modes are, respectively, selected as the 30% CC modes for both designed and METIS substructuring models. The information on localized interfaces for the beam is summarized in Table 4. According to this comparison, it can be inferred that larger accuracy losses compared to the identical number of system-level CC modes are influenced by the partial system coupling, even though a perfectly fair comparison between the proposed and previous hybrid-level is not possible.

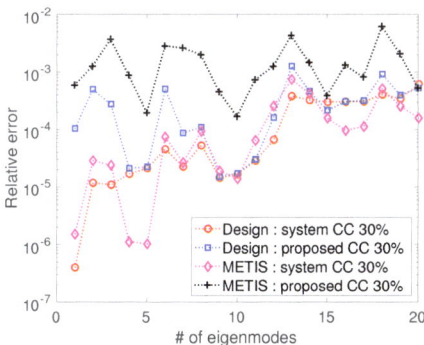

Figure 10. Error verification with respect to substructuring methods.

In Figure 11, additional beam models that have different numbers of substructures are presented for further investigation of applicable modeling ranges with METIS substructuring. In each case, a consistent 30% proportion of CC modes is employed for each localized interface set. The system defined by 6 substructures and 10 interfaces selects 144 CC modes, while the total interface DOFs are 480, in Figure 11a. Regarding the system with 8 substructures in Figure 11b, substructures build 11 localized interfaces, and 170 CC modes are selected from 594 original interface DOFs. More details of the localized interfaces and untransformed DOFs are presented in Table 4.

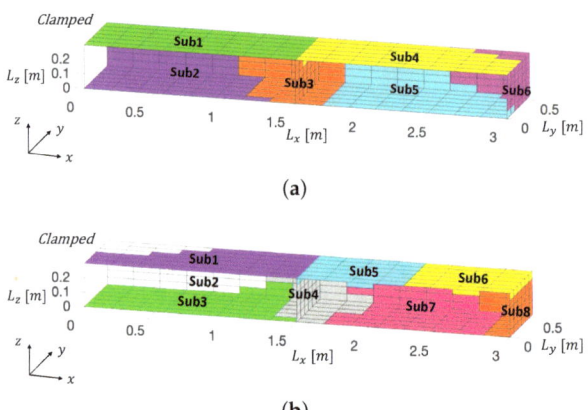

(a)

(b)

Figure 11. METIS design. (**a**) 6 substructuring; (**b**) 8 substructuring.

Table 4. The information of localized interfaces for box–beam.

	Interface DOFs	# of Interface Sets	Untransformed DOFs	# of CC Modes
Design domain	342	3	-	102
METIS: 4 subs	330	5	12	95
METIS: 6 subs	480	10	18	144
METIS: 8 subs	594	11	42	170

Figure 12 presents the relative error comparison with respect to the number of substructures. When the system has four substructures, relative error within 20 modes shows great prediction with figures below 10^{-3}. On the other hand, error levels with a larger number of substructures rise, even the average relative errors are still acceptable as 0.95% and 2.23% for six and eight substructures, respectively. It is important to note that the same percentage of CC modes is applied to each localized interface set for reduction. This implies that the influence of each interface on the entire system is overlooked in this investigation. Consequently, the sensitivity analysis of each interface set would be a possible option to improve the accuracy of the proposed method.

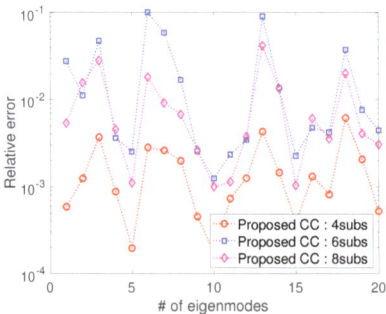

Figure 12. Error verification with respect to the number of substructures.

4.3. Wing Box

The systems presented above are unsuitable to properly demonstrate the efficiency of the proposed method due to their inherently low number of DOFs. Moreover, interface reduction is carried out under limited conditions, with over 30% of CC modes proportional to entire interface DOFs. This limitation arises from the need to include rigid body modes, aiming for higher system reduction than 30% CC modes cannot sufficiently contain rigid body modes.

Accordingly, a large-winged structure with numerous substructures and interfaces is presented as a final example in Figure 13. All substructures in this structure have the same thickness value of 8 mm. The structure consists of 12,560 shell elements and 12,073 nodes, with specific DOFs detailed in Table 2. The system is divided into 10 substructures and 28 localized interfaces by METIS substructuring, as indicated in Table 5. This section focuses on efficiency verification, not only accuracy. Therefore, parametric studies were also performed to evaluate the performance.

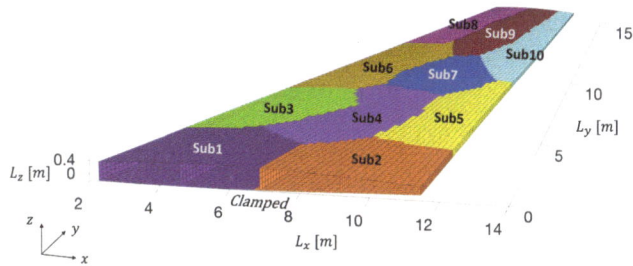

Figure 13. Wing–box modeling.

Table 5. The information of localized interfaces for wing.

	Interface DOFs	# of Interface Sets	Untransformed DOFs	# of CC Modes
Large wing	5184	28	24	578

Figure 14 presents a relative comparison with respect to the percentage of CC modes for wing structures. The relative errors consistently increase, similar to the previous investigations. When 1076 and 1586 CC modes are applied, which is proportional 20% or 30% to entire interface DOFs, reliable error levels are observed with the value of relative errors are approximately 10^{-3}. However, applying 10% CC modes compared to the entire interface DOFs shows 10^{-2} error level, while the system-level method shows great accuracy below 10^{-4}. Nonetheless, the average relative error remains below 1%, specifically at 0.92%.

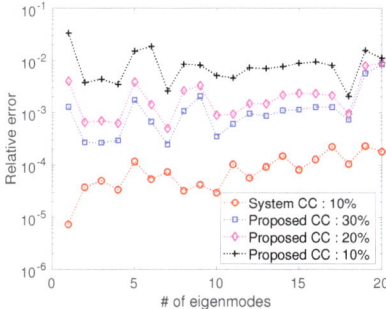

Figure 14. Error verification with respect to CC modes.

To assess the efficiency of the proposed method, the eigenvalue analysis is conducted by using *eigs* function [42] adopted in MATLAB due to significant computational resources. As shown in Figure 15, three values of computation time are presented: full-system, original CMS without interface reduction, and the system reduced using the proposed CC modes method. Despite a considerable interior reduction, there is no significant difference in system computation time between the full system and the original CMS system. On the other hand, the system that employed CC modes shows a great decrease in computation time to 0.12 s. Significant time saving can be achieved with this proposed method—approximately 5.19% of system solving time is taken compared to the original CMS.

For specific comparison in efficiency, the system matrices for CC modes comparison between the system-level and proposed method are presented in Figure 16. Interface region accounting for CC modes computation is marked with a yellow box on the sparsity matrix. Figure 16b–d show partially synthesized stiffness matrices to construct semi-localized interfaces which numbers 1, 2, and 3, and Figure 16a offers the stiffness matrix, which is fully synthesized all substructures. For the system-level interface reduction, the CC modes were computed by considering the system matrix, which has a 9,865,565 non-zero value. On the other hand, the proposed method handles 1,470,616, 1,961,465, and 3,645,419 non-zero matrices for CC modes computation, respectively.

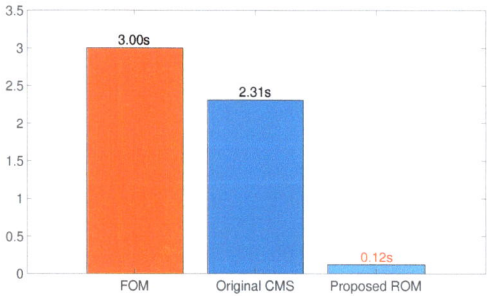

Figure 15. System solving time for wing.

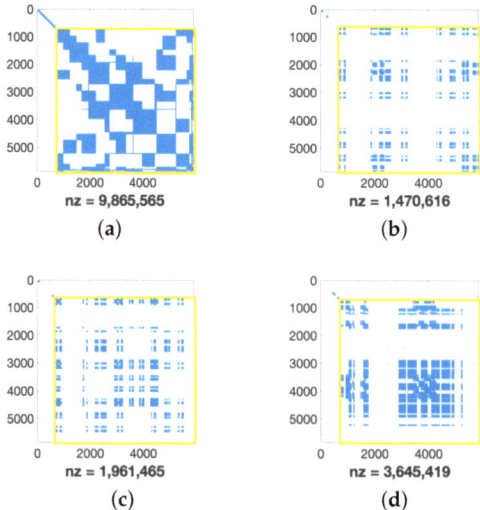

Figure 16. CC modes computation comparison. (**a**) System-level CC modes; (**b**) proposed cc modes—interface 1; (**c**) proposed CC modes: interface 2; (**d**) proposed CC modes: interface 3.

According to the interface matrices comparison presented in Figure 16, the CC modes computation time comparison is also provided in Figure 17. The orange bar represents the secondary eigenvalue analysis time for system-level CC modes computation, while the blue bars indicate individual localized interfaces determined by the proposed method. Most of the localized interfaces require less than 200 s for CC modes computation except for the 13th and 23rd interfaces, while the system-level takes 1066 s. Additionally, this figure also points out that this proposed method enables parallel computation for each interface set. Only several interfaces connected to substructures requiring design modification are considered for design changes, not the full size of the system interface.

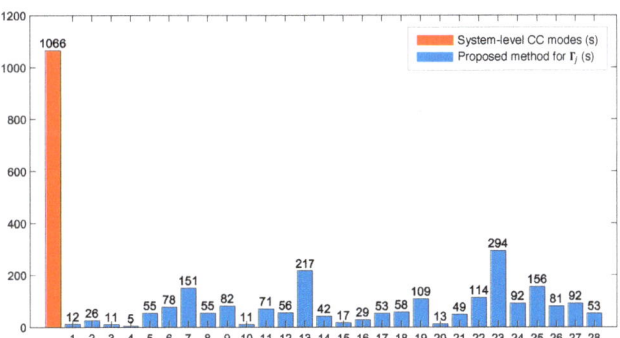

Figure 17. CC modes computation time with respect to each interface.

For further efficiency verification, simple parametric studies have been conducted in this section considering two case scenarios. The thickness of marked substructures varies as [8,10,12] mm, while the previous performance evaluations input consistent thickness for all substructures. The second and eighth substructures are considered for parametric variations following Figure 18a. For the system-level CC modes computation, $3 \times 3 = 9$ times secondary eigenvalue analysis is performed on a fully coupled system. On the contrary, eight semi-localized interface sets are associated with parameter-varied substructures. Therefore, $8 \times 3 = 24$ times CC modes are computed in partially assembled systems. For three substructures with parametric variations according to Figure 18b, the third substructure and five semi-localized interfaces are additionally accounted for CC modes computation; $3 \times 3 = 27$ times and $13 \times 3 = 39$ times secondary eigenvalue analysis are, respectively, performed for system-level and proposed interface-reduction method. The substructure information for constructing each semi-localized interface Γ_j is shown in Table 6.

Figure 19 shows the CC modes computation time comparison for each parametric case studies case. Case 1 represents parametric studies for two substructures shown in Figure 19a, and the system-level CC modes computation took 9592.62 s, including nine repeated computations. Meanwhile, the proposed CC modes computation takes 949.05 s, which is less than 10% compared to the system-level CC modes computation time. Furthermore, in parametric study case 2, the proposed method requires 1944.50 s, while the system-level case takes 28,777.87 s. This figure indicates that approximately 6% of computation time is consumed in comparison to the system-level computation. One of the most significant benefits of the proposed method is the availability of parallel computation. Therefore, only the most time-consuming interface associated with parametric variations is accounted for computation. As a result, it can be expected to achieve at least 61 times computational resource savings according to case 2, which has three parametric varied substructures, when more substructures are associated with parametric studies. The efficiency of CC modes computation with respect to presented parametric studies cases is organized in Tables 7 and 8.

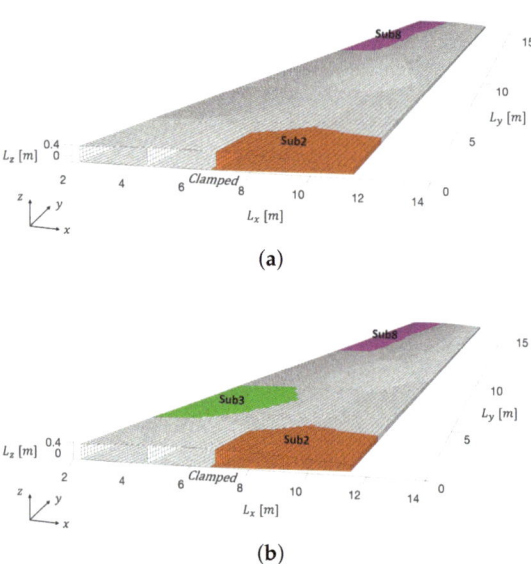

(a)

(b)

Figure 18. Parametric case studies. (**a**) Case 1: 2 substructure varied to parametric variations; (**b**) Case 2: 3 substructure varied to parametric variations.

Table 6. Adjacent substructures to construct interface Γ_j.

	\multicolumn{13}{c}{Localized-Interface Number Γ_j}
	1	2	3	4	6	10	17	18	20	25	26	27	28
Subdomains connectivity	-	-	-	1, 2	1, 2, 4	2, 5	2, 4	-	-	-	-	2, 4, 5	-
	-	3, 6	1, 3	-	-	-	-	3, 4	-	3, 4, 6	1, 3, 4	-	-
	6, 8	-	-	-	-	-	-	-	8, 9	-	-	-	7, 8

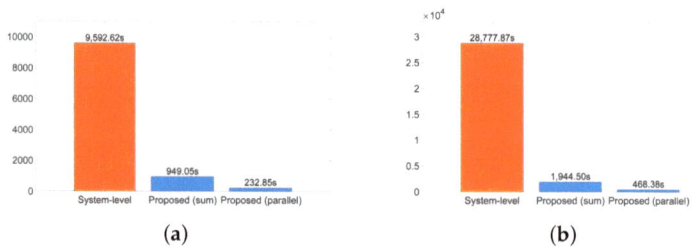

(a)   **(b)**

Figure 19. CC modes computation time comparison. (**a**) Computation time for case 1; (**b**) Computation time for case 2.

Table 7. CC modes computation time comparison: 2subs parametric variations.

	System-Level	Proposed Method (Sum)	Proposed (Parallel)
# of CC modes computation	9	24	3
CC modes computation time	9,592.62 s	949.05 s	232.85 s

Table 8. CC modes computation time comparison: 3subs parametric variations.

	System-Level	Proposed Method (Sum)	Proposed (Parallel)
# of CC modes computation	27	39	3
CC modes computation time	28,777.87 s	1,944.50 s	468.38 s

5. Conclusions

In this paper, an enhanced hybrid-level interface-reduction method was proposed by developing an interface localization algorithm. Although the previous CMS and its variants allow convenient parametric studies by decomposing the main structure into independent subsystems, the methods were limited in using ROM for parametric variations as they primarily focused on the interior reduction, and as a result, the final ROMs were not online-capable size. Since interface reduction is mandatory to be useful for efficient computation, various interface-reduction methods were continuously developed by incorporating secondary eigenvalue analysis. Among them, the methods adopting hybrid-level characteristic constraint (CC) modes verify the feasibility of considering design modifications at the substructural level without much accuracy loss. The proposed method overcomes the limitation of previous hybrid-level interface reduction. Specifically, the previous methods were only applicable to independently defined interfaces and subsystems. In the present work, the interface localization was realized by assigning unique numbers based on substructural-level Boolean operations. As a result, the substructuring and interface reduction became possible regardless of the number of interconnected interfaces and substructures. The performance of the proposed method was demonstrated for both accuracy and efficiency aspects. Compared with the methods at the system-level CC modes, the proposed one requires less than 10 times the CC mode computation time, resulting in a significant enhancement in the efficiency of the constructing ROM for the parametric studies of large dynamical systems.

As a future development, the proposed interface localization method will be applicable to the family of parametric CMS methods. The conventional parametric CMS derives ROMs and their solutions for parametric variations in the online stage by using precomputed offline samples with reduced subsystems. Therefore, the proposed interface localizing method is expected to discard the interface reduction process in the online stage, whereas the previous CMS performs the secondary eigenvalue analysis in the online stage. Additionally, this proposed method is expected to apply to the finite volume method (FVM) expending from the FEM analysis [42–45].

Author Contributions: S.C.: conceptualization, data curation, formal analysis, investigation, methodology, software, validation, visualization, writing—original draft preparation. J.L.: conceptualization, funding acquisition, investigation, methodology, resources, software, supervision, writing—review and editing. All authors have read and agreed to the published version of the manuscript.

Funding: This research was supported by the National Research Foundation of Korea, 2020 (NRF-2020R1C1C1011970), and by the National Research Foundation of Korea (NRF) grant funded by the Korean government (MSIT) (NRF-2018R1A5A7023490).

Data Availability Statement: Data available on request, subject to privacy or ethical considerations.

Conflicts of Interest: The authors declare no conflict of interest.

References

1. Amsallem, D.; Farhat, C. Interpolation method for adapting reduced-order models and application to aeroelasticity. *AIAA J.* **2008**, *46*, 1803–1813. [CrossRef]
2. Amsallem, D.; Farhat, C. An Online Method for Interpolating Linear Parametric Reduced-Order Models. *SIAM J. Sci. Comput.* **2011**, *33*, 2169–2198. [CrossRef]

3. Bui-Thanh, T.; Willcox, K.; Ghattas, O. Model Reduction for Large-Scale Systems with High-Dimensional Parametric Input Space. *SIAM J. Sci. Comput.* **2008**, *30*, 3270–3288. [CrossRef]
4. Negri, F.; Manzoni, A.; Amsallem, D. Efficient model reduction of parametrized systems by matrix discrete empirical interpolation. *J. Comput. Phys.* **2015**, *303*, 431–454. [CrossRef]
5. Lee, J.; Cho, M. An interpolation-based parametric reduced order model combined with component mode synthesis. *Comput. Methods Appl. Mech. Eng.* **2017**, *319*, 258–286. [CrossRef]
6. Lee, J. A parametric reduced-order model using substructural mode selections and interpolation. *Comput. Struct.* **2019**, *212*, 199–214. [CrossRef]
7. Lee, J. A dynamic substructuring-based parametric reduced-order model considering the interpolation of free-interface substructural modes. *J. Mech. Sci. Tech.* **2018**, *32*, 5831–5838. [CrossRef]
8. Zhou, Z.; Zhang, H.; Yang, X. H1-norm error analysis of a robust ADI method on graded mesh for three-dimensional subdiffusion problems. *Numer. Algo.* **2023**, 1–19. [CrossRef]
9. Zhang, H.; Liu, Y.; Yang, X. An efficient ADI difference scheme for the nonlocal evolution problem in three-dimensional space. *J. Appl. Math. Comput.* **2023**, *69*, 651–674. [CrossRef]
10. Tian, Q.; Yang, X.; Zhang, H.; Xu, D. An implicit robust numerical scheme with graded meshes for the modified Burgers model with nonlocal dynamic properties. *Comp. Appl. Math.* **2023**, *42*, 246. [CrossRef]
11. Wang, W.; Zhang, H.; Jiang, X.; Yang, X. A high-order and efficient numerical technique for the nonlocal neutron diffusion equation representing neutron transport in a nuclear reactor. *Ann. Nucl. Energy* **2024**, *195*, 110163. [CrossRef]
12. Hurty, W. Dynamic analysis of structures using substructure modes. *AIAA J.* **1965**, *3*, 678–685. [CrossRef]
13. Craig, R.R.; Bampton, M.C.C. Coupling of substructures for dynamic analyses. *AIAA J.* **1968**, *6*, 1313–1319. [CrossRef]
14. Bennighof, J.K.; Lehoucq, R.B. An automated multilevel substructuring method for eigenspace computation in linear elastodynamics. *SIAM J. Sci. Comput.* **2004**, *25*, 2084–2106. [CrossRef]
15. Kim, J.G.; Lee, P.S. An enhanced craig–bampton method. *Int. J. Numer. Methods Eng.* **2015**, *103*, 79–93. [CrossRef]
16. Craig, R.R.; Kurdila, A.J. *Fundamentals of Structural Dynamics*; John Wiley & Sons: Hoboken, NJ, USA, 2006.
17. Craig, R.R. Substructure Methods in Vibration. *J. Vib. Acoust.* **1995**, *117*, 207–213. [CrossRef]
18. de Klerk, D.; Rixen, D.J.; Voormeeren, S.N. General Framework for Dynamic Substructuring: History, Review and Classification of Techniques. *AIAA J.* **2008**, *46*, 1169–1181. [CrossRef]
19. Peskin, C.S. Numerical analysis of blood flow in the heart. *J. Comput. Phys.* **1977**, *25*, 220–252. [CrossRef]
20. Zhang, L.; Gerstenberger, A.; Wang, X.; Liu, W.K. Immersed finite element method. *Comput. Methods Appl. Mech. Eng.* **2004**, *193*, 2051–2067. [CrossRef]
21. Babuška, I.; Banerjee, U.; Kergrene, K. Strongly stable generalized finite element method: Application to interface problems. *Comput. Methods Appl. Mech. Eng.* **2017**, *327*, 58–92. [CrossRef]
22. Zhang, Q.; Babuška, I. A stable generalized finite element method (SGFEM) of degree two for interface problems. *Comput. Methods Appl. Mech. Eng.* **2020**, *363*, 112889. [CrossRef]
23. Craig , R.R., Jr.; Chang, C.J. *Substructure Coupling for Dynamic Analysis and Testing*; Technical Report; NASA: Washington, DC, USA, 1977.
24. Castanier, M.P.; Tan, Y.C.; Pierre, C. Characteristic constraint modes for component mode synthesis. *AIAA J.* **2001**, *39*, 1182–1187. [CrossRef]
25. Tran, D. Component mode synthesis methods using interface modes. Application to structures with cyclic symmetry. *Comput. Struct.* **2001**, *79*, 209–222. [CrossRef]
26. Tran, D.M. Component mode synthesis methods using partial interface modes: Application to tuned and mistuned structures with cyclic symmetry. *Comput. Struct.* **2009**, *87*, 1141–1153. [CrossRef]
27. Herrmann, J.; Maess, M.; Gaul, L. Substructuring including interface reduction for the efficient vibro-acoustic simulation of fluid-filled piping systems. *Mech. Syst. Signal Process.* **2010**, *24*, 153–163. [CrossRef]
28. Cammarata, A.; Sinatra, R.; Maddio, P.D. Interface reduction in flexible multibody systems using the Floating Frame of Reference Formulation. *J. Sound Vib.* **2022**, *523*, 116720. [CrossRef]
29. Hughes, P.J.; Kuether, R.J. Nonlinear Interface Reduction for Time-Domain Analysis of Hurty/Craig Bampton Superelements with Frictional Contact. *J. Sound Vib.* **2021**, *507*, 116154. [CrossRef]
30. Monteil, M.; Besset, S.; Sinou, J.J. A double modal synthesis approach for brake squeal prediction. *Mech. Syst. Signal Process.* **2016**, *70–71*, 1073–1084; [CrossRef]
31. Lindberg, E.; Hörlin, N.E.; Göransson, P. Component mode synthesis using undeformed interface coupling modes to connect soft and stiff substructures. *Shock Vib.* **2013**, *20*, 157–170. [CrossRef]
32. Lee, S.; Mok, H.; Kim, C.W. On a component mode synthesis on multi-level and its application to dynamics analysis of vehicle system supported with spring-stiffness damper system. *J. Mech. Sci. Tech.* **2011**, *25*, 3115–3121. [CrossRef]
33. Hong, S.K.; Epureanu, B.I.; Castanier, M.P. Next-generation parametric reduced-order models. *Mech. Syst. Signal Process.* **2013**, *37*, 403–421. [CrossRef]
34. Kuether, R.J.; Allen, M.S.; Hollkamp, J.J. Modal Substructuring of Geometrically Nonlinear Finite Element Models with Interface Reduction. *AIAA J.* **2017**, *55*, 1695–1706. [CrossRef]

35. Holzwarth, P.; Eberhard, P. Interface Reduction for CMS Methods and Alternative Model Order Reduction. *IFAC-PapersOnLine* **2015**, *48*, 254–259. [CrossRef]
36. Wu, L.; Tiso, P.; Van Keulen, F. Interface reduction with multilevel Craig Bampton substructuring for component mode synthesis. *AIAA J.* **2018**, *56*, 2030–2044. [CrossRef]
37. Aoyama, Y.; Yagawa, G. Component mode synthesis for large-scale structural eigenanalysis. *Comput. Struct.* **2001**, *79*, 605–615. [CrossRef]
38. Krattiger, D.; Wu, L.; Zacharczuk, M.; Buck, M.; Kuether, R.J.; Allen, M.S.; Tiso, P.; Brake, M.R. Interface reduction for Hurty/Craig Bampton substructured models: Review and improvements. *Mech. Syst. Signal Process.* **2019**, *114*, 579–603. [CrossRef]
39. Karypis, G.; Kumar, V. *METIS: A Software Package for Partitioning Unstructured Graphs, Partitioning Meshes, and Computing Fill-Reducing Orderings of Sparse Matrices*; University of Minnesota: Minneapolis, MN, USA, 1997.
40. Bathe, K.J. *Finite Element Procedures*; Pearson Education: London, UK, 2006.
41. Dvorkin, E.N.; Bathe, K.J. A continuum mechanics based four-node shell element for general non-linear analysis. *Eng. Comput.* **1984**, *1*, 77–88; [CrossRef]
42. Radke, R.J. *A Matlab Implementation of the Implicitly Restarted Arnoldi Method for Solving Large-Scale Eigenvalue Problems*; Rice University: Houston, TX, USA, 1996.
43. Yang, X.; Zhang, H. The uniform l1 long-time behavior of time discretization for time-fractional partial differential equations with nonsmooth data. *Appl. Math. Lett.* **2022**, *124*, 107644. [CrossRef]
44. Yang, X.; Zhang, H.; Zhang, Q.; Yuan, G. Simple positivity-preserving nonlinear finite volume scheme for subdiffusion equations on general non-conforming distorted meshes. *Nonlinear Dyn.* **2022**, *108*, 3859–3886. [CrossRef]
45. Yang, X.; Zhang, H.; Zhang, Q.; Yuan, G.; Sheng, Z. The finite volume scheme preserving maximum principle for two-dimensional time-fractional Fokker–Planck equations on distorted meshes. *Appl. Math. Lett.* **2019**, *97*, 99–106. [CrossRef]

Article

Study of Transversely Isotropic Visco-Beam with Memory-Dependent Derivative

Kulvinder Singh [1], Iqbal Kaur [2] and Eduard-Marius Craciun [3,4,*]

[1] CSE Department, UIET, Kurukshetra University, Kurukshetra 136118, Haryana, India; ksingh2015@kuk.ac.in
[2] Department of Mathematics, Government College for Girls Palwal, Kurukshetra 136118, Haryana, India; bawahanda@gmail.com
[3] Faculty of Mechanical, Industrial and Maritime Engineering, "Ovidius" University of Constanta, 900527 Constanta, Romania
[4] Academy of Romanian Scientists, Ilfov Street, 030167 Bucharest, Romania
* Correspondence: mcraciun@univ-ovidius.ro

Abstract: Based on the modified Moore–Gibson–Thompson (MGT) model, transversely isotropic visco-thermoelastic material is investigated for frequency shift and thermoelastic damping. The Green–Naghdi (GN) III theory of thermoelasticity with two temperatures is used to express the equations that govern heat conduction in deformable bodies based on the difference between conductive and dynamic temperature acceleration. A mathematical model for a simply supported scale beam is formed in a closed form using Euler Bernoulli (EB) beam theory. We have figured out the lateral deflection, conductive temperature, frequency shift, and thermoelastic damping. To calculate the numerical values of various physical quantities, a MATLAB program has been developed. Graphical representations of the memory-dependent derivative's influence have been made.

Keywords: transversely isotropic viscoelastic; beam; memory-dependent derivative; Moore–Gibson–Thompson model; thermoelastic damping; frequency shift

MSC: 74D99; 35D40; 35Q74

Citation: Singh, K.; Kaur, I.; Craciun, E.-M. Study of Transversely Isotropic Visco-Beam with Memory-Dependent Derivative. *Mathematics* **2023**, *11*, 4416. https://doi.org/10.3390/math11214416

Academic Editor: Matjaz Skrinar

Received: 3 October 2023
Revised: 17 October 2023
Accepted: 24 October 2023
Published: 25 October 2023

1. Introduction

In modern engineering structures, materials are often exposed to high temperatures, which makes viscoelastic materials, such as polymer science, of great interest. A certain amount of viscoelastic response is evident in all materials. Among the most common metals are steel, aluminium, and copper. If a material exhibits both viscous and elastic properties when deformed, it is termed viscoelastic. When linear materials show dependency on both time and temperature, they are described as rheological viscoelastic materials. As a consequence of engineering structures' variation in temperature, approximating their material characteristics no longer holds even in an approximation context. Temperature affects the thermal and mechanical properties of materials, so it is necessary to consider the temperature dependence of their properties when performing a thermal stress analysis. Heat conductance is crucial in materials science and related sciences, especially at high working temperatures. Depending on the circumstances, metals and other materials may react differently to temperature changes. Free electrons are the main cause of conductivity in metals. As a general rule, a metal's thermal conductivity (Kelvin) is proportional to its electric conductivity at absolute temperatures.

Visco-thermoelasticity and variational laws in irreversible thermodynamics were discussed by Biot [1]. Using an elastic moduli model and relaxations as parameters, Drozdov [2] developed a thermo-viscoelasticity constitutive model. Applied magneto-thermo-viscoelastic media were studied by Bera [3]. An isotropic visco-thermoelastic model was developed by Ezzat and El-Karamany [4] to investigate volume relaxations in viscoelasticity. Ezzat et al. [5] developed the equation of generalized thermo-viscoelasticity with one relaxation time and two relaxation times, ignoring the volume's relaxation effects. Visco thermoelastic micro-polar transversely isotropic (TI) media were studied by Kumar et al. [6] to determine the effect of viscosity on the amplitude ratios of plane waves. In contrast, Green and Naghdi [7–9] presented Green–Nagdhi (GN) theories of thermoelasticity with and without energy dissipation. A generalized fractional-order thermoelasticity (FOT) model, introduced by Povstenko [10], introduced both classical thermoelasticity and generalized thermoelasticity with GN.

Several academic works have recently analysed and interpreted the Moore–Gibson–Thompson (MGT) equation because of its wide range of applications. There are several important applications of the MGT equation, including fluid dynamics and viscoelasticity [11]. According to Lasiecka and Wang [12], certain fluid dynamics can be modelled by a differential equation of the third order. Quintanilla [13,14] used the MGT equation with 2T to develop a new model of heat conduction. The modified Fourier equation, also known as the MGT equation, is as follows:

$$\left(1 + \tau_0 \frac{\partial}{\partial t}\right) q = -K_{ij} \nabla T - K_{ij}^* \nabla \vartheta, \text{ where, } \dot{\vartheta} = T \tag{1}$$

Later, the memory effect of thermoelasticity was subsequently demonstrated with a better model of MDD (rate of sudden change dependent on past state). "*MDD is defined in an integral form of a common derivative with a kernel function on a slip-in interval*". Wang and Li [15] presented the first-order MDD with respect to time delay $\tau_0 > 0$ for a fixed time t, for the differentiable function $f(t)$:

$$D_{\tau_0} f(t) = \frac{1}{\tau_0} \int_{t-\tau_0}^{t} K(t - \xi) f'(\xi) d\xi, \tag{2}$$

Taylor's series of MDD may be used to extend $q(x, t + \tau_0)$ while ignoring words up to the first order in time delay:

$$q(x, t + \tau_0) = q(x, t) + \tau_0 D_{\tau_0} q(x, t), \tag{3}$$

Thus, Fourier's law in the theory of generalized heat conduction is provided by Ezzat et al. [16] using the Taylor series of MDD.

$$q(x, t) + \tau_0 D_{\tau_0} q(x, t) = -K T_{,i}, (0 < \tau_0 \leq 1), \tag{4}$$

The selection of the kernel functions $K(t - \xi)$ and τ_0 is influenced by the characteristics of the raw materials. Following Ezzat et al. [16–18], the $K(t - \xi)$ is used here in the form

$$K(t - \xi) = 1 - \frac{2\beta}{\tau_0}(t - \xi) + \frac{\alpha^2}{\tau_0^2}(t - \xi)^2 = \begin{cases} 1, & \alpha = 0, \beta = 0, \\ 1 + (\xi - t)/\tau_0, & \alpha = 0, \beta = 1/2, \\ \xi - t + 1, & \alpha = 0, \beta = \tau_0/2, \\ [1 + (\xi - t)/\tau_0]^2, & \alpha = 1, \beta = 1. \end{cases} \tag{5}$$

Despite this, several researchers such as Marin [19,20], Abbas and Marin [21], Kaur et al. [22,23], Van Do et al. [24], Doan et al. [25], Craciun et al. [26], Lata et al. [27], Jafari et al. [28], Craciun et al. [29], Malik et al. [30], and Sharma and Marin [31] studied the theories of thermoelasticity. Besides this, there have not been any studies on frequency shift and thermoelastic damping in visco-beams with the MGT and MDD theories of thermoelasticity.

In this research, the GN III theory of thermoelasticity and the Moore–Gibson–Thompson (MGT) equation have been revisited, and they are adopted to analyse the free vibrations in visco-thermoelastic beams with MDD. EB beam theory has been used to formulate the mathematical simulation for the visco-beams. The effect of MDD on the various quantities is graphically depicted.

2. Basic Equations

The basic equations for an anisotropic thermo-visco-elastic medium without heat sources and body forces [8,32,33] utilizing the MGT and MDD theories are as follows:

1. The stress–displacement–temperature relation:

$$t_{ij} = \tau_m C_{ijkl} e_{kl} - \tau_m \beta_{ij} T, \tag{6}$$

where $\tau_m = 1 + \eta \frac{\partial}{\partial t}$, and η is the viscoelastic relaxation time due to the viscosity.

2. The strain–displacement relation:

$$e_{ij} = \frac{1}{2}(u_{i,j} + u_{j,i}), \quad i, j = 1, 2, 3. \tag{7}$$

3. The MGT thermoelastic heat conduction equation with MDD is

$$K_{ij}\dot{\varphi}_{,ij} + K_{ij}^* \varphi_{,ij} = \left(1 + \tau_0 D_{\tau_0} - \eta^2 \nabla^2\right)\left(\beta_{ij}\tau_m T_0 \ddot{e}_{ij} + \rho C_E \ddot{T}\right), \tag{8}$$

where

$$T = \varphi - a_{ij}\varphi_{,ij}, \tag{9}$$

$$\beta_{ij} = C_{ijkl}\alpha_{ij}, \tag{10}$$

$\beta_{ij} = \beta_i \delta_{ij}$, $K_{ij} = K_i \delta_{ij}$, $K_{ij}^* = K_i^* \delta_{ij}$, i is not summed. C_{ijkl} are elastic parameters and have symmetry $\left(C_{ijkl} = C_{klij} = C_{jikl} = C_{ijlk}\right)$.

3. Mathematical Modelling of the Problem

As illustrated in Figure 1, we have taken a visco-beam with length $(0 \leq x \leq L)$, width $\left(-\frac{b}{2} \leq y \leq \frac{b}{2}\right)$, and thickness $\left(-\frac{h}{2} \leq z \leq \frac{h}{2}\right)$ in Cartesian coordinates. Let the beam's x-axis serve as its axis. Its two endpoints should be at $x = 0$ and $x = h$, and the origin should be located in the middle of the end at $x = 0$. Consider that beam is free from any stress and strain and is at a uniform temperature T_0 in a stable position. Additionally, the upper and bottom surfaces of the beam do not experience any heat transfer; therefore,

$$\frac{\partial \varphi}{\partial z} = 0, \text{ at } z = \pm \frac{h}{2}. \tag{11}$$

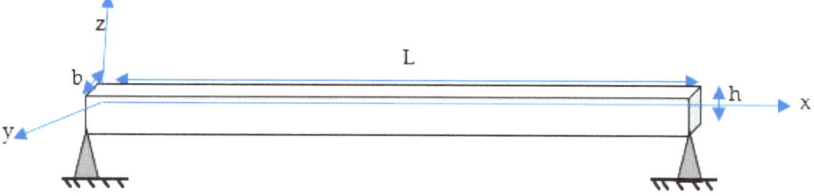

Figure 1. Diagram of the visco-beam.

The EB model describes that "any plane cross-section, initially perpendicular to the axis of the beam remains plane and perpendicular to the neutral surface during bending".

Therefore, according to Youssef et al. [34], the following displacement components are given for small deflection:

$$u(x, y, z, t) = -z\frac{\partial w}{\partial x}, \ \ v(x, y, z, t) = 0, \ \ w(x, y, z, t) = w(x, t), \tag{12}$$

The 1D constitutive Equation (6) using Equation (12) becomes

$$t_{xx} = -C_{11}\tau_m z\frac{\partial^2 w}{\partial x^2} - \beta_1\tau_m T, \tag{13}$$

where $\beta_1 = (C_{11} + C_{13})\alpha_1 + C_{13}\alpha_3$.

The thermoelastic parameter $\beta_3 = 2C_{13}\alpha_1 + C_{33}\alpha_3$ does not exist along the z-axis according to the EB hypothesis.

The flexural moment of the cross-section $M(x, t)$ for the beam is provided by Rao [35] as

$$M(x, t) = -\int_{-\frac{h}{2}}^{\frac{h}{2}}\int_{\frac{-b}{2}}^{\frac{b}{2}} t_{xx}zdzdy = C_{11}\tau_m I\frac{\partial^2 w}{\partial x^2} + \beta_1\tau_m M_T, \tag{14}$$

where

$$M_T = b\int_{\frac{-h}{2}}^{\frac{h}{2}} Tzdz, \tag{15}$$

$$I = \frac{bh^3}{12}. $$

Since $T \equiv T(x, z, t)$ and $\varphi \equiv \varphi(x, z, t)$, the thermodynamic temperature of a transversely isotropic beam from Equation (14) is given by

$$T = \left\{\varphi - \left(a_1\frac{\partial^2\varphi}{\partial x^2} + a_3\frac{\partial^2\varphi}{\partial z^2}\right)\right\}. \tag{16}$$

The equation for the motion of the visco-beam without pressures in the transverse direction [35,36] is written as

$$\frac{\partial^2 M}{\partial x^2} + \rho A\frac{\partial^2 w}{\partial t^2} = 0, \tag{17}$$

where $A = bh$.

Using Equation (14) in Equation (17), we obtain

$$C_{11}I\tau_m\frac{\partial^4 w}{\partial x^4} + \beta_1\tau_m\frac{\partial^2 M_T}{\partial x^2} + \rho A\frac{\partial^2 w}{\partial t^2} = 0. \tag{18}$$

Equation (8), with the help of Equation (12), becomes

$$\left(K_1^* + K_1\frac{\partial}{\partial t}\right)\frac{\partial^2\varphi}{\partial x^2} + \left(K_3^* + K_3\frac{\partial}{\partial t}\right)\frac{\partial^2\varphi}{\partial z^2} = -z\beta_1 T_0(1 + \tau_0 D_{\tau_0})\tau_m\frac{\partial^4 w}{\partial x^2\partial t^2} + \rho C_E(1 + \tau_0 D_{\tau_0})\frac{\partial^2}{\partial t^2}\left\{\varphi - \left(a_1\frac{\partial^2\varphi}{\partial x^2} + a_3\frac{\partial^2\varphi}{\partial z^2}\right)\right\}. \tag{19}$$

The beam's time harmonic behaviour may be described as

$$[w(x, t), \varphi(x, z, t)] = [w(x), \varphi(x, z)]e^{i\omega t}. \tag{20}$$

The dimensionless quantities are given as

$$x' = \frac{x}{L}, \ z' = \frac{z}{L}, \ w' = \frac{w}{L}, h' = \frac{h}{L}, b' = \frac{b}{L}, t' = \frac{c_1}{L}t, \ \eta' = \frac{c_1}{L}\eta, T' = \frac{T}{T_0},$$
$$\varphi' = \frac{\varphi}{T_0}, \ \rho c_1^2 = C_{11}, \ t'_{xx} = \frac{t_{xx}}{\beta_1 T_0}, a'_1 = \frac{a_1}{L^2}, a'_3 = \frac{a_3}{L^2}, M'_T = \frac{M_T}{T_0 L^3}. \tag{21}$$

Equation (21) is applied to Equations (18) and (19) to yield the non-dimensional version of these equations after suppressing the primes, which is represented as

$$I\tau_m^* \frac{\partial^4 w}{\partial x^4} + \tau_m^* \frac{\beta_1 T_0 L^4}{c_{11}} \frac{\partial^2 M_T}{\partial x^2} - AL^2 \omega^2 w = 0, \tag{22}$$

$$\left(K_1^* + K_1 \frac{c_1}{L} i\omega\right) \frac{\partial^2 \varphi}{\partial x^2} + \left(K_3^* + K_3 \frac{c_1}{L} i\omega\right) \frac{\partial^2 \varphi}{\partial z^2} = zc_1^2 \beta_1 \omega^2 (1 + \tau_0 G)\tau_m^* \frac{\partial^2 w}{\partial x^2} - \rho C_E c_1^2 \omega^2 (1 + \tau_0 G)\left\{\varphi - \left(a_1 \frac{\partial^2 \varphi}{\partial x^2} + a_3 \frac{\partial^2 \varphi}{\partial z^2}\right)\right\}. \tag{23}$$

where $\tau_m^* = 1 + \eta i\omega$

$$G = \frac{i}{\omega}\left\{\frac{(1 - e^{i\omega\tau_0})i}{\omega\tau_0} - 2\beta\left[\frac{(1 - i\omega\tau_0)e^{i\omega\tau_0} - 1}{(\omega\tau_0)^2}\right] + \alpha^2\left[\frac{\left(i\left((\omega\tau_0)^2 - 2\right) - 2\tau\omega\right)e^{i\omega\tau_0} - 2i}{(\omega\tau_0)^3}\right]\right\}$$

4. Boundary Conditions

Let us assume that the beam is initially at rest and intact. As a result,

$$w(x,0) = \frac{\partial w(x,0)}{\partial t} = 0, \tag{24}$$

$$\varphi(x,z,0) = \frac{\partial \varphi(x,z,0)}{\partial t} = 0, \tag{25}$$

As considered, the ends of the beam are simply supported; therefore,

$$w(0,t) = w(L,t) = 0, \tag{26}$$

$$\frac{\partial^2 w(0,t)}{\partial x^2} = \frac{\partial^2 w(L,t)}{\partial x^2} = 0. \tag{27}$$

Now imagine that there is no heat transfer between the two surfaces of the beam, i.e., along the bottom surface $z = \frac{h}{2}$ and the upper surface $z = -\frac{h}{2}$, which results in

$$\frac{\partial \varphi}{\partial z}\left(x, \frac{h}{2}, 0\right) = \frac{\partial \varphi}{\partial z}\left(x, \frac{-h}{2}, 0\right) = 0. \tag{28}$$

5. Solution of the Problem along the Thickness Direction

Lifshitz and Roukes [37] state that the thermal gradient is zero in the y-direction. Additionally, "*due to geometry, the thermal gradients in the plane of the cross-section along the thickness direction i.e., z-axis are much larger than those along its axis i.e., x-axis of the -beam*" (i.e., $\frac{\partial^2 \varphi}{\partial x^2} \ll \frac{\partial^2 \varphi}{\partial z^2}$, hence $\frac{\partial^2 \varphi}{\partial x^2}$ can be ignored in Equation (22)), and hence Equation (22) for heat conduction may be changed to

$$\frac{\partial^2 \varphi}{\partial z^2} + \zeta_1^2 \varphi = \frac{\beta_1 \zeta_1^2 \tau_m^*}{\rho C_E} \frac{\partial^2 w}{\partial x^2} z, \tag{29}$$

where

$$\zeta_1 = \sqrt{\frac{\rho C_E c_1^2 \omega^2 (1 + \tau_0 G)}{\left(K_3^* + K_3 \frac{c_1}{L} i\omega - a_3 \rho C_E c_1^2 \omega^2 (1 + \tau_0 G)\right)}}.$$

Equation (29) yields the following solution:

$$\varphi(x,z) = \frac{\beta_1 \tau_m^*}{\rho C_E}\left(z - \frac{\sin \zeta_1 z}{\zeta_1 \cos \frac{\zeta_1 h}{2}}\right) \frac{\partial^2 w}{\partial x^2}. \tag{30}$$

Using Equation (30) in Equation (15) with the aid of Equation (16), we obtain

$$M_T = \frac{I\beta_1 \tau_m^*}{\rho C_E}\left(1 + \left(-1 + a_3\zeta_1^2\right)f(\omega)\right)\frac{\partial^2 w}{\partial x^2}. \tag{31}$$

and using Equation (31) in Equation (22), we obtain

$$L_\omega \frac{\partial^4 w}{\partial x^4} - \omega^2 w = 0, \tag{32}$$

where

$$L_\omega = \frac{I}{AL^2}\tau_m^*\left[1 + \varepsilon_T\left(1 - \left(1 + a_3\zeta_1^2\right)f(\omega)\right)\right],$$
$$\varepsilon_T = \frac{\beta_1^2 T_0 L^4}{\rho C_E},$$
$$f(\omega) = \frac{24}{\zeta_1^3 h^3}\left(\frac{\zeta_1 h}{2} - \tan\frac{\zeta_1 h}{2}\right).$$

Now, Equation (32) can also be written as

$$\frac{\partial^4 w}{\partial x^4} - \zeta^4 w = 0, \tag{33}$$

where

$$\zeta^4 = \frac{\omega^2}{L_\omega}.$$

Applying Laplace transforms defined by

$$\overline{w}(s) = \int_0^\infty w(x)e^{-sx}dx, \tag{34}$$

on Equation (33) and using boundary conditions defined by Equations (26) and (27), we obtain the following solution of Equation (33):

$$\overline{w}(s) = \frac{A_1}{2\zeta}\left(\frac{1}{s^2 + \zeta^2} + \frac{1}{s^2 - \zeta^2}\right) + \frac{A_2}{2\zeta^2}\left(\frac{1}{s^2 - \zeta^2} - \frac{1}{s^2 + \zeta^2}\right). \tag{35}$$

Now, taking the inverse Laplace transform of Equation (35) gives

$$w(x) = \frac{A_1}{2\zeta}(\sin(\zeta x) + \sinh(\zeta x)) + \frac{A_2}{2\zeta^3}(\sinh(\zeta x) - \sin(\zeta x)). \tag{36}$$

After including the dimensionless quantities defined by Equation (21) in the boundary conditions (26) and (27), solving Equation (36) at $x = L$ provides

$$\sin(\zeta)\sinh(\zeta) = 0. \tag{37}$$

which yields $\zeta_n = n\pi$, $n \geq 1$. Thus, the solutions for the lateral deflection from Equation (24) and the thermal moment expressions from Equation (35) for $\zeta_n = n\pi, n \geq 1$ are derived by using (31) as follows:

$$w(x,t) = \frac{1}{2}\sum_n \frac{A_n}{\zeta_n(\sin\zeta_n + \sinh\zeta_n)}\{(\sin\zeta_n + \sinh\zeta_n)(\sin\zeta_n x + \sinh\zeta_n x) - (-\sin\zeta_n + \sinh\zeta_n)(-\sin\zeta_n x + \sinh\zeta_n x)\}e^{i\omega_n t}, \tag{38}$$

$$M_T(x,z,t) = \frac{I\beta_1\tau_m^*}{\rho C_E}(1 + (1 + a_3\zeta_1^2)f(\omega))\sum_n \frac{A_n\zeta_n}{(\sin\zeta_n + \sinh\zeta_n)}\{(\sin\zeta_n + \sinh\zeta_n)(-\sin\zeta_n x + \sinh\zeta_n x) - (-\sin\zeta_n + \sinh\zeta_n)(\sin\zeta_n x + \sinh\zeta_n x)\}e^{i\omega_n t}. \tag{39}$$

From Equation (32), the beam's vibrational frequency is determined by

$$\omega_n = n^2\pi^2\sqrt{L_\omega} = \omega_0\sqrt{1 + \varepsilon_T\left(1 + \left(1 + a_3\zeta_1^2\right)f(\omega)\right)}, \tag{40}$$

where

$$\omega_0 = \frac{hn^2\pi^2}{L\sqrt{12}}$$

If we replace ω with ω_0 and $f(\omega)$ with (ω_0), we obtain the solution for all the media having $\epsilon_T \ll 1$ as follows:

$$\omega^m = \omega_0\sqrt{1 + \varepsilon_T\left(1 + \left(1 + a_3\zeta_1^2\right)f(\omega)\right)}. \tag{41}$$

The thermoelastic damping (TED) quality, also known as the thermal quality Q-factor, may be determined by

$$Q^{-1} = 2\left|\frac{\omega_I^n}{\omega_R^n}\right|, \tag{42}$$

where n is the mode number and is related to the transcendental roots in Equation (37), and ω_R^n and ω_I^n are the real and the imaginary parts of frequency ω^n. Due to thermal variations, the frequency shift (FS) may be given by

$$\omega_S = \left|\frac{\omega_R^n - \omega_0}{\omega_0}\right|. \tag{43}$$

6. Particular Cases

1. We can obtain the solution of physical quantities for simply supported visco-beams with the GN-II theory of thermoelasticity if $K_1 = K_3 = 0$ in Equations (38)–(43).
2. We can obtain the solution of physical quantities for simply supported visco-beams with the classical theory of thermoelasticity if we take $K_1^* = K_3^* = 0$ in Equations (38)–(43).
3. We can obtain the solution of physical quantities for simply supported cubic crystal thermoelastic visco-beams with the GN type-III theory of thermoelasticity if we take $C_{11} = C_{22} = C_{33}$, $C_{12} = C_{13}$, $C_{44} = C_{66}$, $\alpha_1 = \alpha_3 = \alpha'$, $\beta_1 = \beta_3 = \beta'$, $K_1 = K_3 = K$, $K_1^* = K_3^* = K^*$ in Equations (38)–(43).
4. We can obtain the solution of physical quantities for free vibrations in simply supported visco-beams with energy dissipation similar to Abbas [38] if we take $C_{11} = C_{33} = \lambda + 2\mu$, $C_{12} = C_{13} = \lambda$, $C_{44} = 2\mu$, $\alpha_1 = \alpha_3 = \alpha'$, $a_1 = a_3 = a$, $K_1 = K_3 = K$, $K_1^* = K_3^* = K^*$ in Equations (38)–(43).

7. Results and Discussion

Physical information for cobalt material (transversely isotropic) for the beam was selected from Dhaliwal and Singh [39] to illustrate the theoretical results:

$$C_{11} = 3.071 \times 10^{11}\text{Nm}^{-2}, C_{12} = 1.650 \times 10^{11}\text{Nm}^{-2}, C_{13} = 1.027 \times 10^{10}\text{Nm}^{-2},$$

$$C_{33} = 3.581 \times 10^{11}\ \text{Nm}^{-2}, C_{44} = 1.510 \times 10^{11}\ \text{Nm}^{-2}, C_E = 4.27 \times 10^2\ \text{Jkg}^{-1}\text{K}^{-1},$$

$$\beta_1 = 7.04 \times 10^6\ \text{Nm}^{-2}\text{K}^{-1}, \rho = 8.836 \times 10^3\text{kgm}^{-3}, T_0 = 298\ \text{K},$$

$$\beta_3 = 6.90 \times 10^6\ \text{Nm}^{-2}\text{K}^{-1},\ L = 1\text{m}, b = 0.01\text{m}$$

$$K_1 = 0.690 \times 10^2\ \text{Wm}^{-1}\text{K}^{-1}, K_3 = 0.690 \times 10^2\ \text{Wm}^{-1}\text{K}^{-1},$$

$$K_1^* = 0.02 \times 10^2 \text{ NSec}^{-2}\text{K}^{-1}, K_3^* = 0.04 \times 10^2 \text{ NSec}^{-2}\text{K}^{-1},$$

$$\eta = 0.01, \tau_0 = 0.02. \text{ Here, we have taken } A_n = 1.$$

The following physical data for copper, which is an isotropic material, were taken:

$$\lambda = 7.76 \times 10^{10} \text{ Nm}^{-2}, \mu = 3.86 \times 10^{10} \text{ Nm}^{-2}, \rho = 8.954 \times 10^3 \text{ Kgm}^{-3},$$

$$K = 386 \text{ Wm}^{-1}\text{K}^{-1}, \alpha' = 1.78 \times 10^{-5} \text{ K}^{-1}, C_E = 383.1 \text{ JKg}^{-1}\text{K}^{-1}, T_0 = 293 \text{ K},$$

$$K^* = 1.0 \times 10^{10} \text{ Nm}^{-2}$$

A program was developed in MATLAB to determine the numerical values of w, conductive temperature φ, M_T, Q^{-1}, and ω_S, and graphs drawn for different modes of kernel function of MDD are presented in Figures 2–6.

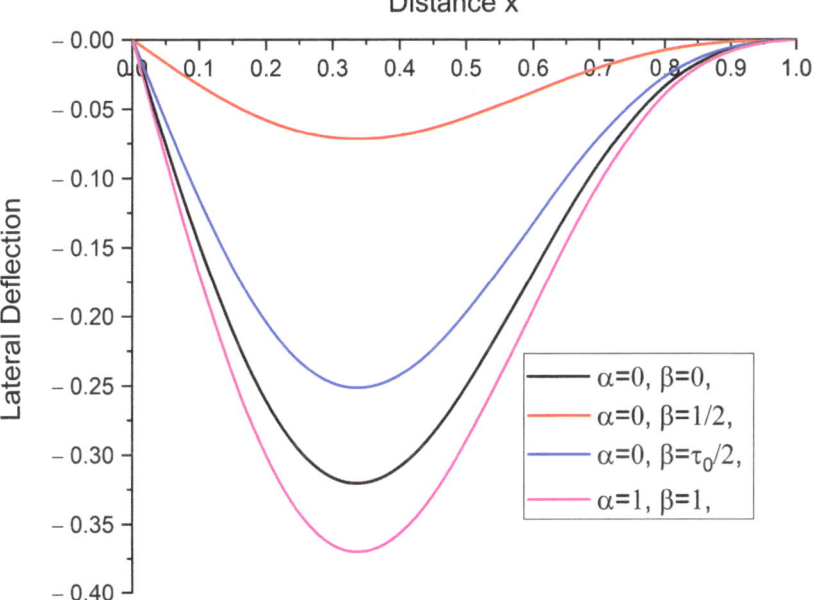

Figure 2. Graph of the lateral deflection w with respect to length of beam with different kernel function of MDD.

Figure 2 demonstrates the variation in the lateral deflection w with respect to the length of the visco-beam for different modes of kernel function $1 - \frac{2\beta}{\tau_0}(t - \xi) + \frac{\alpha^2}{\tau_0^2}(t - \xi)^2$ of MDD based on the values of α and β. As both ends of the visco-beam are simply supported, from the graph, it can be observed that the lateral deflection at $x = 0$ and $x = L$ is zero, which satisfies the boundary conditions. Moreover, for the kernel function $1 + (\xi - t)/\tau_0$ of MDD, the visco-beam shows the minimum variation as compared to when the value of the kernel function is $[1 + (\xi - t)/\tau_0]^2$. Therefore, the memory effect is clearly noticeable from the graph.

Figure 3 shows the variation in thermal moment M_T with the length of the beam for different modes of kernel function $1 - \frac{2\beta}{\tau_0}(t - \xi) + \frac{\alpha^2}{\tau_0^2}(t - \xi)^2$ of MDD based on the values of α and β. As both ends of the visco-beam are simply supported, from the graph, it can be observed that the thermal moment at $x = 0$ and $x = L$ is zero, which satisfies the boundary conditions. Moreover, for the kernel function 1 for $\alpha = 0$ and $\beta = 0$ of MDD, the visco-beam shows the minimum variation, whereas the thermal moment is at its maximum when the value of kernel function is $[1 + (\xi - t)/\tau_0]^2$. Therefore, the memory effect is clearly noticeable from the graph.

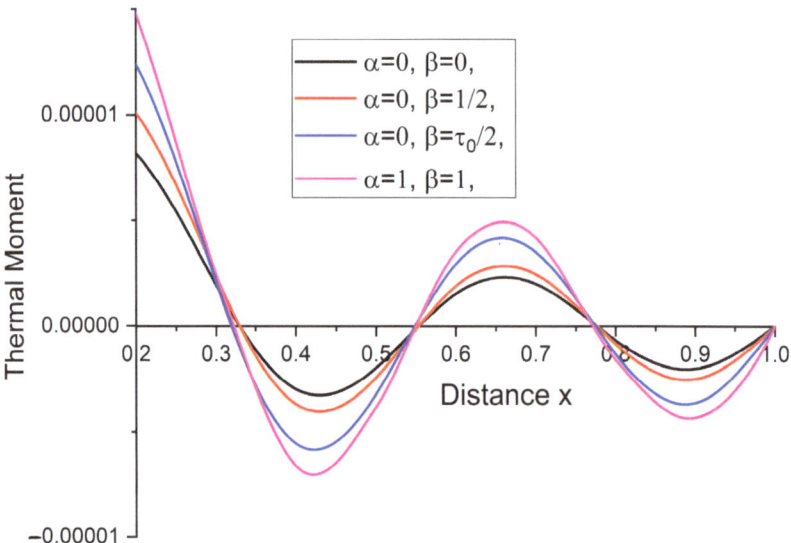

Figure 3. Graph of the thermal moment M_T with length of the beam with different kernel function of MDD.

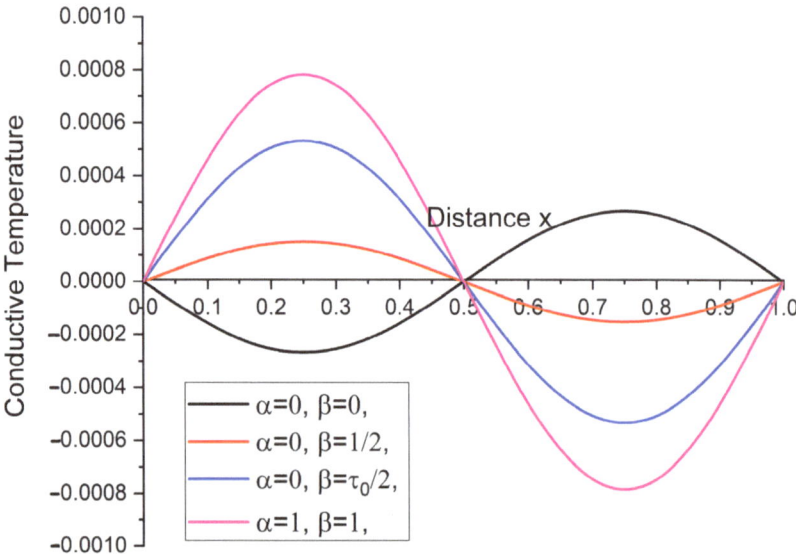

Figure 4. The conductive temperature with length x of beam with different kernel function of MDD.

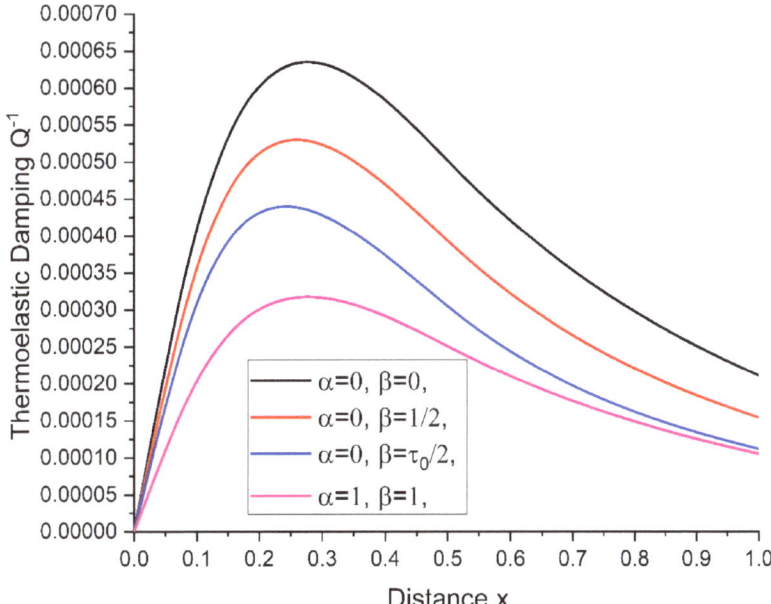

Figure 5. The thermoelastic damping Q^{-1} with length x of beam with different kernel function of MDD.

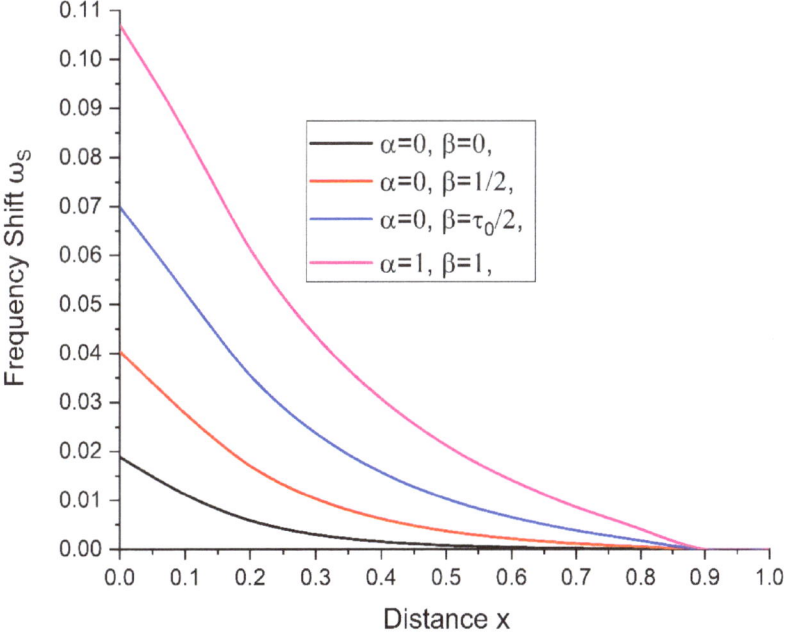

Figure 6. Graph of the frequency shift ω_S with length L of the beam with different kernel function of MDD.

Figure 4 demonstrates the variations in the conductive temperature φ with the length x for different modes of kernel function $1 - \frac{2\beta}{\tau_0}(t - \xi) + \frac{\alpha^2}{\tau_0^2}(t - \xi)^2$ of MDD based on the values of α and β. As both ends of the visco-beam are simply supported, from the graph, it can be observed that the conductive temperature at $x = 0$ and $x = L$ is zero, which satisfies the boundary conditions. Moreover, for the kernel function 1 for $\alpha = 0$ and $\beta = 0$ of MDD, the visco-beam shows the minimum variation in conductive temperature and shows the opposite behaviour to other values of kernel function of MDD, whereas the conductive temperature is at its maximum when the value of kernel function is $[1 + (\xi - t)/\tau_0]^2$. Therefore, the memory effect is clearly noticeable from the graph.

Figure 5 demonstrates the variations in the thermoelastic damping Q^{-1} with the length x for different modes of kernel function $1 - \frac{2\beta}{\tau_0}(t - \xi) + \frac{\alpha^2}{\tau_0^2}(t - \xi)^2$ of MDD based on the values of α and β. For the kernel function 1 for $\alpha = 0$ and $\beta = 0$ of MDD, the visco-beam shows the maximum variation in thermoelastic damping, whereas thermoelastic damping is at its minimum when the value of kernel function is $[1 + (\xi - t)/\tau_0]^2$. Therefore, the memory effect is clearly noticeable from the graph.

Figure 6 exhibits the frequency shift ω_S with length x for different modes of kernel function $1 - \frac{2\beta}{\tau_0}(t - \xi) + \frac{\alpha^2}{\tau_0^2}(t - \xi)^2$ of MDD based on the values of α and β. For the kernel function 1 for $\alpha = 0$ and $\beta = 0$ of MDD, the visco-beam shows the minimum variation in thermoelastic damping, whereas the thermoelastic damping is at its maximum when the value of kernel function is $[1 + (\xi - t)/\tau_0]^2$. Therefore, the memory effect is clearly noticeable from the graph. It is observed that as the length of the beam increases, the frequency shift ω_S abruptly decreases from its highest value to zero.

8. Conclusions

A mathematical model for a simply supported scale beam was formed in a closed form using Euler Bernoulli (EB) beam theory based on the modified Moore–Gibson–Thompson (MGT) model to investigate the frequency shift, thermoelastic damping, and other parameters of visco-beams. The Green–Naghdi (GN) III theory of thermoelasticity with two temperature- and memory-dependent derivatives was used to express the equations that govern heat conduction in deformable bodies. The solutions of PDE were obtained using Laplace transforms.

We came to the following conclusions after the discussion:

- The kernel function of the memory-dependent derivative plays a dominant role. As the kernel function changes, the amplitudes of the lateral deflection and thermal moment increase, but amplitude of the thermoelastic damping factor decreases with change in the kernel function.
- It was noticed that the frequency of time harmonic sources has a significant impact on the various properties of the beam.
- It was observed that the thermoelastic damping Q^{-1} grows first to reach the maximum values before decreasing with length. For the kernel function 1 for $\alpha = 0$ and $\beta = 0$ of MDD, the visco-beam shows the maximum variation in thermoelastic damping, whereas the thermoelastic damping is at its minimum when the value of kernel function is $[1 + (\xi - t)/\tau_0]^2$. Therefore, the memory effect is clearly noticeable from the graph.
- As the length of the beam increases, the frequency shift ω_S decreases from its high value at the beginning to zero.
- Theoretical research and computational results demonstrate that memory effects can amplify the thermoelastic field variations.
- Theoretical research and applications in viscoelastic materials have become crucial for solid mechanics because of the quick development of polymer science and the plastics industry, as well as the widespread use of materials that can withstand high temperatures in contemporary technology, sensing and actuation, mechanical resonators, and the integration of biology and geology into engineering.

Author Contributions: K.S.: conceptualization, effective literature review, experiments and simulation, investigation, methodology, software, supervision, validation, visualization, writing—original draft. I.K.: idea formulation, conceptualization, formulated strategies for mathematical modelling, methodology refinement, formal analysis, validation, writing—review and editing. E.-M.C.: conceptualization, effective literature review, formulated strategies for mathematical modelling, investigation, methodology, supervision, validation, visualization, writing—review and editing. All authors have read and agreed to the published version of the manuscript.

Funding: No fund/grant/scholarship has been taken for this research work.

Data Availability Statement: For the numerical results, silicon material was taken from Mahdy et al. [40].

Conflicts of Interest: The authors declare that they have no conflict of interest.

Nomenclature

δ_{ij}	Kronecker delta
C_{ijkl}	Elastic parameters
β_{ij}	Thermal elastic coupling tensor
T	Absolute temperature
T_0	Reference temperature
φ	Conductive temperature
t_{ij}	Stress tensors
e_{ij}	Strain tensors
u_i	Components of displacement
ρ	Medium density
C_E	Specific heat
a_{ij}	Two temperature parameters
ω	Frequency
I	Moment of inertia
$C_{11}I$	Flexural rigidity of the visco-beam
s	Laplace transform parameter
ε_T	Thermoelastic coupling
A	Area of cross-section
M_T	Thermal moment
$M(x,t)$	Flexural moment
$w(x,t)$	Lateral deflection
t	Time
α_{ij}	Linear thermal expansion coefficient
K_{ij}	Thermal conductivity
K_{ij}^*	Materialistic constant

References

1. Biot, M.A. Theory of Stress-Strain Relations in Anisotropic Viscoelasticity and Relaxation Phenomena. *J. Appl. Phys.* **1954**, *25*, 1385–1391. [CrossRef]
2. Drozdov, A.D. A Constitutive Model in Thermoviscoelasticity. *Mech. Res. Commun.* **1996**, *23*, 543–548. [CrossRef]
3. Bera, R.K. Propagation of Waves in Random Rotating Infinite Magneto-Thermo-Visco-Elastic Medium. *Comput. Math. Appl.* **1998**, *36*, 85–102. [CrossRef]
4. Ezzat, M.A.; El-Karamany, A.S. The Relaxation Effects of the Volume Properties of Viscoelastic Material in Generalized Thermoelasticity. *Int. J. Eng. Sci.* **2003**, *41*, 2281–2298. [CrossRef]
5. Ezzat, M.A. State Space Approach to Generalized Magneto-Thermoelasticity with Two Relaxation Times in a Medium of Perfect Conductivity. *Int. J. Eng. Sci.* **1997**, *35*, 741–752. [CrossRef]
6. Kumar, R.; Sharma, K.D.; Garg, S.K. Reflection of Plane Waves in Transversely Isotropic Micropolar Viscothermoelastic Solid. *Mater. Phys. Mech.* **2014**, *22*, 1–14.
7. Green, A.E.; Naghdi, P.M. A Re-Examination of the Basic Postulates of Thermomechanics. *Proc. R. Soc. Lond. Ser. A Math. Phys. Sci.* **1991**, *432*, 171–194. [CrossRef]
8. Green, A.E.; Naghdi, P.M. On Undamped Heat Waves In An Elastic Solid. *J. Therm. Stress.* **1992**, *15*, 253–264. [CrossRef]
9. Green, A.E.; Naghdi, P.M. Thermoelasticity without Energy Dissipation. *J. Elast.* **1993**, *31*, 189–208. [CrossRef]
10. Povstenko, Y.Z. Fractional Heat Conduction Equation And Associated Thermal Stress. *J. Therm. Stress.* **2004**, *28*, 83–102. [CrossRef]
11. Dreher, M.; Quintanilla, R.; Racke, R. Ill-Posed Problems in Thermomechanics. *Appl. Math. Lett.* **2009**, *22*, 1374–1379. [CrossRef]

12. Lasiecka, I.; Wang, X. Moore-Gibson-Thompson Equation with Memory, Part II: General Decay of Energy. *Anal. PDEs* **2015**, *259*, 7610–7635. [CrossRef]
13. Quintanilla, R. Moore-Gibson-Thompson Thermoelasticity. *Math. Mech. Solids* **2019**, *24*, 4020–4031. [CrossRef]
14. Quintanilla, R. Moore-Gibson-Thompson Thermoelasticity with Two Temperatures. *Appl. Eng. Sci.* **2020**, *1*, 100006. [CrossRef]
15. Wang, J.-L.; Li, H.-F. Surpassing the Fractional Derivative: Concept of the Memory-Dependent Derivative. *Comput. Math. Appl.* **2011**, *62*, 1562–1567. [CrossRef]
16. Ezzat, M.A.; El-Karamany, A.S.; El-Bary, A.A. Generalized Thermo-Viscoelasticity with Memory-Dependent Derivatives. *Int. J. Mech. Sci.* **2014**, *89*, 470–475. [CrossRef]
17. Ezzat, M.A.; El-Karamany, A.S.; El-Bary, A.A. Generalized Thermoelasticity with Memory-Dependent Derivatives Involving Two Temperatures. *Mech. Adv. Mater. Struct.* **2016**, *23*, 545–553. [CrossRef]
18. Ezzat, M.A.; El-Karamany, A.S.; El-Bary, A.A. A Novel Magneto-Thermoelasticity Theory with Memory-Dependent Derivative. *J. Electromagn. Waves Appl.* **2015**, *29*, 1018–1031. [CrossRef]
19. Marin, M. The Lagrange Identity Method in Thermoelasticity of Bodies with Microstructure. *Int. J. Eng. Sci.* **1994**, *32*, 1229–1240. [CrossRef]
20. Marin, M. On Existence and Uniqueness in Thermoelasticity of Micropolar Bodies. *Comptes Rendus Acad. Sci. Paris Ser. II* **1995**, *321*, 475–480.
21. Abbas, I.A.; Marin, M. Analytical Solution of Thermoelastic Interaction in a Half-Space by Pulsed Laser Heating. *Phys. E Low-Dimens. Syst. Nanostructures* **2017**, *87*, 254–260. [CrossRef]
22. Kaur, I.; Lata, P.; Singh, K. Effect of Memory Dependent Derivative on Forced Transverse Vibrations in Transversely Isotropic Thermoelastic Cantilever Nano-Beam with Two Temperature. *Appl. Math. Model.* **2020**, *88*, 83–105. [CrossRef]
23. Kaur, I.; Lata, P. Rayleigh Wave Propagation in Transversely Isotropic Magneto-Thermoelastic Medium with Three-Phase-Lag Heat Transfer and Diffusion. *Int. J. Mech. Mater. Eng.* **2019**, *14*, 12. [CrossRef]
24. Van Do, T.; Hong Doan, D.; Chi Tho, N.; Dinh Duc, N. Thermal Buckling Analysis of Cracked Functionally Graded Plates. *Int. J. Struct. Stab. Dyn.* **2022**, *22*, 2250089. [CrossRef]
25. Doan, D.H.; Zenkour, A.M.; Van Thom, D. Finite Element Modeling of Free Vibration of Cracked Nanoplates with Flexoelectric Effects. *Eur. Phys. J. Plus* **2022**, *137*, 447. [CrossRef]
26. Craciun, E.M.; Baesu, E.; Soós, E. General Solution in Terms of Complex Potentials for Incremental Antiplane States in Prestressed and Prepolarized Piezoelectric Crystals: Application to Mode III Fracture Propagation. *IMA J. Appl. Math. Inst. Math. Its Appl.* **2005**, *70*, 39–52. [CrossRef]
27. Lata, P.; Kaur, I.; Singh, K. Deformation in Transversely Isotropic Thermoelastic Thin Circular Plate Due to Multi-Dual-Phase-Lag Heat Transfer and Time-Harmonic Sources. *Arab J. Basic Appl. Sci.* **2020**, *27*, 259–269. [CrossRef]
28. Jafari, M.; Chaleshtari, M.H.B.; Abdolalian, H.; Craciun, E.-M.; Feo, L. Determination of Forces and Moments Per Unit Length in Symmetric Exponential FG Plates with a Quasi-Triangular Hole. *Symmetry* **2020**, *12*, 834. [CrossRef]
29. Craciun, E.M.; Carabineanu, A.; Peride, N. Antiplane Interface Crack in a Pre-Stressed Fiber-Reinforced Elastic Composite. *Comput. Mater. Sci.* **2008**, *43*, 184–189. [CrossRef]
30. Malik, S.; Gupta, D.; Kumar, K.; Sharma, R.K.; Jain, P. Reflection and Transmission of Plane Waves in Nonlocal Generalized Thermoelastic Solid with Diffusion. *Mech. Solids* **2023**, *58*, 161–188. [CrossRef]
31. Sharma, K.; Marin, M. Reflection and Transmission of Waves from Imperfect Boundary between Two Heat Conducting Micropolar Thermoelastic Solids. *Analele Univ. "Ovidius" Constanta-Ser. Mat.* **2014**, *22*, 151–176. [CrossRef]
32. Youssef, H.M.; El-Bary, A.A. Theory of Hyperbolic Two-Temperature Generalized Thermoelasticity. *Mater. Phys. Mech.* **2018**, *40*, 158–171. [CrossRef]
33. Lata, P.; Kaur, I. Thermomechanical Interactions in a Transversely Isotropic Magneto Thermoelastic Solids with Two Temperatures and Rotation Due to Time Harmonic Sources. *Coupled Syst. Mech.* **2019**, *8*, 219–245. [CrossRef]
34. Youssef, H.M.; El-Bary, A.A.; Elsibai, K.A. Vibration of Gold Nano Beam in Context of Two-Temperature Generalized Thermoelasticity Subjected to Laser Pulse. *Lat. Am. J. Solids Struct.* **2015**, *12*, 37–59. [CrossRef]
35. Rao, S.S. *Vibration of Continuous Systems*; John Wiley & Sons: Hoboken, NJ, USA, 2007; ISBN 0471771716.
36. Sharma, J.N.; Kaur, R. Transverse Vibrations in Thermoelastic-Diffusive Thin Micro-Beam Resonators. *J. Therm. Stress.* **2014**, *37*, 1265–1285. [CrossRef]
37. Lifshitz, R.; Roukes, M.L. Thermoelastic Damping in Micro- and Nanomechanical Systems. *Phys. Rev. B* **2000**, *61*, 5600–5609. [CrossRef]
38. Abbas, I.A. Free Vibrations of Nanoscale Beam Under Two-Temperature Green and Naghdi Model. *Int. J. Acoust. Vib.* **2018**, *23*, 289–293. [CrossRef]
39. Dhaliwal, R.S.; Singh, A. *Dynamic Coupled Thermoelasticity*; Hindustan Publication Corporation: New Delhi, India, 1980.
40. Mahdy, A.M.S.; Lotfy, K.; Ahmed, M.H.; El-Bary, A.; Ismail, E.A. Electromagnetic Hall Current Effect and Fractional Heat Order for Microtemperature Photo-Excited Semiconductor Medium with Laser Pulses. *Results Phys.* **2020**, *17*, 103161. [CrossRef]

Article

Variational Solution and Numerical Simulation of Bimodular Functionally Graded Thin Circular Plates under Large Deformation

Xiao-Ting He [1,2,*], Xiao-Guang Wang [1], Bo Pang [1], Jie-Chuan Ai [1] and Jun-Yi Sun [1,2]

1   School of Civil Engineering, Chongqing University, Chongqing 400045, China;
202116021064t@stu.cqu.edu.cn (X.-G.W.); 202116021032@cqu.edu.cn (B.P.); 202016021052@cqu.edu.cn (J.-C.A.);
sunjunyi@cqu.edu.cn (J.-Y.S.)
2   Key Laboratory of New Technology for Construction of Cities in Mountain Area (Chongqing University),
Ministry of Education, Chongqing 400045, China
*   Correspondence: hexiaoting@cqu.edu.cn; Tel.: +86-(0)23-65120720

Abstract: In this study, the variational method and numerical simulation technique were used to solve the problem of bimodular functionally graded thin plates under large deformation. During the application of the variational method, the functional was established on the elastic strain energy of the plate while the variation in the functional was realized by changing undetermined coefficients in the functional. As a result, the classical Ritz method was adopted to obtain the important relationship between load and maximum deflection that is of great concern in engineering design. At the same time, the numerical simulation technique was also utilized by applying the software ABAQUS6.14.4, in which the bimodular effect and functionally graded properties of the materials were simulated by subareas in tension and compression, as well as the layering along the direction of plate thickness, respectively. This study indicates that the numerical simulation results agree with those from the variational solution, by comparing the maximum deflection of the plate, which verifies the validity of the variational solution obtained. The results presented in this study are helpful for the refined analysis and optimization design of flexible structures, which are composed of bimodular functionally graded materials, while the structure is under large deformation.

Keywords: variational solution; numerical simulation; bimodular effect; functionally graded materials; thin circular plate; large deformation

MSC: 74K20; 74S05

Citation: He, X.-T.; Wang, X.-G.; Pang, B.; Ai, J.-C.; Sun, J.-Y. Variational Solution and Numerical Simulation of Bimodular Functionally Graded Thin Circular Plates under Large Deformation. *Mathematics* **2023**, *11*, 3083. https://doi.org/10.3390/math11143083

Academic Editor: Matjaz Skrinar

Received: 15 June 2023
Revised: 5 July 2023
Accepted: 10 July 2023
Published: 12 July 2023

1. Introduction

In the last ten years, bimodular functionally graded materials have gradually become a new research topic in academic circles. A bimodular material [1] has different elastic moduli in tension or compression, while a single-modulus material has the same modulus in tension or compression. Functionally graded materials [2] (FGMs) are a new type of composite material, generally composed of two materials, and the composition of the two materials presents continuous gradient changes, thus avoiding interface issues effectively. On the basis of functionally graded materials, considering the bimodular characteristics of the material will undoubtedly increase the difficulty of analysis, not to mention the application of this material model to the analysis of flexible structures involving large deformation (for example, flexible thin plates [3,4]). The problem is quite challenging for the combination of nonlinearity of materials and geometrical nonlinearity, especially in terms of the analytical methods. Therefore, in this study, we try to conduct both analytical and numerical research on this problem to enrich and improve existing research works in this field. For this purpose, the review is conducted in the following order to present a complete research background. The first is the bimodular materials, functionally graded materials, and their combination in recent studies; then, we briefly review the basic analytical methods used for plates and shells; finally, the structure of this paper is presented.

Many investigations show that most materials [5,6], such as graphite, rubber, concrete, ceramics, and biomedical materials, present different strains in tension and compression when they are subjected to tensile stress and compressive stress of the same magnitude. These materials have been referred to as bimodular materials by Jones [7]. In the theoretical analysis, there are basically two material models widely adopted: Bert's model [8] and Ambartsumyan's model [9]. Bert's model is mainly used in the analysis of orthotropic materials and laminated composites [10–12], and this model is based on the criterion of positive and negative signs in the strain of longitudinal fibers. Ambartsumyan's model, which is established on the criterion of positive and negatives signs of principal stresses, is mainly applied to isotropic materials. This model is of particular significance in the analysis and design of structures, and our present study is based on this model. In the application of Ambartsumyan's model, the principal stress is generally obtained as a result of the solution but not as a known quantity, which necessarily brings difficulties for describing the stress state of a point. Moreover, there is also a lack of experimental results to describe the elastic coefficient in complex stress states. Analytical solutions are only available in a few simple cases, most of them dealing with plates and beams [13–15]. However, in complex problems, we must turn to the finite element method (FEM) based on an iterative strategy. During each iteration, we need to judge the principal stress state of each element, thus acquiring a new elastic matrix used for the subsequent iteration. In the review of Ye et al. [16], this method is referred to as a direct iterative method of variable stiffness that has widely been used in earlier studies. Thereafter, Ma et al. [17] established a finite element iterative program to obtain buckling critical loads of bimodular rods. Given that the previous iteration of methods struggled because of the convergence difficulty of the constitutive model, Du et al. [18] established a new computational framework. Their works showed that the proposed framework can be successfully applied in solving the problem.

Functionally graded materials are a new type of composite materials, and the characteristic of its composition presents continuous gradient changes along the thickness direction, thus eliminating interface problems and presenting a smooth stress distribution. The material has been successfully used in various engineering fields since its advent, such as micro-electro-mechanical systems [19], aerospace engineering [20], civil engineering [21], and acoustics [22]. There are many works on the analysis of structural elements made of functionally graded materials, most of them dealing with beams and plates (for example, [23]). Among the studies, few consider the bimodular effect from functionally graded materials. As indicated above, most materials will show the bimodular effect (it is just a matter of whether it is obvious or not); thus, functionally graded materials seem to be no exception.

Recently, the bimodular effect of materials was further introduced into the analysis of functionally graded materials, and some works finally emerged, including bimodular FGM beams [24] and bimodular FGM plates [25–28]. Aiming at the bimodular FGM plates, a simplified theory on the neutral layer under small deflection was established in [25]; thereafter, the governing equations of the large-deflection problem of bimodular FGM thin circular plates was derived in [26]. For large-deformation problems, both the deflection and rotation angle will increase with the increase in external loads. For this purpose, a single-parameter perturbation method was used to solve the Föppl–von Kármán equations without the small-rotation-angle assumption in [27], and the biparametric perturbation method was used to solve the same problem in [28]. From the above review, it can be seen that for the analytical solution of this problem, the method is still mostly limited to the perturbation method, although extending from a single-parameter perturbation to a multiple-parameter perturbation. However, the analytical method for this problem is still relatively single. To solve this problem, various analytical methods must be sought.

In general, for plate and shell problems, there are three analytical methods widely used in theoretical analysis. The first one is the so-called series expansion method, in which the series may take all kinds of functional forms, for example, the power function, exponential function, and trigonometric function; the variational method is the second method, which is established on an energy principle (Galerkin method and Ritz method, for example); and the third is the perturbation technique. Each of the three methods has its advantages and disadvantages, which are not discussed in this article.

In large-deformation problems of plates and shells, the applications of the perturbation method and variational method both show their unique advantages. In the perturbation method, the first step is to establish the governing equation expressed in terms of the unknown displacement and stress. Then, the unknown displacement and stress are expanded in the form of ascending powers with respect to a certain small parameter (perturbation parameter). By substituting the expansions into the governing equations and boundary conditions, a set of equations determining the approximate solution of all levels are obtained. Due to the fact that the perturbation parameter either appears explicitly or is introduced artificially, in 1947, Chien [29] first selected the maximum deflection of thin plates as a perturbation parameter to acquire the perturbation solution successfully. Compared with the experimental data, Chien's solution is accurate and regarded as a landmark. For a long period of time, Chien's solution has been cited in subsequent studies. In the variational method, especially in the displacement variational method, that is, the Ritz method, the first step is to prescribe the displacement containing undetermined coefficients, and the prescribed displacement should satisfy the boundary conditions. As the second step, the energy functional is established, in which the total strain energy stored in the elastic body and the work done by external loads are determined in advance. By substituting the prescribed displacement into the energy functional, the so-called variation is realized only by the change in coefficients, thus determining the unknown coefficients and finally obtaining the displacement.

For large-deflection problems of thin circular plates, both Chien's perturbation solution [29] and the corresponding variational solution [30] have given satisfactory results in the literature. Compared with the perturbation method, the variational method has a distinct advantage. Due to the fact that the displacement variational equation itself represents the equilibrium equation and stress boundary conditions, it naturally avoids the consideration for the equilibrium condition of thin plates, while in the perturbation method, the establishment of an equation of equilibrium is necessary and somewhat complicated. Recent studies [31,32] also indicated that the variational method can be successfully used in the analysis of plates and shells. First, Xue et al. [31] adopted the variational method to obtain the critical loads of cantilever vertical plates with different moduli. Thereafter, He et al. [32] also used the variational method to solve bimodular thin shells under large deformation. The studies indicated that the variational method can be used for the analytical investigation of flexible plate and shell structures, but the introduction of nonlinearity of materials will increase the complexity in the analysis. From the currently collected literature, it seems that there is still no application of the variational method to bimodular functionally graded thin plates under large deformation.

In this study, the variational method of displacement is applied to solve the large deformation problem of bimodular functionally graded thin circular plates. The purpose and scope of this work are to seek a feasible analytical method for this problem and, at the same time, this analytical method is verified by the appropriate numerical simulation technique. From point of view of the nonlinearity of problems, the analytical solution for bimodular functionally graded thin plates under large deformation is challenging because the nonlinearities of materials and geometry that are intertwined further makes the obtainment of analytical solution more complicated. To this end, the whole article is organized as follows. In Section 2, the variational method and the bimodular FGM thin circular plate problem are briefly described. In Section 3, the physical equations of bimodular functionally graded materials and the geometrical relations under large deformation are presented. In Section 4, the total strain energy of the plate is derived first and then the Ritz method is adopted to solve the large deformation problem of bimodular functionally graded thin circular plates. Section 5 shows the numerical simulation and the comparisons with the variational solution and the previous perturbation solution. Section 6 shows the corresponding results and discussion, and the concluding remarks are given in Section 7.

2. Method and Problem

2.1. Displacement Variational Method

In a spatial axisymmetric problem of elasticity, the cylindrical coordinate system is established as $O\text{-}r\theta z$, in which O denotes the origin; r and θ denote the radial and circumferential direction, respectively; and z denotes the direction normal to the $rO\theta$ plane, as shown in Figure 1. Let σ_r, σ_θ, and σ_z be the normal stress along the radial, circumferential, and z directions, respectively; and $\tau_{r\theta} = \tau_{\theta r}$, $\tau_{rz} = \tau_{zr}$, and $\tau_{z\theta} = \tau_{\theta z}$ be the three shearing stress components. Due to the axisymmetric characteristic, $\tau_{r\theta} = \tau_{\theta r} = 0$ and $\tau_{z\theta} = \tau_{\theta z} = 0$, and there are four stress components in total remaining, σ_r, σ_θ, σ_z, and $\tau_{rz} = \tau_{zr}$, which are the functions of r and z (please refer to Figure 1). Let ε_r, ε_θ, and ε_z be the normal strain along the radial, circumferential, and z directions, respectively; and let γ_{zr} be the shearing strain of r and z directions. In addition, let u_r, u_θ, and w be the radial, circumferential, and z direction displacements, respectively. Note that, due to the axisymmetry, $u_\theta = 0$.

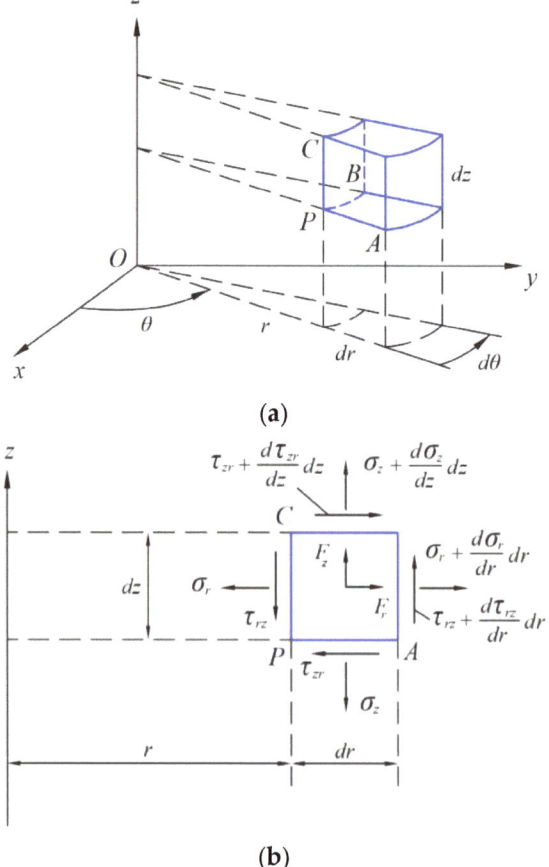

(a)

(b)

Figure 1. *Cont.*

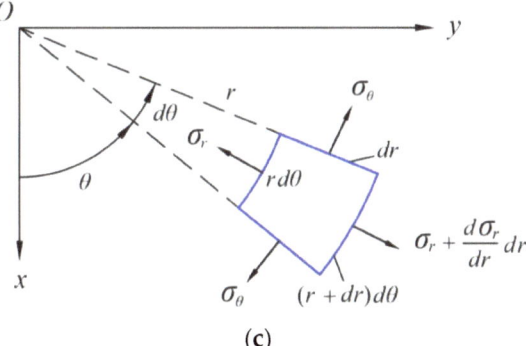

Figure 1. Stresses in a spatial axisymmetric problem in cylindrical coordinate system: (**a**) hexahedron element in cylindrical coordinate system; (**b**) stresses on rOz plane; (**c**) stresses on $rO\theta$ plane.

The geometrical equation of the spatial axisymmetric problem gives [33]

$$\varepsilon_r = \frac{\partial u_r}{\partial r}, \ \varepsilon_\theta = \frac{u_r}{r}, \ \varepsilon_z = \frac{\partial w}{\partial z}, \ \gamma_{zr} = \frac{\partial u_r}{\partial z} + \frac{\partial w}{\partial r}. \tag{1}$$

At the same time, the physical equation of the spatial axisymmetric problem gives [33]

$$\begin{cases} \varepsilon_r = \frac{1}{E}[\sigma_r - \mu(\sigma_\theta + \sigma_z)] \\ \varepsilon_\theta = \frac{1}{E}[\sigma_\theta - \mu(\sigma_z + \sigma_r)] \\ \varepsilon_z = \frac{1}{E}[\sigma_z - \mu(\sigma_r + \sigma_\theta)] \\ \gamma_{zr} = \frac{2(1+\mu)}{E}\tau_{zr} \end{cases}, \tag{2a}$$

where μ and E are the Poisson's ratio and modulus of elasticity, respectively. Alternatively, we may give another form of the physical equation as

$$\begin{cases} \sigma_r = \frac{E}{1+\mu}\left[\frac{\mu}{1-2\mu}(\varepsilon_r + \varepsilon_\theta + \varepsilon_z) + \varepsilon_r\right] \\ \sigma_\theta = \frac{E}{1+\mu}\left[\frac{\mu}{1-2\mu}(\varepsilon_r + \varepsilon_\theta + \varepsilon_z) + \varepsilon_\theta\right] \\ \sigma_z = \frac{E}{1+\mu}\left[\frac{\mu}{1-2\mu}(\varepsilon_r + \varepsilon_\theta + \varepsilon_z) + \varepsilon_z\right] \\ \tau_{zr} = \frac{E}{2(1+\mu)}\gamma_{zr} \end{cases}. \tag{2b}$$

The total strain energy stored in the whole elastic body, U, is expressed in stress and strain as

$$U = \frac{1}{2}\iiint (\sigma_r\varepsilon_r + \sigma_\theta\varepsilon_\theta + \sigma_z\varepsilon_z + \tau_{zr}\gamma_{zr})dV. \tag{3}$$

Obviously, via the geometrical equation and physical equation, the strain potential energy may be expressed in terms of the displacement components, u_r and w, which opens possibilities for the application of the displacement variational method.

Under a cylindrical coordinate system, we suppose that a spatial axisymmetric elastic body is subjected to external forces including the body force and surface force along the r, θ, and z directions; that is, F_r, F_θ, and F_z, as well as $\overline{F_r}$, $\overline{F_\theta}$, and $\overline{F_z}$, and the elastic body are now in equilibrium. The resulting displacements, u_r, u_θ, and w, should satisfy the equation of equilibrium, displacement boundary conditions, as well as stress boundary conditions. If the displacements cause minor changes allowed by the boundary conditions, the new displacements will become (note that, due to the axisymmetry, $u_\theta = 0$)

$$u_r^* = u_r + \delta u_r, \; w^* = w + \delta w, \tag{4}$$

where δu_r and δw are the virtual displacements that occur. During the virtual displacement, if there are no changes in thermal and kinetic energies, according to the principle of energy conservation, the increment in strain potential energy, δU, is equal to the work done by the external forces; therefore, the displacement variational equation may be obtained as follows [33]

$$\delta U = \iiint (F_r \delta u_r + F_z \delta w) dV + \iint (\overline{F}_r \delta u_r + \overline{F}_z \delta w) dS, \tag{5}$$

which is referred to as the Lagrangian variational equation. This variational equation provides an approximate solution to elastic problems. More specifically, if a group of displacements containing a series of unknown coefficients satisfy the displacement boundary conditions, Equation (5) may be used for the determination of these coefficients, thus obtaining the displacement.

The displacement expression is taken as

$$u_r = u_{r0} + \sum_m A_m u_{rm}, \; w = w_0 + \sum_m C_m w_m, \tag{6}$$

where A_m and C_m are the independent coefficients; u_{r0} and w_0 are the specified functions whose boundary value is equal to the known quantity at the boundary; and u_{rm} and w_m are given functions that are equal to zero at the boundary. Therefore, regardless of how A_m and C_m are taken, the displacements u_r and w always satisfy the boundary conditions. Note that because the displacement variation is obtained only by changing A_m and C_m, according to Equation (6), the variation of displacement is

$$\delta u_r = \sum_m u_{rm} \delta A_m, \; \delta w = \sum_m w_m \delta C_m. \tag{7}$$

The variation of strain energy gives

$$\delta U = \sum_m \left(\frac{\partial U}{\partial A_m} \delta A_m + \frac{\partial U}{\partial C_m} \delta C_m \right). \tag{8}$$

Substituting Equations (7) and (8) into Equation (5) will yield

$$\begin{aligned} &\sum_m \left(\frac{\partial U}{\partial A_m} - \iiint F_r u_{rm} dV - \iint \overline{F}_r u_{rm} dS \right) \delta A_m \\ &+ \sum_m \left(\frac{\partial U}{\partial C_m} - \iiint F_z w_m dV - \iint \overline{F}_z w_m dS \right) \delta C_m = 0 \end{aligned} \tag{9}$$

Because the variations δA_m and δC_m are arbitrary and independent from one another, the coefficients of these variations in Equation (9) must be zero, thus obtaining the following two relations:

$$\begin{cases} \frac{\partial U}{\partial A_m} = \iiint F_r u_{rm} dV + \iint \overline{F}_r u_{rm} dS \\ \frac{\partial U}{\partial C_m} = \iiint F_z w_m dV + \iint \overline{F}_z w_m dS \end{cases}, \tag{10}$$

which are used for solving the undermined coefficients; thus, the displacement may be obtained via Equation (6). In many references [30,33,34], the variational method based on displacement is also called the Ritz method.

2.2. Description of Problem

As shown in Figure 2, a bimodular FGM thin circular plate is subjected to a transversely uniformly distributed load q, in which t is the plate thickness and a denotes the radius of the plate. The origin O of cylindrical coordinates system (O-$r\theta z$) is set at the plate center on the neutral layer; r, θ, and z denote the radial, circumferential, and transverse coordinates, respectively. For the reason of axisymmetry, θ is not depicted in Figure 2.

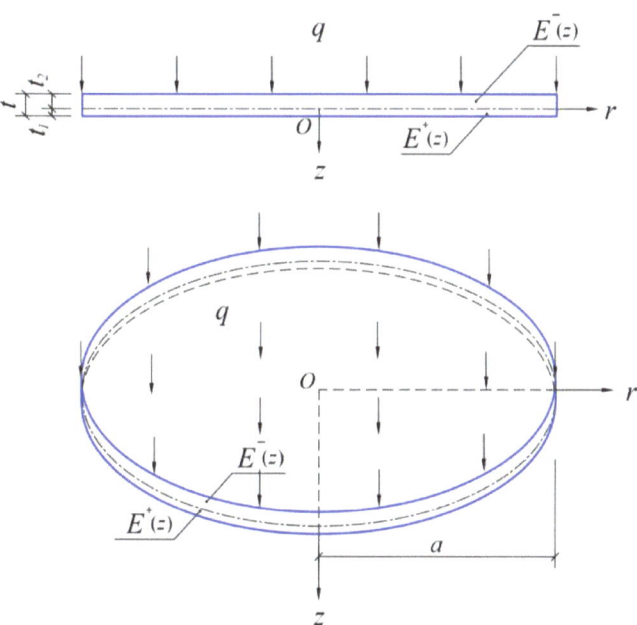

Figure 2. Sketch of bimodular FGM thin circular plate.

Note that in Figure 2, the dot-dashed line stands for the location of the unknown neutral layer of the plate, which is determined next. In general, due to the introduction of bimodular functionally graded materials, the neutral layer does not coincide with the geometrical middle plane of the plate. In Figure 2, t_1 and t_2 are the tensile thickness and compressive thickness, respectively, and the corresponding modulus of the material on the two thicknesses is the tensile modulus $E^+(z)$ and compressive modulus $E^-(z)$, which is a function of z since the functionally graded property is varied along the thickness direction. To facilitate the application of the displacement variational method, the prescribed displacement should satisfy all displacement boundary conditions. Thus, the constraints for the thin circular plate are considered as fully fixed on its peripheral.

For the convenience of differential and integral operations, $E^+(z)$ and $E^-(z)$ are defined as exponent-type functions [25], such that

$$E^+(z) = E_0 e^{\alpha_1 z/t}, \ E^-(z) = E_0 e^{\alpha_2 z/t}, \tag{11}$$

where α_1 and α_2 are two graded indices of the tensile zone and compressive one, respectively, and E_0 is the elastic modulus on the neutral layer. From Equation (11), it is found that when $\alpha_1 = \alpha_2 = 0$ or $z = 0$, $E^+(z) = E^-(z) = E_0$. Meanwhile, according to common practice, the Poisson's ratio is assumed as two constants, μ^+ and μ^-, ignoring the gradient change along the direction of z.

In addition, the determination of the unknown neutral layer (t_1 and t_2) may be via two different conditions, according to our previous study [25]. One is the equilibrium condition, that is, the radial and circumferential normal forces acting on the differential element are zero; the other is the continuity condition, that is, the stresses acting on the neutral layer are continuous. In [25], the equilibrium condition gives

$$\frac{A_1^+}{1 - \mu^+} + \frac{A_1^-}{1 - \mu^-} = 0, \tag{12a}$$

while also in [25], the continuity condition gives

$$\frac{A_1^+}{1-(\mu^+)^2} + \frac{A_1^-}{1-(\mu^-)^2} = 0, \tag{12b}$$

in which

$$\begin{cases} A_1^+ = \int_0^{t_1} z e^{\alpha_1 z/t} dz = \left[\left(\frac{tt_1}{\alpha_1} - \frac{t^2}{\alpha_1^2} \right) e^{\alpha_1 t_1/t} + \frac{t^2}{\alpha_1^2} \right] \\ A_1^- = \int_{-t_2}^0 z e^{\alpha_2 z/t} dz = \left[\left(\frac{tt_2}{\alpha_2} + \frac{t^2}{\alpha_2^2} \right) e^{-\alpha_2 t_2/t} - \frac{t^2}{\alpha_2^2} \right] \end{cases}. \tag{13}$$

The obtainment process in detail for Equation (12a,b) may refer to our previous study [25], so there is no need to repeat the derivation process again. During the obtainment of Equation (12a,b), we first need to give the functional forms of $E^+(z)$ and $E^-(z)$ for the subsequent integral operation, which is also the reason why Equation (11) is given first.

In addition, we note that for the two solutions concerning the neutral layer, it is obvious that the difference between them is slight due to the fact that the values for the Poisson's ratio generally fall into the range of 0 to 0.3; also in Equation (12a,b), there is always a larger number compared to it (here, it is unit 1) before the Poisson's ratio, thus making the influence of Poisson's ratio on the solution small. Moreover, according to our previous study [35], if the influence of Poisson's ratio is completely neglected, both Equation (12a,b) are reduced to $A_1^+ + A_1^- = 0$, which is exactly the solution used for the determination of the unknown neutral axis of bimodular FGM beams.

3. Geometrical and Physical Equations of Thin Circular Plates

Note that in a spatial axisymmetric problem, there exist four stress components in total, σ_r, σ_θ, σ_z, and τ_{rz}, and their corresponding strain components, ε_r, ε_θ, ε_z, and γ_{rz}; thus, the geometrical and physical relations will involve these stresses and strains. In the bending problem of thin plates, according to the classical Kirchhoff hypothesis, ε_z is negligibly small and γ_{rz} may be regarded as zero; thus, the geometrical and physical equations will finally involve the two main stresses, σ_r and σ_θ, as well as the corresponding strains, ε_r and ε_θ. Note that σ_z and τ_{rz} are not zero; they will participate in the equilibrium conditions; however, only the geometric and physical relations are discussed here.

3.1. Geometrical Equations under Large Deformation

The geometrical relation under small-deflection bending may be expressed in terms of the curvature [33] as follows, according to the classical Kirchhoff hypothesis:

$$\varepsilon_{rb} = \frac{z}{\rho_r}, \quad \varepsilon_{\theta b} = \frac{z}{\rho_\theta}, \tag{14}$$

where ε_{rb} and $\varepsilon_{\theta b}$ are the radial and circumferential strain under small-deflection bending, respectively; ρ_r and ρ_θ are the curvature radius along the radial and circumferential directions, respectively; and in the case of small rotation angle, they are the following familiar forms [33]:

$$\frac{1}{\rho_r} = -\frac{d^2w}{dr^2}, \quad \frac{1}{\rho_\theta} = -\frac{1}{r}\frac{dw}{dr}, \tag{15}$$

where w is the transverse displacement or the deflection. Thus, the geometrical relation under small-deflection bending may be expressed in terms of w as follows:

$$\varepsilon_{rb} = -z\frac{d^2w}{dr^2}, \quad \varepsilon_{\theta b} = -z\frac{1}{r}\frac{dw}{dr}. \tag{16}$$

At the same time, the geometrical relation between in-plane displacements and in-plane strain will give [33]

$$\varepsilon_{rm} = \frac{du_r}{dr} + \frac{1}{2}\left(\frac{dw}{dr}\right)^2, \quad \varepsilon_{\theta m} = \frac{u_r}{r}, \tag{17}$$

where ε_{rm} and $\varepsilon_{\theta m}$ are the in-plane strains along the radial and circumferential directions, respectively; u_r and w are the radial displacement and deflection, as indicated above. Finally, the total geometrical relation will give

$$\begin{cases} \varepsilon_r = \varepsilon_{rm} + \varepsilon_{rb} = \frac{du_r}{dr} + \frac{1}{2}\left(\frac{dw}{dr}\right)^2 - z\frac{d^2w}{dr^2} \\ \\ \varepsilon_\theta = \varepsilon_{\theta m} + \varepsilon_{\theta b} = \frac{u_r}{r} - z\frac{1}{r}\frac{dw}{dr} \end{cases}. \tag{18}$$

If the plate is under small deflection, the above relation will change into the form of Equation (16). In the case of small deflection, only the bending effect is considered while the membrane effect is neglected.

3.2. Physical Equations

We suppose the radial and circumferential bending stresses in tensile and compressive zones are $\sigma_{rb}^{+/-}$ and $\sigma_{\theta b}^{+/-}$, respectively, in which the subscript b stands for the bending, and the stress–strain relations, in the tensile zone, will give

$$\begin{cases} \sigma_{rb}^+ = \frac{E^+(z)}{1-(\mu^+)^2}(\varepsilon_{rb} + \mu^+\varepsilon_{\theta b}) \\ \\ \sigma_{\theta b}^+ = \frac{E^+(z)}{1-(\mu^+)^2}(\varepsilon_{\theta b} + \mu^+\varepsilon_{rb}) \end{cases}, at\ 0 \leq z \leq t_1, \tag{19a}$$

and in the compressive zone,

$$\begin{cases} \sigma_{rb}^- = \frac{E^-(z)}{1-(\mu^-)^2}(\varepsilon_{rb} + \mu^-\varepsilon_{\theta b}) \\ \\ \sigma_{\theta b}^- = \frac{E^-(z)}{1-(\mu^-)^2}(\varepsilon_{\theta b} + \mu^-\varepsilon_{rb}) \end{cases}, at\ -t_2 \leq z \leq 0. \tag{19b}$$

At the same time, we note that under large deformation, the in-plane stresses acting on the whole thickness of the cross-section are always tensile; thus. the membrane stress may be changed to σ_{rm}^+ and $\sigma_{\theta m}^+$, in which the subscript m stands for the membrane stress, and the elastic modulus and Poisson's ratio may also be changed to $E^+(z)$ and μ^+, respectively. The physical equation of in-plane deformation may be expressed, along the whole thickness direction, as

$$\begin{cases} \sigma_{rm}^+ = \frac{E^+(z)}{1-(\mu^+)^2}(\varepsilon_{rm} + \mu^+\varepsilon_{\theta m}) \\ \\ \sigma_{\theta m}^+ = \frac{E^+(z)}{1-(\mu^+)^2}(\varepsilon_{\theta m} + \mu^+\varepsilon_{rm}) \end{cases}, at\ -t_2 \leq z \leq t_1. \tag{20}$$

Next, the geometrical and physical equations obtained above are used for the establishment of the functional of energy.

4. Displacement Variational Method

4.1. Total Strain Energy

The total strain energy, U, consists of the energy produced by the bending deformation, U_b, and the energy produced by the deformation of middle surface, U_m, that is [30],

$$U = U_b + U_m, \tag{21}$$

where the subscript b denotes the bending deformation and the subscript m denote the in-plane membrane deformation, which is consistent with the above notational conventions in geometrical and physical equations.

First, the strain energy produced by the middle surface deformation, U_m, is computed as follows [30]:

$$U_m = \frac{1}{2}\iiint\limits_V (\sigma_{rm}^+\varepsilon_{rm} + \sigma_{\theta m}^+\varepsilon_{\theta m})dV. \tag{22}$$

Substituting Equation (20) into Equation (22) and also noticing that the lower limit and upper limit of the integral along the z direction are $-t_2$ and t_1, respectively, and $dV = dzdS$, Equation (22) may be written as

$$U_m = \frac{1}{2}\frac{1}{1-(\mu^+)^2}\int_{-t_2}^{t_1} E^+(z)dz \iint_S \left[(\varepsilon_{rm})^2 + (\varepsilon_{\theta m})^2 + 2\mu^+ \varepsilon_{rm}\varepsilon_{\theta m} \right] dS. \tag{23}$$

Also, substituting Equation (17) into Equation (23) will yield

$$U_m = \frac{1}{2}\frac{1}{1-(\mu^+)^2}\int_{-t_2}^{t_1} E^+(z)dz \iint_S \left\{ \left[\frac{du_r}{dr} + \frac{1}{2}\left(\frac{dw}{dr}\right)^2 \right]^2 + \left(\frac{u_r}{r}\right)^2 + 2\mu^+ \frac{u_r}{r}\left[\frac{du_r}{dr} + \frac{1}{2}\left(\frac{dw}{dr}\right)^2 \right] \right\} dS. \tag{24}$$

Thus, U_m is expressed in terms of u_r and w. Considering Equation (11), we have

$$A_0 = \int_{-t_2}^{t_1} E^+(z)dz = \int_{-t_2}^{t_1} E_0 e^{\alpha_1 z/t}dz = \frac{E_0 t}{\alpha_1}\left(\frac{e^{\alpha_1}-1}{e^{\alpha_1 t_2/t}} \right), \tag{25}$$

and also noting $dS = rd\theta dr$, U_m may be further computed as

$$U_m = \frac{\pi A_0}{1-(\mu^+)^2}\int \left\{ r\left[\frac{du_r}{dr} + \frac{1}{2}\left(\frac{dw}{dr}\right)^2 \right]^2 + \frac{u_r^2}{r} + 2\mu^+ u_r\left[\frac{du_r}{dr} + \frac{1}{2}\left(\frac{dw}{dr}\right)^2 \right] \right\} dr. \tag{26}$$

The energy produced by the bending deformation, U_b, can be derived by the above subareas in tension and compression, that is,

$$U_b = \frac{1}{2}\iiint_{V^+} (\sigma_{rb}^+\varepsilon_{rb} + \sigma_{\theta b}^+\varepsilon_{\theta b})dV + \frac{1}{2}\iiint_{V^-} ((\sigma_{rb}^-\varepsilon_{rb} + \sigma_{\theta b}^-\varepsilon_{\theta b}))dV. \tag{27}$$

Substituting Equation (19a,b) into Equation (27), we have

$$
\begin{aligned}
U_b = {} & \frac{1}{2}\frac{1}{1-(\mu^+)^2}\iiint_{V^+} E^+(z)\left[(\varepsilon_{rb})^2 + (\varepsilon_{\theta b})^2 + 2\mu^+\varepsilon_{rb}\varepsilon_{\theta b} \right]dV \\
& + \frac{1}{2}\frac{1}{1-(\mu^-)^2}\iiint_{V^-} E^-(z)\left[(\varepsilon_{rb})^2 + (\varepsilon_{\theta b})^2 + 2\mu^-\varepsilon_{rb}\varepsilon_{\theta b} \right]dV
\end{aligned}. \tag{28}
$$

Substituting Equation (16) into Equation (28), and also noticing that the range of integrals in the tensile term is from 0 to t_1 while the range in the compressive term is from $-t_2$ to 0, we have

$$
\begin{aligned}
U_b = {} & \frac{1}{2}\frac{1}{1-(\mu^+)^2}\int_0^{t_1} z^2 E^+(z)dz \iint \left[\left(\frac{d^2w}{dr^2}\right)^2 + \left(\frac{1}{r}\frac{dw}{dr}\right)^2 + 2\mu^+\frac{1}{r}\frac{dw}{dr}\frac{d^2w}{dr^2} \right]dS \\
& + \frac{1}{2}\frac{1}{1-(\mu^-)^2}\int_{-t_2}^0 z^2 E^-(z)dz \iint \left[\left(\frac{d^2w}{dr^2}\right)^2 + \left(\frac{1}{r}\frac{dw}{dr}\right)^2 + 2\mu^-\frac{1}{r}\frac{dw}{dr}\frac{d^2w}{dr^2} \right]dS
\end{aligned}. \tag{29}
$$

If we let

$$
\begin{cases}
\begin{aligned}
A_2^+ &= \frac{1}{1-(\mu^+)^2}\int_0^{t_1} z^2 E^+(z)dz = \frac{E_0}{1-(\mu^+)^2}\int_0^{t_1} z^2 e^{\alpha_1 z/t}dz \\
&= \frac{E_0}{1-(\mu^+)^2}\left[\left(\frac{2t^3}{\alpha_1^3} + \frac{t_1^2 t}{\alpha_1} - \frac{2t^2 t_1}{\alpha_1^2} \right)e^{\alpha_1 t_1/t} - \frac{2t^3}{\alpha_1^3} \right] \\
A_2^- &= \frac{1}{1-(\mu^-)^2}\int_{-t_2}^0 z^2 E^-(z)dz = \frac{E_0}{1-(\mu^-)^2}\int_{-t_2}^0 z^2 e^{\alpha_2 z/t}dz \\
&= \frac{E_0}{1-(\mu^-)^2}\left[-\left(\frac{2t^3}{\alpha_2^3} + \frac{t_2^2 t}{\alpha_2} + \frac{2t^2 t_2}{\alpha_2^2} \right)e^{-\alpha_2 t_2/t} + \frac{2t^3}{\alpha_2^3} \right]
\end{aligned}
\end{cases}, \tag{30}
$$

and also noting $dS = rd\theta dr$, U_m may be finally computed as

$$
\begin{aligned}
U_b = \pi A_2^+ \int \left[r\left(\frac{d^2w}{dr^2}\right)^2 + \frac{1}{r}\left(\frac{dw}{dr}\right)^2 + 2\mu^+ \frac{dw}{dr}\frac{d^2w}{dr^2} \right] dr \\
+ \pi A_2^- \int \left[r\left(\frac{d^2w}{dr^2}\right)^2 + \frac{1}{r}\left(\frac{dw}{dr}\right)^2 + 2\mu^- \frac{dw}{dr}\frac{d^2w}{dr^2} \right] dr
\end{aligned}
\tag{31}
$$

Further, Equation (31) may be simplified if the peripheral of the circular plate is fully fixed. Note that the last term of the integrand in Equation (31) may be written as

$$
\int_0^a \frac{d^2w}{dr^2}\frac{dw}{dr} dr = \int_0^a \frac{dw}{dr} d\left(\frac{dw}{dr}\right) = \frac{1}{2}\left(\frac{dw}{dr}\right)^2 \Big|_0^a,
\tag{32}
$$

in which a is the radius of the circular plate, as shown in Figure 2. If the peripheral of the circular plate is fully fixed, we may have $dw/dr = 0$ at $r = a$; at the same time, the axisymmetric condition also gives $dw/dr = 0$ at $r = 0$; it is obvious that, lastly, we have

$$
\int_0^a \frac{d^2w}{dr^2}\frac{dw}{dr} dr = 0.
\tag{33}
$$

Thus, Equation (32) is simplified as

$$
U_b = \pi\left(A_2^+ + A_2^-\right)\int \left[r\left(\frac{d^2w}{dr^2}\right)^2 + \frac{1}{r}\left(\frac{dw}{dr}\right)^2 \right] dr = \pi D^* \int \left[r\left(\frac{d^2w}{dr^2}\right)^2 + \frac{1}{r}\left(\frac{dw}{dr}\right)^2 \right] dr,
\tag{34}
$$

in which D^* is exactly the bending stiffness of the bimodular FGM plate,

$$
D^* = A_2^+ + A_2^-,
\tag{35}
$$

which indicates that the bending stiffness is still obtained via the derivation of bending strain energy, not via the equilibrium relation in our previous study [25].

Finally, we obtain the total strain potential energy, U,

$$
\begin{aligned}
U = U_b + U_m \ = \ & \pi D^* \int \left[r\left(\frac{d^2w}{dr^2}\right)^2 + \frac{1}{r}\left(\frac{dw}{dr}\right)^2 \right] dr \\
& + \frac{\pi A_0}{1-(\mu^+)^2} \int \left\{ r\left[\frac{du_r}{dr} + \frac{1}{2}\left(\frac{dw}{dr}\right)^2\right]^2 + \frac{u_r^2}{r} + 2\mu^+ u_r\left[\frac{du_r}{dr} + \frac{1}{2}\left(\frac{dw}{dr}\right)^2\right] \right\} dr
\end{aligned}
\tag{36}
$$

which is expressed in terms of the displacement components, u_r and w. Note that for the case of small deflection, in Equation (36), only the bending term U_b is retained, while the membrane force term U_m is omitted.

4.2. Ritz Method

For the large-deformation problem of thin circular plates, we take the following displacement components (note that due to the axisymmetry, $u_\theta = 0$):

$$
u_r = \sum_m A_m u_{rm}, \quad w = \sum_m C_m w_m,
\tag{37}
$$

where A_m and C_m are the independent coefficients, and u_{rm} and w_m are the specified functions that are equal to zero on the boundaries. Thus, the displacements, u_r and w, always satisfy displacement boundary conditions. According to the variational method in Section 2.1 and also considering Equation (10), the following two variational equations may be obtained:

$$
\frac{\partial U}{\partial A_m} = \iiint F_r u_{rm} dV + \iint \overline{F}_r u_{rm} dS = 0
\tag{38}
$$

and

$$\frac{\partial U}{\partial C_m} = \iiint F_z w_m dV + \iint \overline{F_z} w_m dS = \iint q w_m dS = 2\pi \int q w_m r dr, \tag{39}$$

where $\overline{F_z} = q$. Equations (38) and (39) are used for solving A_m and C_m. We adopt the following forms of the radial displacement and deflection:

$$u_r = \left(1 - \frac{r}{a}\right)\frac{r}{a}\left[A_0 + A_1\frac{r}{a} + A_2\left(\frac{r}{a}\right)^2 + \cdots\right] \tag{40}$$

and

$$w = \left(1 - \frac{r^2}{a^2}\right)^2\left[C_0 + C_1\left(1 - \frac{r^2}{a^2}\right) + C_2\left(1 - \frac{r^2}{a^2}\right)^2 + \cdots\right]. \tag{41}$$

Obviously, regardless of how the coefficients are chosen, the displacements satisfy the boundary conditions of displacement at the peripheral:

$$u_r = 0, \quad w = 0, \quad \frac{dw}{dr} = 0 \quad at \ r = a, \tag{42}$$

and the axisymmetric conditions at the center:

$$u_r = 0, \quad \frac{dw}{dr} = 0 \quad at \ r = 0. \tag{43}$$

According to the conclusion from [30,33,34], by taking the first few terms, the variational method can give satisfactory results. Thus, in the next computation, for convenience, we take A_0 and A_1 in Equation (40) and C_0 in Equation (41) and then substitute these two displacement formulas into Equation (34):

$$U_b = \frac{32\pi D^*}{3a^2}C_0^2. \tag{44}$$

And substituting these displacement formulas into Equation (26), we have

$$U_m = \frac{E_0 \pi t}{1260[1-(\mu^+)^2]\alpha_1 a^2 e^{\alpha_1 t_2/t}}(e^{\alpha_1} - 1)$$
$$\times \left(\begin{array}{l} 328\mu^+ a A_0 C_0^2 + 176\mu^+ a A_1 C_0^2 + 315 a^2 A_0^2 + 378 a^2 A_0 A_1 \\ -184 a A_0 C_0^2 + 147 a^2 A_1^2 + 16 a A_1 C_0^2 + 384 C_0^4 \end{array}\right). \tag{45}$$

In addition,

$$2\pi \int q w_m r dr = 2\pi q \int_0^a \left(1 - \frac{r^2}{a^2}\right)^2 r dr = \frac{\pi}{3}q a^2. \tag{46}$$

According to Equations (21), (38), and (39), we have

$$\frac{\partial}{\partial A_0}(U_b + U_m) = 0, \quad \frac{\partial}{\partial A_1}(U_b + U_m) = 0, \tag{47}$$

and

$$\frac{\partial}{\partial C_0}(U_b + U_m) = \frac{\pi}{3}q a^2. \tag{48}$$

Substituting Equations (44) and (45) into Equation (47), we have

$$\left\{\begin{array}{l} \dfrac{\partial U}{\partial A_0} = \dfrac{E_0 \pi t}{1260[1-(\mu^+)^2]\alpha_1 a^2 e^{\alpha_1 t_2/t}}(e^{\alpha_1} - 1)\left(\begin{array}{l} 328\mu^+ a C_0^2 + 630 a^2 A_0 \\ +378 a^2 A_1 - 184 a C_0^2 \end{array}\right) = 0 \\[3em] \dfrac{\partial U}{\partial A_1} = \dfrac{E_0 \pi t}{1260[1-(\mu^+)^2]\alpha_1 a^2 e^{\alpha_1 t_2/t}}(e^{\alpha_1} - 1)\left(\begin{array}{l} 176\mu^+ a C_0^2 + 378 a^2 A_0 \\ +294 a^2 A_1 + 16 a C_0^2 \end{array}\right) = 0 \end{array}\right., \tag{49}$$

and then we express A_0 and A_1 with C_0:

$$A_0 = -\frac{C_0^2}{126a}(89\mu^+ - 179), \quad A_1 = \frac{C_0^2}{42a}(13\mu^+ - 79). \tag{50}$$

At the same time, substituting Equations (44)–(46) into Equation (48), we have

$$\frac{E_0\pi t}{1260[1-(\mu^+)^2]\alpha_1 a^2 e^{\alpha_1 t_2/t}}(e^{\alpha_1} - 1)\begin{pmatrix} 656\mu^+ a A_0 C_0 + 352\mu^+ a A_1 C_0 \\ -368a A_0 C_0 + 32a A_1 C_0 + 1536C_0^3 \end{pmatrix}.$$

$$+\frac{64\pi D^*}{3a^2}C_0 - \frac{\pi}{3}qa^2 = 0 \tag{51}$$

Substituting Equation (50) into Equation (51), we finally have

$$HC_0^3 + \frac{64D^*}{3}C_0 = \frac{1}{3}qa^4, \tag{52}$$

where

$$H = -\frac{2E_0 t(e^{\alpha_1} - 1)}{19845[1-(\mu^+)^2]\alpha_1 e^{\alpha_1 t_2/t}}\left[2791(\mu^+)^2 - 4250\mu^+ - 7505\right]. \tag{53}$$

Thus, C_0 may be solved and, according to Equation (50), A_0 and A_1 may also be obtained accordingly. Once the displacements become known, the corresponding stresses and strains may be obtained. Note that C_0 also stands for the central deflection of the thin circular plate; therefore, Equation (52) presents the important relationship of load vs. central deflection. In order to better clarify the solution process of the variational method, we add a flow block diagram for reference (please see Figure 3).

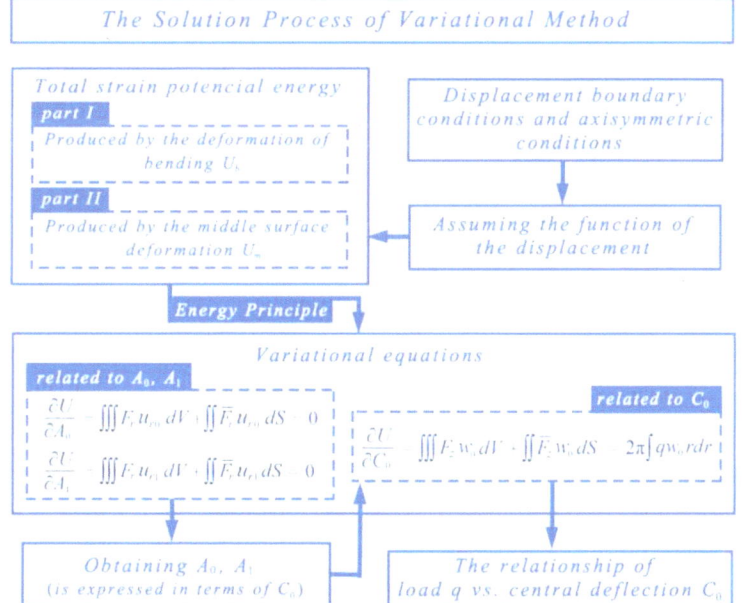

Figure 3. Block diagram of solution process of displacement variational method.

In addition, we note that the above solution is derived on the simple form of the displacement functions u_r and w; that is, A_0 and A_1 are taken in Equation (40), and only C_0 is taken in Equation (41). Although the next comparison with the numerical simulation will show its reliability in the case of small-number terms, for higher precision, more terms in displacement functions u_r and w are necessary; thus, the computation for more terms was also conducted. But, for the sake of coherence of this study, we put this part into Appendix A for interested readers, in which A_0, A_1, and A_2 are taken in Equation (40) and C_0 and C_1 are taken in Equation (41).

5. Numerical Simulation and Comparison with Variational Solution

We use the software ABAQUS6.14.4 to conduct the numerical simulation. When constructing the computational model of a thin circular plate, the first step is to create the three-dimensional solid diagram based on the real shape and size. In our study, the radius of the thin plate, a, is taken as 10 m, and the thickness of the plate, t, is taken as 0.2 m. The peripheral of the circular plate is fully fixed and the load magnitudes take different values, ranging from 10 kPa to 200 kPa, with an interval of 10 kPa. The given values in the numerical simulation are listed in Table 1. A three-dimensional solid element with eight nodes, C3D8, is adopted to conduct the numerical computation. Figure 4 shows the grid division, the loading, and the boundary conditions.

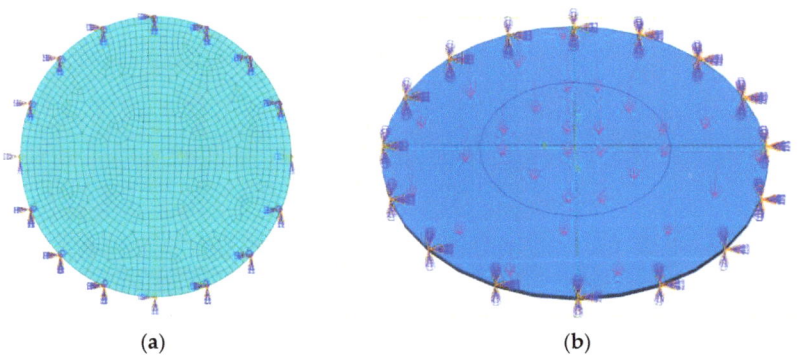

(a)   **(b)**

Figure 4. Thin circular plate model. (**a**) Grid division; (**b**) loading and boundary conditions.

Table 1. Given values in numerical simulation.

Physical Quantities	Taken Values
plate radius a	10 m
plate thickness t	0.2 m
neutral layer modulus E_0	2×10^{10} Pa
load magnitudes q	10 kPa to 200 kPa
tensile grade index α_1	0.5
compressive grade index α_2	0.1
tensile Poisson's ratio μ^+	0.35
compressive Poisson's ratio μ^-	0.25

In our numerical computation, the simulation for bimodular functionally graded materials presents a slight degree of complexity. In ABAQUS6.14.4 software, the realization for functionally graded properties of materials is by layering, but before layering, in consideration of the bimodular effect, we must determine the position of the neutral layer first, that is, only after the subareas are in tension and compression can we effectively layer. To this end, we need to use Equation (12a) or (12b) and the data from Table 1 to determine the tensile thickness and compressive one first, which give $t_1 = 0.4917t$ and $t_2 = 0.5083t$, respectively, where t is the thickness of the plate. Then, the thin circular plate is divided into eight layers along the thickness direction (see Figure 5), taking the middle modulus as the average modulus of this layer. The moduli of elasticity and Poisson's ratios for these eight layers are computed and listed in Table 2, which are used for the property module during the material editing.

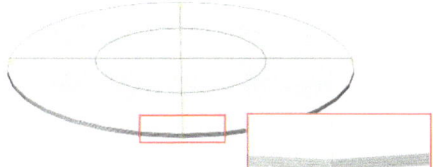

Figure 5. Layering sketch along the direction of plate thickness.

Table 2. Modulus of elasticity of 8-layer plate (*t* is the plate thickness, m).

Distance from Plate Top (m)	Modulus of Elasticity ($\times 10^{10}$ Pa)	Poisson's Ratio
0.0625*t*	1.913	0.25
0.1875*t*	1.937	0.25
0.3125*t*	1.961	0.25
0.4375*t*	1.986	0.25
0.5625*t*	2.055	0.35
0.6875*t*	2.186	0.35
0.8125*t*	2.326	0.35
0.9375*t*	2.475	0.35

Figure 6 shows some representative displacement nephograms under different magnitudes of load, including 20 kPa, 40 kPa, 60 kPa, 80 kPa, 100 kPa, and 120 kPa. From Figure 6, it is easy to see that the maximum deflection occurs at the center of the thin circular plate, as we predicted; the central deflection gradually increases with the increase in load magnitude; and from the center of the plate to the edge of the plate, the deflection gradually decreases, as predicted in our theoretical solution.

Table 3 lists the central deflection values under different load magnitudes (from $q = 10$ kPa to $q = 200$ kPa, with an interval of 10 kPa). For an effective comparison, in Table 3, we also list two other groups of value from different theoretical solutions, the variational solution in this study and the perturbation solution in our previous study [26], in which the results from the variational solution are obtained via Equation (52) in this study; the results from the perturbation solution are based on Equation (104) in [26]. By comparing the values of central deflection in Table 3, it is easily found that the values from the three solutions are basically consistent, but there still exist small differences between them. However, the differences are negligibly small and generally acceptable, which verifies the validity of the variational method.

Table 3. Numerical results of central deflection of three solutions.

q (kPa)	Central Deflection w_0 (m)			
	Result from Analytical Calculations		Result from [26]	Result from FEM
10	0.0898 [1]	0.0897 [2]	0.0895	0.0885
20	0.1538	0.1514	0.1516	0.1491
30	0.2003	0.1953	0.1963	0.1925
40	0.2368	0.2293	0.2311	0.2263
50	0.2670	0.2571	0.2602	0.2542
60	0.2931	0.2808	0.2851	0.2781
70	0.3160	0.3015	0.3070	0.2991
80	0.3366	0.3200	0.3268	0.3179
90	0.3554	0.3367	0.3447	0.3350
100	0.3727	0.3519	0.3613	0.3507
110	0.3887	0.3660	0.3766	0.3653
120	0.4037	0.3790	0.3910	0.3789

Table 3. *Cont.*

q (kPa)	Central Deflection w_0 (m)			
	Result from Analytical Calculations		Result from [26]	Result from FEM
130	0.4178	0.3913	0.4045	0.3917
140	0.4312	0.4028	0.4173	0.4038
150	0.4438	0.4137	0.4294	0.4152
160	0.4558	0.4240	0.4409	0.4262
170	0.4674	0.4338	0.4519	0.4366
180	0.4784	0.4432	0.4625	0.4466
190	0.4890	0.4522	0.4726	0.4562
200	0.4992	0.4608	0.4824	0.4654

[1] Results from the variational solution, in which A_0 and A_1 are taken in Equation (40) and C_0 is taken in Equation (41) (please refer to Section 4.2). [2] Results from the variational solution, in which A_0, A_1, and A_2 are taken in Equation (40), and C_0 and C_1 are taken in Equation (41) (please refer to Appendix A).

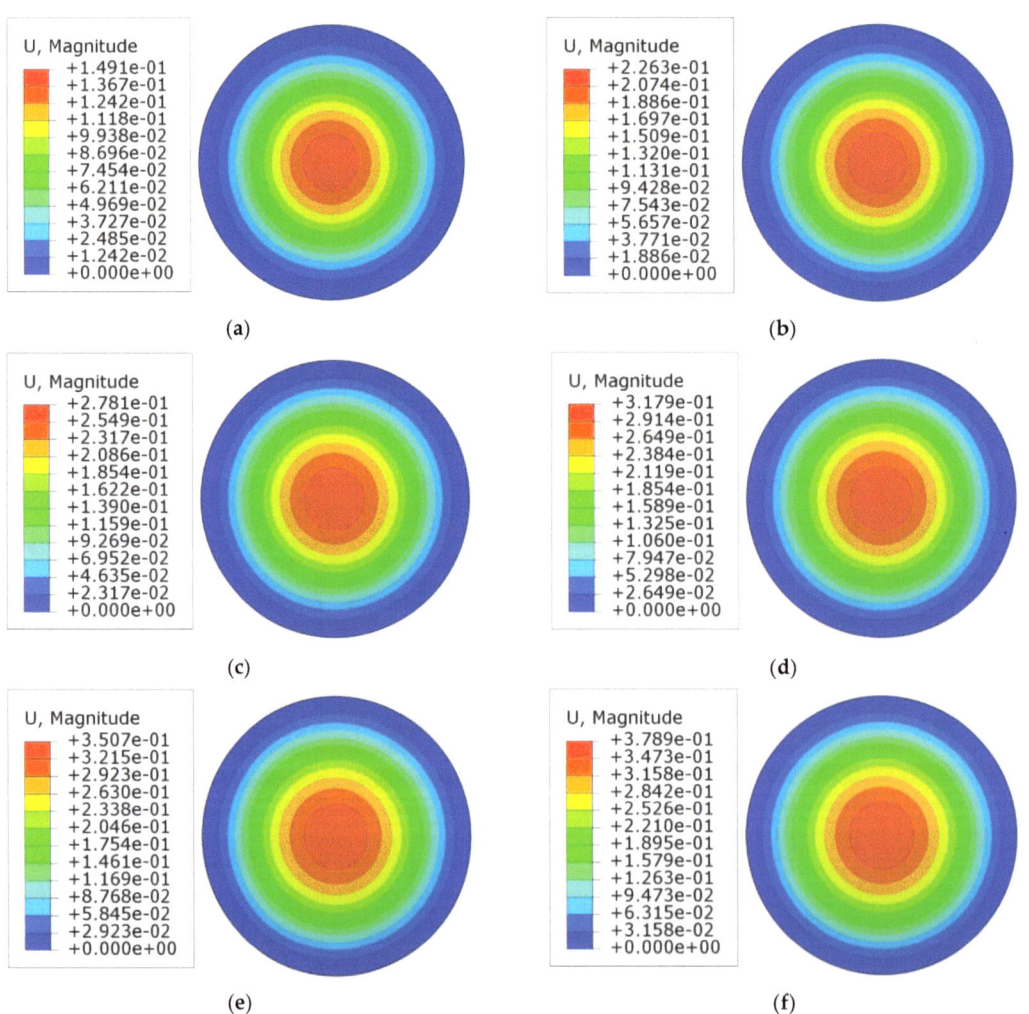

Figure 6. Displacement nephogram under different load magnitudes: (**a**) $q = 20$ kPa; (**b**) $q = 40$ kPa; (**c**) $q = 60$ kPa; (**d**) $q = 80$ kPa; (**e**) $q = 100$ kPa; and (**f**) $q = 120$ kPa.

6. Results and Discussion

6.1. Numerical Comparision of Three Solutions

From the current results, it is found that if the numerical solution can be regarded as a standard to test the validity of two theoretical solutions, the perturbation solution is closest, followed by the variational solution. The values from the variational solution are slightly larger than the values from the perturbation solution, which agrees with the results of classical large-deflection solutions from [29,30]. As indicated in the Introduction, in the literature, both Chien's perturbation solution [29] and the variational solution [30] give satisfactory results. In Chien's perturbation solution [29], the relationship between load and maximum deflection gives

$$\frac{qa^4}{64D} = w_0 \left[1 + 0.544 \left(\frac{w_0}{t} \right)^2 \right], \tag{54}$$

while, in the variational solution [30], the same relationship is

$$\frac{qa^4}{64D} = w_0 \left[1 + 0.486 \left(\frac{w_0}{t} \right)^2 \right], \tag{55}$$

where a is the radius of a thin circular plate, t is the plate thickness, w_0 is the central deflection, q is the uniformly distributed loads, and D is the bending stiffness of the plate. It is readily found that they are quite close. In addition, we note that if other quantities in this relationship take the same values, the value of the maximum deflection from the variational solution is a little greater than the value from the perturbation solution.

The above conclusion is drawn on the basis of the variation solution with fewer terms. If the variation solution with more terms is taken, another phenomenon should be noticed. From the data of the second column marked with footer 2, it is easy to see that if more terms in the displacement functions are taken, the precision of the variational solution will be significantly improved, even exceeding that of the perturbation solution.

It should be noted here that the observed discrepancies resulting from the variational method and FEM method may come down to the fact that, apart from differences in the calculation methods themselves, it comes from different simulated models of the material properties. In the Ritz method, the bimodular functionally graded properties are considered as, for the bimodular effect, the subarea in tension and compression is used, while for the functionally graded property, in each tensile or compressive area, two smooth and continuous functions ((Equation (11)) are adopted. At the same time, in the FEM method, the subarea in tension and compression is still used for the bimodular effect, but the functionally graded property is realized by the layering along the direction of plate thickness; thus, the difference is inevitable. We can speculate that if more layers are adopted, the simulation of materials is likely to be closer to the continuous function change, like Equation (11). However, considering the computational efforts and time, only eight layers were adopted in our present study. In future work, more layers can be adopted to obtain a more precise result.

6.2. Stress Variation along Plate Thickness

In order to investigate the influence of plate thickness on the radial and circumferential stresses, we take three different thickness values, 0.1 m, 0.2 m, and 0.3 m, to carry out the numerical computation, and other taken values may refer to Table 1, in which the load intensity is taken as 10 kPa. At the same time, we take two different survey locations, that is, $r = a/4$ and $r = 3a/4$, where a is the radius of the circular plate, to investigate the influence of different radial locations on stresses. The numerical results are plotted in Figure 7, in which Figure 7a–c correspond to the thickness cases of $t = 0.1$ m, $t = 0.2$ m, and $t = 0.3$ m.

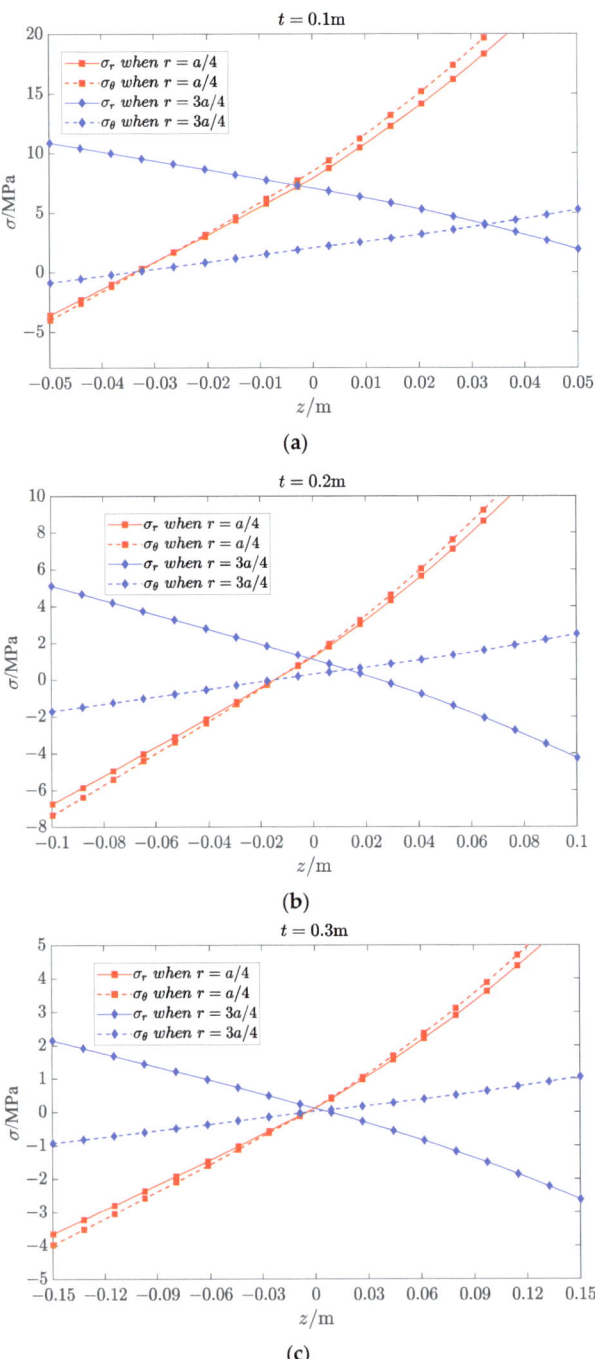

Figure 7. Radial and circumferential stresses under different radial locations and thicknesses: (**a**) $t = 0.1$ m; (**b**) $t = 0.2$ m; (**c**) $t = 0.3$ m.

From Figure 7, the following two trends may be found. (i) The stress distribution trend of radial and circumferential stresses under different plate thicknesses is basically the same, that is, when $r = a/4$ (near the plate center), the differences between the radial and circumferential stresses tend to be smaller; when $r = 3a/4$ (near the plate edge), the differences between the radial and circumferential stresses tend to be larger, which may be due to the influence of boundary constraints. (ii) When the plate becomes thinner ($t = 0.1$ m), the radial and circumferential stresses both tend to be tensile, indicating that the membrane stress is dominant in thinner plates; when the plate becomes thicker ($t = 0.3$ m), the tensile area and compressive area appear distinct, showing that the bending stress is dominant in thicker plates. This phenomenon is also consistent with our expectations.

7. Conclusions

In this paper, the displacement variational method is used to solve the large-deformation problem of bimodular functionally graded thin plates. In order to facilitate the application of the variational method, the physical equations of the bimodular functionally graded material and the geometric equation under large deformation are first given. The total strain potential energy is expressed as the displacement component, which opens up the possibility for the realization of the Ritz method. Finally, the analytical result is verified by numerical simulation. The following three conclusions can be drawn.

(i)   The numerical simulation results verify the validity of the perturbation solution obtained in our previous study and the variational solution presented in this study.

(ii)   The perturbation method and variational method are both, in terms of nature, theoretical, being able to give useful analytical expressions that are convenient for use in the analysis and design. However, the variational method based on the energy principle avoids the establishment of an equation of equilibrium, which is necessary in the perturbation method yet.

(iii)   Compared with the traditional variational method, the improvement on this method in this study lies mainly in such a fact that the derivation of total strain energy is somewhat complicated due to the introduction of bimodular functionally graded materials and structural large deformation. In addition, the bending stiffness of the bimodular FGM plate may also be obtained from the derivation of total strain energy, but not necessarily from the conditions of equilibrium.

The results presented in this study are helpful for the refined analysis and optimized design of flexible thin plate structures, which are composed of functionally graded materials, while at the same time, the bimodular effect of materials is relatively obvious and cannot be ignored.

In the end, it should be pointed out again that Ambartsumyan's bimodular model is established on the criterion of positive–negative signs of principal stresses. This fact makes it very difficult to use this model in structural analysis, because, except for a very few cases, the state of principal stress at any point in the structure is different each other under the action of external load. Fortunately, the proposal of a simplified mechanical model on a subarea in tension and compression makes it possible to use Ambartsumyan's bimodular model in structural analysis. While, at the same time, the material model also deviates from the original definition, this may be seen as an imperfection of the method. In the future, we will try to establish a simplified mechanical model that satisfies the requirements of structural analysis and is closer to the original material model. This work is in progress.

Author Contributions: Conceptualization, X.-T.H. and J.-Y.S.; methodology, X.-T.H., X.-G.W. and J.-C.A.; software, X.-G.W., B.P. and J.-C.A.; formal analysis, X.-T.H., X.-G.W. and J.-C.A.; writing—original draft preparation, X.-T.H. and X.-G.W.; writing—review and editing, B.P., J.-C.A. and J.-Y.S.; visualization, X.-G.W., B.P. and J.-C.A.; funding acquisition, X.-T.H. and J.-Y.S. All authors have read and agreed to the published version of the manuscript.

Funding: The research described in this paper was financially supported by the National Natural Science Foundation of China (Grant Nos. 11572061 and 11772072).

Data Availability Statement: Not applicable.

Conflicts of Interest: The authors declare no conflict of interest.

Appendix A

If more terms in displacement functions u_r and w are taken, that is, A_0, A_1, and A_2 are taken in Equation (40), and C_0 and C_1 are taken in Equation (41), we have the following displacement:

$$u_r = \left(1 - \frac{r}{a}\right)\frac{r}{a}\left[A_0 + A_1\frac{r}{a} + A_2\left(\frac{r}{a}\right)^2\right] \tag{A1}$$

and

$$w = \left(1 - \frac{r^2}{a^2}\right)^2\left[C_0 + C_1\left(1 - \frac{r^2}{a^2}\right)\right]. \tag{A2}$$

Substituting them into Equations (34) and (26), respectively, we have

$$U_b = \frac{32\pi D^*}{3a^2}C_0^2 + \frac{16\pi D^*}{a^2}C_0C_1 + \frac{48\pi D^*}{5a^2}C_1^2. \tag{A3}$$

and

$$U_m = \frac{E_0\pi t}{[1-(\mu^+)^2]\alpha_1 e^{\alpha_1 t_2/t}}\left(e^{\alpha_1} - 1\right)\times$$

$$\left[\begin{array}{l} \frac{13}{168}A_2^2 + \frac{7}{60}A_1^2 + \frac{3}{10}A_0A_1 + \frac{1}{5}A_0A_2 + \frac{19}{105}A_1A_2 + \frac{32}{105a^2}C_0^4 + \frac{18}{55a^2}C_1^4 + \frac{6}{5a^2}C_0C_1^3 + \frac{1}{4}A_0^2 \\[2mm] +\frac{1}{3465a}\left(284\mu^+A_2C_0^2 + 212A_2C_0^2\right) + \frac{1}{315a}\left(44\mu^+A_1C_0^2 + 82\mu^+A_0C_0^2 - 46A_0C_0^2 + 4A_1C_0^2\right) \\[2mm] +\frac{1}{385a}\left(\begin{array}{c}102\mu^+A_1C_0C_1 \\ +206\mu^+A_0C_0C_1\end{array}\right) + \frac{1}{5005a}\left(\begin{array}{c}886A_2C_0C_1 + 1467\mu^+A_0C_1^2 + 678\mu^+A_1C_1^2 + 346\mu^+A_2C_1^2 \\ +722\mu^+A_2C_0C_1 - 69A_0C_1^2 + 526A_2C_1^2 + 498A_1C_1^2\end{array}\right) \\[2mm] +\frac{1}{77a}\left(10A_1C_0C_1 - 10A_0C_0C_1\right) + \frac{1}{7a^2}\left(12C_0^2C_1^2 + 8C_0^3C_1\right)\end{array}\right]. \tag{A4}$$

In addition,

$$\begin{cases} 2\pi\int qw_{m=0}rdr = 2\pi q\int_0^a\left(1 - \frac{r^2}{a^2}\right)^2 rdr = \frac{\pi}{3}qa^2 \\[2mm] 2\pi\int qw_{m=1}rdr = 2\pi q\int_0^a\left(1 - \frac{r^2}{a^2}\right)^3 rdr = \frac{\pi}{4}qa^2 \end{cases} \tag{A5}$$

According to Equations (21), (38), and (39), we have

$$\begin{cases} \frac{\partial}{\partial A_0}(U_b + U_m) = 0 \\[2mm] \frac{\partial}{\partial A_1}(U_b + U_m) = 0 \\[2mm] \frac{\partial}{\partial A_2}(U_b + U_m) = 0 \end{cases} \tag{A6}$$

and

$$\begin{cases} \frac{\partial}{\partial C_0}(U_b + U_m) = \frac{\pi}{3}qa^2 \\[2mm] \frac{\partial}{\partial C_1}(U_b + U_m) = \frac{\pi}{4}qa^2 \end{cases}. \tag{A7}$$

Substituting Equations (A3) and (A4) into Equation (A6), we have

$$
\begin{cases}
\dfrac{\partial U}{\partial A_0} = \dfrac{E_0 \pi t}{[1-(\mu^+)^2]\alpha_1 e^{\alpha_1 t_2/t}}(e^{\alpha_1}-1)
\begin{pmatrix}
\frac{1}{2}A_0 + \frac{206\mu^+}{385a}C_0C_1 + \frac{3}{10}A_1 + \frac{1}{5}A_2 + \frac{82\mu^+}{315a}C_0^2 \\[2mm]
+ \frac{1467\mu^+}{5005a}C_1^2 - \frac{10}{77a}C_0C_1 - \frac{46}{315a}C_0^2 - \frac{69}{5005a}C_1^2
\end{pmatrix} = 0 \\[8mm]
\dfrac{\partial U}{\partial A_1} = \dfrac{E_0 \pi t}{[1-(\mu^+)^2]\alpha_1 e^{\alpha_1 t_2/t}}(e^{\alpha_1}-1)
\begin{pmatrix}
\frac{7}{30}A_1 + \frac{102\mu^+}{385a}C_0C_1 + \frac{3}{10}A_0 + \frac{19}{105}A_2 + \frac{44\mu^+}{315a}C_0^2 \\[2mm]
+ \frac{678\mu^+}{5005a}C_1^2 + \frac{10}{77a}C_0C_1 + \frac{4}{315a}C_0^2 + \frac{498}{5005a}C_1^2
\end{pmatrix} = 0 \\[8mm]
\dfrac{\partial U}{\partial A_2} = \dfrac{E_0 \pi t}{[1-(\mu^+)^2]\alpha_1 e^{\alpha_1 t_2/t}}(e^{\alpha_1}-1)
\begin{pmatrix}
\frac{13}{84}A_2 + \frac{722\mu^+}{5005a}C_0C_1 + \frac{1}{5}A_0 + \frac{19}{105}A_1 + \frac{284\mu^+}{3465a}C_0^2 \\[2mm]
+ \frac{886}{5005a}C_0C_1 + \frac{346\mu^+}{5005a}C_1^2 + \frac{212}{3465a}C_0^2 + \frac{526}{5005a}C_1^2
\end{pmatrix} = 0
\end{cases}
\tag{A8}
$$

And then we express A_0, A_1, and A_2 with C_0 and C_1:

$$
\begin{cases}
A_0 = -\dfrac{1}{180,180a}
\begin{pmatrix}
93,990\mu^+ C_0^2 + 249,516\mu^+ C_0 C_1 + 167,931\mu^+ C_1^2 \\[2mm]
-206,050C_0^2 - 553,824C_0C_1 - 350,145C_1^2
\end{pmatrix} \\[8mm]
A_1 = -\dfrac{1}{25,740a}
\begin{pmatrix}
11,050\mu^+ C_0^2 + 5508\mu^+ C_0 C_1 - 8307\mu^+ C_1^2 \\[2mm]
+19,890C_0^2 + 149,328C_0C_1 + 124,425C_1^2
\end{pmatrix} \\[8mm]
A_2 = \dfrac{8}{6435a}
\begin{pmatrix}
520\mu^+ C_0^2 + 891\mu^+ C_0 C_1 + 306\mu^+ C_1^2 \\[2mm]
-780C_0^2 + 1341C_0C_1 + 1980C_1^2
\end{pmatrix}
\end{cases}
\tag{A9}
$$

At the same time, substituting Equations (A3) and (A4) into Equation (A7), we have

$$
D^*\left(\frac{16\pi}{a^2}C_1 + \frac{64\pi}{3a^2}C_0\right) + \frac{E_0 \pi t}{[1-(\mu^+)^2]\alpha_1 e^{\alpha_1 t_2/t}}(e^{\alpha_1}-1)
$$

$$
\times
\begin{pmatrix}
\frac{722\mu^+}{5005a}A_2C_1 + \frac{102\mu^+}{385a}A_1C_1 + \frac{206\mu^+}{385a}A_0C_1 + \frac{128}{105a^2}C_0^3 \\[2mm]
+\frac{568\mu^+}{3465a}A_2C_0 + \frac{88\mu^+}{315a}A_1C_0 + \frac{164\mu^+}{315a}A_0C_0 + \frac{886}{5005a}A_2C_1 \\[2mm]
+\frac{10}{77a}A_1C_1 - \frac{10}{77a}A_0C_1 - \frac{92}{315a}A_0C_0 + \frac{8}{315a}A_1C_0 \\[2mm]
+\frac{424}{3465a}A_2C_0 + \frac{24}{7a^2}C_0C_1^2 + \frac{24}{7a^2}C_0^2C_1 + \frac{6}{5a^2}C_1^3
\end{pmatrix}
= \frac{\pi q a^2}{3}
\tag{A10}
$$

and

$$
D^*\left(\frac{16\pi}{a^2}C_0 + \frac{96\pi}{5a^2}C_1\right) + \frac{E_0 \pi t}{[1-(\mu^+)^2]\alpha_1 e^{\alpha_1 t_2/t}}(e^{\alpha_1}-1)
$$

$$
\times
\begin{pmatrix}
\frac{722\mu^+}{5005a}A_2C_0 + \frac{102\mu^+}{385a}A_1C_0 + \frac{206\mu^+}{385a}A_0C_0 + \frac{72}{55a^2}C_1^3 \\[2mm]
+\frac{1356\mu^+}{5005a}A_1C_1 + \frac{886}{5005a}A_2C_0 + \frac{2934\mu^+}{5005a}A_0C_1 + \frac{10}{77a}A_1C_0 \\[2mm]
-\frac{10}{77a}A_0C_0 + \frac{692\mu^+}{5005a}A_2C_1 - \frac{138}{5005a}A_0C_1 + \frac{24}{7a^2}C_0^2C_1 \\[2mm]
+\frac{8}{7a^2}C_0^3 + \frac{1052}{5005a}A_2C_1 + \frac{996}{5005a}A_1C_1 + \frac{18}{5a^2}C_0C_1^2
\end{pmatrix}
= \frac{\pi q a^2}{4}
\tag{A11}
$$

Substituting Equation (A9) into Equations (A10) and (A11), we finally obtain the expressions of C_0 and C_1. Since the expressions are too complex, they are not given here. At the same time, according to Equation (A2), if we let $r = 0$, the central deflection or the maximum deflection of the circular plate will be

$$
w_0 = C_0 + C_1.
\tag{A12}
$$

References

1. Jones, R.M. Stress-strain relations for materials with different moduli in tension and compression. *AIAA J.* **1977**, *15*, 16–23. [CrossRef]
2. Koizumi, M. Functionally gradient materials the concept of FGM. *Ceram. Trans.* **1993**, *34*, 3–10.

3. Gong, Y.; Mei, Y.; Liu, J. Capillary adhesion of a circular plate to solid: Large deformation and movable boundary condition. *Int. J. Sci. Mech.* **2017**, *126*, 222–228. [CrossRef]
4. Huang, X.; Wang, M.; Feng, Y.; Wang, X.; Qiu, X. Finite deformation analysis of the elastic circular plates under pressure loading. *Thin-Walled Struct.* **2023**, *188*, 110864. [CrossRef]
5. Barak, M.M.; Currey, J.D.; Weiner, S.; Shahar, R. Are tensile and compressive Young's moduli of compact bone different? *J. Mech. Behav. Biomed. Mater.* **2009**, *2*, 51–60. [CrossRef] [PubMed]
6. Destrade, M.; Gilchrist, M.D.; Motherway, J.A.; Murphy, J.G. Bimodular rubber buckles early in bending. *Mech. Mater.* **2010**, *42*, 469–476. [CrossRef]
7. Jones, R.M. Apparent flexural modulus and strength of multimodulus materials. *J. Compos. Mater.* **1976**, *10*, 342–354. [CrossRef]
8. Bert, C.W. Models for fibrous composites with different properties in tension and compression. *ASME J. Eng. Mater. Technol.* **1977**, *99*, 344–349. [CrossRef]
9. Ambartsumyan, S.A. *Elasticity Theory of Different Moduli*; Wu, R.F.; Zhang, Y.Z., Translators; China Railway Publishing House: Beijing, China, 1986.
10. Reddy, J.N.; Chao, W.C. Nonlinear bending of bimodular material plates. *Int. J. Solids Struct.* **1983**, *19*, 229–237. [CrossRef]
11. Zinno, R.; Greco, F. Damage evolution in bimodular laminated composite under cyclic loading. *Compos. Struct.* **2001**, *53*, 381–402. [CrossRef]
12. Khan, A.H.; Patel, B.P. Nonlinear periodic response of bimodular laminated composite annular sector plates. *Compos. Part B-Eng.* **2019**, *169*, 96–108. [CrossRef]
13. Yao, W.J.; Ye, Z.M. Analytical solution for bending beam subject to lateral force with different modulus. *Appl. Math. Mech. (Engl. Ed.)* **2004**, *25*, 1107–1117.
14. Zhao, H.L.; Ye, Z.M. Analytic elasticity solution of bi-modulus beams under combined loads. *Appl. Math. Mech. (Engl. Ed.)* **2015**, *36*, 427–438. [CrossRef]
15. He, X.T.; Cao, L.; Wang, Y.Z.; Sun, J.Y.; Zheng, Z.L. A biparametric perturbation method for the Föppl-von Kármán equations of bimodular thin plates. *J. Math. Anal. Appl.* **2017**, *455*, 1688–1705. [CrossRef]
16. Ye, Z.M.; Chen, T.; Yao, W.J. Progresses in elasticity theory with different moduli in tension and compression and related FEM. *Mech. Eng.* **2004**, *26*, 9–14.
17. Du, Z.L.; Zhang, Y.P.; Zhang, W.S.; Guo, X. A new computational framework for materials with different mechanical responses in tension and compression and its applications. *Int. J. Solids Struct.* **2016**, *100–101*, 54–73. [CrossRef]
18. Ma, J.W.; Fang, T.C.; Yao, W.J. Nonlinear large deflection buckling analysis of compression rod with different moduli. *Mech. Adv. Mater. Struct.* **2019**, *26*, 539–551. [CrossRef]
19. Almajid, A.; Taya, M.; Hudnut, S. Analysis of out-of-plane displacement and stress field in a piezocomposite plate with functionally graded microstructure. *Int. J. Solids Struct.* **2001**, *38*, 3377–3391. [CrossRef]
20. Kumar, S.; Murthy Reddy, K.V.V.S.; Kumar, A.; Rohini Devi, G. Development and characterization of polymer–ceramic continuous fiber reinforced functionally graded composites for aerospace application. *Aerosp. Sci. Technol.* **2013**, *26*, 185–191. [CrossRef]
21. Maalej, M.; Ahmed, S.F.U.; Paramasivam, P. Corrosion durability and structural response of functionally-graded concrete beams. *J. Adv. Concr. Technol.* **2003**, *1*, 307–316. [CrossRef]
22. Rabbani, V.; Hodaei, M.; Deng, X.; Lu, H.; Hui, D.; Wu, N. Sound transmission through a thick-walled FGM piezo-laminated cylindrical shell filled with and submerged in compressible fluids. *Eng. Struct.* **2019**, *197*, 109323. [CrossRef]
23. Van Vinh, P.; Van Chinh, N.; Tounsi, A. Static bending and buckling analysis of bi-directional functionally graded porous plates using an improved first-order shear deformation theory and FEM. *Eur. J. Mech. Solid.* **2022**, *96*, 104743. [CrossRef]
24. Xue, X.-Y.; Wen, S.-R.; Sun, J.-Y.; He, X.-T. One- and two-dimensional analytical solutions of thermal stress for bimodular functionally graded beams under arbitrary temperature rise modes. *Mathematics* **2022**, *10*, 1756. [CrossRef]
25. He, X.T.; Pei, X.X.; Sun, J.Y.; Zheng, Z.L. Simplified theory and analytical solution for functionally graded thin plates with different moduli in tension and compression. *Mech. Res. Commun.* **2016**, *74*, 72–80. [CrossRef]
26. He, X.-T.; Li, X.; Yang, Z.-X.; Liu, G.-H.; Sun, J.-Y. Application of biparametric perturbation method to functionally graded thin plates with different moduli in tension and compression. *Z. Angew. Math. Mech.* **2019**, *99*, e201800213. [CrossRef]
27. Li, X.; He, X.-T.; Ai, J.-C.; Sun, J.-Y. Large deformation problem of bimodular functionally-graded thin circular plates subjected to transversely uniformly-distributed load: Perturbation solution without small-rotation-angle assumption. *Mathematics* **2021**, *9*, 2317. [CrossRef]
28. He, X.-T.; Pang, B.; Ai, J.-C.; Sun, J.-Y. Functionally graded thin circular plates with different moduli in tension and compression: Improved Föppl–von Kármán equations and its biparametric perturbation solution. *Mathematics* **2022**, *10*, 3459. [CrossRef]
29. Chien, W.Z. Large deflection of a circular clamped plate under uniform pressure. *Chin. J. Phys.* **1947**, *7*, 102–113.
30. Xu, Z.L. *Elasticity*, 5th ed.; Higher Education Press: Beijing, China, 2016.
31. Xue, X.-Y.; Du, D.-W.; Sun, J.-Y.; He, X.-T. Application of variational method to stability analysis of cantilever vertical plates with bimodular effect. *Materials* **2021**, *14*, 6129. [CrossRef]
32. He, X.-T.; Chang, H.; Sun, J.-Y. Axisymmetric large deformation problems of thin shallow shells with different moduli in tension and compression. *Thin-Walled Struct.* **2023**, *182*, 110297. [CrossRef]
33. Timoshenko, S.; Woinowsky-Krieger, S. *Theory of Plates and Shells*; McGraw-Hill: New York, NY, USA, 1959.

34. Volmir, A.C. *Flexible Plates and Shells*; Lu, W.D.; Huang, Z.Y.; Lu, D.H., Translators; Science Press: Beijing, China, 1959.
35. He, X.-T.; Li, W.-M.; Sun, J.-Y.; Wang, Z.-X. An elasticity solution of functionally graded beams with different moduli in tension and compression. *Mech. Adv. Mater. Struct.* **2018**, *25*, 143–154. [CrossRef]

MDPI AG
Grosspeteranlage 5
4052 Basel
Switzerland
Tel.: +41 61 683 77 34

Mathematics Editorial Office
E-mail: mathematics@mdpi.com
www.mdpi.com/journal/mathematics

www.ingramcontent.com/pod-product-compliance
Lightning Source LLC
LaVergne TN
LVHW072341090526
838202LV00019B/2457